THE PRACTICE OF
business communication

1st canadian edition

THE PRACTICE OF
business communication

1st canadian edition

MARY ELLEN GUFFEY

Professor of Business Emerita
Los Angeles Pierce College

RICHARD ALMONTE

George Brown College

THOMSON ™
NELSON

Australia   Canada   Mexico   Singapore   Spain   United Kingdom   United States

THOMSON

NELSON

The Practice of Business Communication, First Canadian Edition

by Mary Ellen Guffey and Richard Almonte

**Associate Vice President,
Editorial Director:**
Evelyn Veitch

**Editor-in-Chief,
Higher Education:**
Anne Williams

Executive Editor:
Cara Yarzab

Acquisitions Editor:
Bram Sepers

Marketing Manager:
Shelley Collacutt Miller

Developmental Editor:
Linda Sparks

**Photo Researcher
and Permissions Coordinator:**
Daniela Glass

**Senior Content Production
Manager:**
Natalia Denesiuk Harris

Production Service:
Graphic World Publishing Services

Copy Editor:
Wendy Thomas

Proofreader:
Wayne Herrington

Indexer:
Graphic World Publishing Services

Production Coordinator:
Ferial Suleman

Interior and Cover Design:
Liz Harasymczuk

Cover Image:
©Nikolai Punin/Images.com

Printer:
Courier

**Library and Archives Canada
Cataloguing in Publication Data**

Guffey, Mary Ellen

    The practice of business communication / Mary Ellen Guffey, Richard Almonte — 1st Canadian ed.

Includes bibliographical references and index.

ISBN-13: 978-0-17-625155-0
ISBN-10: 0-17-625155-3

    1. Business communication—Textbooks. 2. Business writing—Textbooks.

I. Almonte, Richard II. Title.

HF5718.3.G82 2007a   651.7
C2006-907025-3

Contents

Preface

THIS TEXTBOOK TAKES a new approach to covering the topic of Business Communication. The approach is known as Problem-Based Learning (PBL). Most instructors will have heard of this approach, whereas it may be a new phrase to students. PBL is one of numerous active learning approaches (case studies are another) currently gaining pedagogical favour in postsecondary institutions. In this preface we would like to briefly explain the PBL approach so that students and instructors can make the most of this textbook.

According to leading theorists of this approach to teaching, PBL is "a method of learning in which the learners first encounter a problem, followed by a systematic, student-centred enquiry process."[1] In other words, PBL is a new way of teaching and learning in our classrooms. Instead of the traditional method in which the instructor lectures on material and students emulate models in take-home assignments, or instead of the workshop method in which the instructor models material and students emulate the modelled material in a lab or in class, the PBL method poses a real-world problem that students try to solve using the skills they currently have. The problem is designed to get students thinking about material the instructor is about to cover.

The PBL approach was first introduced in Canada at McMaster University's medical school in the late 1960s. Increasingly, however, this teaching methodology is gaining favour at universities and community colleges across the curriculum, including in the arts and humanities and sciences and social sciences. Research has shown that PBL effectively increases students' abilities in a number of important areas. One critic argues that among PBL's virtues is its ability to foster self-directed learning, to require students to be active in the classroom, and to promote learning through collaboration.[2] Other critics note PBL's ability to enhance "students' motivation … and [change] students' attitudes."[3] Not surprisingly, as with any change in teaching methodology, some challenges may arise when using the PBL approach. These challenges include getting students to solve problems before they have all the necessary content knowledge, combatting the perception that PBL is an easy out for lazy instructors who'd rather not lecture or lead the class, through to the notion that it's too difficult for instructors to come up with well-designed "real-world" problems on a regular basis.

Of course, as experienced teachers know, most challenges can be turned into excellent teaching opportunities. Furthermore, the PBL approach is best used, at least in the Business Communication classroom, as *one* method in the instructor's pedagogical toolkit. In other words, a typical three-hour class solely devoted to the PBL approach is probably going to cause some problems, notably an inability to cover material. Yet, if PBL is used consistently as *one part* of a more traditional or workshop-based classroom, everyone involved stands to gain through the variety of approaches. Below we briefly describe the ideal characteristics of a well-designed PBL approach as well as the process students should go through when they are given a problem to solve in a PBL classroom.

According to Renee E. Weiss, an expert in the PBL approach, an instructor choosing to use the PBL approach should go through a two-stage process when designing problems. First, the instructor has to determine the purpose of the problem. As Weiss states, unless instructors "address this question, they are likely to end up with problems that do not serve their intended purpose."[4] Some of the most common purposes for using PBL include "guiding, testing, illustrating important principles, concepts, or procedures, fostering the processing of content; and providing a stimulus for activity."[5] In our own experience, all five purposes are important, although the first—guiding or previewing—and the last—providing a stimulus for activity—seem to be the most useful. Once you've determined the purpose of the problem, it's time to design it. Weiss argues there are four important criteria to a well-designed PBL problem.

Problems must be appropriate for students; in other words they should contain a mix of what students already know and what they might not yet know, in order to provide a challenge. Problems must also—and this is sometimes challenging for instructors—be "ill-structured." What this means is that in order for higher-order thinking skills to be fostered, problems, like those encountered in the world outside the classroom, should not necessarily have an easy or obvious solution. There should be imperfection and grey areas in well-designed PBL problems. Also, problems must be collaborative. This means that decision making has to be part of the process. According to Weiss, some researchers have even claimed that well-designed problems should not just be collaborative, but they should "engender controversy among members of the group."[6] Finally, problems must also be authentic. This means that they should be both realistic in that they stem from some experience students can understand and they should replicate what actually goes on in the work world that students will be entering.

So what happens in the PBL classroom? It usually looks something like this: the instructor either has students self-divide into groups or else divides them into groups. The problem is then presented, either orally, visually, or more commonly, in a handout that can be referred to by students throughout the PBL portion of the class. The problem description can be as short as a paragraph and as long as a page. Anything longer tends to be too complex for the undergraduate level and too demanding of time in a classroom where PBL may not be the only delivery approach. Once students have digested the problem, they follow an in-class problem-solving model first articulated by John Dewey in 1924 and summarized more recently by Bonwell and Eison:

1. Define the problem
2. Diagnose possible reasons for the problem
3. Search for alternative solutions
4. Evaluate the alternatives and choose the most appropriate solution[7]

Instructors may choose to make the process more fleshed out than this bare-bones approach. For example, many PBL instructors ask, in stage 4, for some sort of product, either written or oral, to be produced as part of the solution. In a business communication problem, the most appropriate solution may be a memo that goes out to staff at a company explaining a new e-mail etiquette policy to be followed. In other problems, the most appropriate solution is a presentation or a meeting or a one-on-one discussion. The possibilities are endless.

In the next section we describe the features of this textbook that allow instructors and students to implement a PBL approach in their Business Communication classroom.

FEATURES OF THIS TEXTBOOK

In order to facilitate the PBL approach discussed previously, this textbook has been designed in the following way:

1. Each chapter begins with a current article from the Canadian press highlighting a business communication–related problem.
2. The article is followed by a suggested in-class PBL activity that instructors may use to lead off their class.
3. The article and the problem stemming from it lead into a chapter that is devoted to discussing the skills highlighted by the article. At various points in the chapter, the article is mentioned to reinforce the centrality of the PBL approach.
4. Each chapter ends with a set of five problems that can be used in class, as a take-home assignment, or in a test situation.
5. Each chapter concludes with a chapter review, a grammar/style review, and a communication lab (related to the chapter-opening article), which can be completed in a computer lab, on a notebook computer, in the classroom in written fashion, or at home as an assignment.
6. Extra problems are found on this textbook's website, in case those at the end of the chapter are not sufficient in variety.

Using the classification of pedagogical styles discussed earlier (lecture, workshop, problem-based), the Guffey series of business communication textbooks, which now numbers four, can be seen as offering the ultimate amount of flexibility in fulfilling the needs of instructors who teach in various ways. *Essentials of Business Communication* and *Canadian Business English* work well to facilitate a traditional lecture-and-model classroom. *Business Communication: Process and Product* is unrivalled as a resource for workshop-based classrooms. This new text, *The Practice of Business Communication,* completes the trio of pedagogical approaches by featuring the more student-centred/active learning PBL method. Of course, all four books can be modified by a professional instructor to suit his or her preferred mix of teaching methodologies. The choice is the instructor's.

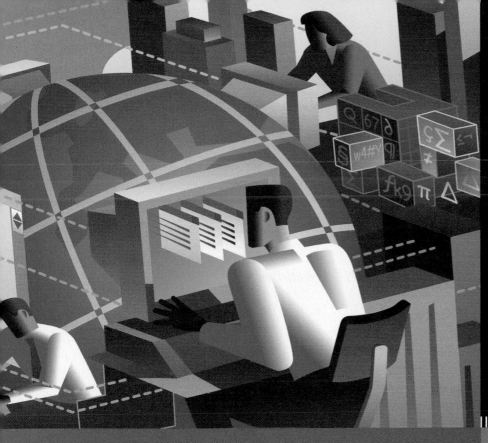

Analyzing Communication

CHAPTER 1

A Theory of Communication

Police Exam Unsuitable: Race Committee Members

BY NIKHAT AHMED, *THE STARPHOENIX*, MONDAY, NOVEMBER 14, 2005

AN EXAM GIVEN to potential police officers got a failing grade from some members of the city's cultural diversity and race relations committee who took the test last week.

The committee had the opportunity to take the Sigma exam to help determine whether it presents cultural barriers, and the initial reaction wasn't good.

"It was confusing," said Nesar Rajput, a committee member. "Especially for people who are not born English-speaking, it was difficult."

The 35-minute American aptitude test has been used by Saskatchewan police forces for about two years. The test requires a score of at least 60 per cent and roughly half of Saskatoon applicants fail.

Earlier this year, police Chief Russ Sabo and the police service diversity advisory committee said the Sigma test needed to be changed because it was keeping visible minorities from earning a badge.

Rajput said he thinks high school kids, especially those who go to schools on reserves, aren't taught the grammar skills that are needed to pass the test. The test includes questions on spelling, grammar and simple math, as well as a passage of the American Criminal Code which candidates must prove they understand.

Candidates who pass the test go through background and reference checks, a physical test, interviews and a polygraph test to reinforce questions about any criminal past or drug use.

Andrew Mason, committee chair, said he found the Sigma test "had very Euro-centric language," and visible minorities would find the language difficult.

Mason said he recognizes "good communication is important in any job," but there was "too much emphasis on language skills."

"There were a lot of words there that are not commonly used," he said, such as the word "admonished."

He added the test often required reading through paragraphs of examples before getting to the question, which might make test-takers think "they were trying to trick you." He said he believes the exam "weighs heavily against people that we are trying to recruit." Filling vacancies in the police service has been difficult in recent years, particularly with minority candidates. Mason, a lawyer, said he thinks he'll pass the test, but he wasn't able to finish in time. Jim Balfour, a committee member, agreed the test isn't easy for those with English as a second language. He said the exam should "screen for respect or understanding of different cultures," and he didn't completely feel the test accomplished that task.

Instead, the exam focused on vocabulary skills, he said, which don't always "reflect a person's ability."

Balfour said the exam could be designed by using examples of aboriginal history, issues that face minorities and the values and beliefs of cultural groups. "There are ways to put that in there," he said.

"The police service is a human service," and a candidate exam should find recruits that can interact well with people, Balfour said. He said he was very happy that the police service approached the committee for help in assessing the exam and determining what, if any, changes should be made. Not all members of the committee took the Sigma test. Saskatchewan police forces used the Otis test until the commission replaced it because of a perceived test bias against aboriginals.

DIAGNOSING THE PROBLEM

Using the classic method for solving a problem discussed in this book's Preface, what can we say about the situation described by Nikhat Ahmed? First of all, we need to define the problem. We could say that the problem described here is that over half of all people from Saskatoon writing the aptitude test to become a police officer in the province of Saskatchewan are failing the test. Furthermore, they're failing because they can't understand the language used in the test. Some reasons for the existence of this problem are offered in the article: the test requires a knowledge of English grammar that may not be taught in aboriginal schools in Saskatchewan. Similarly, the test may be skewed toward people who have highly effective English-language vocabulary skills, even though such skills are not necessarily used daily by the police, especially not in aboriginal communities. Another reason the article hints at but does not discuss is the fact that the Saskatchewan police forces are using an American test. Is it possible that some of the examples or the language in an American test might not be understandable to Canadians? What other information do we require to assess the problem that the article doesn't provide? For example, why does the article focus so much on aboriginal people? Are the majority of people failing the test from aboriginal backgrounds? How many people of aboriginal background are passing the test?

What solutions might exist to this problem? The obvious one would be to develop a new test, right? Or maybe not. Perhaps another solution would be to modify the current test so that its examples or its language are more in line with the lived reality of people in Saskatchewan. Still another solution might be to change the testing model. Why does a police officer candidate need to pass a written test if writing is only a small part of the job? Wouldn't it make more sense for him or her to pass a more detailed interview? There are probably other solutions you can think of, but we'll leave it there for the moment. The difficult job is evaluating different possible solutions and choosing the most appropriate one. This is as good a place as any for you to start using your problem-solving skills...

in class
activity 1

WORKING IN SMALL groups of three to four, students will discuss the analysis of the problem above and evaluate the solutions offered in order to choose the most appropriate one. Is the analysis provided above complete? What will an appropriate solution look like? Why did your group choose this solution? What pluses and minuses are there in choosing this solution? Report back to the class within 20 minutes.

Now that you've presented your solution to the rest of the class, you're ready to discover some of the theory that exists behind the situation you've just examined. At the end of this chapter, you will be presented with some more problems that you may be asked to analyze, evaluate, and explain.

THE LASSWELL AND SHANNON/WEAVER MODELS OF COMMUNICATION

Just what is communication? For our purposes, communication is the transmission of information and meaning from one individual or group (the sender) to another (the receiver). It follows, therefore, that business communication is the transmission of information and meaning between individuals and groups in the workplace. The crucial element in both definitions is meaning. Communication has as its central objective the transmission of meaning. The process of communication is successful only when the receiver understands an idea as the sender intended it. Think of the last time you received an e-mail or an instant message that you didn't understand. What is she talking about, you may have thought to yourself. In this case, transmission of meaning did not occur. In fact, because you had to send your co-worker another e-mail or instant message to find out what she meant, the main objective of communication had not been met.

The classic theory of communication was first articulated by the Greek philosopher Aristotle, in his well-known text *Rhetoric*. Aristotle argued that any time communication occurs, there is a speaker, a speech, and an audience. Most people would not disagree with Aristotle's formulation, although not all communication is spoken and listened to, of course. When you read the words on this page, who is the speaker? It appears that the book you are reading is both speaker and speech, while you are the audience. This type of flexibility with regard to definitions is important, because the theorists that came after Aristotle developed more detailed, but still very fixed theories to explain how communication takes place.

The best known of Aristotle's successors are the so-called transmission model theorists of the middle 20th century. Three of these theorists are especially important, and all three were Americans: Harold Lasswell and the team of Claude E. Shannon and Warren Weaver. The transmission model of communication was first described by sociologist Harold Lasswell in 1948 and later expanded upon by mathematicians Claude E. Shannon and Warren Weaver in 1949. A useful summary and critique of the work of these theorists is available on the Communication, Cultural and Media Studies website, <www.ccms-infobase.com>, by searching under "Shannon-Weaver model." Their theoretical process of communication generally involves five steps, discussed here and shown in Figure 1.1.

- **Sender forms an idea.** The idea may be influenced by the sender's mood, frame of reference, background, and culture, as well as the context of the situation. (For example, an accountant realizes income tax season is about to begin.)
- **Sender encodes the idea in a message.** Encoding means converting the idea into words or gestures that will convey meaning. A major problem in communicating any message is that words have different meanings for different people. That's why skilled communicators try to choose familiar words with concrete meanings on which both senders and receivers agree. (For example, the accountant writes a letter asking all her clients to begin scheduling income tax appointments.)
- **Message travels over a channel.** The medium over which the message is transmitted is the channel. Messages may be sent by computer, telephone, fax, portable handheld device like a BlackBerry, traditional mail, or website blog. Because both verbal and nonverbal messages are carried, senders must choose channels carefully. Any barrier that disrupts the transmission of a message in the communication process is called noise. Channel noise ranges

Figure 1.1 ▶
Communication Process

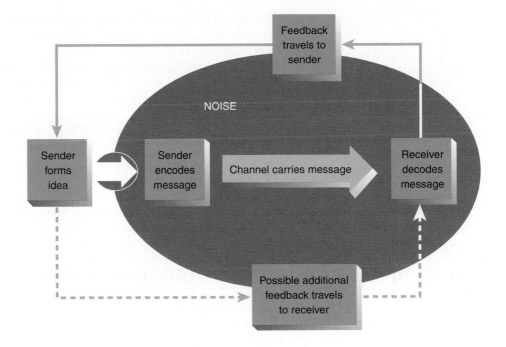

from static that disrupts a telephone conversation to spelling and grammar errors in an e-mail message, to e-mails that are not sent because of firewalls. Such errors can damage the credibility of the sender. (For example, the accountant's assistant sends the letter to 125 clients via traditional mail in early January.)

- **Receiver decodes message.** The person for whom a message is intended is the receiver. Translating the message into meaning involves decoding. Successful communication takes place only when a receiver understands the meaning intended by the sender. Such success is often hard to achieve because barriers and noise may disrupt the process. (For example, a client opens the letter, reads it, and decides to do his taxes himself this year.)

- **Feedback travels to sender.** The response of the receiver creates feedback, a vital part of the entire communication process, and one that Lasswell and Shannon/Weaver did not include in their original model. Feedback helps the sender know that the message was received and understood. Senders can encourage feedback by including statements such as "Please let me know what you think as soon as possible." Senders can further improve feedback by delivering the message at a time when receivers can respond. Senders should also provide only as much information as a receiver can handle. Receivers can improve the process by paraphrasing the sender's message. They might say, "Thanks for your e-mail explaining the new safety procedure." (For example, the client calls the accountant and leaves a voice mail thanking her for her letter but letting her know he's going to do his taxes himself this year.)

The transmission model of communication described above has been critiqued and fine-tuned over the past 50 years by other well-known theorists like the Canadian professor Marshall McLuhan. Like many theories, the transmission model of communication has been persuasive because of its clarity and elegance and because it appears to cover most communication situations. For example, the problem described in the article at the beginning of the chapter is a classic case of barriers (lack of English grammar and vocabulary skills) getting in the way of the decoding of communication.

However, commentators have increasingly begun to point out that the transmission model does not account for all communication situations. For example, the most commonly cited criticism is that the transmission model is based on a metaphor of "transmission" that is increasingly unconvincing in the Internet age when messages travel incredibly quickly. In other words, because communication today is instantaneous and ever-present (how many e-mails did you receive today?), the idea that there is a process of communication that can be broken down into discrete steps (as above) might be misleading. Despite this and other criticisms of the theory, it is still the most effective way for understanding the dynamic between two people (or two machines!) that have chosen to talk, write, gesture, or listen to each other.

COMMUNICATION IN THE KNOWLEDGE ECONOMY

Understanding the transmission model of communication remains vital precisely because the world of work is changing dramatically. The kind of work you'll do, the tools you'll use, the form of management you'll work under, the environment in which you'll work, the people with whom you'll interact—all are undergoing a pronounced transformation. Many of the changes revolve around processing and communicating information. It's logical that the most successful players in this new world of work will be those with highly developed communication skills. The following business trends illustrate the importance of excellent communication skills.

- **Innovative communication technologies.** E-mail, instant messaging, the Web, mobile technologies, audio- and videoconferencing—all these technologies mean that you will be communicating more often and more rapidly than ever before. Your writing and speaking skills will be showcased and tested as never before.
- **Flattened management hierarchies.** To better compete and to reduce expenses, businesses have for years been trimming layers of management. This means that as a frontline employee, you will have fewer managers. You will be making decisions and communicating them to customers, to fellow employees, and to executives.
- **More participatory management.** Gone are the days of command-and-control management. Now, even new employees will be expected to understand and contribute to the success of the organization. Improving productivity and profitability will be everyone's job, not just management's.
- **Increased emphasis on self-directed work and project teams.** Businesses today are often run by cross-functional teams of peers. You can expect to work with a team in gathering information, finding and sharing solutions, implementing decisions, and managing conflict. Good communication skills are extremely important in working together successfully in a team environment.
- **Heightened global competition.** Because Canadian companies are required to move beyond local markets, you may be interacting with people from many different cultures. At the same time, because of increased immigration, you may be expected to interact with people from many cultures in your local market as well as in your organization.[1] As a successful business

communicator, you will want to learn about other cultures. You'll also need to develop interpersonal skills, including sensitivity, flexibility, patience, and tolerance.

- **New work environments.** Mobile technologies and the desire for better work/family balance have resulted in flexible working arrangements. You may become part of the 1.5 million Canadians engaged in full- or part-time telecommuting.[2] Working away from the office requires exchanging even more messages in order to stay connected.
- **The move to a knowledge economy.** As Statistics Canada researchers Desmond Beckstead and Tara Vinodrai show in their paper "Dimensions of Occupational Changes in Canada's Knowledge Economy, 1971–1996," the decrease in the importance of sectors like manufacturing and agriculture has taken place at the same time as "the importance of knowledge occupations has continuously increased over the last three decades."[3] By definition, such "knowledge occupations," many of which are in business, require excellent communication skills.

OVERCOMING BARRIERS TO EFFECTIVE COMMUNICATION

The communication process is successful only when the receiver understands the message as intended by the sender. It sounds quite simple. Yet it's not. How many times have you thought that you delivered a clear message, only to learn later that your intentions were totally misunderstood? Most messages that we send reach their destination, but many are only partially understood. Another factor in the success of communication is time. It's one thing for a receiver to clearly understand what a message means, but what happens if the message is one of 45 he has received that day, and he finds himself physically unable to respond to the volume of communication?

You can improve your chances of communicating successfully by learning to recognize barriers that are known to disrupt the process. The most significant barriers for individuals are bypassing, frames of reference, lack of language skill, and distractions.

- **Bypassing.** One of the biggest barriers to clear communication involves words. Each of us attaches a little bundle of meanings to every word, and these meanings are not always similar. *Bypassing* happens when people miss each other with their meanings.[4] Bypassing can lead to major miscommunication because people assume that meanings are contained in words. Actually, meanings are in people. For communication to be successful, the receiver and sender must attach the same symbolic meanings to their words.
- **Differing frames of reference.** Another barrier to clear communication is your *frame of reference*. Everything you see and feel in the world is translated through your individual frame of reference. Your unique frame is formed by a combination of your experiences, education, culture, expectations, personality, and many other elements. As a result, you bring your own biases and expectations to any communication. Because your frame of reference is totally different from everyone else's, you will never see things exactly as others do. The article at the beginning of the chapter is an excellent example of how differing frames of reference (aboriginal vs. Eurocentric) affect communication in a workplace. Wise business communicators strive to prevent communication failure by being alert to both their own frames of reference and those of others.

- **Lack of language skill.** No matter how extraordinary the idea, it won't be understood or fully appreciated unless the communicators involved have good language skills. Each individual needs an adequate vocabulary, a command of basic punctuation and grammar, and skill in written and oral expression. Again, in reference to the article above, we could have a healthy debate over whether it is the police officer candidates' lack of language skills that caused them to fail the test or whether it was mismatched frames of reference (and hence the police force's responsibility) that caused the high failure rate. Moreover, poor listening skills can prevent us from hearing oral messages clearly and thus responding properly.

- **Distractions.** Other barriers include emotional interference and physical distractions. Shaping an intelligent message is difficult when you're feeling joy, fear, resentment, hostility, sadness, or some other strong emotion. To reduce the influence of emotions on communication, both senders and receivers should focus on the content of the message and try to remain objective. Physical distractions such as faulty acoustics, noisy surroundings, or a poor cell phone connection can disrupt oral communication. Similarly, sloppy presentation, poor printing, careless formatting, and typographical or spelling errors can disrupt written messages. Finally, as mentioned above, the stress of overwhelming volumes of communication is an important factor.

What can we do to lessen this stress? Careful communicators can conquer barriers in a number of ways. Half the battle in communicating successfully is recognizing that the entire process is sensitive and susceptible to breakdown. Like a defensive driver anticipating problems on the road, a good communicator anticipates problems in encoding, transmitting, and decoding a message. Effective communicators also focus on the receiver's environment and frame of reference. They ask themselves questions such as "How is that individual likely to react to my message?" or "Does the receiver know as much about the subject as I do?"

Misunderstandings are less likely if you arrange your ideas logically and use words precisely. But communicating is more than expressing yourself well. A large part of successful communication is listening.

Overcoming interpersonal barriers often involves questioning your preconceptions. Successful communicators continually examine their personal assumptions, biases, and prejudices. The more you pay attention to subtleties and know "where you're coming from" when you encode and decode messages, the better you'll communicate.

Finally, effective communicators create an environment for useful feedback. In oral communication this means asking questions such as "Do you understand?" and "What questions do you have?" as well as encouraging listeners to repeat instructions or paraphrase ideas. As a listener, it means providing feedback that describes rather than evaluates. And in written communication it means asking questions and providing access: "Do you have my telephone number in case you have questions?" or "Here's my e-mail address so that you can give me your response immediately."

THEORY INTO PRACTICE: COMMUNICATING AT WORK

Until now, you've probably been thinking about the communication you do personally. But business communicators must also be concerned with the bigger picture, and that involves sharing information in organizations. Creating and exchanging knowledge are critical to fostering innovation, the key challenge in today's knowledge economy. On the job you'll be exchanging information by communicating internally and externally. Internal communication includes sharing ideas and messages with superiors, co-workers, and subordinates. When those messages must be written, you'll probably choose e-mail or a memo. When you are communicating externally with customers, suppliers, government, and the public, you will generally send letters on company stationery.

Some of the functions of internal communication are to issue and clarify procedures and policies, inform management of progress, develop new products and services, persuade employees or management to make changes or improvements, coordinate activities, and evaluate and reward employees. External communication functions are to answer inquiries about products or services, persuade customers to buy products or services, clarify supplier specifications, issue credit, collect bills, respond to government agencies, and promote a positive image of the organization.

In all of these tasks employees and managers use a number of communication skills: reading, listening, speaking, and writing. You probably realize that you need to improve these skills to the proficiency level required for success in today's knowledge society. This book and this course will provide you with practical advice on how to do just that.

If we look back over the preceding discussion of internal and external functions of communication in organizations, there appear to be a large number of diverse business communication functions. In fact, we can classify these various functions into three easy-to-understand categories: to inform, to persuade, and/or to promote goodwill.

The flattening of organizations coupled with the development of sophisticated information technology has greatly changed the way we communicate internally and externally. We're seeing a major shift away from one-sided and rather slow forms of communication, such as memos and letters, to more interactive, fast-results communication. Speeding up the flow of communication are technologies such as e-mail, instant messaging (IM), text messaging, voice mail, cell phones, and wireless fidelity (Wi-Fi) networks. Wi-Fi lets mobile workers connect to the Internet at ultra-fast speeds without cables. Using IM, workers can communicate simultaneously with clients, colleagues, and friends. Many workers also rely on text messaging on their cell phones, laptops, or handheld devices. In addition to dependence on IM, many businesspeople rely on their cell phones. Unfortunately, cell phones have proliferated so rapidly that their careless use has become an annoyance in many public places and business communication situations such as meetings. Chapter 12 discusses cell phone etiquette among other business etiquette topics.

Other forms of interactive communication include intranets (internal company versions of the Internet), websites, video transmission, and videoconferencing. You'll be learning more about some of these forms of communication in subsequent chapters. Despite the range of interactive technologies, communicators are still working with two basic forms of communication: oral and written. Each has advantages and disadvantages.

- **Oral communication.** Nearly everyone agrees that the best way to exchange information is orally in face-to-face conversations or meetings. Oral communication has many advantages. For one thing, it minimizes misunderstandings because communicators can immediately ask questions to clarify uncertainties. For another, it enables communicators to see each other's facial expressions and hear voice inflections, further improving the process. Oral communication is also an efficient way to develop consensus when many people must be consulted. Finally, most of us enjoy face-to-face interpersonal communication because it's easy, feels warm and natural, and promotes friendships.

The main disadvantages of oral communication are that it produces no written record, sometimes wastes time, and may be inconvenient. When individuals meet face to face or speak on the telephone, someone's work has to be interrupted. And how many of us are able to limit a conversation to just business? Nevertheless, oral communication has many advantages.

- **Written communication.** Written communication is impersonal in the sense that two communicators cannot see or hear each other and cannot provide immediate feedback. Most forms of business communication—including e-mail, memos, faxes, letters, newsletters, reports, proposals, and manuals—fall into this category. Organizations rely on written communication for many reasons. It provides a permanent record, a necessity in these times of increasing litigation and extensive government regulation. Writing out an idea instead of delivering it orally enables communicators to develop an organized, well-considered message. Written documents are also convenient. They can be composed and read when the schedules of both communicators permit, and they can be reviewed if necessary.

  Written messages have drawbacks, of course. They require careful preparation and sensitivity to audience and anticipated effects. Words spoken in conversation may soon be forgotten, but words committed to hard or soft copy become a public record—and sometimes an embarrassing or dangerous one.

  Another drawback to written messages is that they are more difficult to prepare. They demand good writing skills, and such skills are not inborn. But writing proficiency can be learned. Because as much as 90 percent of all business transactions may involve written messages and because writing skills are so important to your business success, you will be receiving special instruction in becoming a good writer and a good communicator.

Although technology provides a myriad of communication channel choices, the sheer volume of messages is overwhelming many employees. The average North American worker receives 54 e-mails per day, and this number seems to have stabilized. However, the number of nonessential messages has increased by 41 percent. According to Christina Cavanagh, a professor at the Richard Ivey School of Business, the cost of e-mail overload is approximately 12 percent of yearly corporate payrolls.[5]

Additionally, meaning may also be lost since reading on a computer screen has been shown to yield just 75 percent of the comprehension of reading on paper.[6]

IMPROVING COMMUNICATION AT WORK

Information overload and resulting productivity meltdown are becoming serious problems for workers and their employers. While some software programs can now automatically sort messages into limited categories, one expert says that "human brainpower"—not new technology—is the key to managing e-mail overload.[7] Suggestions for controlling the e-mail monster are discussed in Chapter 4.

Information within organizations flows through formal and informal communication channels. A free exchange of information helps organizations respond rapidly to changing markets, increase efficiency and productivity, build employee morale, serve the public, and take full advantage of the ideas of today's knowledge workers. Barriers, however, can obstruct the flow of communication.

Formal Channels

Formal channels of communication generally follow an organization's hierarchy of command. Information about policies and procedures originates with executives and flows down through managers to supervisors and finally to lower-level employees. Many organizations have formulated official communication policies that encourage regular open communication, suggest means for achieving it, and spell out responsibilities. Official information among workers typically flows through formal channels in three directions: downward, upward, and horizontally.

Downward flow. Information flowing downward generally moves from decision makers, including the CEO and managers, through the chain of command to workers. This information includes job plans, policies, and procedures. Managers also provide feedback about employee performance and instill a sense of mission in achieving the organization's goals.

One obstacle that can impede the downward flow of information is distortion resulting from long lines of communication. If, for example, the CEO wanted to change an accounting procedure, she or he would probably not send a memo directly to the staff or cost accountants who would implement the change. Instead, the CEO would relay the idea through proper formal channels—from the vice president for finance, to the accounting manager, to the senior accountant, and so on—until the message reached the affected employees. Obviously, the longer the lines of communication, the greater the chance that a message will be distorted.

To improve communication and to compete more effectively, many of today's companies have "reengineered" themselves into smaller operating units and work teams. Rather than being bogged down with long communication chains, management speaks directly to team leaders, thus speeding up the entire process.[8] Management is also improving the downward flow of information through newsletters, announcements, meetings, videos, and company intranets. Instead of hoarding information at the top, today's managers recognize how essential it is to let workers know how well the company is doing and what new projects are planned.

Upward flow. Information flowing upward provides feedback from non-management employees to management. Subordinate employees describe progress in completing tasks, report roadblocks encountered, and suggest methods for improving efficiency. Channels for upward communication include phone messages, e-mail, memos, reports, departmental meetings, and suggestion systems. Ideally, the heaviest flow of information should be upward, with information being fed steadily to decision makers.

A number of obstacles, however, can interrupt the upward flow of communication. Employees who distrust their employers are less likely to communicate openly. Employees cease trusting managers if they feel they are being tricked, manipulated, criticized, or treated unfairly. Unfortunately, some employees today no longer have a strong trusting attitude toward employers. Downsizing, cost-cutting measures, the tremendous influx of temporary workers, discrimination and harassment suits, substantial compensation packages for chief executives, and many other factors have eroded the feelings of trust and pride that employees once felt toward their employers and their jobs. Other obstacles include fear of reprisal for honest communication, lack of adequate communication skills, and differing frames of reference. Imperfect communication may result when individuals are not using words or symbols with similar meanings, when they cannot express their ideas clearly, or when they come from different backgrounds.

To improve the upward flow of communication, some companies are hiring communication coaches to train employees, asking employees to report customer complaints, encouraging regular meetings with staff, providing a trusting, non-threatening environment in which employees can comfortably share their observations and ideas with management, and offering incentive programs that encourage employees to collect and share valuable feedback. Companies are also building trust by setting up hotlines for anonymous feedback to management and by installing ombudsman programs. An *ombudsman* is a mediator who hears employee complaints, investigates, and seeks to resolve problems fairly.

Horizontal flow. Lateral channels transmit information horizontally among workers at the same level. These channels enable individuals to coordinate tasks, share information, solve problems, and resolve conflicts. Horizontal communication takes place through personal contact, telephone, e-mail, memos, voice mail, and meetings. Most traditional organizations have few established regular channels for the horizontal exchange of information. Restructured companies with flattened hierarchies and team-based management, however, have discovered that when employees combine their knowledge with that of other employees, they can do their jobs better. Much of the information in these organizations is travelling horizontally among team members.[9]

Obstacles to the horizontal flow of communication, as well as to upward and downward flow, include poor communication skills, prejudice, ego involvement, and turf wars. Some employees avoid sharing information if doing so might endanger their status or chances for promotion within the organization. Competition within units and an uneven reward system may also prevent workers from freely sharing information.

To improve horizontal communication, companies are training employees in teamwork and communication techniques, establishing reward systems based on team achievement rather than individual achievement, and encouraging full participation in team functions. However, employees must also realize that they are personally responsible for making themselves heard, for really understanding what other people say, and for getting the information they need. Developing those business communication skills is exactly what this book and this course will do for you.

Informal Channels

Not all information within an organization travels through formal channels. Often, it travels in informal channels known as the *grapevine*. These channels are usually based on social relationships in which individuals talk about work when they are having lunch, meeting at the water cooler, working out, golfing, or carpooling to work. Alert managers find the grapevine an excellent source of information about employee morale and problems. They have also used the grapevine as a "break it to them gently" device, planting "rumours," for example, of future layoffs or other changes.

Researchers studying communication flow within organizations know that the grapevine can be a major source of information. Is this bad? It depends. The grapevine can be a fairly accurate and speedy source of organization information. However, grapevine information is often incomplete because it travels in headlines. When employees obtain most of their company news from the grapevine, it's a pretty sure bet that management is not releasing sufficient information through formal channels. The truth is that most employees want to know what's going on. In fact, one study found that regardless of how much information organization members reported receiving, they wanted more.[10] Many companies today have moved away from a rigid authoritarian management structure in which only managers were privy to vital information, such as product success and profit figures. Employees who know the latest buzz feel like important members of the team.[11] Through formal lines of communication, smart companies are keeping employees informed. Thus, the grapevine is reduced to carrying gossip about who's dating whom and what restaurant is trendy for lunch.

ETHICAL BUSINESS COMMUNICATION

It's not just how communication flows within and outside a company that is important, however. The content of that communication is increasingly being scrutinized. Many businesses have begun to recognize that ethical practices make good business sense. Ethical companies endure less litigation, less resentment, and less government regulation.[12] As a result, companies are adding ethics officers, hotlines, workshops, training programs, and codes of conduct. If you go to work for a large company, chances are good that you'll be asked to comply with its code of conduct.

Despite this trend, however, the business world continues to be plagued by unethical behaviour and a poor public image. With downsized staffs and fewer resources, employees feel pressure to increase productivity—by whatever means. Knowingly or not, managers under pressure to make profit quotas may send the message to workers that it's acceptable to lie, cheat, or steal to achieve company goals.[13] Couple these pressures with a breakdown in the traditional attitudes of trust and loyalty toward employers, and it's easy to see why ethical lapses are causing concern in the workplace.

Business communicators can minimize the danger of falling into ethical traps by setting specific ethical goals. Although the following goals hardly comprise a formal code of conduct, they will help business writers maintain a high ethical standard.

- **Telling the truth.** Ethical business communicators do not intentionally make statements that are untrue or deceptive. We become aware of dishonesty in business when violators break laws, notably in advertising, packaging, and marketing. Half-truths, exaggerations, and deceptions constitute unethical communication. But conflicting loyalties in the workplace sometimes blur the line between right and wrong.
- **Labelling opinions.** Sensitive communicators know the difference between facts and opinions. Facts are verifiable and often are quantifiable; opinions are beliefs held with confidence but without substantiation. Stating opinions as if they were facts is unethical.
- **Being objective.** Ethical business communicators recognize their own biases and strive to keep them from distorting a message. Honest reporting means presenting the whole picture and relating all facts fairly.
- **Communicating clearly.** Ethical business communicators feel an obligation to write clearly so that receivers understand easily and quickly. Many organizations, such as banks and insurance companies, have even created "Plain

English" guidelines to ensure that policies, warranties, and contracts are in language comprehensible to average readers. Plain English means short sentences, simple words, and clear organization. Communicators who intentionally obscure the meaning with long sentences and difficult words are being unethical. A thin line, however, separates unethical communication from ethical communication. Some might argue that writers and speakers who deliver wordy, imprecise messages requiring additional correspondence or inquiry to clarify the meaning are acting unethically. However, the problem may be one of experience and skill rather than ethics. Such messages waste the time and resources of both senders and receivers. However, they are not unethical unless the intent is to deceive.

- **Giving credit.** As you probably know, using the published ideas of others without giving proper credit is called *plagiarism*. Ethical communicators give credit for ideas by referring to originators' names within the text, using quotation marks, and documenting sources with internal references or endnotes and footnotes. In school or on the job, stealing ideas or words from others is unethical.

CONCLUSION

This chapter described the importance of becoming an effective business communicator in the knowledge economy. Many of the changes in today's dynamic workplace revolve around processing and communicating information. Flattened management hierarchies, participatory management, increased emphasis on work teams, heightened global competition, and innovative communication technologies are all trends that increase the need for good communication skills. To improve your skills, you should understand the communication process. Communication doesn't take place unless senders encode meaningful messages that can be decoded by receivers. However, various barriers may get in the way of effective communication. You also learned about the flow of communication in organizations, and about ethical challenges facing business communicators today.

The following chapter looks more broadly at the process of communication. You will learn about aural communication, which means listening skills. You will also learn about non-spoken and non-written communication, which includes gestural communication. Finally, you will learn about communicating in special situations, for example, in workplace teams or in cross-cultural workplaces.

Chapter Review

As a way of studying the material in this chapter, imagine you are at a job interview for your dream entry-level job after college or university. You've prepared answers for all the classic interview questions, but to your surprise, your interviewer also asks a number of questions based on communication theory. How would you answer the following six questions?

1. We've advertised communication skills as being very important to this position. What does communication mean to you?
2. Why do you think we advertised communication skills at the top of our list of necessary qualifications?
3. Can you tell us about two or three situations in your past work experience where communication broke down? Please tell us what you did to improve the situation.

4. Describe some different types of communication or communication situations you think you might find yourself in at our company.
5. What's your opinion on best practices in communication in an organization like ours? Are there any negative communication challenges you can foresee?
6. We're big proponents of ethical communication at our company. What do you think we mean by "ethical communication"?

⋮⋮ *Problems*

Solve the following problems using the method described in the Preface of this book. Keep in mind that your instructor may ask you to solve the problem in a number of ways. For example, you may be asked to role-play part of the solution. Or you may be asked to debate two opposing viewpoints from your analysis of the problem. Or you may be asked to write a part of the solution. Be creative!

1. Each year, Manulife Financial takes in between 20 and 30 co-op students from various colleges and universities near its Canadian head office in Waterloo, Ontario. The co-op process requires a significant investment of time (interviewing, correspondence) and money (honoraria, training for employees) on the part of the company. As a result, Manulife expects the colleges and universities sending students out on co-op interviews to have screened the applicants to make sure they have excellent communication skills. This past year, the director of Human Resources, who oversees the co-op program for Manulife, began to notice a frustrating trend. Of the three colleges and universities working with Manulife over the past five years, two (one college, one university) have become lax in their screening process. The evidence is that almost all the cover letters and résumés sent to Manulife by these institutions were poorly written and obviously not edited, because they were full of grammar and style mistakes. Being a good corporate citizen, Manulife wants to continue its co-op participation with the colleges and universities, but it can't afford to hire students whose communication skills are so poor that they cannot be trusted to perform even the most basic tasks in the workplace. As the director of Human Resources at Manulife, you need to find a solution to this situation by the next round of interviews, which is in four months.
   <**www.manulife.ca**>

2. As a marketing manager at Vancouver-based Lions Gate Entertainment, you are responsible for a number of products within a specific category, which is DVDs. Your main responsibility is making sure the company's sales representatives have all the material they need to properly sell Lions Gate DVDs across Canada. Each year, Lions Gate holds a national sales conference at which all the marketing managers and all the sales reps get together to attend presentations on new products. Over the past couple of sales conferences—at which you had to give multiple presentations to multiple audiences—you've noticed that sales reps are increasingly not listening to your presentation. Instead, they're using various communication devices (PDAs, cell phones, tablet PCs) to communicate or do work. You consider this a rude interruption, especially because once one audience member starts using a BlackBerry the concentration of the whole room seems to evaporate. At the same time, you recognize that being sales reps, your audience members have to be communicating all the time. Still, you're pretty close to approaching your boss, the VP of Marketing, to ask her about drafting a sales conference policy that would ban the use of communication devices during presentations. What is the main problem in this situation and how can it be solved?
   <**www.lionsgatefilms.com**>

3. Keilhauer is a leading Canadian manufacturer of contemporary office and residential furniture. Located in Toronto, the company is a family-owned business that has won numerous national and international awards. Besides family members, the company employs designers and sales reps on a freelance or contract basis. The corporate structure includes a CEO, Byron Keilhauer, who founded the company in 1981. Although he has remained in that role, Keilhauer currently takes a passive approach to managing the company. His children, Veronica, Leonard, and William, oversee the day-to-day running of the firm. Veronica is the VP of Marketing and Sales, Leonard is the VP of Operations, and William is the VP of Design. A cousin, Nancy, is VP of Finance. Recently, during board meetings (all the above-mentioned people are on the board), arguments have broken out between Byron Keilhauer's children about the direction of the company. Veronica has accused William of bypassing her on numerous occasions and communicating directly via e-mail with their father about important marketing decisions. Similarly, Leonard is angry at William because William apparently phones their father on a weekly basis to complain about various production issues, all of which are Leonard's responsibility. Nancy also voices a concern about promises William has made to various designers that have not been cleared by her. Clearly, the CEO has an important communication problem on his hands. What is the problem and what should he do about it?
   <www.keilhauer.com>

4. The food service industry has increasingly become integrated, with many chain restaurants across the country owned and operated by large companies. A good example is Cara Operations Limited of Toronto, which owns the Swiss Chalet, Harvey's, Second Cup, and Kelsey's chains. As the owner of privately held Beavertails Inc. of Montreal, you have recently been in talks with Peter Suurtamm, VP of Corporate Development for Cara Operations Limited. Cara has been interested in purchasing Beavertails Inc. for a number of years now, especially because Beavertails' outlets are located in high-traffic locations in major malls and tourist destinations across Canada. The talks with Suurtamm have been ongoing—and secret—for over a year now. Only your partner, the co-owner of Beavertails, knows about the talks with Cara. Or so you thought. One morning, you open the business section of the Montreal *Gazette* to find an article titled "Beavertails Moving to Toronto?" Since Beavertails is a Quebec-headquartered company, the possibility of being sold to an English-Canadian company is politically sensitive. You have no idea who leaked the news to the media, and it doesn't take long for gossip to start making its way around head office. Your anger over the leak to the media takes a back seat to the reality of what's going on at your office: your voice mail is inundated with employees who want to talk to you. People are stopping you outside your office and asking if the media reports are true. Soon, you're near the end of your rope and having difficulty functioning properly. Something has to be done. What is the solution and how should it be implemented?
   <www.cara.com.> <www.beavertailsinc.com>

5. As a small business owner, you're used to running things the way you like at your company. The company you own, Cows Inc., enjoys a favourable reputation with almost all Canadians (and many Americans, Japanese, and Germans) who've come into contact with the well-known ice cream brand on trips to Prince Edward Island or to other well-known tourist destinations like Banff. Cows is one of Canada's best-known ice cream companies, just as

famous for its bright graphic T-shirts and other clothing products as it is for its ice cream. No trip to P.E.I. is complete without a visit to Green Gables and to one of the Cows' locations for a tasty ice cream cone. The company's well-deserved reputation has been tested recently by a story that appeared in the Charlottetown *Guardian* in which reporter Brian McKay alleges that Cows' famous T-shirts and sweatshirts are being produced in "third-world sweat-shops in countries such as Haiti, Guatemala, and Thailand." The firm you've subcontracted with in Montreal to provide you with T-shirts and sweatshirts assured you in a verbal conversation that all its clothing products were man-ufactured in "certified factories" in which "good wages" are paid and "good conditions" are ensured. Whatever the truth of the situation, you need to prepare a communication strategy (website? press release? media inter-views?) to do damage control and ensure future business success through customer loyalty.

<www.cows.ca>

Grammar/Style Review 1

As you learned in this chapter, one of the major barriers to effective communication is a lack of language skills. As a way of bolstering your language skills, each chapter in this book contains a Grammar/Style Review that targets one of the top mistakes found in students' writing. Each Review contains a typical business document with a number of mistakes. Your task is to proofread the document and identify and fix the mistakes, using the proofreading marks found in Appendix B.

In this review, you will be practising identifying subject-verb agreement mistakes. There are five mistakes in total. For a brief explanation of this grammar problem, please read the explanation on page 323. Besides completing the exercise below, be on the lookout for subject-verb agreement mistakes in your own writing.

To: mauletti@bmo.ca

From: ksmythe@bmo.ca

Re: Training materials for new hires

Hi Marco,

The new training handbook, along with the brochures and posters, are going to the printer on Friday. What this means is that the copy edit and the proofread is going to be due on the Monday before, which is the 16th. This also means that either you or the members of your team is going to have to put in some extra hours next week. I realize that each of your team members are working at full capacity, so I'd ask you to prioritize your non-handbook tasks. The handbook team are behind you all the way, so just let me know if you need any help over the next week as we work towards this deadline.

Regards,

Kathleen

∴ *Business Communication Lab 1*

Depending on your instructor and your course delivery style, you may be asked to complete this Business Communication Lab in a computer lab during class time, at home as homework, in class the old-fashioned way (pen and paper), or in class as a presentation.

You are the sales manager for Canassessment Services Inc., a Winnipeg-based consulting company that specializes in producing custom testing materials. You've just come across Nikhat Ahmed's article in the Saskatoon *StarPhoenix*. Obviously, you see a sales opportunity here to provide a customized testing product for the Saskatoon Police Force. After some research on the topic, you decide to write a letter to Lisa Olson, Director of Human Resources, Saskatoon Police Service, P.O. Box 1728, Saskatoon, SK, S7K 3R6. To help with this lab, you may want to visit the following websites: <**http://www.police.saskatoon.sk.ca/index.html**> <**http://www.mackayedge.com**>

CHAPTER 2

Nonverbal, Listening, Team, and Cross-Cultural Communication

Workers bring culture to their cubicle

As more employees express their ethnicity in their clothing, and more compa-nies recognize their diverse work forces, such dress still raises issues about acceptance in the workplace

BY APARITA BHANDARI, *THE GLOBE AND MAIL,* WEDNESDAY, SEPTEMBER 28, 2005

WHEN PARAMJIT KAUR Mangat arrives for work at Royal Bank of Canada's Toronto head office, she's often dressed in a *salwar-kameez.*

"I wear my cultural clothes as often as I can," says Ms. Mangat of the long tunic, pants and stole outfit she refers to by its Urdu name.

"I am Punjabi by culture and Sikh by faith. My dress reflects who I am."

The assistant manager in the corporate treasury department sees her dress as a reflection of the changing face of Canada.

And changing it is. The country's visible minority population more than tripled to nearly four million, or 13 per cent of the population, from 1.1 million, or 5 per cent, in 1981, according to Statistics Canada's most recent census data.

By 2016, one in five Canadian workers will belong to a visible minority, a study by the Conference Board of Canada last year predicted.

"As more and more Canadians become comfort-able in their skins, they are outwardly expressing their ethnicity by wearing particular clothing," says Cynthia Reyes, vice-president of DiversiPro Inc., a Toronto-based consulting firm specializing in diversity.

At the same time, "as organizations and compa-nies become more culturally competent, they are allowing their employees to wear certain clothes so long as it does not pose a safety risk on the job or conflict with the image the company is trying to pro-ject to its customers."

And, Ms. Reyes adds, "For some people, wearing ethnic-specific clothing is not a fashion statement or an occasion to celebrate a particular holiday. It's a natural extension of who they are. They want to pre-sent their whole selves on the job."

Blending cultural or religious dress with more tra-ditional corporate wear is growing more common, Ms. Reyes says.

Beyond combining Muslim, Jewish or Sikh reli-gious head wear with a suit, say, "a man may decide to wear an African top or a *kurta* [Indian tunic] with dress pants, a woman may decide to integrate a Chinese silk blouse into her outfit or top off that busi-ness suit with a beautiful scarf made from African kinte cloth," she adds.

Yet, even as more people choose to express their ethnicity by donning a sari, mandarin or dashiki top—or even a kilt to the office—it raises many issues about acceptance.

On the one hand, people sporting ethnic clothing are expressing their individuality, and such wear "can be taken as a perception of your flexibility, your ability to adapt, and your comfort in the Canadian workplace," says Janice Steele, an employability sup-port counsellor at the Ryerson Career Centre in Toronto.

Wearing different clothing can also make you stand out in a positive way, inviting curiosity, conversation and understanding, says Monica Belcourt, director of the graduate program in human resources management at York University in Toronto.

And more employers are recognizing clothing as a way to celebrate their diverse work forces.

RBC, as one example, is guided by principles of diversity, and its policy is to respect clients and employees in dealing with dress code issues, says media relations manager Judi Levita.

"We do welcome diversity, and it would reflect in attire," Ms. Levita says.

On the other hand, bringing your culture to your cubicle "can also be used as a way to discriminate against you," Ms. Steele warns.

And standing out also has its negatives.

Employers are always looking for organizational fits, and if you wear something different, you may send unconscious signals that you don't understand the culture of the organization, Ms. Belcourt adds.

"People who decide to wear ethnic clothes on the job should be aware there could be some push-backs from co-workers in some environments," Ms. Reyes says.

Image consultant Nyla Ibrahim, director of Oakville, Ont.-based Professional Edge Image Consulting, contends that, unless it's absolutely nec-essary—say, a religious requirement—you're better off sticking to professional work wear.

To an observer, no matter how liberal, ethnic wear will give off signals that you defy authority or don't know how to behave professionally, she suggests.

"You are limiting your career opportunities," she warns.

"Just like when someone wears outdated clothes, you think the person is outdated."

Jyoti Rana can relate to that.

Several years ago, when she worked at the Toronto branch of a U.S. software production company as a technical resource manager, she wore a sari to work and received compliments from colleagues.

But a few hours into the day, Ms. Rana got called on by a senior executive.

"She told me that my dress was inappropriate because it was ethnic," she recalls.

"I said I'm showing less skin than the short skirt you're wearing. She didn't take it well."

Certainly, the law is on the side of those who want to reflect their culture through their clothes.

Unless there's an occupational requirement or a safety issue, the banning of ethnic clothing could be grounds for a human rights complaint of discrimination on the basis of ethnic origin, says Donald Eady, an employment lawyer and partner at Paliare Roland LLP.

DIAGNOSING THE PROBLEM

It's clear that much of the above article is about positive, not problematic, aspects of nonverbal communication (in this case the signals sent out by the clothes we wear at work). Yet we can also say that a problem exists, which is that dressing in non-standard business wear such as ethnic clothing can lead to miscommunication. As image consultant Nyla Ibrahim argues, non-standard business wear can be interpreted as unprofessional and defying authority, and it may hamper promotion opportunities within a company. In essence, it may mark you as "not fitting in" to the company's culture. Does the article furnish us with reasons for why the problem exists? In fact, it offers two clear reasons. First, the demographic reality in Canada is changing, with immigrants from non-Western cultures and visible minority groups set to make up 20 percent of the Canadian workforce within a decade. Also, companies are liberalizing their policies on workplace dress, and these policies are backed up by legislation that makes it against the law to discriminate against someone based on ethnic origin, according to lawyer Donald Eady.

So even though the communications problem is not clear-cut, what sorts of solutions might be appropriate? There's obviously a spectrum of possibilities. On one end, we could argue that the norm in a professional Canadian environment is traditional business wear—dress clothes like button-down shirts, suit jackets, and ties for men, and blouses, skirts, dress pants, and jackets for women—and that this standard must be adhered to by all. Another solution might be to do the opposite: to proclaim, as the Canadian courts have done, that it's our right as Canadians to dress how we want to at any time or in any place, as long as someone else's safety or well-being is not affected. Perhaps an even more subtle solution would be to accept that this problem is not so much about what's legal and what's not. Rather, this problem is about what is seen as acceptable and what is accepted as "normal" in Canadian businesses. If it's legal for people to wear Indian-style clothing to their job, but they know that if they do so, gossip will spread throughout the firm before the first morning break, then what is the benefit of dressing in Indian clothing? Perhaps the solution is to encourage dialogue in the workplace about changing realities in Canada and how that might affect what people wear to work. There are probably other solutions you can think of, but we'll leave it there for the moment. The task now is to evaluate different possible solutions and choose the most appropriate one. This is where you and your team come in...

in-class activity 2

WORKING IN SMALL groups of three to four, students will discuss the analysis of the problem provided above and evaluate the solutions offered in order to choose the most appropriate one. Is the analysis provided above complete? What will an appropriate solution look like? Why did your group choose this solution? What pluses and minuses are there in choosing this solution? Report back to the class within 30 minutes.

Now that you've presented your solution to the rest of the class, you're ready to discover some of the theory that exists behind the situation you've just examined. At the end of this chapter, you will be presented with more problems that you may be asked to analyze, evaluate, and explain.

NONVERBAL COMMUNICATION

Understanding messages often involves more than listening to spoken words. Nonverbal cues also carry powerful meanings. Nonverbal communication includes all unwritten and unspoken messages, both intentional and unintentional. Eye contact, facial expression, body movements, space, time, distance, appearance—all of these nonverbal cues influence the way a message is interpreted, or decoded, by the receiver. Many of the nonverbal messages that we send are used intentionally to accompany spoken words. But people can also communicate nonverbally even when they don't intend to. And not all messages accompany words.

Because nonverbal communication is an important tool for you to use and control in the workplace, you need to learn more about its functions and forms.

Functions of Nonverbal Communication

Nonverbal communication functions in at least five ways to help convey meaning. As you become more aware of the following functions of nonverbal communication, you will be better able to use these silent codes to your advantage in the workplace.

- **To complement and illustrate.** Nonverbal messages such as gestures can amplify, modify, or provide details for a verbal message.
- **To reinforce and accentuate.** Skilled speakers raise their voices to convey important ideas, but they whisper to suggest secrecy. A grimace forecasts painful news, while a big smile intensifies good news.
- **To replace and substitute.** Many gestures substitute for words: nodding your head for "yes," giving a "V" for victory. In fact, a complex set of gestures totally replaces spoken words in sign language.
- **To control and regulate.** Nonverbal messages are important regulators in conversation. Shifts in eye contact, slight head movements, changes in posture, raising of eyebrows, nodding of the head, and voice inflection—all these cues tell speakers when to continue, to repeat, to elaborate, to hurry up, or to finish.
- **To contradict.** To be sarcastic, a speaker might hold his nose while stating that your new perfume is wonderful. In the workplace, individuals may send contradictory messages with words or actions.

In the workplace, people may not be aware that they are sending contradictory messages. Researchers have found that when verbal and nonverbal messages contradict each other, listeners tend to believe and act on the nonverbal message.

Effective communicators must make sure that all their nonverbal messages reinforce their spoken words and their professional goals. To make sure that you're on the right track to nonverbal communication competency, let's look more carefully at the specific forms of nonverbal communication.

Forms of Nonverbal Communication

Instead of conveying meaning with words, nonverbal messages carry their meaning in a number of different forms ranging from facial expressions to body language and even clothes, as you learned in the article by Aparita Bhandari. Each of us sends and receives thousands of nonverbal messages daily in our business and personal lives. As you learn about the messages sent by eye contact, facial expressions, posture, and gestures, as well as the use of time, space, territory, and appearance, think about how you can use these nonverbal cues positively in your career.

Eye contact. Communicators consider the eyes to be the most accurate predictor of a speaker's true feelings and attitudes. Most of us cannot look another person straight in the eyes and lie. As a result, we tend to believe people who look directly at us. We have less confidence in and actually distrust those who cannot maintain eye contact. Sustained eye contact suggests trust and admiration; brief eye contact signifies fear or stress. Prolonged eye contact, however, can be intrusive and intimidating.

Good eye contact enables the message sender to determine whether a receiver is paying attention, showing respect, responding favourably, or feeling distress. From the receiver's perspective, good eye contact reveals the speaker's sincerity, confidence, and truthfulness. Since eye contact is a learned skill, however, you must be respectful of people who do not maintain it. You must also remember that nonverbal cues, including eye contact, have different meanings in various cultures.

Facial expression. The expression on a communicator's face can be almost as revealing of emotion as the eyes. Researchers estimate that the human face can display over 250 000 different expressions.[1] Although a few people can control these expressions and maintain a "poker face" when they want to hide their feelings, most of us display our emotions openly. Raising or lowering the eyebrows, squinting the eyes, swallowing nervously, clenching the jaw, smiling broadly—these voluntary and involuntary facial expressions supplement or entirely replace verbal messages.

Posture and gestures. An individual's general posture can convey anything from high status and self-confidence to shyness and submissiveness. Leaning toward a speaker suggests attraction and interest; pulling away or shrinking back denotes fear, distrust, anxiety, or disgust. Similarly, gestures can communicate entire thoughts via simple movements. But remember that these nonverbal cues may have vastly different meanings in different cultures.

In the workplace, a simple way to leave a good impression is to make sure your upper body is aligned with the person to whom you're talking. Erect posture sends a message of confidence, competence, diligence, and strength. Gestures are also important, if used effectively.

Time. How we structure and use time tells observers about our personality and attitudes. For example, when someone gives a visitor a prolonged interview, she signals her respect for, interest in, and approval of the visitor or the topic to be discussed. By sharing her valuable time, she sends a clear nonverbal message. Likewise, when an individual twice arrives late for a meeting, it could mean that the meeting has low priority to him, that he is a self-centred person, or that he has little self-discipline. These are assumptions that typical North Americans might make. In other cultures and regions, though, punctuality is viewed differently.

In the North American workplace you can send positive nonverbal messages by being on time for meetings and appointments, staying on task during meetings, and giving ample time to appropriate projects and individuals.

Space. How we arrange things in the space around us tells something about ourselves and our objectives. Whether the space is a dorm room, an office, or a department, people reveal themselves in the design and grouping of furniture within that space. Generally, the more formal the arrangement, the more formal and closed the communication environment.

Territory. Each of us has certain areas that we feel are our own territory, whether it's a specific spot or just the space around us. We all maintain zones of privacy in which we feel comfortable. Figure 2.1 categorizes the four zones of social interaction among North Americans, as formulated by anthropologist Edward T. Hall.

Appearance of business documents. The way an e-mail, letter, or report looks can have either a positive or a negative effect on the receiver. Documents can look neat, professional, well organized, and attractive—or just the opposite. Among the worst offenders are poorly written e-mail messages.

Figure 2.1 ▶
Four Space Zones for Social
Interaction

Zone	Distance	Uses
Intimate	0 to 45 cm (1.5 feet)	Reserved for members of the family and other loved ones.
Personal	45 cm to 123 cm (1.5 to 4 feet)	For talking with friends privately. The outer limit enables you to keep someone at arm's length.
Social	123 cm to 360 cm (4 to 12 feet)	For acquaintances, fellow workers, and strangers. Close enough for eye contact yet far enough for comfort.
Public	360 cm and over (12 feet and over)	For use in the classroom and for speeches before groups. Nonverbal cues become important as aids to communication.

Although they seem like conversation, e-mails are business documents that create a permanent record and often a bad impression. Sending an e-mail message full of errors conveys a damaging nonverbal message. The receiver immediately doubts the credibility of the sender. How much faith can you put in someone who can't spell, capitalize, or punctuate and won't make the effort to communicate clearly?

Appearance of people. The way you look—your clothing, grooming, and posture—sends an instant nonverbal message about you. Based on what they see, viewers make quick judgments about your status, credibility, personality, and potential. Business communicators who look the part are more likely to be successful in working with superiors, colleagues, and customers. Given what you learned in *The Globe and Mail* article above, this reality may sound like a harsh truth, but most people's experience does bear it out.

Especially if you are a new or potential employee, invest in appropriate, professional-looking clothing and accessories; quality is more important than quantity. Rules of thumb in business include avoiding flashy or too-informal clothes, clunky jewellery, garish makeup, and overpowering colognes, and paying attention to good grooming, including a neat hairstyle, body cleanliness, polished shoes, and clean nails. That said, once you are an established employee, you may choose to inject some of your own personality (or ethnic origin) into your clothing as outlined in the article above. Above all, project confidence in your posture, both standing and sitting.

Although the current trend is toward one or more days per week of casual dress at work, casual clothes change the image you project and also may affect your work style. A recent survey found that 70 percent of employees feel that workplace attire affects an employee's state of mind, behaviour, and productivity. The survey also reported that 69 percent of employees would prefer a more professional dress code, and they would be willing to give up casual attire if it would help their career progression.[2]

THE LISTENING PROCESS AND ITS BARRIERS

Another type of communication that we don't often think of (because writing and speaking are so omnipresent)—though it's incredibly important—is listening. Like the transmission model of communication discussed in Chapter 1, we can describe the listening process in steps. Listening takes place in four steps: perception, interpretation, evaluation, and action, as illustrated in Figure 2.2. A number of barriers, however, can obstruct the listening process.

- **Perception.** The listening process begins when you hear sounds and concentrate on them. The conscious act of listening begins when you focus on the sounds around you and select those you choose to hear. You tune in when you sense that the message is important, are interested in the topic, or are in the mood to listen. Perception is reduced by impaired hearing, noisy surroundings, inattention, and pseudolistening. *Pseudolistening* occurs when listeners "fake" it. They look as if they are listening, but their minds are wandering far off.
- **Interpretation.** Once you have focused your attention on a sound or message, you begin to interpret, or decode, it. As described in Chapter 1, interpretation of a message is affected by your cultural, educational, and social frames of reference. The meanings you attach to the speaker's words are filtered through your expectations and life experiences. Thus, your interpretation of the speaker's meaning may be quite different from what the speaker intended because your frame of reference is different. Interpretation can be reduced by language skill. For example, if English is not your first language, you will find it takes more concentration to interpret what someone who is speaking quickly is saying.
- **Evaluation.** After interpreting the meaning of a message, you analyze its merit and draw conclusions. To do this, you attempt to separate fact from opinion. Good listeners try to be objective, and they avoid prejudging the message. Thus, to evaluate a message accurately and objectively, you should consider all the information, be aware of your own biases, and avoid jumping to hasty conclusions.
- **Action.** Responding to a message may involve storing the message in memory for future use, reacting with a physical response (a frown, a smile, a laugh), or supplying feedback to the speaker. Listener feedback is essential because it helps clarify the message so that it can be decoded accurately. Feedback also helps the speaker to find out whether the message is getting through clearly. In one-to-one conversation, of course, no clear distinction exists between the roles of listener and speaker—you give or receive feedback as your role alternates.

Figure 2.2 ▶
The Listening Process and Its Barriers

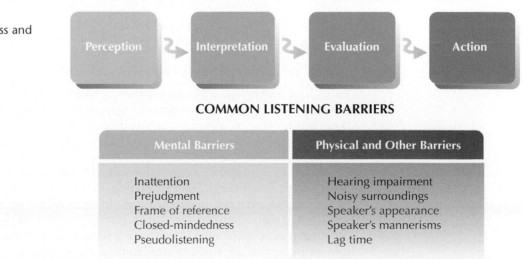

COMMON LISTENING BARRIERS

Mental Barriers	Physical and Other Barriers
Inattention	Hearing impairment
Prejudgment	Noisy surroundings
Frame of reference	Speaker's appearance
Closed-mindedness	Speaker's mannerisms
Pseudolistening	Lag time

Unfortunately, most of us will be able to recall only 50 percent of information we heard a day earlier and only 20 percent after two days.[3] How can we improve our retention? Memory training specialists say that effective remembering involves three factors: deciding to remember, structuring the incoming information to form relationships, and reviewing. In the first step, you determine what information is worth remembering. Once you have established a positive mindset, you look for a means of organizing the incoming information to form relationships. Chain links such as acronyms or rhymes can help you associate the unfamiliar with something familiar.

One of the most reliable ways to improve retention is to take notes of the important ideas to be remembered. Rewriting within ten minutes of completing listening improves your notes and takes advantage of peak recall time, which immediately follows listening. The final step in improving retention is reviewing your notes, repeating your acronym, or saying your rhyme to move the targeted information into long-term memory. Frequent reviews help strengthen your memory connections.

LISTENING IN THE WORKPLACE

Employers say that listening is a critical employee and management skill. Most workers spend 30 to 45 percent of their communication time listening,[4] while executives spend 60 to 70 percent of their communication time listening.[5] Studies report that good listeners make good managers and that good listeners advance more rapidly in their organizations.[6] In addition, listening to customers takes on increasing importance as our economy becomes ever more service-oriented.

Poor Listening Habits

Although executives and workers devote the bulk of their communication time to listening, research suggests that they're not very good at it. Poor listening habits may result from several factors. Lack of English-language experience is one significant reason, as is lack of training in listening. Few schools give as much emphasis to listening as they do to the development of reading, speaking, and writing skills. In addition, our listening skills may be less than perfect because of the large number of competing sounds and stimuli in our lives that interfere with concentration. Finally, we are inefficient listeners because we are able to process speech much faster than others can speak. While most speakers talk at about 125 to 250 words per minute, listeners can think at 1000 to 3000 words per minute.[7] The resulting lag time fosters daydreaming, which clearly reduces listening efficiency.

Types of Workplace Listening

Entry-level employees are most concerned with listening to superiors. As you advance in your career and enter the ranks of management, you will also need skills for listening to colleagues and teammates. Finally, the entire organization must listen to customers to compete in today's service-oriented economy.

Listening to superiors. One of your most important tasks will be listening to instructions, assignments, and explanations about how to do your work. You will be listening to learn and to comprehend. To focus totally on the speaker, be sure you are not distracted by noisy surroundings or other tasks. Don't take phone calls, and don't try to complete another job while listening with one ear. Show your interest by leaning forward and striving for good eye contact.

Above all, take notes. Don't rely on your memory. Details are easy to forget. Taking selective notes also conveys to the speaker your seriousness about hearing accurately and completely. Don't interrupt. When the speaker finishes, paraphrase the instructions in your own words. Ask pertinent questions in a nonthreatening manner. And don't be afraid to ask "dumb" questions, if it means you won't have to do a job twice. Avoid criticizing or arguing when you are listening to a superior. Your goals should be to hear accurately and to convey an image of competence.

Listening to colleagues and teammates. Much of your listening will result from interactions with fellow workers and teammates. In these exchanges two kinds of listening are important. *Critical listening* enables you to judge and evaluate what you are hearing. You will be listening to decide whether the speaker's message is fact, fiction, or opinion. You will also be listening to decide whether an argument is based on logic or emotion. Critical listening requires objectivity, particularly when you disagree with what you are hearing. Control your tendency to prejudge. Let the speaker have a chance to complete the message before you evaluate it. *Discriminative listening* is necessary when you must understand and remember. It means you must identify main ideas, understand a logical argument, and recognize the purpose of the message. This is the kind of listening you do at a lecture or presentation.

Three listening strategies will be useful to you in team and group interactions: dampening, redirecting, and reflecting.[8] *Dampening* involves listening with minimal response and maximum acceptance. It is particularly necessary when group members are in conflict. If one team member is unhappy about something, it is often best to let that person vent without interrupting. Dampening is also appropriate in situations requiring politeness. You listen courteously, for example, when team members are introducing themselves or when a valued employee describes a stressful encounter with a customer. *Redirecting* involves asking questions, restating the message, and getting the speaker back on track. For example, "Jeff, I believe that our goal is to find a way to reduce travel expenses. Although your comments on airport delays are interesting, do you have specific suggestions for cutting back travel expenses?"

Reflecting is useful to clarify both content and feeling as well as a helpful tool in managing conflict. By reflecting emotions, you are better able to interpret a message in the proper context. A wise strategy, for instance, is to repeat the speaker's message and acknowledge the feeling that goes with it. Paraphrase what has been said and check with the speaker to make sure you understand. For example, "I understand, Holly, that you were upset because we changed the meeting date without consulting you. Is that correct?"

Listening to customers. Although dampening, redirecting, and reflecting are listening techniques that work well in group interactions, they are equally effective in listening to customers. The new management mantra in North America has become "customers rule." Many organizations are just learning that listening to customers results in increased sales and profitability as well as improved customer acquisition and retention. As one salesperson says, "Price is almost always the number one factor for the buyer. But once you develop a relationship, even if your price is a little high, the customers will want to find a reason to stay with you."[9] The truth is that consumers feel better about companies that value their opinions. Listening is an acknowledgment of caring and is a potent retention tool. Customers want to be cared about, thus fulfilling a powerful human need.

IMPROVING WORKPLACE LISTENING

Listening on the job is more difficult than listening in classes where professors present organized lectures and repeat important points. Workplace listening is more challenging because information is often exchanged casually. It may be disorganized, unclear, and cluttered with extraneous facts. Moreover, your co-workers are sometimes also friends. Because they are familiar with one another, they may not be as polite and respectful as they are with strangers. Friends tend to interrupt, jump to conclusions, and take each other for granted. So how can organizations improve their customer listening techniques? Try using the following listening skills next time you're in a conversation, in a meeting, or on the phone.

Control external and internal distractions. Move to an area where you can hear without conflicting noises or conversations. Block out surrounding physical distractions. Internally, try to focus totally on the speaker. If other projects are on your mind, put them on the back burner temporarily. When you are emotionally upset, whether angry or extremely happy, it's a good idea to postpone any serious listening.

Become actively involved. Show that you are listening closely by leaning forward and maintaining eye contact with the speaker. Don't fidget or try to complete another task at the same time you are listening. Listen to more than the spoken words. How are they said? What implied meaning, reasoning, and feelings do you hear behind the spoken words? Does the speaker's body language (eye contact, posture, movements) support or contradict the main message?

Separate facts from opinions. Facts are truths known to exist; opinions are statements of personal judgments or preferences. Some opinions are easy to recognize because speakers preface them with statements such as "I think," "It seems to me," and "As far as I'm concerned."[10] Often, however, listeners must evaluate assertions to decide their validity. Good listeners consider whether speakers are credible and speaking within their areas of competence. They don't automatically accept assertions as facts.

Identify important facts. Speakers on the job often intersperse critical information with casual conversation. Unrelated topics pop up—sports scores, a customer's weird request, a computer glitch, the boss's extravagant new SUV. Your task is to select what's important and register it mentally. What step is next in your project? Who does what? What is your role?

Don't interrupt. While someone else has the floor, don't interrupt with a quick reply or opinion. And don't show nonverbal disagreement such as negative head shaking, rolling eyes, sarcastic snorting, or audible sighs. Good listeners let speakers have their say. Interruptions are not only impolite, but they also prevent you from hearing the speaker's complete thought. Listeners who interrupt with their opinions sidetrack discussions and cause hard feelings.

Ask clarifying questions. Good listeners wait for the proper moment and then ask questions that do not attack the speaker. Instead of saying, "But I don't understand how you can say that," a good listener seeks clarification with questions such as "Please help me understand by explaining more about...." Because questions can put you in the driver's seat, think about them in advance. Use open questions (those without set answers) to draw out feelings, motivations, ideas, and suggestions. Use closed fact-finding questions to identify key factors in a discussion.[11] People whose first language is not English, and who are having particular trouble listening effectively, should never be afraid to ask clarifying questions.

Paraphrase to increase understanding. To make sure you understand a speaker, rephrase and summarize a message in your own words. Be objective and nonjudgmental. Remember, your goal is to understand what the speaker has said—not to show how mindless the speaker's words sound when parroted. Remember, too, that other workplace listeners will also benefit from a clear summary of what was said.

Capitalize on lag time. While you are waiting for a speaker's next idea, use the time to review what the speaker is saying. Separate the central idea, key points, and details. Sometimes you may have to supply the organization. You can also use lag time to silently rephrase and summarize the speaker's message in your own words. Most important, keep your mind focused on the speaker and her or his ideas—not on all the other work waiting for you.

Take notes to ensure retention. Don't trust your memory. If you have a hallway conversation with a colleague and don't have a pencil handy, make a mental note of the important items. Then write them down as soon as possible. Even with seemingly easily remembered facts or instructions, jot them down to ease your mind and also to be sure you understand them correctly. Two weeks later you'll be glad you did. Be sure you have a good place to store notes of various projects, such as file folders, notebooks, or computer files.

Be aware of gender differences. Men tend to listen for facts, whereas women tend to perceive listening as an opportunity to connect with the other person on a personal level.[12] Men tend to use interrupting behaviour to control conversations, while women generally interrupt to communicate assent, to elaborate on an idea of another group member, or to participate in the topic of conversation.[13] Women listeners tend to be attentive, provide steady eye contact, remain stationary, and nod their heads.[14] Male listeners are less attentive, provide sporadic eye contact, and move around. Being aware of these tendencies will make you a more sensitive and knowledgeable listener.

COMMUNICATING IN TEAMS

As organizations in the 1990s were downsized, restructured, and reengineered, one reality became increasingly clear: companies were expected to compete globally, meet higher standards, and increase profits—but often with fewer people and fewer resources.[15] Striving to meet these seemingly impossible goals, organizations began developing groups and teams for the following specific reasons:

- **Better decisions.** Decisions are generally more accurate and effective because group and team members contribute different expertise and perspectives.
- **Faster response.** When action is necessary to respond to competition or to solve a problem, small groups and teams can act rapidly.
- **Increased productivity.** Because they are often closer to the action and to the customer, team members can see opportunities for improving efficiencies.

- **Greater "buy-in."** Decisions derived jointly are usually better received because members are committed to the solution and are more willing to support it.
- **Less resistance to change.** People who have input into making decisions are less hostile, aggressive, and resistant to change.
- **Improved employee morale.** Personal satisfaction and job morale increase when teams are successful.
- **Reduced risks.** Responsibility for a decision is diffused, thus carrying less risk for any individual.[16]

Teams can be very effective in solving problems; however, they don't solve all workplace problems, and with regard to communication, they may even create new ones of their own. As a result, some major organizations have retreated from teams, finding that they slowed decision making, shielded workers from responsibility, and created morale and productivity problems.[17] Yet, in most models of future organizations, teams, not individuals, function as the primary performance unit.[18] Some organizations are even creating *virtual teams*, which are connected by the Internet, intranets, and electronic media.

CHARACTERISTICS OF SUCCESSFUL TEAMS

Experts who have studied team workings and decisions have discovered that effective teams share some or all of the following characteristics.

Small size, diverse makeup. For most functions, the best teams range from two to twenty-five members, although four or five is optimum for many projects. Larger groups have trouble interacting constructively, much less agreeing on actions.[19]

Agreement on purpose. An effective team begins with a common purpose. Working from a general purpose to specific goals typically requires a huge investment of time and effort. Meaningful discussions, however, motivate team members to "buy into" the project.

Agreement on procedures. The best teams develop procedures to guide them. They set up intermediate goals with deadlines. They assign roles and tasks, requiring all members to contribute equivalent amounts of real work.

Ability to confront conflict. Poorly functioning teams avoid conflict, preferring sulking, gossip, or backstabbing. A better plan is to acknowledge conflict and address the root of the problem openly.

Use of good communication techniques. The best teams exchange information and contribute ideas freely in an informal environment. Team members speak clearly and concisely, avoiding generalities. They encourage feedback. Listeners become actively involved, read body language, and ask clarifying questions before responding. Tactful, constructive disagreement is encouraged.

Ability to collaborate rather than compete. Effective team members are genuinely interested in achieving team goals instead of receiving individual recognition. They contribute ideas and feedback unselfishly. They monitor team progress, including what's going right, what's going wrong, and what to do about it. They celebrate individual and team accomplishments.

Acceptance of ethical responsibilities. Teams as a whole have ethical responsibilities to their members, to their larger organizations, and to society. Members have a number of specific responsibilities to each other. As a whole, groups have a responsibility to represent the organization's view and respect its privileged information.

Shared leadership. Effective teams often have no formal leader. Instead, leadership rotates to those with the appropriate expertise as the team evolves and moves from one phase to another. Many teams operate under a democratic approach. This approach can achieve agreement with team decisions, boost morale, and create fewer hurt feelings and less resentment. But in times of crisis, a strong team member may need to step up as leader.

Demonstration of good workplace manners. Rudeness and bad manners have become alarmingly common in the North American workplace. Successful team members treat each other and colleagues politely and respectfully. This may involve a few more *pleases* and *thank yous,* as well as showing consideration for others. Good team members are aware of noise levels when colleagues are trying to concentrate. They offer support to colleagues with heavy workloads, and they respect others' boundaries and need for privacy.

TEAM-BASED WRITING AND PRESENTING

Companies form teams for many reasons. The goal of some teams is an oral presentation to pitch a new product or to win a high-stakes contract. The goal of other teams is to investigate a problem and submit recommendations to decision makers in a report. The end product of any team is often a written report or an oral presentation.

Guidelines for Team Writing and Oral Presentations

Whether your team's project produces written reports or oral presentations, you generally have considerable control over how the project is organized and completed. If you've been part of team efforts before, you also know that such projects can be very frustrating—particularly when some team members don't carry their weight or when members cannot resolve conflict. On the other hand, team projects can be harmonious and productive when members establish ground rules and follow guidelines related to preparing, planning, collecting information for, organizing, rehearsing, and evaluating team projects.

Preparing to work together. Before you begin talking about a specific project, it's best to discuss some of the following issues with regard to how your group will function.

- Name a meeting leader to plan and conduct meetings, a recorder to keep a record of group decisions, and an evaluator to determine whether the group is on target and meeting its goals.
- Decide whether your team will be governed by consensus (everyone must agree), by majority rule, or by some other method.
- Compare schedules of team members in order to set up the best meeting times. Plan to meet often. Make team meetings a top priority. Avoid other responsibilities that might cause disruption during these meetings.

- Discuss the value of conflict. By bringing conflict into the open and encouraging disagreement, your team can prevent personal resentment and group dysfunction. Confrontation can actually create better final products by promoting new ideas and avoiding groupthink. Conflict is most beneficial when team members are allowed to air their views fully.
- Discuss how you will deal with team members who are not pulling their share of the load.

Planning the document or presentation. Once you've established ground rules, you're ready to discuss the final document or presentation. Be sure to keep a record of the following decisions your team makes.

- Establish the specific purpose for the document or presentation. Identify the main issues involved.
- Decide on the final format. For a report, determine what parts it will include, such as an executive summary, figures, and an appendix. For a presentation, decide on its parts, length, and graphics.
- Discuss the audience(s) for the product and what questions it would want answered in your report or oral presentation. If your report is persuasive, consider what appeals might achieve its purpose.
- Develop a work plan. Assign jobs. Set deadlines. If time is short, work backward from the due date. For oral presentations, build in time for content and creative development as well as for a series of rehearsals.
- For oral presentations, give each team member a written assignment that details his or her responsibilities for researching content, producing visuals, developing handout materials, building transitions between segments, and showing up for rehearsals.
- For written reports, decide how the final document will be composed: individuals working separately on assigned portions, one person writing the first draft, the entire group writing the complete document together, or some other method.

Collecting information. The following suggestions help teams generate and gather accurate information. Unless facts are accurate, the most beautiful report or the best high-powered presentation will fail.

- Brainstorm for ideas; consider cluster diagramming.
- Assign topics. Decide who will be responsible for gathering what information.
- Establish deadlines for collecting information.
- Discuss ways to ensure the accuracy of the information collected.

Organizing, writing, and revising. As the project progresses, your team may wish to modify some of its earlier decisions.

- Review the proposed organization of your final document or presentation and adjust it if necessary.
- Compose the first draft of a written report or presentation. If separate team members are writing segments, they should use the same word processing and/or presentation graphics program to facilitate combining files.
- Meet to discuss and revise the draft(s) or rehearse the presentation.
- If individuals are working on separate parts of a written report, appoint one person (probably the best writer) to coordinate all the parts, striving for

consistent style and format. Work for a uniform look and feel to the final product.

- For oral presentations be sure each member builds a bridge to the next presenter's topic and launches it smoothly. Strive for logical connections between segments.

Editing, rehearsing, and evaluating. Before the presentation is made or the final document is submitted, complete the following steps.

- For a written report give one person responsibility for finding and correcting grammatical and mechanical errors.
- For a written report meet as a group to evaluate the final document. Does it fulfill its purpose and meet the needs of the audience? Is there any evidence of plagiarism? Successful group documents emerge from thoughtful preparation, clear definition of contributors' roles, commitment to a group-approved plan, and willingness to take responsibility for the final product.
- For oral presentations assign one person the task of merging the various files, running a spell checker, and examining the entire presentation for consistency of design, format, and vocabulary.
- Schedule at least five rehearsals, say the experts.[20] Consider videotaping one of the rehearsals so that each presenter can critique his or her own performance.
- Schedule a dress rehearsal with an audience at least two days before the actual presentation. Practise fielding questions.

CROSS-CULTURAL COMMUNICATION

Understanding the verbal and nonverbal meanings of a message is sometimes difficult even when communicators are from the same culture. But when they are from different cultures, special sensitivity and skills are necessary. Negotiators for a Canadian company learned this lesson when they were in Japan looking for a trading partner. The Canadians were pleased after their first meeting with representatives of a major Japanese firm. The Japanese had nodded assent throughout the meeting and had not objected to a single proposal. The next day, however, the Canadians were stunned to learn that the Japanese had rejected the entire plan. In interpreting the nonverbal behavioural messages, the Canadians made a mistake. They assumed the Japanese were nodding in agreement as fellow Canadians would. In this case, however, the nods of assent indicated comprehension—not approval.

Every country has a common heritage, joint experience, and shared learning that produce its culture. These elements give members of that culture a complex system of shared values and customs. The system teaches them how to behave; it conditions their reactions. Comparing Canadian values with those in other cultures will broaden your world view. This comparison should also help you recognize some of the values that shape your actions and judgments of others.

Comparing Key Cultural Values

While it may be difficult to define a typical Canadian, one poll found that Canadians are convinced that a unique national identity exists—even if they are unable to agree on what it is. When asked what makes Canadian individuals distinct, respondents highlighted the tendency toward nonviolence and tolerance of others. When asked what makes Canada as a country distinct, respondents cited social programs and a nonviolent tradition as the two leading factors that make Canada different from the United States and other countries.[21] Research shows that Canadians tend to be more collective, conforming, and conservative than their U.S. neighbours. Canadians are more supportive of civil and political institutions and collective decision making. Americans, on the other hand, tend to be much more supportive of individual decision making and questioning of collective decisions.[22]

Despite the differences outlined above, most Canadians have habits and beliefs similar to those of other members of Western, technologically advanced societies. It's impossible to fully cover the many habits and beliefs of Western culture here, but we can look at four of the crucial ones that characterize the Canadian context.

Individualism versus collectivism. One of the most identifiable characteristics of Western culture is its built-in tension between individualism, an attitude of independence and freedom from control, and collectivism, the idea that the group or nation is more important than its individual citizens. Political scientist Seymour Martin Lipset has persuasively argued that Canadians are more collectivist than Americans (e.g., they support universal health care).[23] Today, however, regional tensions over health care, for example, between some parts of western Canada and central Canada, demonstrate that Canadians' collectivist past may not be as assured in the future. Some non-Western cultures are even more collectivist than Canada. They encourage membership in organizations, groups, and teams and acceptance of group values, duties, and decisions. Members of these cultures sometimes resist independence because it fosters competition and confrontation instead of consensus.

Formality. A second significant dimension of Canadian culture is its attitude toward formality. Canadians place less emphasis on tradition, ceremony, and social rules than do people in some other cultures. We dress casually and are soon on a first-name basis with others. Our lack of formality is often characterized by directness in our business dealings. Indirectness, we feel, wastes time, a valuable commodity.

Communication style. A third important dimension of our culture relates to communication style. We value straightforwardness, are suspicious of evasiveness, and distrust people who might have a "hidden agenda" or who "play their cards too close to the chest." Canadians also tend to be uncomfortable with silence and impatient with delays. Moreover, we tend to use and understand words literally.

Time orientation. A fourth dimension of our culture relates to time orientation. Canadians consider time a precious commodity to be conserved. We equate time with productivity, efficiency, and money. Keeping people waiting for business appointments wastes time and is also rude. In other cultures, time may be perceived as an unlimited and never-ending resource to be enjoyed.

Controlling Ethnocentrism and Stereotyping

The process of understanding and accepting people from other cultures is often hampered by two barriers: ethnocentrism and stereotyping. These two barriers, however, can be overcome by developing tolerance, a powerful and effective aid to communication.

Ethnocentrism. The belief in the superiority of one's own culture is known as ethnocentrism. This attitude is found in all cultures. If you were raised in Canada, the values just described probably seem "right" to you, and you may wonder why the rest of the world doesn't function in the same sensible fashion. A Canadian businessperson in a foreign country might be upset at time spent over coffee or other social rituals before any "real" business is transacted. In many cultures, however, personal relationships must be established and nurtured before earnest talks may proceed.

Ethnocentrism causes us to judge others by our own values. We expect others to react as we would, and they expect us to behave as they would. Misunderstandings naturally result. A Canadian who wants to set a deadline for completion of a deal may be considered pushy overseas. Similarly, a foreign businessperson who prefers a handshake to a written contract is seen as naive and possibly untrustworthy by a Canadian. These ethnocentric reactions can be reduced through knowledge of other cultures and development of flexible, tolerant attitudes.

Stereotypes. Our perceptions of other cultures sometimes cause us to form stereotypes about groups of people. A stereotype is an oversimplified behavioural pattern applied to entire groups. For example, the Swiss are hard working, efficient, and neat; Germans are formal, reserved, and blunt; Americans are loud, friendly, and impatient; Canadians are polite, trusting, and tolerant; Asians are gracious, humble, and inscrutable. These attitudes may or may not accurately describe cultural norms. But when applied to individual business communicators, such stereotypes may create misconceptions and misunderstandings. Look beneath surface stereotypes and labels to discover individual personal qualities.

Tolerance. Working among people from other cultures demands tolerance and flexible attitudes. As global markets expand and as our multicultural society continues to develop, tolerance becomes critical. Tolerance does not mean "putting up with" or "enduring," which is one part of its definition. Instead, tolerance is used in a broader sense. It means having sympathy for and appreciating beliefs and practices differing from our own.

One of the best ways to develop tolerance is by practising empathy. This means trying to see the world through another's eyes. It means being nonjudgmental, recognizing things as they are rather than as they "should be." It includes the ability to accept others' contributions in solving problems in a culturally appropriate manner.

When a few Canadian companies began selling machinery in China, an Asian adviser suggested that the companies rely less on legal transaction and more on creating friendships. Why? In China, the notion of friendship implies a longer-term relationship of trust and loyalty where business obligations are transacted. Instead of insisting on what "should be" (contracts and binding agreements), these companies adopted successful approaches by looking at the challenge from another cultural point of view.[24] Making the effort to communicate with sensitivity across cultures can be very rewarding in both your work life and your personal life. The suggestions below provide specific tips for preventing miscommunication in transactions across cultures.

Minimizing Cross-Cultural Miscommunication

When you have a conversation with someone from another culture, you can reduce misunderstandings by following these tips:

- **Use simple English.** Speak and write in short sentences (under 15 words) with familiar, short words. Eliminate puns, specific cultural references, slang, and jargon (special business terms). Be especially alert to idiomatic expressions that can't be translated, such as "burn the midnight oil" and "under the weather."

- **Speak slowly and enunciate clearly.** Avoid fast speech, but don't raise your voice. Overpunctuate with pauses. Always write numbers for all to see.
- **Encourage accurate feedback.** Ask probing questions, and encourage the listener to paraphrase what you say. Don't assume that a yes, a nod, or a smile indicates comprehension or assent.
- **Check frequently for comprehension.** Avoid waiting until you finish a long explanation to request feedback. Instead, make one point at a time, pausing to check for comprehension. Don't proceed to B until A has been grasped.
- **Observe eye messages.** Be alert to a glazed expression or wandering eyes. These tell you the listener is lost.
- **Accept blame.** If a misunderstanding results, graciously accept the blame for not making your meaning clear.
- **Listen without interrupting.** Curb your desire to finish sentences or to fill out ideas for the speaker. Keep in mind that Canadian listening and speaking habits may not be familiar to other cultures.
- **Remember to smile.** Roger Axtell, international behaviour expert, calls the smile the single most understood and most useful form of communication in either personal or business transactions.
- **Follow up in writing.** After conversations or oral negotiations, confirm the results and agreements with follow-up letters or e-mails. For proposals and contracts, engage a translator to prepare copies in the local language.

Capitalizing on Workforce Diversity

As global competition opens world markets, Canadian businesspeople will increasingly interact with customers and colleagues from around the world. At the same time, as we saw in the article on ethnic clothing in the workplace, the Canadian workforce is also becoming more diverse—in race, ethnicity, age, gender, national origin, physical ability, and countless other characteristics.

The majority of new entrants to the workforce are women, First Nations, new Canadians, and other visible-minority groups. The Canadian workforce is getting older as the baby boom generation ages. By the year 2016, half of the Canadian population will be over 40 and 16 percent over 65. At the same time, the proportion of people under 15 will shrink to 19 percent from the current 25 percent.[25]

A diverse work environment has many benefits. Customers want to deal with companies that reflect their values and create products and services tailored to their needs. Organizations that hire employees with different experiences and backgrounds are better able to create the customized products these customers desire. In addition, businesses with diverse workforces suffer fewer human rights complaints, fewer union clashes, and less interpersonal conflict. That's why diversity is viewed by a growing number of companies as a critical bottom-line business strategy to improve employee relationships and to increase productivity.

For some businesses, diversity also makes economic sense. As Virginia Galt reports in *The Globe and Mail*, "There is one token Canadian on Western Union's national marketing team in Canada. The rest come from China, India, Colombia, Poland, the Philippines." According to Galt, while "Western Union may be further along than most employers in diversifying its work force ... others are planning to follow suit, driven by a competitive need to expand into international markets and serve the increasingly diverse population at home."[26]

Tips for Effective Communication with Diverse Workplace Audiences

Capitalizing on workplace diversity is a challenge for most organizations and individuals. Harmony and acceptance do not happen automatically when people who are dissimilar work together. The following suggestions can help you become a more effective communicator as you enter a rapidly evolving workplace with diverse colleagues and clients.

- **Understand the value of differences.** Diversity makes an organization innovative and creative. Sameness fosters "groupthink," an absence of critical thinking sometimes found in homogeneous groups. Diversity in problem-solving groups encourages independent and creative thinking.
- **Don't expect conformity.** Gone are the days when businesses could demand that new employees or customers simply conform to the existing organization's culture. Today, the value of people who bring new perspectives and ideas is recognized. But with those new ideas comes the responsibility to listen and to allow those new ideas to grow.
- **Create zero tolerance for bias and stereotypes.** Cultural patterns exist in every identity group, but applying these patterns to individuals results in stereotyping. Assuming that Canadians of African descent are good athletes or that women are poor at math fails to admit the immense differences in people in each group. Check your own use of stereotypes and labels. Don't tell sexist or ethnic jokes at meetings. Avoid slang, abbreviations, and jargon that imply stereotypes. Challenge others' stereotypes politely but firmly.
- **Practise focused, thoughtful, and open-minded listening.** Much misunderstanding can be avoided by attentive listening. Listen for main points; take notes if necessary to remember important details. The most important part of listening, especially among diverse communicators, is judging ideas, not appearances or accents.
- **Invite, use, and give feedback.** As you learned earlier, a critical element in successful communication is feedback. You can encourage it by asking questions such as "Is there anything you don't understand?" When a listener or receiver responds, use that feedback to adjust your delivery of information. Does the receiver need more details? A different example? Slower delivery? As a good listener, you should also be prepared to give feedback. For example, summarize your understanding of what was said or agreed on.
- **Make fewer assumptions.** Be careful of seemingly insignificant, innocent workplace assumptions. For example, don't assume that everyone wants to observe the holidays with a Christmas party and a decorated tree. Celebrating only Christian holidays in December and January excludes those who honour Hanukkah, Chinese New Year, and Ramadan. Moreover, in workplace discussions don't assume that everyone is married or wants to be or is even heterosexual, for that matter. For invitations, avoid phrases such as "managers and their *wives.*" *Spouses* or *partners* is more inclusive. Valuing diversity means making fewer assumptions that everyone is like you or wants to be like you.
- **Learn about your cultural self.** Knowing your own cultural biases helps you become more objective and adaptable. Begin to recognize the reactions and thought patterns that are automatic to you as a result of your upbringing. Become more aware of your own values and beliefs. That way you can see them at work when you are confronted by differing values.
- **Seek common ground.** Look for areas where you and others not like you can agree or share opinions. Be prepared to consider issues from many perspectives,

all of which may be valid. Accept that there is room for different points of view to coexist peacefully. Although you can always find differences, it's much harder to find similarities. Look for common ground in shared experiences, mutual goals, and similar values. Professor Nancy Adler of McGill University offers three useful methods to help diverse individuals find their way through conflicts made more difficult by cultural differences: look at the problem from all participants' points of view, uncover the interpretations each side is making on the basis of their cultural values, and create agreement by working together on a solution that works for both sides.[27] Looking for common ground and mutual goals can help each of you reach your objectives even though you may disagree on how.

CONCLUSION

This chapter described a number of specific business communication tasks that are less-often thought of than writing and speaking. Nonverbal communication, the things we tell each other through our eyes, face, and body, is just as important as anything we might write or say. Similarly, our gestures, posture, and use of space, time, and territory also send nonverbal messages. Listening is also a business communication skill that can be learned and improved. Good listeners don't interrupt speakers, they ask clarifying questions at appropriate times, and they paraphrase to ensure they understand what the speaker has said. Taking notes is another important part of listening effectively.

Communicating in teams is also an important skill that can be learned. It involves clear delineation of responsibilities among team members, and also shared responsibility for the quality of the final product whether that be a report or a presentation. Finally, in the contemporary workplace, cross-cultural communication skills are also necessary. These include tolerance and empathy and a willingness not to engage in ethnocentrism and stereotyping. Specific suggestions for communicating in a cross-cultural environment include simplifying and clarifying communication by avoiding ambiguity, and embracing brevity. Workplace diversity requires the seeking of common ground among employees of different backgrounds.

The following chapter looks in detail at one of the two primary modes of communication: writing. You will learn an effective strategy to write any business communication in any channel.

:: *Chapter Review*

As a way of studying the material in this chapter, imagine you are at a job interview for your dream entry-level job after college or university. You've prepared answers for all the classic interview questions, but to your surprise, your interviewer also asks a number of questions based on special communications situations. How would you answer the following six questions?

1. At this company we have a formal dress code policy. What are your feelings about such policies?

2. In this position you will be meeting with clients daily. Can you tell us what communication strategies besides good speaking skills would make your meetings go smoothly?

3. You probably know that our company slogan is "Listening to learn." Can you comment on why it is important to listen to co-workers and clients, and why this may sometimes be challenging?

4. You'll be working on various project teams if you are successful in attaining this position. Can you give us one positive and one negative example of teamwork from your past experience and explain which experience taught you more?

5. Because we're located in Vancouver, diversity is a fact of life at our company. What background or training do you have that allows you to function in an environment where many of your colleagues may be of different cultural and ethnic backgrounds?

6. A large number of our clients are South Asian and East Asian immigrants. In your phone conversations and in-person conversations with these clients, how might you deal with a situation in which you didn't understand what a client said to you?

:: Problems

1. Blayne Peterson is close to completing his Marketing and Advertising Management program at Holland College, and he's looking for an entry-level position. He asks his mother for help. Blayne's mother, Sheila, is a deputy minister in the Prince Edward Island Ministry of Tourism: the top-level civil servant in that ministry. One day, Sheila hears that the ministry is looking to hire five customer service representatives for a six-month contract for the busy May to October tourist period. She suggests that Blayne apply for one of these positions. Sheila has also heard, through her friend Bob Tyson, who manages the Rogers call centre, that Rogers may be hiring up to a dozen full-time customer service representatives. So she suggests Blayne send an application to Rogers. (Rogers is a telecommunications company that operates a number of call centres across the country, including one in Charlottetown.) Within a couple of weeks, Blayne has heard from both the ministry and Rogers; both have asked to schedule an interview with him. At this point Blayne is busy with final exams, and he is not concentrating as much on interview preparation as he should. He shows up at the ministry on a Monday morning five minutes late for his interview, wearing a button-down shirt, which he has tucked into his jeans. He's also wearing running shoes. He has not showered. The interview at Rogers is scheduled to begin one hour after the one at the ministry ends (so that the interviews won't conflict with his exams). By the time he arrives at Rogers, he's 15 minutes late for his interview. His shoelaces are untied and he's out of breath and red in the face. Both the hiring director at the ministry and Bob Tyson at Rogers are unimpressed by Blayne's lack of respect for the interview process. At the same time, he is bright and energetic, and his mother is one of the most influential public servants in the province. What should the two employers do?
   <www.rogers.ca> <www.gov.pe.ca/tourism/index.php3>

2. Mirko Blazic is a salesman for Transcontinental, one of the largest printing companies in the world, printing everything from newspapers and books to catalogues, flyers, and magazines. His sales territory is the Prairie provinces and includes northwestern Ontario. He makes sales calls twice a year, and at this time he finds himself in Calgary, making a number of new sales calls and visiting existing customers like Grant MacEwan College and the

Calgary Herald. Mirko has been Transcontinental's rep in this territory for just over two years and this is his most important selling season ever. The reason is that Mirko has almost closed negotiations on a contract to service all of the Government of Alberta's printing needs for a five-year period. This contract has been valued at between $20 and $50 million. The potential bonus for Mirko is quite large, as is the prestige business for Transcontinental. But there's just one problem. Two senior managers at the Government of Alberta printing office have complained to Mirko's boss in Quebec about his "pushy behaviour" and "intimidating tactics" during negotiation. For example, Bill Fraser, one of the government managers, has e-mailed Mirko's boss that on one particularly tense evening, Mirko slammed the door to the room in which they were negotiating, and then moved his chair right up next to his own, so that Mirko's shoulders were touching Bill's. Bill found this uncomfortable and intimidating. Bill's problem is that Transcontinental's prices are significantly lower than the competition, and part of Bill's mandate in these negotiations is to secure a contract that saves the government at least 15 percent over current printing expenses. How should Mirko's boss respond to Bill's e-mail? What should Bill and Mirko do next?

<www.transcontinental-printing.com> <www.qp.gov.ab.ca>

3. Weekly meetings are a chore for many employees at DFS Architects in Montreal. The man who runs the meetings, Marc Hebert, is well-known for his pompous and long-winded speaking style. Still, he is the managing partner of the firm, and most people—especially those who have been with the firm for a long time—excuse Marc's speaking style because they only have to listen to him once a week for about an hour. "He's a nice guy" is the general consensus at the firm. Sylvia Callaghan has just been hired by DFS, straight out of her architecture program at the University of Waterloo. Sylvia won a number of prizes at Waterloo, and she had her choice of jobs after interviews with a number of firms. She chose DFS because of its location in Montreal (a city she's always wanted to live in), and because of the calibre of the projects DFS is involved in, which include historical restorations and educational and corporate projects, among others. Sylvia knows only one other person at DFS, her friend Geneviève Morency, who went to Waterloo too, but was a year ahead of Sylvia. At her first weekly meeting, Sylvia sits next to Geneviève at the back of the room and starts talking to her about her apartment hunting on the weekend—all this while Marc Hebert is speaking. Geneviève participates in the conversation. A number of architects around the table cast glances back toward Sylvia—trying to make her understand she should be listening—but Sylvia doesn't seem to notice. She keeps whispering with Geneviève. Finally Marc notices the whispering and says loudly, "Excuse me but is there something you'd like to tell the group?" Sylvia turns red, as does Geneviève. Who should do what at this point? Are there any longer-term solutions to this problem?

<www.dfsarch.com>

4. National Investor Relations in Toronto is well known as a leading corporate communications firm. It counts among its top-notch clients such blue-chip Canadian firms as Loblaws, BCE, Royal Bank of Canada, and Inco. The majority of National's business comes from the writing and design of annual and semi-annual corporate reports, which are the main investor relations tools for these corporations. In fact, National's work for Loblaws won the company its third CICA Corporate Reporting Award in the Consumer

Products and Services category. It has a high reputation in the corporate communications industry. This year, National has run into an embarrassing and serious problem. A newspaper reporter in Kitchener-Waterloo has sued National for alleged plagiarism. The reporter claims that in one of the annual corporate reports it wrote and designed last year for Canadian Tire, National plagiarized from one of his business articles in the *Kitchener-Waterloo Record*. It turns out that the three-person team assigned to write and design the Canadian Tire report did not work well together at all. Two of the three team members who worked on the report have been let go by National, and the third, Karen Sunohara, has taken sick leave. Before she left on sick leave, however, she had a long and emotional meeting with her boss. In the meeting she claimed that all the "research for the Canadian Tire report was done by Larry" (one of the former employees). As Karen's boss, you're being pressured to pin the blame on one person, even though it looks as though a team was involved. What measures can you take in the short term and in the long term to deal with the situation described above?

5. Japan-Canada Tours is Canada's leading tour company specializing in tours of western Canada for tourists from Japan. For over 25 years, Japan-Canada Tours has led the market with its "Best of the Canadian West" packages that feature three nights at luxurious hotels in Banff and Lake Louise, Alberta, followed by a day-long drive through the Rockies and the B.C. interior, capped off with three nights in Vancouver and one night in Victoria. Over the past few years, Japan-Canada Tours' Japanese sales office has been reporting that the "Best of the Canadian West" packages are starting to decrease in popularity because it is felt by many Japanese tourists that the drive from Banff to Vancouver (12 hours with only a one-hour lunch break in Kamloops) is too strenuous. Japan-Canada Tours is therefore looking for an experience to add to its "Best of the Canadian West" package that would make it easier for the Japanese tourists, while still retaining their interest. As the VP of Product Development for Japan-Canada Tours, you begin to research the possibilities for a one-day break somewhere between the Rockies and Vancouver. You decide that what might interest Japanese tourists would be a visit to Nk'Mip Cellars, the award-winning winery located in the Okanagan and run by the Osoyoos Indian Band. The exposure to Okanagan First Nations culture and the opportunity to tour a beautiful and successful winery are probably exactly what Japanese tourists would be interested in. When you e-mail your proposal to Japan-Canada's Director of Marketing in Kyoto, you receive a surprising e-mail back from him in which he says that "despite potential interest in the Okanagan wine region, it would be hard to drum up interest in anything too Indian, if you know what I mean." Balancing the needs of the business and your own convictions about what's right in this situation, how would you reply to the Director of Marketing in Kyoto and what would be your next step?

Grammar/Style Review 2

In this review, you will be practising identifying pronoun-antecedent agreement mistakes. There are five mistakes in total. For a brief explanation of this grammar problem, please read the explanation on page 324. Besides completing the exercise below, be sure to be on the lookout for pronoun-antecedent agreement mistakes in your own writing.

To: lzhou@sobeys.ca

From: gcarere@sobeys.ca

Re: Mistakes in last week's flyer

Hi Lucy,

Last week's flyer (Atlantic region) contained so many mistakes that we had to have it reprinted at the last minute. Sobeys stands for quality; their flyers can't be full of mistakes. Unfortunately, each of the pages has their fair share of mistakes. Let me give you some examples:

- Page 2: The 12-pack of chicken burgers was listed at $6.98 when they should have been listed at $5.98

- Page 4: The juicepacks and cheesesticks were both on sale, but it was on sale for $0.99 cents, not $1.98

- Page 5: "Every customer receives $1 off their first prescription order" has a spelling mistake (missing t...)

Please ensure that correct proofreading procedure is followed this week.

Best,

George

:: *Business Communication Lab 2*

Depending on your instructor and your course delivery style, you may be asked to complete this Business Communication Lab in a computer lab during class time, at home as homework, in class the old-fashioned way (pen and paper), or in class as a presentation.

As the CEO of the Newfoundland and Labrador Credit Union, the largest credit union in that province, one of your responsibilities is to be aware of issues that may require changes in your organization. Recently, there have been two high-profile human rights cases, one in New Brunswick and one in Nova Scotia, in which two credit unions were taken to court by people claiming they were fired because they wore ethnic clothing to work. Although you don't have a high number of non-white employees (in fact there are only two out of two hundred and twenty), you don't want the same thing to happen in your own credit union. Therefore, you e-mail your assistant and ask her to do some research on Canadian diversity consultants who could be hired to help Newfoundland and Labrador Credit Union foster diversity within its organization. As the CEO's assistant, reply in an e-mail that includes some research and a recommendation. To help with this lab you may want to visit the following websites:
<www.nlcu.com> <www.diversipro.com>

The Writing Process

Constipated Mommies and Plush Upholstery

BY RICHARD H. LEVEY, *DIRECT MAGAZINE,* JULY 17, 2005

MARKETING COPYWRITERS, MIND your modifiers! Take a lesson from the Ottawa furniture store that sent out a Mother's Day flier advertising "Soft Stools for Mom." The company was not launching a pharmaceutical division.

Oops, indeed. "They are communicating a message different from the one they intended," says Simon Hanington, COO of BackDraft (www.backdraft.org), a professional writing consultancy based in Ottawa, ON.

This is only one example of 40 common fumbles that account for 95% of writers' troubles, as characterized by BackDraft. According to Hanington, the blunder came when the company lost control of how the mailing piece's recipient perceived the message.

For Hanington, what actually comes across is the company's sloppiness, making the customer wonder whether the company was even describing its furniture accurately, or how it might handle a shipping error.

American furniture marketers have their share of flawed communication as well. One upstate New York firm noted that it only shipped within the "Untied States," and went on to apologize for any "incontinence."

Punctuation mistakes can also raise some unpleasant questions. Take quotation marks, which people often, but mistakenly, use for emphasis. When not applied to a literal quotation, they can cast doubt upon the phrase between the marks.

Take, for instance, a restaurant direct mail piece with the message 'Try our "Chicken Soup."' This, Hanington said, would make the eater wonder what

was actually at the end of his spoon. He also recalled a newspaper article about the war in Iraq which cited the number of people "killed," suggesting, perhaps, that those deemed casualties might actually be alive and well, and vacationing in Malibu.

BackDraft employs a combination of in-person instructors and online tutorial programs to strengthen professionals' writing ability. Hanington feels that the industry is reaching a tipping point regarding the need for proper communication skills. With the ubiquity of computers and e-mail, people are writing now more than at any point in history. Two-thirds of American professionals must write to do their jobs, he says, yet one-third of these do not do so proficiently.

Reporters are by no means immune to these fumbles: when a Canadian newspaper stated that a traffic accident was caused by high tech writers, Hanington wondered whether these were high-tech writers (scribes who specialize in creating computer manuals), or merely tech-writers who had smoked one too many maple leafs before getting behind the wheel.

What about those upper-level executives who consider themselves God's gift to copywriting? While BackDraft employees will ultimately follow any rule they are given, "We pummel them with better knowledge," says Hanington.

Take the CEO who announced, "You are never allowed to use the verb 'to be' in any of my speeches. It makes the writing look weak." The BackDraft consultant replied, "The verb 'to be' is like an equals sign. If you prohibit the verb 'to be,' there will be no way you will tell any audience member about what you are, how you think or feel, and you will never establish a relationship between you and the audience. Are you cool with that?"

Before accepting BackDraft's criticism, many potential clients feel the need to test the firm's mettle. One client asked Hanington to demonstrate the past pluperfect subjunctive tense, and was rewarded with both an example of it and a discourse on why it passed out of the English language in 1410.

If the two-year-old company doesn't work out, Hanington has a backup plan to support himself. The department store Zellers used to feature signs in its lobby proclaiming "This store has been equipped with an electronic shoplifting device."

As Hanington put it, such a machine would relieve him of the need to work for a living, and probably could be programmed not to rat him out to the authorities.

DIAGNOSING THE PROBLEM

If we read carefully between the lines, the situation described in Richard Levey's article includes more than one problem. The first problem is the obvious one: companies in Canada and the United States are finding their employees don't have strong writing skills. As Levey notes, one-third of workers are not writing correctly, and one of the consequences of such poor business communication skills is that companies are seen as sloppy by their customers and potential customers. While there isn't any hard data on to what degree sloppiness in writing turns off customers, numerous researchers have been able to prove that within companies, poor writing is increasingly leading to miscommunication and frustration, which affects both productivity and employee stress levels. But another problem lies below the surface of what Levey discusses in his article. Companies like Ottawa-based BackDraft are capitalizing on the problem of poor writing by creating businesses that offer support (via writing training) to companies around North America and Europe. Why is the increasing number of such businesses a problem?

Once again we have a problem that is not simply negative. While BackDraft is doing very well, thank you very much, providing its specialized writing services to corporations, these same corporations are having to find room in their budget (which perhaps they didn't have to 20 or 30 years ago) to spend on writing training. Again, this sort of budget item might seem to be a problem to some, while others might argue that the best marketing tool a company has is proficient communicators. Are there solutions to these problems we can agree on? Perhaps one solution would be to mandate the introduction of Professional Communication courses more widely—in universities as well as in colleges, in all programs, not just in business programs. Another solution may be for major corporations to start a trend of "zero tolerance" policies for grammar and other writing mistakes, supported by workplace training for employees who don't meet the standard. Perhaps another solution is to lobby the government to give companies that spend money on writing and communications training a tax credit. Or maybe the solution goes back even further to elementary and high schools and involves weaning students away from their keyboards and other tech-savvy toys and back to writing with pen and pencil.

Either way, the solution to the problem of poor writing skills in the workplace is multi-layered and complex. In fact, you can probably think of other solutions that were not suggested above. Working with your team, it's time for you to evaluate all possible solutions and choose the most appropriate one ...

in-class
activity 3

WORKING IN SMALL groups of three to four, students will discuss the analysis of the problem provided above and evaluate the solutions offered in order to choose the most appropriate one. Is the analysis provided above complete? What will an appropriate solution look like? Why did your group choose this solution? What pluses and minuses are there in choosing this solution? Report back to the class within 20 minutes.

Now that you've presented your solution to the rest of the class, you're ready to discover some best practices in business writing that could help solve the situation you've just examined. At the end of this chapter, you will be presented with some more problems that you may be asked to analyze, evaluate, and explain.

BASICS OF BUSINESS WRITING

While it's true that oral communication (speaking), aural communication (listening), nonverbal communication (gestures, body language), as well as reading, are all important in the world of work, perhaps the most important skill you can learn is how to improve your writing in business situations. When we say improve your writing, we don't just mean writing with few grammar and style and spelling and punctuation mistakes, although that is a large part of it. What we mean is that writing correctly is a process with three discrete stages. As a student, it's your responsibility to learn about and internalize these three stages because sometimes in the real world of work, you will not have the time to divide your writing tasks into three stages. As a student, however, you do have the luxury of separating the written communication process into its three important stages, which are prewriting, writing, and revising.

The ultimate goal for you as a business writer is to connect with your audience, not to confuse, anger, or intimidate it. An Ipsos Reid study conducted among Canadian CEOs indicated that CEOs devote half of their time (49 percent) communicating with a variety of audiences, including both external stakeholders, such as investors, government, the media, and customers, and internal audiences, such as employees and management.[1] All members of the organization, from the CEO to front-line staff, must concern themselves with their audience. This is what leads us to claim that effective business writing exhibits three main characteristics or "basics":

- **Audience oriented.** Write to satisfy the receiver, not yourself.
- **Purposeful.** Fulfill a clear purpose in each written message. Don't waste receivers' time.
- **Economical.** Present ideas clearly but concisely. Length is *not* rewarded in business communication.

The ability to prepare audience-centred, purposeful, and concise messages does not come naturally. Because you received an "A" in high school English does not mean you will be a natural business communicator, for example. Few people, especially beginners, can sit down and compose an effective letter or report without training. Whether you are writing an e-mail, instant message, memo,

Figure 3.1 ▶
The Business Writing
Process

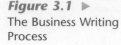

Figure 3.1 ▶
The Business Writing
Process

letter, or report, the writing process will be easier if you follow a systematic plan. As mentioned above, our plan breaks the entire task into three separate phases: prewriting, writing, and revising, as shown in Figure 3.1.

THE PREWRITING PHASE

As a general rule, any time you're going to write something at work, you should spend a significant amount of time on prewriting. Let's say you're the leader of a new project and you're about to send an important e-mail inviting team members to their first meeting in a week's time. The poor business communicator sends the e-mail in two minutes without thinking about it or checking it before pressing the send button. Within four minutes she receives her first e-mail back saying "Thanks for your e-mail, Sue, but you didn't tell us what time we're meeting on Monday. Also, the whole Marketing group is at an off-site next Monday so Bob and I probably won't be able to make it to your meeting."

Obviously, the two minutes spent sending this important e-mail wasn't enough. Sue should have added an extra prewriting phase to her construction of the e-mail. In this phase, she could have done a number of important things. For example, she could have thought about her audience, the receivers of the e-mail. Are any of them going to be busy on Monday? Obviously Sue also forgot to build in time for revising and proofreading her e-mail. If she had built in the time, she would have noticed that her meeting invitation was missing perhaps its most important piece—the time of the meeting. For now, we'll concentrate on the prewriting phase, which includes all the things Sue should have done before writing and sending her e-mail. This phase includes understanding your purpose for writing, choosing the correct channel, anticipating how your audience will react, and adapting your message to the audience.

Identifying Your Purpose

As you begin to compose a message, ask yourself two important questions: why am I sending this message and what do I hope to achieve? Your responses will determine how you organize and present your information.

Your message may have primary and secondary purposes. For college work, your primary purpose may be merely to complete the assignment; secondary purposes might be to make yourself look good and to get a good grade. The primary purposes for sending business messages are typically to inform, to persuade, and to instruct. A secondary purpose is to promote goodwill: you and your organization want to look good in the eyes of your audience.

Selecting the Best Channel

After identifying the purpose of your message, you need to select the most appropriate communication channel. Some information is most efficiently and effectively delivered orally. Other messages should be written, and still others are best delivered electronically. Whether to set up a meeting, send a message by e-mail, or write a report depends on some of the following factors: importance of the message, amount and speed of feedback required, necessity of a permanent record, cost of the channel, degree of formality desired, and best practices in your company. These six factors will help you decide which of the channels shown in Figure 3.2 is most appropriate for delivering a message.

Figure 3.2 ▶   Choosing Communication Channels

Channel	Best Use
Written	
E-mail	When you wish to deliver routine or urgent messages quickly and inexpensively across time zones or borders. Appropriate for small, large, local, or dispersed audiences. Quickly becoming preferred channel replacing hard-copy memos and many letters. Printout provides permanent record.
Instant message	When you need to have a brief conversation with a trusted colleague or customer at a distance. The question does not warrant a telephone call and should be about something you are working on at that moment. Expected to overcome e-mail as the most preferred channel within organizations for exchanging routine messages.
Fax	When your message must cross time zones or international boundaries, when a written record is significant, or when speed is important.
Memo	When you want a written record to explain policies clearly, discuss procedures, or collect information within an organization.
Letter	When you need a written record of correspondence with customers, the government, suppliers, or others outside an organization.
Report or proposal	When you are delivering considerable data internally or externally.
Spoken	
Telephone call	When you need to deliver or gather information quickly, when nonverbal cues are unimportant, and when you cannot meet in person.
Voice mail message	When you wish to leave important or routine information that the receiver can respond to when convenient.
Face-to-face conversation	When you want to be persuasive, deliver bad news, or share a personal message.
Face-to-face group meeting	When group decisions and consensus are important. Inefficient for merely distributing information.
Video- or teleconference	When group consensus and interaction are important but members are geographically dispersed.

Technology and competition continue to accelerate the pace of business today. As a result, communicators are switching to ever-faster means of exchanging information. In the early to mid-20th century, business messages within organizations were delivered largely by hard-copy memos. Responses would typically take a couple of days. But that's too slow for today's communicators. Cell phones, faxes, websites, e-mail, and instant messaging can deliver that information much faster than traditional channels of communication.

In fact, according to business writer Don Tapscott, within some organizations and between colleagues at different organizations, instant messaging is being added to e-mail as a popular channel choice. Tapscott even names some large companies like IBM that have abandoned e-mail in favour of instant messaging.[2] Instant messaging software alerts colleagues in distant locations that a co-worker is prepared to participate in an online exchange. Once signed in, individuals or entire groups can carry on and manage two-way discussions. Instant messaging resembles a conversation: a sender types a one- or two-sentence note followed by the receiver typing his or her response to the note. Responses appear next to the original message for both sender and receiver to see. Through instant messaging, an entire conversation can be completed online without the time delay that can occur when sending and responding to e-mail. A few years ago, *The Globe and Mail* reported that instant messaging would soon surpass e-mail as the primary way in which people interact electronically. Although this prediction has not yet come true, experts like Tapscott signal that instant messaging is certainly a force to be reckoned with, especially because it is already so much a part of many young people's personal lives.[3]

Within many organizations, hard-copy memos are still written, especially for messages that require persuasion, permanence, or formality. But the channel of choice for corporate communicators today is clearly e-mail. It's fast, cheap, and easy. Thus fewer hard-copy memos are being written. Fewer letters are also being written. That's because many customer service functions are now being managed through Web-based customer relationship management tools or by e-mail. Interestingly, the fact that fewer memos and letters are being written does *not* make knowing how to write one less important. In fact, it makes it more important. This is because novice business communicators often assume business e-mails can be as informal as their personal e-mails. The reality is that business e-mails should be nearly as structured as memos and letters have always been. Whether your channel choice is e-mail, hard-copy memo, or report, you'll be a more effective writer if you spend sufficient time in the prewriting phase.

Anticipating the Audience

A good writer anticipates the audience for each message: What is the reader like? How will the reader react to the message? Although you can't always know exactly who the reader is, you can imagine some characteristics of the reader. Even writers of direct mail sales letters have a general idea of the audience they wish to target. Picturing a typical reader is important in guiding what you write. By profiling your audience and shaping a message to respond to that profile, you are more likely to achieve your communication goals.

Visualizing your audience is a pivotal step in the writing process. The questions in Figure 3.3 will help you profile your audience. How much time you devote to answering these questions depends on your message and its context. An analytical report that you compose for management or an oral presentation before a big group would, of course, demand considerable audience anticipation. On the other hand, an e-mail message to a co-worker or a letter to a familiar supplier might

Figure 3.3 ▶ Asking the Right Questions to Profile Your Audience

Primary Audience
Who is my primary reader or listener?
What is my personal and professional relationship with that person?
What position does the individual hold in the organization?
How much does that person know about the subject?
What do I know about that person's education, beliefs, culture, and attitudes?
Should I expect a neutral, positive, or negative response to my message?
Secondary Audience
Who might see or hear this message in addition to the primary audience?
How do these people differ from the primary audience?

require only a few moments of planning. No matter how short your message, though, spend some time thinking about the audience so that you can adjust your words appropriately for your readers or listeners. "The most often unasked question in business and professional communication," claims a writing expert, "is as simple as it is important: *Have I thought enough about my audience?*"[4]

Profiling your audience helps you make decisions about shaping the message. You'll discover what kind of language is appropriate, whether you're free to use specialized technical terms, whether you should explain everything, and so on. You'll decide whether your tone should be formal or informal, and you'll select the most desirable channel. Imagining whether the receiver is likely to be neutral, positive, or negative will help you determine how to organize your message.

Another advantage of profiling your audience is considering the possibility of a secondary audience. For instance, you might write a report that persuades your boss to launch a website for customers. Your boss is the primary reader, and he is familiar with many of the details of your project. But he will need to secure approval from his boss, and that person is probably unfamiliar with the project details. Because your report will be passed along to secondary readers, it must include more background information and more extensive explanations than you included for the primary reader, your boss. Analyzing the task and anticipating the audience assists you in adapting your message so that it will accomplish what you intend.

Adapting the Message to the Audience

After analyzing your purpose and anticipating your audience, you must convey your purpose to that audience. Adaptation is the process of creating a message that suits your audience.

One important aspect of adaptation is tone. Tone, conveyed largely by the words in a message, determines how a receiver feels on reading or hearing it. Skilled communicators create a positive tone in their messages by using a number of adaptive techniques, some of which are unconscious. These include spotlighting audience benefits, cultivating a polite "you" attitude, sounding conversational, and using inclusive language. Additional adaptive techniques include using positive expression and preferring plain language with familiar words.

Audience benefits. Smart communicators know that the chance of success of any message is greatly improved by emphasizing reader benefits. This means making readers see how the message affects and benefits them personally.

Adapting your message to the receiver's needs means temporarily putting yourself in that person's shoes. This skill is known as empathy. Empathic senders think about how a receiver will decode a message. They try to give something to the receiver, solve the receiver's problems, save the receiver money, or just understand the feelings and position of that person. Which of the following messages is more appealing to the audience?

SENDER-FOCUSED   *To enable us to update our shareholder records, we ask that the enclosed card be returned.*

AUDIENCE-FOCUSED   *So that you may promptly receive dividend cheques and information related to your shares, please return the enclosed card.*

SENDER-FOCUSED   *The Human Resources Department requires that the online survey be completed immediately so that we can allocate our training resource funds.*

AUDIENCE-FOCUSED   *By filling out the online survey, you can be one of the first employees to sign up for the new career development program.*

Polite "you" view. Notice how many of the previous audience-focused messages included the word *you*. In concentrating on receiver benefits, skilled communicators naturally develop the "you" view. They emphasize second-person pronouns (*you, your*) instead of first-person pronouns (*I/we, us, our*). Whether your goal is to inform, persuade, or promote goodwill, the most attention-getting words you can use are *you* and *your*. Compare the following examples.

"I/WE" VIEW   *We have shipped your order by courier, and we are sure it will arrive in time for the sales promotion January 15.*

"YOU" VIEW   *Your order will be delivered by courier in time for your sales promotion January 15.*

"I/WE" VIEW   *As a financial planner, I care about my clients' well-being.*

"YOU" VIEW   *Your well-being is the most important consideration for financial planners like me.*

Readers appreciate genuine interest; on the other hand, they resent obvious attempts at manipulation. Some sales messages, for example, become untrustworthy when they include *you* dozens of times in a direct mail promotion. Furthermore, the word can sometimes create the wrong impression. Consider this statement: *You cannot return merchandise until you receive written approval.* The word *you* appears twice, but the reader feels singled out for criticism. In the revised version the message is less personal and more positive: *Customers may return merchandise with written approval.* In short, avoid using *you* for general statements that suggest blame and could cause ill will.

In recognizing the value of the "you" view, however, writers do not have to sterilize their writing and totally avoid any first-person pronouns or words that show their feelings. Skilled communicators are able to convey sincerity, warmth, and enthusiasm by the words they choose. Don't be afraid to use phrases such as "I'm happy" or "We're delighted," if you truly are. When speaking face to face, communicators show sincerity and warmth with nonverbal cues such as a smile and pleasant voice tone. In letters, memos, and e-mail messages, however, only expressive words and phrases can show these feelings. These phrases suggest hidden messages that say to readers and customers "You are important, I am listening, and I'm honestly trying to please you."

Conversational but professional. Most business e-mails, letters, memos, and reports are most effective when they convey an informal, conversational tone instead of a formal, pretentious tone. But messages should not become so conversational that they sound overly casual and unprofessional. With the increasing use of e-mail, a major problem has developed. Sloppy, unprofessional expression appears in many e-mail messages. You'll learn more about e-mail in Chapter 4. At this point, though, we urge you to strive for a warm, conversational tone that does not include slang or overly casual wording. The following examples should help you distinguish between three levels of diction.

UNPROFESSIONAL	CONVERSATIONAL	FORMAL
(low-level diction)	(mid-level diction)	(high-level diction)
badmouth	criticize	denigrate
ticked off	upset	provoked
rat on	inform	betray
rip off	steal	embezzle or appropriate

UNPROFESSIONAL	*If we just hang in there, we can snag the contract.*
CONVERSATIONAL	*If we don't get discouraged, we can win the contract.*
FORMAL	*If the principals persevere, they can acquire the contract.*

Your goal is a warm, friendly tone that sounds professional. Talk to the reader with words that are comfortable to you. Avoid long and complex sentences. Use familiar pronouns such as *I*, *we*, and *you* and an occasional contraction, such as *we're* or *I'll*. Stay away from third-person constructions such as *the undersigned, the writer*, and *the affected party*. Also avoid legal terminology and technical words. Your writing will be easier to read and understand if it sounds like the following conversational examples:

FORMAL   *The writer wishes to inform the above-referenced individual that subsequent payments may henceforth be sent to the address cited below.*

CONVERSATIONAL   *Your payments should now be sent to us in Sudbury.*

FORMAL   *To facilitate ratification of this agreement, your negotiators urge that the membership respond in the affirmative.*

CONVERSATIONAL   *We urge you to approve the agreement by voting yes.*

Positive language. The clarity and tone of a message are considerably improved if you use positive rather than negative language. Positive language generally conveys more information than negative language. Moreover, positive messages are uplifting and pleasant to read. Positive wording tells what is and what can be done rather than what isn't and what can't be done. For example, "Your order cannot be shipped by January 10" is not nearly as informative as "Your order will be shipped January 20." Notice in the following examples how you can revise the negative tone to reflect a more positive impression.

NEGATIVE   *We are sorry that we must reject your application for credit at this time.*

POSITIVE   *At this time we can serve you on a cash basis only.*

NEGATIVE   *Although I've never had a paid position before, I have completed a work placement in a law office as an administrative assistant while completing my diploma.*

POSITIVE   *My work placement experience in a lawyer's office and my recent training in legal procedures and computer applications can be assets to your organization.*

Inclusive language. A business writer who is alert and empathic will strive to create messages that include rather than exclude people. Referring to a letter carrier as a *mailman*, for example, reinforces the stereotype that mail delivery is carried out only by men. This stereotype creates a barrier for women who want to be letter carriers and can exclude them from a career delivering mail. By using inclusive language such as *letter carrier*, we battle an inappropriate stereotype and show we are aware that a person who delivers the mail could be either a woman or a man.

When creating your messages, identify or address people first as individuals, and then mention the group to which they belong only if that information is relevant. Job titles should describe the role rather than who is best to assume the role. Using terms such as *manager, sales clerk,* or *flight attendant* suggests that anyone can be considered an appropriate candidate for these roles.

Some words have been called sexist because they seem to exclude women or refer to women in ways the sender would not use to refer to a man. Notice the use of the masculine pronouns *he* and *his* in the following sentence: *Every homeowner must read his insurance policy carefully.* This sentence illustrates an age-old grammatical rule called "common gender." When a speaker or writer did not know the gender (sex) of an individual, masculine pronouns (such as *he* or *his*) were used. Masculine pronouns were understood to indicate both men and women. Today, however, writers and speakers striving for clarity replace common-gender pronouns with inclusive constructions. You can use one of four alternatives.

SEXIST   *Every lawyer has ten minutes for his summation.*

ALTERNATIVE 1   *All lawyers have ten minutes for their summations. (Use a plural noun and plural pronoun.)*

ALTERNATIVE 2   *Lawyers have ten minutes for summations. (Omit the pronoun entirely.)*

ALTERNATIVE 3   *Every lawyer has ten minutes for a summation. (Use an article instead of a pronoun.)*

ALTERNATIVE 4   *Every lawyer has ten minutes for his or her summation. (Use both a masculine and a feminine pronoun.)*

Note that the last alternative, which includes a masculine and a feminine pronoun, is wordy. Don't use it too frequently.

Plain language. Business communicators who are conscious of their audience try to use plain language that expresses clear meaning. They do not use showy words and ambiguous expressions in an effort to dazzle or confuse readers. They write to express ideas, not to impress others.

Some business, legal, and government documents are written in an inflated style that obscures meaning. This style of writing has been given various terms, such as *jargon, legalese, federalese, bureaucratese, doublespeak,* and *the official style.* It may be used intentionally to mask meaning. It may be an attempt to show off the writer's intelligence and education. It may be the traditional or accepted way of writing in that field. Or it may result from lack of training. What do you think the manager's intention is in the following message: *Personnel assigned vehicular space in the adjacent areas are hereby advised that access will be suspended temporarily Friday morning*?

Employees will probably have to read that sentence several times before they understand that they are being advised not to park in the lot next door on Friday morning. To overcome this pretentious style, the federal government requires public servants to use plain language to inform the public about government policies, programs, and services. This means a clear, simple style that uses everyday words. But the plain-English movement goes beyond word choice. It can also mean writing that is easy to follow and organized into segments with appropriate headings.

The important thing to remember is not to be impressed by important-sounding language and legalese, such as *herein, thereafter, hereinafter, whereas,* and similar expressions. Your writing will be better understood if you use plain language.

Familiar words. Clear messages contain words that are familiar and meaningful to the receiver. How can we know what is meaningful to a given receiver? Although we can't know with certainty, we can avoid long or unfamiliar words that have simpler synonyms. Whenever possible in business communication, substitute short, common, simple words. Don't, however, give up a precise word if it says exactly what you mean.

LESS FAMILIAR WORDS	SIMPLE ALTERNATIVES	LESS FAMILIAR WORDS	SIMPLE ALTERNATIVES
ascertain	*find out*	*option*	*choice*
conceptualize	*see*	*perpetuate*	*continue*
encompass	*include*	*perplexing*	*troubling*
hypothesize	*guess*	*reciprocate*	*return*
leverage	*make use of*	*stipulate*	*require*
monitor	*check*	*terminate*	*end*
operational	*working*	*utilize*	*use*

THE WRITING PHASE

Once you've prewritten your message and considered the points discussed above, you're ready to move into the writing phase. This phase is made up of three sub-processes, namely, researching, organizing, and composing. The processes are described in detail below.

Researching

No smart businessperson begins writing a message before collecting the needed information. Some of the consequences of not doing so are mentioned in the Levey article above, embarrassing mistakes being the most obvious. We call this collection process research. Research is necessary before beginning to write because the information you collect helps shape the message. Discovering significant information after a message is completed often means starting over and reorganizing. To avoid frustration and inaccurate messages, collect information that answers this primary question:

- What does the receiver need to know about this topic?

When the message involves action, search for answers to secondary questions:

- What is the receiver to do?
- How is the receiver to do it?
- When must the receiver do it?
- What will happen if the receiver doesn't do it?

Whenever your communication problem requires more information than you have in your head or at your fingertips, you must conduct research. This research may be formal or informal.

Formal research methods. Long reports and complex business problems generally require some use of formal research methods. Let's say you are a market specialist for a major soft drink manufacturer, and your boss asks you to evaluate the impact on cola sales of generic ("no name") soft drinks. Or let's assume you must write a term paper for a college class. Both tasks require more data than you have in your head or at your fingertips. To conduct formal research, you could do one or more of the following:

- **Search electronically.** Much of the world's printed material (books, magazines, newspapers, journals) is now contained in searchable electronic databases available through the Internet. College and public libraries subscribe to retrieval services that permit you to access most periodical literature. You can also find extraordinary amounts of information, though not always of the best quality, by searching the Web. You'll learn more about using electronic sources in Chapter 8.
- **Go to the source.** For firsthand information, go directly to the source. For the cola sales report, for example, you could find out what consumers really think by conducting interviews or surveys or by organizing focus groups. Formal research includes structured sampling and controls that enable investigators to make accurate judgments and valid predictions.
- **Conduct experiments.** Instead of asking for the target audience's opinion, researchers can choose to present choices with controlled variables. Let's say, for example, that a brand-name soft-drink manufacturer wants to determine at what price and under what circumstances consumers would switch from the brand name to a generic brand. The results of such experimentation would provide valuable data for managerial decision making.

Because formal research techniques are particularly necessary for reports, you'll study them more extensively in Chapter 8.

Informal research and idea generation. Most routine tasks—such as composing e-mails, memos, letters, informational reports, and oral presentations—require data that you can collect informally. Here are some techniques for collecting informal data and for generating ideas:

- **Search company files.** If you are responding to an inquiry, you often can find the answer by investigating your company's files or by consulting colleagues.
- **Talk with your boss.** Get information from the individual who assigned you the work. What does that person know about the topic? What slant should be taken? What other sources would he or she suggest?
- **Interview the target audience.** Consider talking with individuals at whom the message is aimed. They can provide clarifying information that tells you what they want to know and how you should shape your remarks.
- **Conduct an informal survey.** Gather unscientific but helpful information via questionnaires or telephone surveys. In preparing a memo report predicting the success of a proposed fitness centre, for example, circulate a questionnaire asking for employee reactions.
- **Brainstorm for ideas.** Alone or with others, discuss ideas for the writing task at hand, and record at least a dozen ideas without judging them. Small groups are especially fruitful in brainstorming because people spin ideas off one another.

Organizing the Message

Once you've collected data, you must find a way to organize it in your message. Organizing includes two processes: grouping and patterning. Well-organized messages group similar items together so that ideas follow a sequence that helps the reader understand relationships and accept the writer's views. Unorganized messages proceed without structure or pattern, jumping from one thought to another. Such messages fail to emphasize important points. Puzzled readers can't see how the pieces fit together, and they become frustrated and irritated. Many communication experts regard poor organization as the greatest failing of business writers. A simple technique can help you organize data: the outline.

Outlining. In developing simple messages, some writers make a quick ideas list of the topics they wish to cover. They then compose a message at their computers directly from the list. Most writers, though, need to organize their ideas—especially if the project is complex—into a hierarchy, such as an outline. The beauty of preparing an outline is that it gives you a chance to organize your thoughts before you start to choose specific words and sentences. Figure 3.4 shows a format for an outline.

Choosing a direct or indirect pattern. After preparing an outline, you will need to decide where in the message you will place the main idea. Placing the main idea at the beginning of the message is called the direct pattern. In the direct pattern the main idea comes first, followed by details, explanation, or evidence. Placing the main idea later in the message (after the details, explanation, or evidence) is called the indirect pattern. The pattern you select is determined by how you expect the audience to react to the message, as shown in Figure 3.5.

In preparing to write any message, you need to anticipate the audience's reaction to your ideas and frame your message accordingly. When you expect the reader to be pleased, mildly interested, or, at worst, neutral—use the direct pattern.

Figure 3.4 ▶ Sample Outline

Awards Ceremony Costs

I. Venue
    A. Rentals
        1. Microphone
        2. Screen projector
        3. Tablecloths
    B. Extra staff
        1. Security guard
        2. Set-up, clean-up staff
II. Food
    A. Pre-awards
        1. Nonalcoholic beverages
        2. Appetizers
    B. Post-awards
        1. Alcohol
        2. Dinner
        3. Dessert
III. Awards
    A. Certificates
    B. Cash prizes

Tips for Writing Outlines

- **Define the main topic in the title.**
- **Divide the topic into major components, preferably three to five.**
- **Break the components into subpoints.**
- **Use details, illustrations, and evidence to support subpoints.**
- **Don't put a single item under a major component if you have only one subpoint; integrate it with the main item above it or reorganize.**
- **Strive to make each component exclusive (no overlapping).**

Figure 3.5 ▶   Audience Response Determines Pattern of Organization

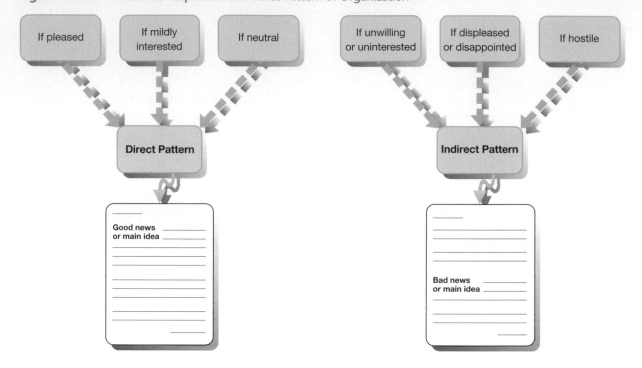

That is, put your main point in the first or second sentence. Compare the direct and indirect patterns in the following memo openings. Notice how long it takes to get to the main idea in the indirect opening.

> INDIRECT OPENING   *Bombardier is seeking to improve the process undertaken in producing its annual company awards ceremony. To this end, the Marketing Department, which is in charge of the event, has been refining last year's plan, especially with regard to the issue of rental costs and food and beverage costs.*

> DIRECT OPENING   *The Marketing Department at Bombardier suggests cutting costs for the annual awards ceremony by adjusting the way we order food and the way we handle rentals.*

Explanations and details should follow the direct opening. What's important is getting to the main idea quickly. This direct method, also called *frontloading*, has at least three advantages:

- **Saves the reader time.** Many businesspeople can devote only a few moments to each message. Messages that take too long to get to the point may lose their readers along the way.
- **Sets a proper frame of mind.** Learning the purpose upfront helps the reader put the subsequent details and explanations in perspective. Without a clear opening, the reader may be thinking, "Why am I being told this?"
- **Prevents frustration.** Readers forced to struggle through excessive text before reaching the main idea become frustrated. They resent the writer. Poorly organized messages create a negative impression of the writer.

This direct strategy works best with audiences that are likely to be receptive to or at least not likely to disagree with what you have to say. Typical business messages that follow the direct pattern include routine requests and responses, orders and acknowledgments, non-sensitive memos, e-mails, informational reports, and informational oral presentations. All these tasks have one element in common: none has a sensitive subject that will upset the reader.

When you expect the audience to be uninterested, unwilling, displeased, or perhaps even hostile, the indirect pattern is more appropriate. In this pattern you don't reveal the main idea until after you have offered explanation and evidence. This approach works well with three kinds of messages: bad news, ideas that require persuasion, and sensitive news, especially when being transmitted to superiors. The indirect pattern has these benefits:

- **Respects the feelings of the audience.** Bad news is always painful, but the pain can be lessened when the receiver is prepared for it.
- **Encourages a fair hearing.** Messages that may upset the reader are more likely to be read when the main idea is delayed. Beginning immediately with a piece of bad news or a persuasive request, for example, may cause the receiver to stop reading or listening.
- **Minimizes a negative reaction.** A reader's overall reaction to a negative message is generally improved if the news is delivered gently.

Typical business messages that could be developed indirectly include letters and memos that refuse requests, deny claims, and disapprove credit. Persuasive requests, sales letters, sensitive messages, and some reports and oral presentations also benefit from the indirect strategy. You'll learn more about how to use the indirect pattern in Chapter 6.

Composing the First Draft

Once you've researched any information you need to write your message correctly, and once you've decided how it will be organized, you're ready to write the first draft of your message. Communicators who haven't completed the preparatory work often suffer from "writer's block" and sit staring at the computer screen. It's easier to get started if you have organized your ideas and established a plan. Composition is also easier if you have a quiet environment in which to concentrate. Businesspeople with messages to compose often set aside a given time and do not allow calls, visitors, or other interruptions. This is a good technique for students as well.

As you begin composing, keep in mind that you are writing the first draft, not the final copy. Experts suggest that you write quickly (sprint writing). According to one university writing centre, "The purpose of the initial draft is to produce raw material, not to dazzle the critics with your finely shaped prose."[5] As you work your way through the draft, imagine that you are talking to the receiver. Don't let yourself get bogged down. If you can't think of the right word, insert a substitute or type "find perfect word later."[6] Sprint writing works especially well for those composing on a computer, because it's simple to make changes at any point of the composition process. If you are handwriting the first draft, double-space so that you have room for changes.

While the ability to type written business communications into an e-mail or word processing program has made us more efficient writers, it has also made us lazier writers. There's something about typing and seeing the words appear in front of us instantaneously on a screen that leads us to believe that the message is all right the way it is. This moment—when you've put words on the screen for the first time—is probably the most important moment described in this whole book.

We say this because before you click "send," before you attach that word-processed document to an e-mail, or before you print it out and hand it in to someone, you should do something very important—wait. Step back and remember that what you've written is just a first draft. This first draft deserves to be considered carefully. Take some time (at least as much as it took you to compose the draft, if not more) to see whether your message includes any of the common writing mistakes described below. This process is called revising.

THE REVISING PHASE

Revising means improving the content and sentence structure of your message. It may include adding to, cutting, and changing what you've written. Proofreading involves correcting the grammar, spelling, punctuation, format, and mechanics of your messages. Both revising and proofreading require a little practice to develop your skills. Some business writers compose the first draft quickly without worrying about grammar, style, or punctuation. Then they revise and proofread extensively. Other writers prefer to revise and proofread as they go—particularly for shorter business documents. Unsuccessful writers omit this third phase of the writing process completely and often suffer the embarrassing consequences described in Richard Levey's article. Whether you revise and proofread as you go or do it when you finish a document, you'll need to learn a bit about how to professionally revise and proofread.

How to Proofread Documents

For routine messages like e-mails the most efficient way to revise and proofread is to do so on-screen. If we were to print each e-mail we draft before sending it out in order to revise and proofread it, we'd be using up incredible amounts of paper. Instead, it's easier to scroll back to the top of your e-mail before clicking send, and begin revising and proofreading. Use the down arrow to reveal one line of your e-mail at a time. Look carefully for spelling, grammar, and punctuation mistakes, many of which are described in detail later in this section. When you are satisfied that the e-mail is correct not just in its grammar and style, but also in its tone (friendly or neutral instead of angry and curt), format (does it include a short salutation and closing such as "Hi Bob" or "Cheers"?), and structure (does it divide long paragraphs into easier-to-manage chunks of text; does it use bullets and numbering and spacing to make it easier on the reader's eyes?), you can feel confident in clicking the send button.

For other non-e-mail messages such as letters, memos, reports, and proposals, a more effective proofreading method is revising from a printed copy. Even though word processing programs like Microsoft Word have sophisticated proofreading features built into their software (e.g., the "track changes" feature in the Tools menu, or the Comment feature in the Insert menu), which you should be able to use if asked to, many professional editors continue to use the tried and tested paper-based method. In this method, a pen or pencil is used, and the text is marked up using standard proofreading marks shown in Figure 3.6.

The process is straightforward: print a copy of what you've just written (or what a team member or other colleague has written), preferably double-spaced, and set it aside for some time. You'll be more alert after a breather. Then give yourself adequate time to proofread carefully. A common excuse for sloppy proofreading is lack of time, especially in team-writing situations where the final product is being compiled by a number of people all of whom have their own pressures and deadlines. Be prepared to find errors. One student confessed, "I can find other people's errors, but I can't seem to locate my own." Psychologically, we don't expect to find errors, and we don't want to find them. You can overcome this obstacle by anticipating errors and congratulating, not criticizing, yourself each time you find one.

Read the document at least twice—once for revisions (things you think should be changed or added or deleted) and once for grammar and mechanics (mistakes like spelling and verb agreement). For long documents (such as proposals or reports), read a third time to verify consistency. For example, is the writer using the phrase "Dr. Smith" for two-thirds of the document, but then using the word phrase "Bob Smith" the other third of the time? If yes, indicate that the writer should make references to Dr. Smith consistent. For documents that must be perfect, have someone read parts of or all of it aloud. Although this sounds like an inefficient method, it's anything but. You'll find mistakes you never would have if you only read the document to yourself silently. Finally, use the standard proofreading marks shown in Figure 3.6 to indicate changes. A more complete list of proofreading marks appears in Appendix B.

Young business communicators today often protest that the revising and proofreading phase isn't necessary because their word processing program includes a style or grammar checker. Such programs analyze aspects of your writing style, including readability level and use of passive voice, trite expressions, split infinitives, and wordy expressions. Most use sophisticated technology (and a lot of computer memory) to identify significant errors. In addition to finding spelling and typographical errors, grammar checkers can find subject-verb non-agreement, word misuse, spacing irregularities, punctuation problems, and many other faults. But they won't find everything. The checklist in Figure 3.7 lists all the things you should look for when you proofread. Grammar and spell checkers cannot find all of these elements. You are ultimately the final proofreader. You are responsible for your own or your team's work.

Figure 3.6 ▶
Proofreading Marks

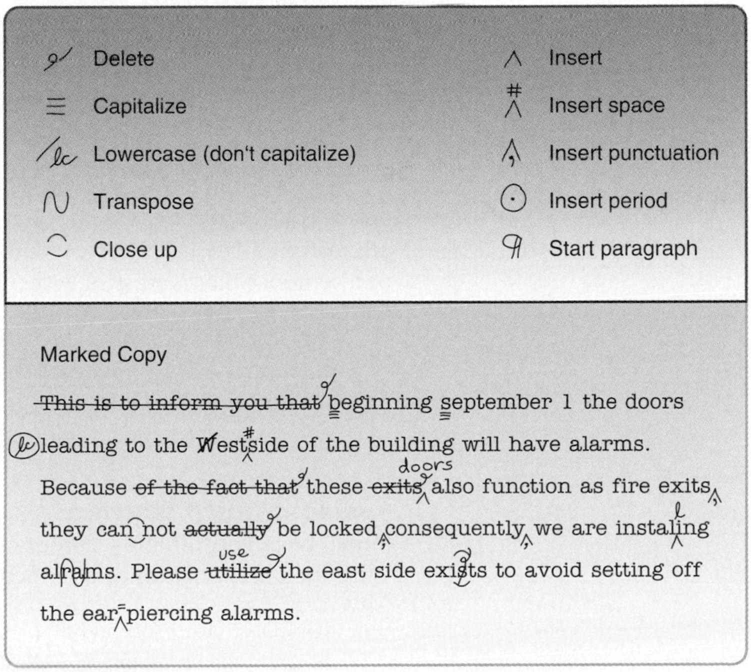

Figure 3.7 ▶
A Proofreading Checklist

- **Spelling.** Now's the time to consult the dictionary. Is *recommend* spelled with one or two *c*'s? Do you mean *affect* or *effect*? Use your computer spell checker, but don't rely on it.
- **Grammar.** Locate sentence subjects. Do their verbs agree with them? Do pronouns agree with their antecedents? Review the principles outlined in Appendix A.
- **Punctuation.** Make sure that introductory clauses are followed by commas. In compound sentences put commas before coordinating conjunctions (*and*, *or*, *but*, *nor*). Double-check your use of semicolons and colons.
- **Names and numbers.** Compare all names and numbers with their sources, because inaccuracies are not immediately visible. Especially verify the spelling of the names of individuals receiving the message. Most of us immediately dislike someone who misspells our name.
- **Format.** Be sure that letters, printed memos, and reports are balanced on the page. Compare their parts and format with those of standard documents shown in Appendix C. If you indent paragraphs, be certain that all are indented.
- **Consistency.** Make sure all words are spelled and formatted the same way throughout your document. For example, spelling *cheque* the Canadian way three times and then twice the American way (*check*) reduces your credibility as a business writer and confuses readers.

Mistakes to Correct When Revising and Proofreading

The rest of the chapter offers brief explanations and examples of the 12 most typical writing mistakes found in both students' and professionals' writing. You should be able to recognize when these mistakes have occurred, and be able to suggest a correction. There are, of course, other mistakes that writers make (many of which are covered in the Grammar/Style Reviews at the ends of chapters in this book). Be on the lookout for them too.

Sentence fragment. One of the most common errors writers make is punctuating a fragment as if it were a complete sentence. A fragment is a broken-off part of a sentence that is missing either a subject or a verb.

> FRAGMENT   *The interviewer requested a writing sample. Even though the candidate seemed to communicate well.*

> CORRECTION   *The interviewer requested a writing sample even though the candidate seemed to communicate well.*

Run-on or fused sentence. A sentence with two independent clauses must be joined by a coordinating conjunction (*and*, *or*, *nor*, *but*) or by a semicolon (;). Without a conjunction or a semicolon, the result is a run-on sentence.

> RUN-ON   *Most job seekers present a printed résumé some are also using websites as electronic portfolios.*

CORRECTION 1   *Most job seekers present a printed résumé, but some are also using websites as electronic portfolios.*

CORRECTION 2   *Most job seekers present a printed résumé; some are also using websites as electronic portfolios.*

Sentence and paragraph length. Because your goal is to communicate clearly, you're better off limiting your sentences to 20 or fewer words. Thus, in crafting your sentences, think about the relationship between sentence length and comprehension:

SENTENCE LENGTH	COMPREHENSION RATE
8 words	100%
15 words	90%
19 words	80%
28 words	50%

Business readers want to grasp ideas immediately. They can do that best when thoughts are separated into short sentences. On the other hand, too many monotonous short sentences will sound unprofessional and may bore or even annoy the reader. Strive for a balance between longer sentences and shorter ones.

Although no rule regulates the length of paragraphs, business writers recognize the value of short paragraphs. Paragraphs with eight or fewer printed lines look inviting and readable. Long, solid chunks of print appear formidable. If a topic can't be covered in eight or fewer printed lines (not sentences), consider breaking it into smaller segments.

Emphasis. When you are talking with someone, you can emphasize your main ideas by saying them loudly or by repeating them slowly. You could pound the table if you want to show real emphasis. Another way you could signal the relative importance of an idea is by raising your eyebrows or by shaking your head or whispering in a low voice. But when you write, you must rely on other means to tell your readers which ideas are more important than others. Emphasis in writing can be achieved in two ways: mechanically or stylistically.

To emphasize an idea using mechanics, a writer may employ any of the following devices:

UNDERLINING   <u>Underlining</u> draws the eye to a word.

ITALICS AND BOLDFACE   Use *italics* or **boldface** for special meaning and emphasis.

ALL CAPS   Printing words in ALL CAPS is like shouting them.

DASHES   Dashes—if used sparingly—can be effective in capturing attention.

TABULATION   Listing items vertically makes them stand out:

1. First item
2. Second item
3. Third item

Other means of achieving mechanical emphasis include the arrangement of space, colour, lines, boxes, columns, titles, headings, and subheadings. Although mechanical means are often appropriate (especially in complex documents like reports, but also in routine documents like e-mails), a writer may also achieve emphasis stylistically. That is, the writer chooses words carefully and constructs sentences skillfully to emphasize main ideas and de-emphasize minor or negative ideas. Here are four suggestions for emphasizing ideas stylistically:

- **Use vivid words.** Vivid words are emphatic because the reader can picture ideas clearly.

  GENERAL *A customer said that he wanted the contract returned soon.*

  VIVID *Mr. LeClerc insisted that the contract be returned by July 1.*

- **Label the main idea.** If an idea is significant, tell the reader.

  UNLABELLED *Explore the possibility of leasing a site, but also hire a consultant.*

  LABELLED *Explore the possibility of leasing a site; but most important, hire a consultant.*

- **Place the important idea first or last in the sentence.** Ideas have less competition from surrounding words when they appear first or last in a sentence. Observe how the concept of productivity is emphasized in second example:

  UNEMPHATIC *Profit-sharing plans are more effective in increasing productivity when they are linked to individual performance rather than to group performance.*

  EMPHATIC *Increased productivity occurs when profit-sharing plans are linked to individual performance rather than to group performance.*

- **Place the important idea in a simple sentence or in an independent clause.** Don't dilute the effect of the idea by making it share the spotlight with other words and clauses.

  UNEMPHATIC *Although you are the first trainee whom we have hired for this program, we had many candidates and expect to expand the program in the future. (Main idea is lost in a dependent clause.)*

  EMPHATIC *Although we considered many candidates, you are the first trainee whom we have hired for this program. (Independent clause contains main idea.)*

Sometimes as a business communicator, especially when sending bad news, you'll want to de-emphasize some parts of your message. There are two ways to de-emphasize something in writing:

- **Use general words.**

  SPECIFIC *Our records indicate that you were recently fired. ("fired" is specific)*

  GENERAL *Our records indicate that your employment status has changed recently. ("status has changed" is general)*

- **Place the bad news in a dependent clause connected to an independent clause with something positive.** In sentences with dependent clauses, the main emphasis is always on the independent clause.

  EMPHASIZES BAD NEWS *We cannot issue you credit at this time, but we do have a plan that will allow you to fill your immediate needs on a cash basis.*

  DE-EMPHASIZES BAD NEWS *We have a plan that will allow you to fill your immediate needs on a cash basis since we cannot issue credit at this time.*

Active voice vs. passive voice.   In English, verbs are written in one of two voices: active and passive. In the active voice, the subject does the action (e.g., Mr. Wong completed his tax return before the April 30 deadline). In the passive voice, action is done to the subject (e.g., Mr. Wong's tax return was completed before the April 30 deadline). In business writing, you need to know when to use the active instead of the passive voice. In general, use the following guidelines:

- **Use the active voice for most business writing.** It clearly tells what the action is and who is performing that action.
  The sales reps broke numerous records this quarter.

- **Use the passive voice to emphasize an action or the recipient of the action.**
  You have been selected to represent us.

- **Use the passive voice to de-emphasize negative news.**
  Your watch has not been repaired.

- **Use the passive voice to conceal the doer of an action.**
  A major error was made in the estimate.

Parallelism. Effective business writing includes balanced sentences. Sentences written so that their parts are balanced or parallel are easy to read and understand. To achieve parallel construction, use similar structures to express similar ideas. For example, the words *computing, coding, recording,* and *storing* are parallel because they all end in *-ing.* To express the list as *computing, coding, recording,* and *storage* is wrong because the last item is not what the reader expects. Try to match nouns with nouns, verbs with verbs, and clauses with clauses. Avoid mixing active-voice verbs with passive-voice verbs. Your goal is to keep the wording balanced in expressing similar ideas.

LACKS PARALLELISM *The market for industrial goods includes manufacturers, contractors, wholesalers, and those in the retail trades.*

CORRECTION *The market for industrial goods includes manufacturers, contractors, wholesalers, and retailers. (Parallel construction matches nouns.)*

LACKS PARALLELISM *Our primary goals are to increase productivity, reduce costs, and the improvement of product quality.*

CORRECTION *Our primary goals are to increase productivity, reduce costs, and improve product quality. (Parallel construction matches verbs.)*

LACKS PARALLELISM *We are scheduled to meet in Toronto on January 5, we are meeting in Montreal on the 15th of March, and in Burlington on June 3.*

CORRECTION *We are scheduled to meet in Toronto on January 5, in Montreal on March 15, and in Burlington on June 3. (Parallel construction matches phrases.)*

Unity. Unified sentences contain thoughts that are related to only one main idea. The following sentence lacks unity because the first clause has little or no relationship to the second clause:

LACKS UNITY *Our insurance plan is available in all provinces, and you may name anyone as a beneficiary for your coverage.*

CORRECTION *Our insurance plan is available in all provinces. What's more, you may name anyone as a beneficiary for your coverage.*

The ideas in a sentence are better expressed by separating the two dissimilar clauses and by adding a connecting phrase.

Coherence. A paragraph is a group of sentences with a controlling idea, usually stated first. Paragraphs package similar ideas into meaningful groups for readers. Effective paragraphs are coherent; that is, they hold together. But coherence does not happen accidentally. It is achieved through effective organization and repetition of key ideas, use of pronouns, and use of transitional expressions.

- **Repetition of key ideas or key words.** Repeating a word or key thought from a preceding sentence helps guide a reader from one thought to the next. This redundancy is necessary to build cohesiveness into writing.

  EFFECTIVE REPETITION   *Quality problems in production are often the result of inferior raw materials. Some companies have strong programs for ensuring the quality of incoming production materials and supplies.*

The second sentence of the preceding paragraph repeats the key idea of *quality*. Moreover, the words *incoming production materials and supplies* refer to raw materials mentioned in the preceding sentence. Good writers find similar words to describe the same idea, thus using repetition to clarify a topic for the reader.

- **Use of pronouns.** Pronouns such as *this, that, they, these,* and *those* promote coherence by connecting the thoughts in one sentence to the thoughts in a previous sentence. To make sure that the pronoun reference is clear, consider joining the pronoun with the word to which it refers, thus making the pronoun into an adjective.

  PRONOUN REPETITION   *Xerox has a four-point program to assist suppliers. This program includes written specifications for production materials and components.*

  Be careful, though, in using pronouns. A pronoun without a clear antecedent can be annoying. That's because the reader doesn't know precisely to what the pronoun refers.

  VAGUE PRONOUN   *When company profits increased, employees were given either a cash payment or company stock. This became a real incentive to employees. (Is* This *the cash or the stock or both?)*

  CORRECTION   *When company profits increased, employees were given either a cash payment or company stock. This profit-sharing plan became a real incentive to employees.*

- **Use of transitional expressions.** One of the most effective ways to achieve paragraph coherence is through transitional expressions. These expressions act as road signs: they indicate where the message is headed, and they help the reader anticipate what is coming. Here are some of the most effective transitional expressions. They are grouped according to use.

  TIME ASSOCIATION: *before, after, first, second, third, meanwhile, next, until, when*

  CONTRAST: *although, but, however, instead, nevertheless, on the other hand*

  ILLUSTRATION: *for example, in this way, in the following way*

  CAUSE/EFFECT: *consequently, for this reason, therefore, hence, as a result*

  ADDITIONAL IDEA: *furthermore, in addition, likewise, moreover*

Imprecision. For business writing to be effective, it has to be understood. Often, writers use imprecise language. This could be words that are used incorrectly or in a non-standard way, clichés that are empty of meaning because they have become overused, and words whose meaning is not clear because there are more precise alternatives available.

- **Misused words.** For example: The hearts of our customers will soar when they learn of our new product. (Typical ESL-type mistake in which "hearts...will soar" is a translation from another language but inappropriate in the English context. Writer probably meant "Our customers will be intrigued" or "fascinated.")
- **Clichés.** For example: You won't find another product like it—it's one in a million. (Where "one in a million" is meaningless through overuse. A better phrase might be "the only one of its kind on the market at this point.")
- **Unclear words and phrases.** For example: Verbs like "do" used instead of more interesting verbs like "complete" or "finish"; adjectives like "nice" used instead of more interesting adjectives like "relaxing" or "friendly."

Slang. Slang is the use of informal words with arbitrary and extravagantly changed meanings. Slang words quickly go out of fashion because they are no longer appealing when everyone begins to understand them. Consider the following excerpt from an e-mail sent by a ski resort company president to his executive team: "Well u guys, the results of our customer survey are in and I'm stoked by what I'm hearing. Our customers are jazzed with the goods. Congratulations to all my peeps on a job well done!" The meaning here is considerably obscured by the use of slang. Good communicators, of course, aim at clarity and avoid unintelligible slang. Watch out especially for transferring informal Internet-based chat slang (brb, lol, etc.) into formal business documents.

Jargon. Except in certain specialized contexts, you should avoid jargon and unnecessary technical terms. Jargon is special terminology that is peculiar to a particular activity or profession. For example, geologists speak knowingly of *exfoliation*, *calcareous ooze*, and *siliceous particles*. Engineers are familiar with phrases such as *infrared processing flags*, *output latches*, and *movable symbology*. Telecommunication experts use words and phrases such as *protocol*, *mode*, and *asynchronous transmission*. Business professionals are especially prone to using jargon, with words and phrases such as *leverage*, *ramp up*, *in the pipeline*, *drill down*, *cascade*, *pushback*, and *bullish* or *bearish* being just a few of the many you may find in the business section of the newspaper or in your office.

Every field has its own special vocabulary. Using that vocabulary within the field is acceptable and even necessary for accurate, efficient communication. Don't use specialized terms, however, if you have reason to believe that your reader or listener may misunderstand them.

Wordiness. Wordiness is a common writing problem. It usually appears in three different ways: unnecessary repetition, redundancy, and unnecessary words and phrases.

- **Unnecessary repetition.** Communicators who want to create vibrant sentences vary their words to avoid unintentional repetition. Notice how monotonous the following personnel announcement sounds:

Employees will be able to elect an additional six employees to serve with the four previously elected employees who currently comprise the employees' board of directors. To ensure representation, shift employees will be electing one shift employee as their sole representative.

In this example the word *employee* is used six times. In addition, the last sentence begins with the word *representation* and ends with the similar word *representative.* An easier-to-read version follows:

Employees will be able to elect an additional six representatives to serve with the four previously elected members of the employees' board of directors. To ensure representation, shift workers will elect their own board member.

In the second version, synonyms (*representatives, members, workers*) replaced *employee*. The last sentence was reworked by using a pronoun (*their*) and by substituting *board member* for the repetitious *representative*. Variety of expression can be achieved by searching for appropriate synonyms and by substituting pronouns. Good writers are also alert to the overuse of the articles *a, an,* and particularly *the.* Often the word *the* can simply be omitted, particularly with plural nouns.

WORDY   *The committee members agreed on many rule changes.*

CORRECTION   *Committee members agreed on many rule changes.*

- **Redundancy.** The needless repetition of words whose meanings are clearly implied by other words is a writing fault called redundancy. For example, in the expression *final outcome,* the word *final* is redundant and should be omitted, since *outcome* implies finality. Learn to avoid redundant expressions such as the following: *absolutely* essential, adequate *enough, grateful* thanks, *advance* warning, *mutual* cooperation, *basic* fundamentals, *necessary* prerequisite, big *in size, new* beginning, combined *together, past* history, consensus *of opinion,* reason *why,* continue *on,* red *in colour,* each *and every,* refer *back, exactly* identical, repeat *again,* few *in number, true* facts.
- **Unnecessary words and phrases.** These usually come in three types: old-fashioned expressions no longer current (e.g., "you are in receipt of" instead of "you've received"); needless adverbs that make your writing sound too informal (e.g., "We didn't truly give his plan a really fair hearing" instead of "We didn't give his plan a fair hearing"); and fillers—those words and phrases that take up space but which are not necessary (e.g., "There are three VPs who report to the President" instead of "Three VPs report to the President").

CONCLUSION

In this chapter you learned that good business writing is audience-centred, purposeful, and economical. To achieve these results, business communicators should follow a systematic writing process. This process includes three phases: prewriting, writing, and revising. In the prewriting phase, communicators analyze the task and the audience. They select an appropriate channel to deliver the message, and they consider ways to adapt their message to the task and the audience. The second phase of the writing process includes researching, organizing, and composing. Before beginning a message, business writers collect data, either formally or informally. Information for a message is then organized into a list or an outline. Depending on the expected reaction of the receiver, the message can be organized directly (for positive reactions) or indirectly (for negative reactions or when persuasion is necessary).

After composing the first draft, business writers leave enough time for the third process, revision. In this important part of the writing process, writers revise their work to check that sentences are correct and complete. They look for clarity and conciseness, wordy phrases that can be shortened (such as *more or less*), as well as repetitious words and redundancies (such as *combined together*). They eliminate jargon unless it will be clear to receivers, and they avoid slang and clichés altogether. After revising their message, business writers proofread their work, which means catching errors in spelling, grammar, punctuation, names and numbers, format, and consistency. Although routine messages like e-mails may be proofread on the screen, you will have better results if you proofread from a printed copy. Complex documents should be printed, put away for a while, and then proofread several times.

In the next chapter, you will learn about short routine business messages, including e-mails, memos, and letters, as well as non-routine short business messages like persuasive and negative messages.

Chapter Review

As a way of studying the material in this chapter, imagine you are at a job interview for your dream entry-level job after college or university. You've prepared answers for all the classic interview questions, but to your surprise, your interviewer also asks a number of questions based on written business communications. How would you answer the following six questions?

1. We've advertised the four main competencies for this position, and the first one is excellent business communication. Can you tell us how you define top-notch business communication?

2. I'd say that 90 percent of the communicating you'll be doing in this job is e-mail-based. One of the common complaints we hear around the office is that people don't seem to think too much before sending out e-mails, which results in e-mail overload for many employees. Can you comment on this situation?

3. Our customer service department, which you'll be working with closely, sometimes receives customer complaints about e-mails that are not customer-friendly. What do you think might be causing these complaints?

4. We held a communications training seminar last year for employees, and the facilitator, after looking at employee writing samples, said that many of them tended to "beat around the bush" and "not get to the point." What's your philosophy about being direct vs. being indirect in business communication?

5. There's a temptation to reply to e-mails as soon as they're received. Do you see any possible problems with this?

6. As part of the training seminar I mentioned earlier, we were all encouraged to set aside one or two minutes for each e-mail—before it's sent—for editing. What do you think goes into the editing process and why is it so important?

Problems

1. Rob Dipchan is a managing forensic auditor with KPMG in Fredericton. Each tax season, he is assigned a team of colleagues, also forensic auditors, who will work on a handful of "problem clients" who are being investigated for one reason or another. This is Rob's second year as a managing forensic auditor, and while he's an excellent auditor (which explains his promotion to the managerial position), he's turning out to be not as excellent a manager. For example, according to one of his teammates, Melanie Bonysteel, all of Rob's e-mails are "pretentious" and "over the top." She claims that in his beginning-of-week e-mail to the team, he routinely uses phrases like "I find it surprising that ..." or "I'm amazed that some of you...." Also, another of Rob's teammates, Sean Kennedy, has complained that he can't get his auditing work done because Rob sends, on average, about 30 e-mails per week, all of which he expects to be answered within three or four hours, and many of which, according to Sean "are repetitive requests for status reports—he wants status reports every day!" Finally, by his own admission, Rob is prone to writing long-winded e-mails that often take up more than one e-mail screen.

Reading and responding to these e-mails is causing his teammates a huge headache. At the same time, Rob has a say in making recommendations for year-end bonuses, and he's very well liked by his immediate supervisor, the director of Auditing. What should Rob's teammates do?
<www.kpmg.ca/en>

2. Jenny Green just graduated from the Faculty of Education at the University of British Columbia. She has landed her first full-time job at a private high school in downtown Vancouver, named Canada One Academy. Canada One offers the standard B.C. high school curriculum and is ministry-approved. The school is run as a business: it charges a fairly hefty tuition, pays its teachers less than they would receive if they worked in one of the government-funded systems, and counters any negative criticism by pointing to the low teacher-student ratio of its classes. Jenny's boss, the school's principal Reg Schacter, is also the school's owner. His method of dealing with complaints (and there are many, ranging from "My mark needs to be higher" to "That teacher doesn't know how to teach"—from both students and parents) is to send e-mails to his teachers, like Jenny, whenever there's a complaint. Typically, he takes the side of the complainant (the student or parent) and asks the teacher to defend him- or herself against the charges. The tone of his e-mails is usually belligerent, and this attitude has caused a high stress level in the workplace for Jenny and her fellow teachers. For some reason, Reg doesn't seem to want to or be able to discuss complaints in person, as most of the teachers think it should be done. For example, Reg has discontinued the practice of weekly staff meetings and has proclaimed that his e-mail communication with teachers should be sufficient. Last week, an official complaint was registered with the British Columbia College of Teachers by one of Jenny's colleagues, Ted Chu, and it looks like an investigation is going to take place in the near future. What advice would you give Reg Schacter?

3. A memo written and distributed by Sandy Nichols is causing her boss and her co-workers a big headache. This is the situation: Sandy is the manager of Customer Service at Art Knapp Plantland in Prince George, B.C. At a meeting of all customer service reps last week, Sandy listened to Bill McPhee, the store's manager, describe the new point-of-sale software that was being introduced in March, in time for the busy planting season. McPhee told the customer service reps that they would be receiving paid training in the new software at the end of February and that a memo with more details would be sent with their mid-February pay stub. Sandy stepped out of the meeting to use the washroom at the point where McPhee had talked about the paid training. Later that week, Sandy typed up a memo in which she encouraged all customer service reps to sign up for "Voluntary Microsoft Retail Management System training within the next week. A sign-up sheet is posted in the staff room by the water cooler. Thanks for your cooperation!" Customer service reps were left scratching their heads. A number of them thought they should just go straight to McPhee and ask for clarification, but then they remembered the case of Todd Martini. Todd had been a customer service rep last summer. He had had a bit of a run-in with his boss, Sandy, about taking too much time during breaks. He thought Sandy was being unfair, so he left a complaint voice mail at McPhee's extension. When Sandy found out about the voice mail, she promptly fired Todd. The customer service reps remember this incident and don't want to lose their jobs for questioning Sandy. What should be done in this situation?

4. The situation is tense across the province of Manitoba as provincial civil servants approach a strike deadline. With one week to go before the deadline, negotiations with the province are continuing, though reports claim that there has been no tangible movement by either side in over six weeks. At one Winnipeg union local, in the Food Safety Branch, the local union steward, Marek Szczygula, has been sending out daily update e-mails to his members about the state of the negotiations. Because the strike deadline is a week away, Marek is required to set in motion the procedures by which workers in the Food Safety Branch become ready for picket duty. The procedure is as follows: a meeting is convened and members are invited to sign up for a minimum of 20 hours of picket duty per week during a strike. To be eligible for strike pay, workers must sign up and attend picket duty. Marek composes the following e-mail:

To: All Local 4332 Members

From: Marek Szczygula

Date: March 5, 2007

Re: Picket duty sign-up

Hello members,

I remain cautiously optimistic that a negotiated settlement will occur sometime between today and next Monday's deadline. However, in the event that a strike goes ahead, we must be prepared for picket duty here at the Food Safety Branch. Therefore, we are holding a sign-up session for all union members tomorrow, TUESDAY MARCH 6, 2007 in the main lobby of the building. Please sign-up for picket duty. The attached document outlines the strike pay available to union members depending on the number of dependants living with them at home.

Regards,

Marek

Marek spends about ten minutes composing the above e-mail and then clicks the send button. He leaves his office for the day. When he checks his e-mail the next day around 11 a.m., 57 e-mails are in his in-box from union members at the Food Safety Branch complaining or requesting clarification. Marek sends out another e-mail hoping to clarify the situation, but by this time it's already noon and most of the branch's employees are away at an off-site workshop session on mad cow disease. A huge opportunity has been missed. What were the 57 complaint e-mails about and how could Marek improve his communication strategy next time he sends a group e-mail? <www.gov.mb.ca/agriculture/food.html>

5. Bay and Northumberland Ferries Inc. is a Charlottetown-headquartered company that provides ferry services between the Maritime provinces and between Nova Scotia and the state of Maine. Each year, more than 200 000 people take a trip aboard one of its ferries, especially in the busy summer

tourist season. As part of the company's drive to be more profitable and more responsive to both customer and corporate communications, Bay and Northumberland decided a year ago to purchase personal digital assistants (PDAs) for each member of its management team. The management team includes 15 people in both the Charlottetown head office and the various ferry terminals in Digby, Saint John, Bar Harbor, Yarmouth, and Pictou. The point of purchasing the PDAs was to make communication more efficient, but the company has noticed the opposite trend in the past year. President Mark MacDonald has personally received so many badly written messages that he's considering getting rid of the PDAs and returning to the old method of communication, which included e-mails from laptops and phone calls. Before making the decision, he invites his manager of Communications, Rachel Rolfe, to his office to discuss the situation. "You wouldn't believe the crappy e-mails I'm seeing on a daily basis, Rachel," he says as Rachel enters his office. "I'm sorry, Mark, but what do you mean exactly—e-mails from customers or e-mails from staff?" "E-mails from staff," he responds. "And what makes them crappy?" she asks. "Well, I'll show you," Mark says, gesturing toward his BlackBerry. "Take a look for yourself." Rachel leans over to read the e-mail on the tiny screen. It's from Terminal Manager Jim McDaniel in Yarmouth. It reads: "i don't know if u heard of this yet Mark but theres talk here bout a competitor startin a service from BH to Yar next summer. somthin u mite wanna look into... jim." Mark looks at Rachel. "Do you see what I mean? I get dozens of these-a-day! What am I going to do?" As Rachel, provide your boss Mark MacDonald with some realistic options.
\<www.nfl-bay.com\>

Grammar/Style Review 3

In this review, you will be practising identifying run-on sentence and sentence fragment mistakes. There are five such mistakes plus some other typical mistakes. For a brief explanation of fragments and run-on sentences, please read the explanation on page 326. Besides completing the exercise below, be sure to be on the lookout for fragments and run-on sentence mistakes in your own writing.

To: malamsah@harryrosen.ca

From: cbrillstein@harryrosen.ca

Re: Corporate retreat

Hi Mira,

Can we talk about the corporate retreat? First the hotel. Then the accommodations. And also probably the food. Last year's event went really well, Dave thinks we should use the same place in Niagara-on-the-Lake, as last year. Harry also told me that if we could bring in the top-selling employees from all stores this time around that we could do a small awards ceremony in order to recognize there achievements.

Let me know what you think.

Carl

∴ *Business Communication Lab 3*

The article by Richard Levey at the beginning of this chapter ends with an amusing anecdote about a sign in a Zellers store that included an important writing mistake, lack of precision. The sign reads, "This store has been equipped with an electronic shoplifting device." Obviously, the way the sign is worded makes it sound as if somewhere in the Zellers store there is an electronic device that will help you to shoplift. Most customers either didn't notice the mistake or else noticed it and sighed to themselves without doing anything about it. On the other hand, there are always some customers who feel it's their duty to inform a business owner when poor English has been used in one of its advertisements, brochures, or in-store signs. Imagine you are one such customer. You check out the Zellers website and see that it's not easy to find a street address to which you can mail a letter. Instead, the company has a Web-based form with fields that can be filled out for customer service-related questions. You decide to draft a short complaint letter about the poor English usage in the store sign. As part of your letter, you would like to stress the importance of upholding good English usage. You also have a suggestion for what the sign should say instead. Once you've written the e-mail, pretend you are the receiver of that e-mail. As Brenda Pupatello, the customer service representative whose job it is to respond to your complaint, draft a response to your customer complaint. You will find the following websites useful:

\<**www.hbc.com/zellers/**\>
\<**www.entrepreneur.com/article/0,4621,317323,00.html**\>

Writing Shorter Business Documents: E-Mails, Letters, and Memos

Routine Business Messages

You've Got Too Much Mail

BY KATHERINE MACKLEM, *MACLEAN'S,* JANUARY 30, 2006

ALMOST A YEAR ago, Jon Coleman set an ambitious and anachronistic goal for his department of 300 people. He asked his staff to reduce their email volume by 25 per cent over the course of 12 months. A vice-president with the pharma giant Pfizer Inc., Coleman felt that email had gotten out of control. "Many people judge their productivity based on how many emails they've responded to," he says. "That's a ridiculous measure."

Coleman isn't alone in his view. Originally billed as a time saver for office workers, email has emerged as the scourge of the modern workplace. With that upbeat dling—the tonal equivalent of a happy face—announcing the arrival of every message, email has upped stress levels in cubicles around the world. It demands ever-increasing hours. It's provided a bully pulpit for the overzealous and a hiding place for the anti-social. It can even be credited with introducing new forms of rudeness, as emailers thumb messages below the table on wireless handheld devices during meetings or conferences or, yes, dinner.

Now the backlash is growing. "We've gotten to the point where people stay in their offices and send an email rather than get up out of their chair to cross the hall," says Coleman. And so, largely at the urging of an employee committee on office wellness, he's leading a charge to rein in the habit. He brought in email trainers to provide tips on efficient email use. He keeps a file of inappropriate emails, "not to pick on anyone," he says, but to provide examples of what not to do. In July, his group introduced Freedom Six to Six, a ban on email messages between 6 p.m. and

6 a.m., and on weekends. "The spirit of the whole idea is to enable employees to disconnect when they go home, so they are all the more productive when they get back to work," he explains.

Coleman's instincts about email are backed up by research. A survey conducted by TNS Research for Hewlett Packard found that two out of three office workers check email after office hours and when on holiday. A recent Reuters survey of 1,300 business people around the world revealed that executives are suffering from an overload of information, much of it delivered by email. Two-thirds said that the stress had damaged their personal relationships, increased tension with colleagues, and contributed to a decline in job satisfaction. Email has become so indispensable that the idea of a system failure makes IT managers quake. A survey conducted for Veritas Software Corp., a U.S. storage software provider, found that one-third of IT managers would see an email collapse at their company on par with a car wreck or a divorce, in terms of stress levels.

The new technology has even spawned an addiction. In what's considered a first, a 19-year-old in Scotland was referred to counselling last year after his employer discovered he was sending up to 300 messages a day—8,000 over three months—most of them to his girlfriend. (It seems she didn't reciprocate—the two are no longer together.) After the man mistakenly sent a message intended for the girlfriend to an office colleague, he quit his job rather than face disciplinary action. "He was suffering from severe anxiety when he wasn't getting any reply, which was causing him to text and email even more," Philip Irvine, project leader of Renfrewshire Council on Alcohol Trust, where the man is being treated, told the Guardian Weekly. "This patient has all the hallmarks of any classic addict, where mental health problems such as depression, low self-esteem and relationship difficulties occur as a result of the addiction." The man, who wasn't identified by name, told the BBC there was something comforting about receiving messages. "It's like a game of ping-pong," he said, "as you send one and then get one back."

The constant flow of email can feed emotional dependence and narcissism. "We are seduced by the idea that our importance is linked to how busy we are—which is rubbish," says Ann Searles, a Montreal-based consultant with the Institute for Business Technology. Searles's client list includes heavyweights such as Cirque du Soleil and Bombardier. "We coach people every day on how to manage the double-edged sword of email," she says. One client called Searles after discovering 10,000 messages in an employee's inbox, 8,000 of them unanswered. Searles's client sought her advice. But before Searles could connect with the worker, he quit. "When someone is drowning, or close to burning out, they are likely to bite the hand that comes to help," Searles says. "They see it as a threat."

The other problem is the loss of productivity from all the interruptions. Email traffic around the world clocks in at 141 billion messages a day, up from 5.1 billion five years ago, according to the Radicati Group, a technology and market research firm in Palo Alto, Calif. The typical business worker is interrupted six to eight times a day, leading one researcher to conclude that email consumes about 28 per cent of a knowledge worker's day, or 28 billion hours per year in the United States. At an average cost of $21 an hour, the cost to U.S. business is $588 billion. "Only recently have we started to look at the dark side of email," says Ashish Gupta, a visiting assistant professor at Oklahoma State University who studied group interaction within an email environment for his Ph.D. dissertation. "There are so many problems cropping up due to email use. How frequent are the interruptions? How much time is wasted when an email comes in and disrupts a user? It's much more than most people think."

"It's a major killer for executives," says Searles. "Leaders get battered to death by email." The "cc" button is part of the problem, as employees copy their bosses on low-priority messages, also known as CYA (Cover Your Ass) emailing. When Searles first started consulting, about 10 years ago, she advised clients to check email first thing in the morning. Now, as part of an email-management strategy, she tells executives to focus on something strategically important for the first hour of their day—and to keep their email turned off.

It's not so much the interruption itself that takes up time, but rather the delay between handling the interruption and getting back to where you were. Especially in an era of multiple windows on computer screens, people often forget what they were doing. Mary Czerwinski, a computer scientist at Microsoft who studies how computers affect human behaviour, says knowledge workers constantly flit from one project to another like bees in a rose garden. After dealing with an interruption, workers jump to a new project about 40 per cent of the time, rather than return to the original task. On average, it takes 25 minutes to hop through all the subsequent interruptions, and finally return to what you were doing in the first place. All because of one email.

Czerwinski's research isn't pure academics. It will eventually feed design ideas for new computers. In experiments with oversized 42-inch screens, for instance, volunteer subjects found it easier to organize their various windows when they could see them all displayed on a large surface. Office workers already do this in an ad hoc sort of way—witness the halo of Post-It notes around many a monitor. A bigger screen, of course, won't eliminate email; but it might help people use it in smarter ways.

That would be important, as email may currently be making us stupid. Glenn Wilson, a psychiatrist at King's College, London University, monitored office workers and found that as they juggled email interruptions with the rest of their work, their IQ fell by a "shocking" 10 points—the equivalent damage of losing a night's sleep, or more than double the four-point mean drop found in pot smokers. The onslaught of messages left them more befuddled and slow. "We have found that this obsession with looking at messages, if unchecked, will damage a worker's performance by reducing their mental sharpness," Wilson reports. "This is a very real and widespread phenomenon."

But it's wrong to blame email for all our office woes, says Richard Smith, a professor of communication at B.C.'s Simon Fraser University. It's really up to users to set their own limits on the technology. "They have a choice," Smith points out. People can turn off the instant notification of new messages and check messages less frequently, he says. Email is still a new technology, he adds, and we should be cautious about making pronouncements on its social impact. We are still at a stage in which people misuse email, for instance, by typing in capital letters, the print equivalent of shrieking, or sending emails to unintended recipients. "Most of these are the kind of thing that you could expect from someone who is just learning how to use something," he says. "As more people learn, the mistakes and problems will diminish."

Pfizer's Coleman agrees the advantages of email outweigh its irritants. "Blaming RIM for email overload is like blaming BMW for speeding," he says. But he insists that a cultural shift has to take place, to keep workers from being swamped by incessant messages. "Here's a tool that's all about speeding up communication, but does exactly the opposite when used in the wrong way," he points out. "If we want to be more innovative in launching new products or competing with our competitors, I have to make sure my employees are spending as little time as possible focused on email, and as much time as possible innovating new products. By reducing the volume of email in our organization, we allow people to focus on business building and not on paper shuffling." Coleman won't know how successful his campaign has been until the spring, when he'll receive data on email usage for his group. But already, his own inbox is lighter, he says, and demands less of his time. Which means more time for more substantial work—what email was supposed to liberate office workers to do in the first place.

DIAGNOSING THE PROBLEM

It's hard to recognize, especially for young people who grew up with e-mail if not instant messaging, that there was a time not long ago when these types of communication did not exist. It was a slower time, when people would communicate by telephone, or in person-to-person conversations. Instead of arriving at your desk, turning on your computer, and looking at the dozens of e-mails you've received overnight, in the past the work day would just begin. You started to do work, and interruptions like phone calls were dealt with more easily. There were pluses to the pre-e-mail age (less stress, fewer misunderstandings), but there were also minuses, such as an inability to easily send documents to people anywhere at anytime (as we now do with e-mail attachments). Unfortunately, as Katherine Macklem describes in the article above, we appear to be entering a period in history when our routine business communication—the e-mails we write every day at work—are threatening to make us both unhealthy and stressed, as well as unproductive. Why are we dealing with this difficult situation? As the article points out, the main problem is volume. E-mail has multiplied communication to the point where it appears to be beyond many humans' ability to deal with it (as with the employee who had 8000 unanswered e-mails). Another problem not discussed by Macklem but that other studies have found just as important is that many of the millions of e-mails that are being sent each day are poorly written and actually miscommunicate instead of communicating.

Macklem describes what one Canadian company, Pfizer, is doing to combat the problem. Pfizer has decided to attack the issue of e-mail volume by mandating that its employees use e-mail less often and send fewer messages. This is one good idea, but perhaps it's an idea that would not work for all companies and in all situations. Perhaps it's an idea with serious limitations. It's time for you to think about this problem in more detail and, with your team, propose a solution.

in class
activity 4

WORKING IN SMALL groups of three to four, students will discuss the analysis of the problem provided above and evaluate the solutions offered in order to choose the most appropriate one. Is the analysis provided above complete? What will an appropriate solution look like? Why did your group choose this solution? What pluses and minuses are there in choosing this solution? Report back to the class within 20 minutes.

Now that you've presented your solution to the rest of the class, you're ready to discover some best practices in routine business writing that could help solve the problem you've just examined. At the end of this chapter, you will be presented with some more problems that you may be asked to analyze, evaluate, and explain.

WHAT IS A ROUTINE BUSINESS MESSAGE?

For most people, a day at work is spent completing two kinds of tasks. On one hand are tasks related directly to one's position (e.g., a sales representative making a sales call, a chef buying food supplies). On the other hand are all those common or routine tasks that happen in between the job-specific tasks, many of which involve communication. For example, knowing how to make small talk on an elevator with colleagues or managers is a routine oral communication task. Similarly, a Human Resources director who e-mails her staff weekly to remind them about their end-of-week meeting is writing a routine business message. Or a Customer Service manager who e-mails students at local community colleges three times a year to offer them co-op positions is writing another kind of routine message.

What defines routine messages is that they are regularly repeated: weekly, daily, monthly, or quarterly. Another defining element of routine messages is that they're written quickly, and these days, often while we're on the go—in the subway, on an airplane, in a restaurant. If you're in a position to manage other employees, chances are that one of your routine messages will be to communicate with employees about meetings. If you're in a position of reporting to a manager, chances are that one of your routine messages will be to communicate with that manager any time you can't make it to work, or when you're going to be late for work, or when you've been asked to complete a task, or when you need to ask for time off work. There are an infinite number of routine communication situations—probably at least as many as there are different jobs in the world—and obviously not all of them can be summarized in this book. The important point with routine business messages is that both when writing them and responding to them, you should stick to a clear, concise plan and use that plan each time you sit down to type one.

Routine messages are most often communicated via three channels: e-mail, memo, and letter. In this chapter, we will look at best practices using each of these three channels, in a number of routine situations. Our intention is to equip you with the skills to make your routine communications effective, so that you don't contribute to the situation described in the *Maclean's* article above.

HOW TO WRITE ROUTINE BUSINESS E-MAILS

E-mails are significant not so much because of their "new-ness" (they've been around for a few decades now) but because of their multi-functionality. With an e-mail, you have the ability to do things such as send attachments and cut and paste from other electronic texts, features that can make getting your job done much more efficient. No longer do you have to send that long contract in the mail; you can simply convert it to a PDF file and attach it to an e-mail. It gets sent to your client in three seconds, instead of three days. It's for this reason—a vast savings in time—that e-mail has become vastly more popular than more traditional channels of communication like the telephone and person-to-person conversations.[1]

Until the mid-1990s, hard-copy memos, telephone calls, and person-to-person meetings were the most common channel for exchanging routine messages at work. Today, however, e-mail is the favoured medium. Businesspeople are writing more messages than ever before and using e-mail to distribute those messages more often. Although we write e-mails up to hundreds of times a day and thus they begin to feel "routine," e-mails still require preparation because they may travel farther than you expect. Preparing an e-mail just as you would a letter or a report is also a good habit to get into so that you don't end up doing what some of the people described in Macklem's article above did—become addicted to the ease of responding to e-mails largely without thinking about them.

A novice market researcher in Calgary, for example, was eager to please her boss. When asked to report on the progress of her project, she quickly e-mailed a summary of her work. It contained numerous grammatical mistakes. Later that week, a vice president asked her boss how the project was progressing. Her boss forwarded the market researcher's hurried e-mail memo. Unfortunately, the resulting poor impression was difficult for the new employee to overcome.

Developing skill in writing e-mails brings you two important benefits. First, well-written documents are likely to achieve their goals. Second, such documents enhance your image within the organization. Individuals identified as competent, professional writers are noticed and rewarded; most often, they are the ones promoted into management positions.

Business e-mails generally fall into two types. The first type is the e-mail that's part of an already-established chain. For example, your friend Mike e-mails you to ask whether you know where the meeting is happening this afternoon. Obviously, because Mike is a friend and co-worker instead of a client or manager or boss, your e-mail back to him is going to be more informal than it would be if you were writing to someone outside the company or someone more senior than you. Generally, this first type of e-mail follows a quick three-part formula.

Writing Plan for E-Mails in an Already-Established Chain

- **Salutation.** Usually something informal like "Hey Mike," or just "Mike."
- **Message.** Often a one-sentence paragraph like "The meeting's happening in 314A."
- **Brief closing.** Most commonly an informal word like "Cheers," or "Bye," followed by the writer's first name.

Not surprisingly, because of the high volume of e-mails many of us receive at work these days, even this simple three-part formula for writing routine e-mails in a

Figure 4.1 ▶ Informal E-Mail

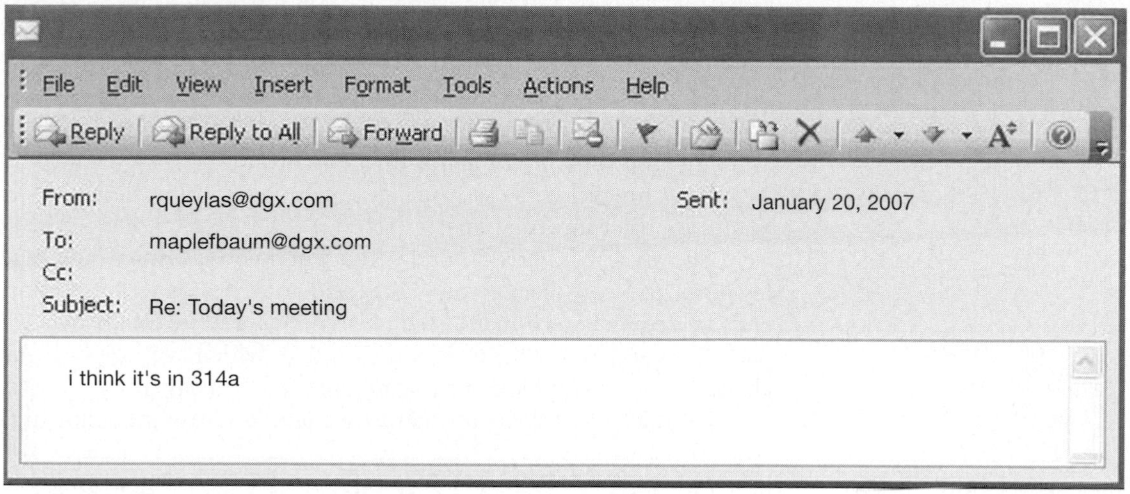

chain sometimes goes by the wayside, and what we encounter instead is something like the e-mail shown in Figure 4.1.

After reading this book and finishing your Business Communication course, one of the main things you should take away with you is that the above e-mail is *not* acceptable in a business environment. It's your responsibility as a business communicator to wean yourself away from the kind of informality displayed in the above example. Of course, this kind of e-mail informality is perfectly fine when you're using your personal instant messaging or personal e-mail address with friends. But you need to continually distinguish between the personal context and the workplace context—keep your audience in mind—because informality is not going to help you succeed in the world of work.

Figure 4.2 ▶ Revised Informal E-Mail

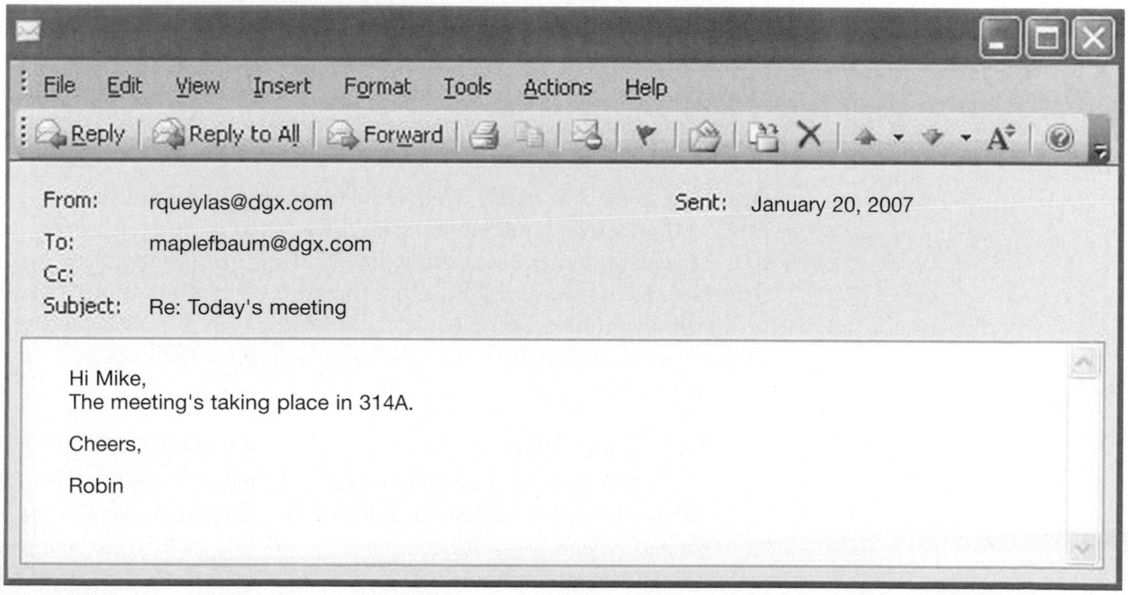

In the personal context, your non-capitalized, non-grammatical, non-formal e-mail is acceptable. It may even make you look "cool." But in a business context, your non-capitalized, non-grammatical, non-formal e-mail makes you look like you don't know how to write proper English and like you don't have the extra time it takes to write properly, thus being respectful of the person you're writing to. No business professional should ever put him- or herself in this position. Take a look at the revised version of the informal e-mail shown in Figure 4.2.

How much longer do you think it took to write the above revised version than the earlier informal one?

The answer is three seconds. And when you consider how much more professional and considerate you will appear to Mike (as well as to anyone else who ends up seeing your e-mail), it's three seconds well invested.

A second type of e-mail is the kind in which you are beginning an e-mail chain. In such a situation (e.g., writing to request a day off, writing to a customer), it's advisable to notch the formality up a level and use the following strategy.

Writing Plan for E-Mails That Begin a Chain

- **Subject line.** Summarize your message.
- **Opening.** State the main idea.
- **Body.** Provide background information and explain the main idea.
- **Closing.** Request action, summarize message, or present closing thought.

Writing the subject line. Possibly the most important part of an e-mail is the subject line. It should summarize the central idea and provide quick identification. It is usually written in an abbreviated style, often without articles (*a*, *an*, *the*). It need not be a complete sentence, and it does not end with a period. E-mail subject lines are particularly important, since meaningless ones may cause readers to delete a message without ever opening it. Good subject lines, such as the following, are specific, eye-catching, and talking (that is, they contain a verb form):

SUBJECT: *How to Fund Your Youth Health and Safety Internship Program [Instead of just Funding]*

SUBJECT: *Recommendations to Improve Network Security [Instead of just Recommendations]*

SUBJECT: *Staff Meeting to Discuss Summer Vacation Schedules [Instead of just Staff Meeting]*

Opening with the main idea. Most e-mails cover routine, non-sensitive information that can be handled in a straightforward manner. Begin by frontloading—that is, reveal the main idea immediately. Even though the purpose of an e-mail is summarized in the subject line, that purpose should be restated—and amplified—in the first sentence. Some readers skip the subject line and plunge right into the first sentence. Notice how the following indirect e-mail openers can be improved by frontloading.

INDIRECT OPENING	IMPROVED DIRECT OPENING
This is to inform you that for the past six months we have been examining benefits as part of our negotiation package under a contract that expires soon.	*Please review the following four changes in our benefits package and let us know your preference by January 1.*

As you may know, employees in Document Production have been complaining about eye fatigue as a result of the overhead fluorescent lighting in their centre.

To improve lighting in Document Production, I recommend that we purchase high-intensity desk lamps.

Explaining clearly in the body. In the body of the message, explain the main idea. If you are asking for detailed information, arrange your questions in logical order. If you are providing information, group similar information together. When a considerable amount of information is involved, use a separate paragraph for each topic. Use effective transitions between paragraphs.

Design your data for easy comprehension by using bulleted lists, headings, and tables. All these techniques make readers understand important points quickly. Compare the following two versions of the same e-mail body. Notice how the graphic devices of bullets, columns, headings, and white space make the main points easier to comprehend.

HARD-TO-READ PARAGRAPH

Effective immediately are the following air travel guidelines. Between now and December 31, only account executives may take company-approved trips. These individuals will be allowed to take a maximum of two trips per year, and they are to travel economy class or discount airline only.

EASY-TO-READ PARAGRAPH

Effective immediately are the following air travel guidelines:

- *Who may travel: Account executives only*
- *How many trips: A maximum of two trips yearly*
- *By when: Between now and December 31*
- *Air class: Economy or discount airline only*

In addition to highlighting important information, pay attention to the tone of your message. Although e-mails are generally informal, they should also be professional. Remember that e-mail messages are not telephone conversations. Don't be overly casual, funny, or blunt. Do attempt to establish a conversational tone by using occasional contractions (*won't, didn't, couldn't*) and personal pronouns (*I, me, we*).

Closing the message. Generally, end an e-mail or memo with action information, dates, or deadlines; a summary of the message; or a closing thought. Here again the value of thinking through the message before actually writing it becomes apparent. The closing is where readers look for deadlines and action language. An effective e-mail closing might be "Please submit your report by June 1. We need to review your recommendations before our July planning session."

In more complex messages, a summary of main points may be an appropriate closing. If no action request is made and a closing summary is unnecessary, you might end with a simple concluding thought ("I'm happy to provide answers to your questions" or "This project sounds like a good idea"). Although you needn't close messages to co-workers with goodwill statements such as those found in letters to customers or clients, some closing thought is often necessary to prevent a feeling of abruptness.

Closings can show gratitude or encourage feedback with remarks such as "Thanks for your help on this project" or "Do you have any suggestions on this proposal?" Other closings look forward to what's next, such as "How would you like to proceed?" Avoid trite expressions, such as "Please let me know if I may be of further assistance."

Whenever possible, the closing paragraph of a request should be end-dated. An end date sets a deadline for the requested action and gives a reason for this action to be completed by the deadline. Such end-dating prevents procrastination and allows the reader to plan a course of action to ensure completion by the date given. Giving a reason adds credibility to a deadline: "Please submit your order by December 1. We need to know the number of labels required for mailing the year-end reports January 15."

The e-mail shown in Figure 4.3 is the first draft of a message Cynthia Chomsky wrote to her team leader. Although it contains solid information, the first version is so wordy and poorly organized that the reader has trouble grasping its significance. Cynthia's revised message opens directly. Both the subject line and the first sentence explain the purpose for writing. Notice how much easier the revised version is to read. Bullets and boldfaced headings emphasize the actions necessary to solve the database problems. Notice, too, that the revised version ends with a deadline and refers to the next action to be taken.

THE CHALLENGES OF USING E-MAIL

In 2000, the Internet handled about 10 billion e-mails a day. More recent estimates indicate e-mail use has now reached 62 billion messages per day.[2] Statistics Canada reports that 60 percent of Canadians use a computer in their job with the majority (78 percent) using one daily. A full 54 percent of those workers used their computer for Internet access and e-mail.[3] Suddenly, companies find that e-mail has become an indispensable means of internal communication as well as an essential link to customers and suppliers.

At the same time, as a recent high-profile case demonstrates, companies are also finding the widespread use of e-mail is causing problems. A major Canadian bank recently sued ten of its former employees for what it claimed was illegal use of BlackBerrys it had assigned these employees.[4] The employees used the communication devices to send each other e-mails in which they discussed setting up a new and rival company to the bank. The employees obviously didn't realize that the e-mails sent using the BlackBerrys were not private and that the bank was fully within its rights to store—and read—these e-mails.

Today, the average e-mail message may remain in the company's computer system for several years. And, in an increasing number of cases, the only impression a person has of the e-mail writer is from a transmitted message; they never actually meet. That's why it's important to take the time to organize your thoughts, compose carefully, and ensure correct grammar and punctuation.

Savvy e-mail business communicators are also learning e-mail's dangers. They know that their messages can travel (intentionally or unintentionally) to unexpected destinations. A quickly drafted note may end up in the boss's mailbox or forwarded to an unintended receiver. Making matters worse, computers—like elephants—never forget. Even erased messages can remain on disk drives. The case involving the bank discussed above is a cautionary tale for any company-employed business writer naive enough to assume e-mail is a simple, private, two-way communication system.

Figure 4.3 ▶ Revising a Draft Memo

Before

From:	Sent:
To:	Susan Hsu
Cc:	
Subject:	

This is in response to your recent inquiry about our customer database. Your message of May 9 said that you wanted to know how to deal with the database problems.

I can tell you that the biggest problem is that it contains a lot of outdated information, including customers who haven't purchased anything in five or more years. Another problem is that the old database is not compatible with the new Access database that is being used by our mailing service, and this makes it difficult to merge files.

I think I can solve both problems, however, by starting a new database. This would be the place where we put the names of all new customers. And we would have it entered into the Access database. The problem with outdated information could be solved by finding out if the customers in our old database wish to continue receiving our newsletter and product announcements. Finally, we would rekey the names of all active customers into the new database.

Fails to reveal purpose quickly and concisely

Does not help reader see the two problems or the three recommendations

Forgets to conclude with next action and end date

After

From:	Susan Hsu, Team Leader Sent: May 15, 2007
To:	Cynthia Chomsky, Marketing Associate
Cc:	
Subject:	IMPROVING OUR CUSTOMER DATABASE

As you requested, here are my recommendations for improving our customer database. The database has two major problems. First, it contains many names of individuals who have not made purchases in five or more years. Second, the format is not compatible with the new Access database used by our mailing service. The following procedures, however, should solve both problems:

- **Start a new database.** Effective immediately, enter the names of all new customers in a new Access database.

- **Determine the status of customers in our old database.** Send out a mailing asking whether recipients wish to continue receiving our newsletter and product announcements.

- **Rekey the names of active customers in the new database.** Enter the names of all responding customers in our new database so that we have only one active database.

These changes will enable you, as team leader, to request mailings that go only to active customers. Please respond by May 20 with suggestions or other alternatives I could review. I will then investigate costs.

Subject line summarizes and identifies purpose

Opening states purpose concisely

Body organizes main points for readability

Closing mentions key benefit, provides deadline, and looks forward to next action

Smart E-Mail Practices

Despite its dangers and limitations, e-mail is increasingly the channel of choice for sending routine business messages. In large part, this increased popularity is a result of the advent of personal digital assistants (PDAs—BlackBerry and Palm Pilot are the best-known brands) that make it possible for people to carry their e-mail with them wherever they go. However, other channels of communication like phone calls and person-to-person conversations are still more effective for complex data or sensitive messages. The following pointers will help you get off to a good start in using e-mail safely and effectively:

- **Get the address right.** E-mail addresses can be long and complex, often including letters, numbers, dashes, and underscores. As with an address on an envelope, e-mail addresses are also unforgiving. Omit one character or mis-read the letter *l* for the number *1*, and your message will be returned. Solution: use your electronic address book frequently and use the reply feature in your e-mail program. Most e-mail programs include the correct e-mail address from the original message in the reply message. And double-check every address that you key in manually.

- **Avoid misleading subject lines.** With an abundance of "spam" (junk e-mail) clogging in-boxes and the fear of computer viruses that are spread by e-mail attachments, many e-mail users ignore or delete messages with unclear subject lines. Make sure your subject line is specific and helpful. Generic tags such as "HELLO" and "GREAT DEAL" may cause your message to be deleted before it is opened.

  Although e-mail seems as casual as a telephone call, it's not. A telephone call has its own set of rules, as does a letter, but neither of these sets of rules applies to e-mail. Concentrating on tone, content, and correctness will help to reduce the potential for misinterpretation of e-mail messages. As well, since e-mail also produces a permanent record, think carefully about what you say and how you say it.

- **Be concise and use graphic highlighting.** Don't burden readers with unnecessary information. Many e-mail recipients read dozens or even hundreds of e-mails every day. A concise message is appreciated. If you're making more than one point in your e-mail, use graphic highlighting such as a bulleted or numbered list. A list is always easier to read than a dense paragraph of information. Organized and compelling messages will help to hold the reader's interest even if the e-mail contains many ideas. Below are some examples of what we mean:

INSTEAD OF THIS...

On May 16 we will be in Regina, and Dr. Susan Dillon is the speaker.

On June 20, we will be in Saskatoon and Dr. Diane Minger is the speaker.

...TRY THIS

Date	City	Speaker
May 16	*Regina*	*Dr. Susan Dillon*
June 20	*Saskatoon*	*Dr. Diane Minger*

INSTEAD OF THIS...

Here are the instructions for operating the copy machine. First, you insert your copy card in the slot. Then you load paper in the upper tray. Last, copies are fed through the feed tray.

...TRY THIS

Follow these steps to use the copy machine:
1. Insert your copy card in the slot.
2. Load paper in the upper tray.
3. Feed copies through the feed tray.

- **Send only appropriate information.** Because e-mail seems like a telephone call or a person-to-person conversation, writers sometimes send sensitive, confidential, inflammatory, or potentially embarrassing messages. Information you consider appropriate, funny, or appealing may not be interpreted the same way by your audience. By sending an inappropriate message, you are also creating a permanent record that often does not go away even when deleted. Every message sent at work is a corporate communication for which both you and your employer are responsible.

- **Don't use e-mail to avoid contact.** Breaking bad news or resolving an argument through e-mail is not recommended. With e-mail you cannot rely on nonverbal communication, active listening techniques, and other face-to-face communication methods to ensure correct understanding of emotion and meaning. Imagine being fired by e-mail or having your job performance evaluated through e-mail. It's also not a good channel for dealing with conflict with supervisors, subordinates, or colleagues. If there's any possibility of hurt feelings, pick up the telephone or pay the person a visit.

- **Never respond when you're angry.** Always allow some time to compose yourself before responding to an upsetting message. You often come up with different and better alternatives after thinking about what was said. If possible, iron out differences in person.

- **Care about correctness.** People are still judged by their writing, whether electronic or paper-based. Sloppy e-mail messages (with missing apostrophes, haphazard spelling, and stream-of-consciousness writing) make readers work too hard. Readers quickly lose respect for writers of poor e-mails.

- **Resist humour and personal jokes.** Without the nonverbal cues conveyed by your face and your voice, humour can easily be misunderstood.

Although e-mail is an evolving communication channel, a number of rules of polite online interaction apply:

- **Limit the tendency to copy to your distribution list.** Send copies only to people who really need to see a message. It is unnecessary to document every business decision and action with an electronic paper trail.

- **Limit the tendency to reply to the entire cc list.** You should think carefully about whether your reply needs to be seen by everyone or just the person who sent you the message.

- **Don't automatically forward junk e-mail.** Internet jokes and other unnecessary messages such as warnings about new viruses, chain letters, or unusual fundraising campaigns are tiresome and valueless.

- **Consider using identifying labels.** When appropriate, add one of the following labels to the subject line: "ACTION" (action required, please respond); "FYI" (for your information, no response needed); "RE" (this is a reply to another message); "URGENT" (please respond immediately). These labels should be agreed upon among employees.

- **Use capital letters only for emphasis or for titles.** Avoid writing entire messages in all caps, which is equivalent to shouting.

- **Announce attachments.** If you're sending a lengthy attachment, tell your receiver. Consider summarizing or highlighting important aspects of the attachment briefly in the e-mail. Make sure the receiver can open the attachment you send. Some file formats cannot be opened on all computers.

- **Consider asking for permission before forwarding.** For messages containing private or project-specific information, obtain approval before forwarding to others.

The following tips can save you time and frustration when answering messages:

- **Scan all messages in your in-box before replying to each individually.** Because subsequent messages often affect the way you respond, read them all first, especially all those from the same sender.
- **Don't automatically return the sender's message.** When replying, cut and paste the relevant parts. Avoid irritating your recipients by returning the entire "thread" or sequence of messages on a topic, unless the thread needs to be included to provide context for your remarks.
- **Revise the subject line if the topic changes.** When replying or continuing an e-mail exchange, revise the subject line as the topic changes.
- **Respond to messages quickly and efficiently.** Read them, then answer, delete, or file into a project-specific folder.

Remember that office computers are meant for work-related communication:

- **Don't use company computers for personal matters.** Unless your company specifically allows it, never use your employer's computers for personal messages, personal shopping, or entertainment.
- **Assume that all e-mail is monitored.** Employers can and do monitor e-mail.

Depending on your messages and audience, the following tips promote effective electronic communication:

- **Use graphic highlighting to improve readability of longer messages.** When a message is longer, help the reader with headings, bulleted lists, and perhaps an introductory summary that describes what will follow. Although these techniques lengthen a message, they shorten reading time.
- **Consider cultural differences.** When using this global tool, be especially clear and precise in your language. Remember that figurative clichés (*pull up stakes, playing second fiddle*), sports references (*hit a home run, play by the rules, level playing field*), and slang (*cool, stoked*) can cause confusion abroad and at home for multicultural audiences.
- **Double-check before hitting the send button.** Finally and most importantly, never press the send button without reading your e-mail over at least once. In business, e-mails should be proofread before they're sent. The costs of not proofreading can be high. For instance, have you included all the information? Is your tone neutral and polite instead of angry and frustrated? Have you edited out typical grammar and style mistakes and reread for fluency before sending? At all costs, avoid the necessity of sending a second message, which makes you look careless.

HOW TO WRITE ROUTINE BUSINESS MEMOS

This is the shortest section of this book for the simple fact that hard-copy memos are a dying business communication format. Before the widespread use of e-mail, memos were a regular way of communicating in business. Today, however, they are becoming more rare, with some people going months or years without seeing one in their mailbox. The reason memos are no longer used is that e-mail has made them redundant. E-mails have largely replaced memos because they do exactly what a memo has always done, but they do it much more quickly and efficiently. While memos can be written on a computer, they are generally transmitted by hand, whereas e-mails, which perform the exact function of a memo, are written on *and* transmitted by computer, instantaneously.

A memo, short for memorandum, is traditionally used to communicate important internal company information between employees or between managers and employees. For example, if the health benefits plan at a company is about to change (e.g., if rates are increasing on January 1), the Human Resources department at the company may decide that instead of sending everyone an e-mail (adding to their already-packed in-boxes), it will act more formally by sending a memo. How does it go about doing this?

Today, writing a memo is easy because most word processing programs have easy-to-use memo templates built in. Whereas business communication students in the 1960s, 1970s, and 1980s had to learn to create memos from scratch (see Appendix C for instructions), today students simply choose a template in their word processing program (e.g., Microsoft Word's Professional Memo template) and begin filling in their content. Once in the workforce, employees are usually encouraged to use a company memo template.

The example in Figure 4.4 (page 88) shows what a typical business memo looks like. Note its similarities to an e-mail (i.e., To line, From line, Date line, Subject line) and note its differences from an e-mail (i.e., lack of a closing such as "Cheers" or "Best"). If you are asked to write a memo in your business career, simply use the writing plans discussed in the e-mail section above—they work for memos and e-mails interchangeably. The secret is not to forget the four important components: a well-thought-out subject line, a to-the-point opening sentence or paragraph, a body that explains the main idea found in the opening, and a closing that requests action by using dates and times.

HOW TO WRITE ROUTINE BUSINESS LETTERS

Letters that fail to get to the point or are badly written are a concern for employees and managers everywhere. For example, a bank's profitability can depend on the quality of information it provides to its customers. Without clear, well-written messages that transmit information concisely, banks and insurance companies risk alienating current customers and losing potential customers. This fact was demonstrated by the work of the Government of Canada's Task Force on the Future of the Canadian Financial Services Sector. In one of its research reports, "Assessing Financial Documents for Readability," the task force concluded that based on "readability scores, almost all the documents assessed in these studies are Difficult and Complex."[5] Since then, financial services companies have strived to use plain language in both their internal and external messages. Messages that meander slowly toward their point have little appeal for most of us. Readers want to know why a message was written and how it involves them. And they want that information upfront.

Letters are a form of routine external communication. In other words, they are business messages that travel outside a company. Even though e-mail has largely taken the place of letters (as it has memos), there are still numerous occasions when employees need to use letters. Generally, any time you need a formal record of an inquiry, response, or complaint, letters are the best communication channel. Routine letters can go to suppliers, government agencies, other businesses, and, most important, customers. Customer letters are given high priority because these messages encourage product feedback, project a favourable image of the company, and promote future business.

Like e-mails and memos, letters are easiest to write when you have a plan to follow. As with memos, today's sophisticated word processing software includes

Figure 4.4 ▶
Typical Business Memo

Memorandum

To: All Full-time Staff

From: Brent Ng, Compensation & Benefits Manager

Date: January 1, 2007

Re: Group Insurance Benefits Rate Adjustment

This is to inform you that the Compensation Committee has completed, with the assistance of a benefits consultant, its review of the rate adjustments provided by Sun Life. The proposed adjustments have been approved by Management Committee. The following rates are effective February 1, 2007:

Basic Life Insurance	Rate increased	$0.27 per $1000
Accidental Death	Rate unchanged	$0.02 per $1000
Dependant Life	Rate decreased	$1.59 per unit
Vision & Hearing	Rate unchanged	Single $55.20
		Family $150.10

Please note the above rates are exclusive of the provincial sales tax. If you have any questions about these changes, please contact me at extention 11610 or at bng@magna.ca.

numerous letter-writing templates. We encourage you to write letters using these templates, such as Microsoft Words' Professional Letter template. However, your company may have its own template that you will be expected to use. The standard template for a business letter (which you can use in situations where a computer may not be close to hand) is found in Appendix C. The writing plan for routine letters is straightforward and described below. Letters requiring persuasion or the delivery of bad news require special skills that will be discussed in the next two chapters.

Writing Plan for a Routine Letter

- **Formal inside and outside address.** Make sure your letter includes both the full address of your company and the full address of the person you're writing to.
- **Opening.** The first paragraph is a short summary of the purpose of your letter.

- **Body.** The body of the letter (often one paragraph but sometimes two or three) provides details that explain the purpose of your letter.
- **Closing.** The final paragraph motivates your reader to action, summarizes your letter, and sometimes offers a parting thought.

An example of a well-formatted typical business letter is found in Figure 4.5. Obviously it's important to understand when to choose e-mail, memo, or letter as a channel for your routine message. The sections in Chapter 3, "Selecting the Best Channel" and "Anticipating the Audience," should help you make this decision. For most business communicators today, the default choice is e-mail. We use memos and letters only for specific formal situations—either because we need to

Figure 4.5 ▶ Block Letter Style

**Block style
Open punctuation**

island*graphics* ─────────────────────────────── Letterhead
893 Dillingham Boulevard, Vancouver, BC V5A 1B1

↓ line 13 or 1 blank line below letterhead
September 13, 2007 ──────────────────────────── Dateline

↓ 1 to 9 blank lines

Mr. T. M. Wilson, President
Visual Concept Enterprises ─────────────────── Inside address
2166 Ocean Forest Drive
Surrey, BC V3A 7K2
↓ 1 blank line
Dear Mr. Wilson ──────────────────────────────── Salutation
↓ 1 blank line
SUBJECT: BLOCK LETTER STYLE ─────────────────── Subject line
↓ 1 blank line
This letter illustrates block letter style, about which you asked. All typed lines begin at the left margin. The date is usually placed 5 cm from the top edge of the paper or two lines below the last line of the letterhead, whichever position is lower.

This letter also shows open punctuation. No colon follows the salutation, and no comma follows the complimentary close. Although this punctuation style is efficient, we find that most of our customers prefer to include punctuation after the salutation and the complimentary close. ─────────────── Body

If a subject line is included, it appears two lines below the salutation. The word *SUBJECT* is optional. Most readers will recognize a statement in this position as the subject without an identifying label. The complimentary close appears two lines below the end of the last paragraph.
↓ 1 blank line
Sincerely ──────────────────────────────────── Complimentary
close
↓ 3 blank lines
Mark H. Wong
Graphics Designer ──────────────────────────── Signature
↓ 1 blank line   block
MHW:pil

communicate an important inter-company change or event or rule (memo) or because we need to communicate an important out-of-company message, often to customers, suppliers, or government agencies (letters).

COMMON ROUTINE BUSINESS MESSAGES

Not everybody's routine is the same. In some businesses, a routine message is an invitation. For example, one of your regular duties as a financial adviser's assistant may be to draft and send invitation letters to customer financial planning seminars. In other businesses, a routine message is a note of thanks. For example, if you work in the fundraising department of a university and a group of donors has requested not to be contacted by e-mail, you'll need to develop a letter that is sent via regular mail to these donors. Other businesses require employees to routinely respond to customer queries or comments in letter format. In this section, we provide examples of the seven most common routine business messages: information/instruction messages, information/action requests, claim/adjustment requests, information/action responses, claim/adjustment responses, recommendations, and goodwill messages such as thanks, congratulations, sympathy, condolences.

It's important to recognize that most of these seven typical messages can be expressed using any of the three channels we've talked about above: e-mail, memo, or letter. For example, a claim request can be made via e-mail as well as via letter. A message of thanks can be written in memo format or in e-mail format. But a letter of condolence cannot be written as a memo. It's up to you as a business communicator to understand your needs, your receiver's needs, and your company's needs when deciding which channel to choose. Even though e-mail is the primary channel in business today, it doesn't mean it is the channel you should always use.

Information/Instruction Message

Many of the routine e-mails and memos that are sent within a business are about sharing information or instructions. Whether it's a message reminding employees about the annual company picnic, or one that announces a change in fire safety regulations within the company's plant, the following general writing plan can be followed.

Writing Plan for an Information/Instruction Message

- **Opening**—State the main reason for writing the message.
- **Body**—Explain details of the information or details of the new or changed process.
- **Closing**—Tell readers they can get back to you for more details or if they don't understand the instructions.

Information/Action Request

Many business messages are written to request information or action. Although the specific subject of each inquiry may differ, the similarity of purpose in routine requests enables writers to use the following writing plan.

Writing Plan for an Information/Action Request

- **Opening**—Ask the most important question first or express a polite command.
- **Body**—Explain the request logically and courteously. Ask other questions if necessary.

Figure 4.6 ▶
Information/Instruction
Message via Memo

Memo

To: All Tenants

From: Fred Dalvecchio, Facilities Department x 4566

Date: September 1, 2007

Re: Change in Fire Procedures

As a result of new regulations adopted last month by the city of Hamilton, all public buildings, such as the one we work in, must follow new procedures in case of a fire.

The main new regulation is that all publicly accessible rooms/areas must have a telephone. As you may have noticed, we have recently complied with this new regulation by installing emergency telephones in a number of areas of the building including the food court, the entrance to the movie theatres, and all entrances to the mall. If you are in one of these areas and witness the outbreak of a fire, please do the following:

1. Call 911.

2. State the name of the building: "Limeridge Mall" and the name of the room/area, e.g., "Food court."

3. Exit the building using the nearest exit (usually one of the mall entrances).

Please let me know if you have any questions or concerns. My extension is 4566.

● **Closing**—Request a specific action with an end date, if appropriate, and show appreciation.

Information/Action Response

Often, your messages will respond favourably to requests for information or action. A customer wants information about a product. A supplier asks to arrange a meeting. Another business inquires about one of your procedures. But before responding to any inquiry, be sure to check your facts and figures carefully. Any letter written on company stationery is considered a legally binding contract. If a policy or procedure needs authorization, seek approval from a supervisor or executive before writing the letter. In complying with requests, you'll want to apply the same direct pattern you used in making requests.

Writing Plan for an Information/Action Response Letter

● **Subject line**—Identify previous correspondence.
● **Opening**—Deliver the most important information first.
● **Body**—Arrange information logically, explain and clarify it, provide additional information if appropriate, and build goodwill.
● **Closing**—End pleasantly.

Figure 4.7 ▶ Letter That Requests Information

Letterhead ——————————•

GEOTECH

770 Cherry Avenue
Corner Brook, NF A2L 3W5

Dateline ——————————•

August 20, 2007

Inside address ——————————•

Ms. Jane Mangrum, Manager
Vancouver Hilton Hotel
6333 North Scottsdale Road
Vancouver, BC V5H 1W4

Salutation ——————————•

Dear Ms. Mangrum:

Direct opening ——————————•

Can the Vancouver Hilton provide meeting rooms and accommodations for about 250 GeoTech sales representatives from May 25 through May 29?

Your hotel received strong recommendations because of its excellent resort and conference facilities. Our spring sales conference is scheduled for next May, and I am collecting information for our planning committee. Will you please answer these additional questions regarding the Vancouver Hilton.

- Does the hotel have a banquet room that can seat 250?

Body ——————————•

- Do you have at least four smaller meeting rooms, each to accommodate a maximum of 75?

- What kind of computer facilities are available for presentations?

- Is there a shuttle from the airport to the hotel?

Closing ——————————•

I would appreciate answers to these questions and any other information you can provide about your resort facilities by September 1. Our planning committee meets in mid-September to finalize details.

Sincerely,

Marlene Frederick

Author's name and
identification ——————————•

Marlene Frederick
Corporate Travel Administrator

Reference initials ——————————•

MF:gdr

Tips for Formatting Letters

Most business writers today use a software template such as Microsoft Word's Professional Letter template, and simply pour in their content. If you don't have access to a template, follow the steps below.

- **Start the date on line 13 or 1 blank line below the letterhead.**
- **For block style like the letter above, begin all lines at the left margin.**
- **For modified block style like the letter on page 95, begin the date and closing lines at the centre.**
- **Leave side margins of 2.5 to 3 cm (1 to 1.5 inches) depending on the length of the letter.**
- **Single-space the body and double-space between paragraphs.**

1 PREWRITING

Analyze: The purpose of this letter is to provide helpful information and to promote company products.

Anticipate: The reader is the intelligent owner of a small business who needs help with personnel administration.

Adapt: Because the reader requested this data, he will be receptive. Use the direct pattern.

2 WRITING

Research: Gather facts to answer the business owner's questions. Consult brochures and pamphlets.

Organize: Prepare a scratch outline. Plan for a fast, direct opening. Use numbered answers to the business owner's three questions.

Compose: Write the first draft on a computer. Strive for short sentences and paragraphs.

3 REVISING

Revise: Eliminate jargon and wordiness. Look for ways to explain how the product fits the reader's needs. Revise for "you" view.

Proofread: Double-check the form of numbers (*July 12, page 6, 8 to 5 PST*).

Evaluate: Does this letter answer the customer's questions and encourage an order?

Figure 4.8 ▶ Customer Reply Letter

Office Headquarters, Inc.
777 Raymer Road
Kelowna, BC V1W 1H7
www.OHQ.ca

July 15, 2007

Mr. Jeffrey M. White
White-Rather Enterprises
220 Telford Court
Leduc, AB T9E 5M6

Dear Mr. White:

SUBJECT: YOUR JULY 12 INQUIRY ABOUT PERSONNEL SOFTWARE

Yes, we do offer personnel record-keeping software specially designed for small businesses like yours. Here are answers to your three questions about this software:

1. Our Personnel Manager software provides standard employee forms so that you are always in compliance with current government regulations.

2. You receive an interviewer's guide for structured employee interviews, as well as a scripted format for checking references by telephone.

3. Yes, you can update your employees' records easily without the need for additional software, hardware, or training.

This software was specially designed to provide you with expert forms for interviewing, verifying references, recording attendance, evaluating performance, and tracking the status of your employees. We even provide you with step-by-step instructions and suggested procedures. You can treat your employees as if you had a professional human resources specialist on your staff.

On page 6 of the enclosed pamphlet you can read about our Personnel Manager software. To receive a preview copy or to ask questions about its use, just call 1-800-354-5500. Our specialists are eager to help you weekdays from 8 to 5 PST. If you prefer, visit our website to receive more information or to place an order.

Sincerely,

Amy Villanueva

Amy Villanueva
Senior Marketing Representative

Enclosure

Annotations (left):
- Puts most important information first
- Lists answers to sender's questions in order asked
- Helps reader find information by citing pages

Annotations (right):
- Identifies previous correspondence and subject
- Emphasizes "you" view
- Links sales promotion to reader benefits
- Makes it easy to respond

Claim/Adjustment Request

In business many things can go wrong—promised shipments are late, warranted goods fail, or service is disappointing. When you as a customer must write to identify or correct a wrong, the letter is called a *claim*. Straightforward claims are those to which you expect the receiver to agree readily. But even these claims often require a letter. While your first action may be a telephone call or a visit to submit your claim, you may not get the results you seek. Written claims are generally taken more seriously, and they also establish a record of what happened. Claims that require persuasion are presented in Chapter 5. In this chapter you'll learn to apply the following writing plan for a straightforward claim that uses a direct approach.

Writing Plan for a Claim/Adjustment Request

- **Opening**—Describe clearly the desired action.
- **Body**—Explain the nature of the claim, explain the claim is justified, and provide details regarding the action requested.
- **Closing**—End pleasantly with a goodwill statement and include an end date if appropriate.

Claim/Adjustment Response

As you learned earlier, when an organization receives a claim, it usually means that something has gone wrong. In responding to a claim, you have three goals:

- To rectify the wrong, if one exists
- To regain the confidence of the customer
- To promote future business and goodwill

If you decide to grant the claim, your response letter will represent good news to the reader. Use the direct strategy described in the following writing plan.

Writing Plan for Granting a Claim or Making an Adjustment

- **Subject line (optional)**—Identify the previous correspondence.
- **Opening**—Grant request or announce the adjustment immediately. Include resale or sales promotion if appropriate.
- **Body**—Provide details about how you are complying with the request. Try to regain the customer's confidence, and include resale or sales promotion if appropriate.
- **Closing**—End positively with a forward-looking thought, express confidence in future business relations, and avoid referring to unpleasantness.

Recommendation

Letters of recommendation may be written to nominate people for awards and for membership in organizations. More frequently, though, they are written to evaluate present or former employees. The central concern in these messages is honesty. Thus, you should avoid exaggerating or distorting a candidate's qualifications to cover up weaknesses or to destroy the person's chances. Ethically and legally, you have a duty to the candidate as well as to other employers to describe that person truthfully and objectively. You don't, however, have to endorse everyone who asks. Since recommendations are generally voluntary, you can—and should—resist writing letters for individuals you can't truthfully support. Ask these people to find other recommenders who know them better.

Some businesspeople today refuse to write recommendations for former employees because they fear lawsuits. Other businesspeople argue that recommendations are useless because they're always positive. Despite the general avoidance

Figure 4.9 ▶ Direct Claim Letter

Before

Sounds angry; jumps
to conclusions

Forgets that mistakes
happen

Fails to suggest
solution

Dear Sweet Sounds:

You call yourselves Sweet Sounds, but all I'm getting from your service is sour notes! I'm furious that you have your salespeople slip in unwanted service warranties to boost your sales.

When I bought my Panatronic DVD player from Sweet Sounds, Inc., in August, I specifically told the salesperson that I did NOT want a three-year service warranty. But there it is on my credit card statement this month! You people have obviously billed me for a service I did not authorize. I refuse to pay this charge.

How can you hope to stay in business with such fraudulent practices? I was expecting to return this month and look at flat-screen TVs, but you can be sure I'll find an honest dealer this time.

Sincerely,

Brent K. Royer

After

1201 North Plum Street
Steinbach, MB R3L 2N7
September 3, 2007

Personal business
letter style

Mr. Sam Lee, Customer Service
Sweet Sounds, Inc.
2003 East Street
Toronto, ON M2T 1G5

Dear Mr. Lee:

Please credit my VISA account, No. 0000-0046-2198-9421, to correct an erroneous charge of $299.

States simply and
clearly what to do

On August 8 I purchased a Panatronic DVD player from the Sweet Sounds, Inc., outlet in Steinbach. Although the salesperson discussed a three-year extended warranty with me, I decided against purchasing that service for $299. However, when my credit card statement arrived this month, I noticed an extra $299 charge from Sweet Sounds, Inc. I suspect that this charge represents the warranty I declined.

Explains objectively
what went wrong

Doesn't blame or
accuse

Enclosed is a copy of my sales invoice along with my VISA statement on which I circled the charge. Please authorize a credit immediately and send a copy of the transaction to me at the above address.

Documents facts

I'm enjoying all the features of my DVD player and would like to be shopping at Sweet Sounds for a flat-screen TV shortly.

Uses friendly tone
Suggests continued
business once problem
is resolved

Sincerely,

Brent K. Royer

Brent K. Royer

Enclosure

Figure 4.10 ▶ Customer Claim Response

Before

Sir:

In response to your recent complaint about a missing shipment, it's very difficult to deliver merchandise when we have been given the wrong address.

Our investigators looked into your problem shipment and determined that it was sent immediately after we received the order. According to the shipper's records, it was delivered to the warehouse address given on your stationery: 3590 University Avenue, Saint John, New Brunswick E2M 1G7. Unfortunately, no one at that address would accept delivery, so the shipment was returned to us. I see from your current stationery that your company has a new address. With the proper address, we probably could have delivered this shipment.

Although we feel that it is entirely appropriate to charge you shipping and restocking fees, as is our standard practice on returned goods, in this instance we will waive those fees. We hope this second shipment finally catches up with you.

Sincerely,

Amy Hopkins

Fails to reveal good news immediately; blames customer

Creates ugly tone with negative words and sarcasm

Sounds grudging and reluctant in granting claim

After

E_W ELECTRONIC WAREHOUSE
930 Abbott Park Place
Saint John, New Brunswick E3L 0T7

February 21, 2007

Mr. Jeremy Garber
Sound, Inc.
2293 Second Avenue
Saint John, NB E3M 2R5

Dear Mr. Garber:

SUBJECT: YOUR FEBRUARY 20 LETTER ABOUT YOUR PURCHASE ORDER

You should receive by February 28 a second shipment of the speakers, VCRs, headphones, and other electronic equipment that you ordered January 20.

The first shipment of this order was delivered January 28 to 3590 University Avenue, Saint John, NB. When no one at that address would accept the shipment, it was returned to us. Now that I have your letter, I see that the order should have been sent to 2293 Second Avenue, Saint John, New Brunswick E3M 2R5. When an order is undeliverable, we usually try to verify the shipping address by telephoning the customer. Somehow the return of this shipment was not caught by our normally painstaking shipping clerks. You can be sure that I will investigate shipping and return procedures with our clerks immediately to see if we can improve existing methods.

As you know, Mr. Garber, our volume business allows us to sell wholesale electronics equipment at the lowest possible prices. However, we do not want to be so large that we lose touch with valued customers like you. Over the years our customers' respect has made us successful, and we hope that the prompt delivery of this shipment will earn yours.

Sincerely,

Amy Hopkins

Amy Hopkins
Distribution Manager

c David Cole
Shipping Department

Uses customer's name in salutation

Announces good news immediately

Regains confidence of customer by explaining what happened and by suggesting plans for improvement

Closes confidently with genuine appeal for customer's respect

of negatives, well-written recommendations do help match candidates with jobs. Hiring companies learn more about a candidate's skills and potential. As a result, they are able to place a candidate properly. Therefore, you should learn to write such letters because you will surely be expected to do so in your future career.

Writing Plan for a Letter of Recommendation

- **Opening** —Identify the applicant, the position, and the reason for writing. State that the message is confidential. Establish your relationship with the applicant. Describe the length of employment or relationship.
- **Body** —Describe job duties. Provide specific examples of the applicant's professional and personal skills and attributes. Compare the applicant with others in his or her field.
- **Closing** —Summarize the significant attributes of the applicant. Offer an overall rating. Draw a conclusion regarding the recommendation.

Goodwill Messages

Goodwill messages, which include thanks, recognition, and sympathy, seem to intimidate many communicators. Finding the right words to express feelings is sometimes more difficult than writing ordinary business documents. Writers tend to procrastinate when it comes to goodwill messages, or else they send a ready-made card or pick up the telephone. Remember, though, that the personal sentiments of the sender are always more expressive and more meaningful to readers than are printed cards or oral messages. Taking the time to write gives more importance to our well-wishing. Personal notes also provide a record that can be reread and treasured.

In expressing thanks, recognition, or sympathy, you should always do so promptly. These messages are easier to write when the situation is fresh in your mind. They also mean more to the recipient. And don't forget that a prompt thank-you note carries the hidden message that you care and that you consider the event to be important. Generally, there are four kinds of goodwill messages—thanks, congratulations, praise, and sympathy. Instead of writing plans for each of them, we recommend that you concentrate on the five Ss. Goodwill messages should be

- **Selfless.** Be sure to focus the message solely on the receiver not the sender. Don't talk about yourself; avoid such comments as "I remember when I ...."
- **Specific.** Personalize the message by mentioning specific incidents or characteristics of the receiver. Telling a colleague "Great speech" is much less effective than "Great story about RIM marketing in Washington." Take care to verify names and other facts.
- **Sincere.** Let your words show genuine feelings. Rehearse in your mind how you would express the message to the receiver orally. Then transform that conversational language to your written message. Avoid pretentious, formal, or flowery language ("It gives me great pleasure to extend felicitations on the occasion of your firm's 20th anniversary").
- **Spontaneous.** Keep the message fresh and enthusiastic. Avoid canned phrases ("Congratulations on your promotion," "Good luck in the future"). Strive for directness and naturalness, not creative brilliance.
- **Short.** Although goodwill messages can be as long as needed, try to accomplish your purpose in only a few sentences. What is most important is remembering an individual. Such caring does not require documentation or wordiness. Individuals and business organizations often use special note cards or stationery for brief messages.

Figure 4.11 ▶   Employment Recommendation Letter

Kelowna Health Sciences Centre

2404 Euclid Avenue   Kelowna, BC V1Y 4S3   Phone: 250 768-3434 www.khsc.bc.ca

March 2, 2007

Vice President, Human Resources
Healthcare Enterprises
1200 Riel Blvd. N.
Winnipeg, MB R3C 2X4

Illustrates simplified letter style ——→

RECOMMENDATION OF LANCE W. OLIVER

Identifies applicant and position ——→

At the request of Lance W. Oliver, I submit this confidential information in support of his application for the position of assistant director in your Human Resources Department. Mr. Oliver served under my supervision as assistant director of Patient Services at Kelowna Health Sciences Centre for the past three years.

←—— Mentions confidentiality of message

←—— Tells relationship to writer

Supports general qualities with specific details ——→

Mr. Oliver was in charge of many customer service programs for our 770-bed hospital. A large part of his job involved monitoring and improving patient satisfaction. Because of his personable nature and superior people skills, he got along well with fellow employees, patients, and physicians. His personnel record includes a number of "Gotcha" citations, given to employees caught in the act of performing exemplary service.

Mr. Oliver works well with a team, as evidenced by his participation on the steering committee to develop our "Service First Every Day" program. His most significant contributions to our hospital, though, came as a result of his own creativity and initiative. He developed and implemented a patient hotline to hear complaints and resolve problems immediately. This enormously successful telephone service helped us improve our patient satisfaction rating from 7.2 last year to 8.4 this year. That's the highest rating in our history, and Mr. Oliver deserves a great deal of the credit.

←—— Describes and interprets accomplishments

Summarizes main points and offers evaluation ——→

We're sorry to lose Mr. Oliver, but we recognize his desire to advance his career. I am confident that his resourcefulness, intelligence, and enthusiasm will make him successful in your organization. I recommend him without reservation.

Mary E. O'Rourke
MARY E. O'ROURKE, DIRECTOR, Patient Services

MEO:rtd

Tips for Writing Letters of Recommendation

- **Identify the purpose and confidentiality of the message.**
- **Establish your relationship with the applicant.**
- **Describe the length of employment and job duties, if relevant.**
- **Provide specific examples of the applicant's professional and personal skills.**
- **Compare the applicant with others in his or her field.**
- **Offer an overall rating of the applicant.**
- **Summarize the significant attributes of the applicant.**
- **Draw a conclusion regarding the recommendation.**

Thanks

When someone has done you a favour or when an action merits praise, you need to extend thanks or show appreciation. Letters of appreciation may be written to customers for their orders, to hosts and hostesses for their hospitality, to individuals for kindnesses performed, and especially to customers who complain. After all, complainers are actually providing you with "free consulting reports from the field." Complainers who feel that they were listened to often become the greatest promoters of an organization.[6]

Figure 4.12 ▶ Thank-You for a Favour

The Canada-Japan Society of British Columbia

302-1107 Homer Street, Vancouver, BC V6B 2Y1   www.canadajapansociety.bc.ca   604 681-0295

March 20, 2007

Mr. Bryant Huffman
Marketing Manager
Ballard Power Systems
4343 North Fraser Way
Burnaby, BC V5J 5J9

Dear Bryant:

You have our sincere gratitude for providing The Canada-Japan Society of B.C. with one of the best presentations our group has ever heard.　　● — Tells purpose and delivers praise

Your description of the battle Ballard Power waged to begin marketing products in Japan was a genuine eye-opener for many of us. Nine years of preparation establishing connections and securing permissions seems an eternity, but obviously such persistence and patience pay off. We now understand better the need to learn local customs and nurture relationships when dealing in Japan.　　● — Personalizes the message by using specifics rather than generalities

In addition to your good advice, we particularly enjoyed your sense of humour and jokes—as you must have recognized from the uproarious laughter. What a great routine you do on faulty translations!　　● — Spotlights the reader's talents

We're grateful, Bryant, for the entertaining and instructive evening you provided our marketing professionals. Thanks!　　● — Concludes with compliments and thanks

Cordially,

Judy Hayashi

Judy Hayashi
Program Chair, CJSBC

JRH:grw

Because the receiver will be pleased to hear from you, you can open directly with the purpose of your message. The letter in Figure 4.12 thanks a speaker who addressed a group of marketing professionals. Although such thank-you notes can be quite short, this one is a little longer because the writer wants to lend importance to the receiver's efforts. Notice that every sentence relates to the receiver and offers enthusiastic praise. And, by using the receiver's name along with contractions and positive words, the writer makes the letter sound warm and conversational.

Written notes that show appreciation and express thanks are significant to their receivers. In expressing thanks, you generally write a short note on special notepaper or heavy card stock. If you're expressing thanks to a colleague, however, an e-mail is okay too. Figures 4.13 and 4.14 provide models for expressing thanks for a recommendation and for hospitality.

Response

Should you respond when you receive a congratulatory note or a written pat on the back? By all means. These messages are attempts to connect personally; they are efforts to reach out, to form professional and/or personal bonds. Failing to respond to notes of congratulations and most other goodwill messages is like failing to say "You're welcome" when someone says "Thank you." Responding to such messages is simply the right thing to do, and it's easy to do if you follow the models in Figures 4.15 and 4.16. Avoid minimizing your achievements with comments that suggest you don't really deserve the praise or that the sender is exaggerating your good qualities.

Sympathy

Most of us can bear misfortune and grief more easily when we know that others care. Notes expressing sympathy are probably more difficult to write than any other kind of message. Commercial "In sympathy" cards make the task easier—but they are far

Figure 4.13 ▶ Thank-You E-Mail for a Recommendation

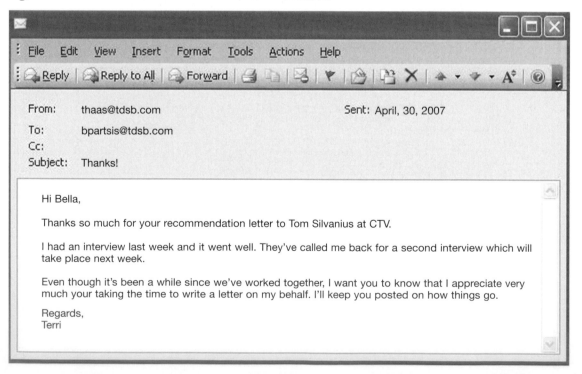

Figure 4.14 ▶ Thank-You Card for Hospitality

Dear Susan,

Jeff and I want you to know how much we enjoyed the dinner party on Saturday night.

It was great to meet your husband Patrick and let me say again how beautiful the renovations are that you've done to your house. And of course the food was wonderful!

We look forward to having you over to our place in the near future. Thanks for including a co-worker at such a special dinner party.

Best,
Tim

less meaningful. Grieving friends want to know what you think—not what Hallmark's card writers think. To help you get started, you can always glance through cards expressing sympathy. They will supply ideas about the kinds of thoughts you might wish to convey in your own words. In writing a sympathy note, refer to the death or misfortune sensitively, using words that show you

Figure 4.15 ▶ E-Mail Answer to a Congratulatory Note

From: sbielinski@accouontex.ca   Sent: December 15, 2007
To: kkasim@accountex.ca
Cc:
Subject: Thank you

Hi Khalida,
Thanks for your kind words regarding my promotion, and thanks also for sending me the newspaper clipping. I truly appreciate your thoughtfulness and best wishes.

Best,
Stan

Figure 4.16 ▶ E-Mail Response to a Pat on the Back

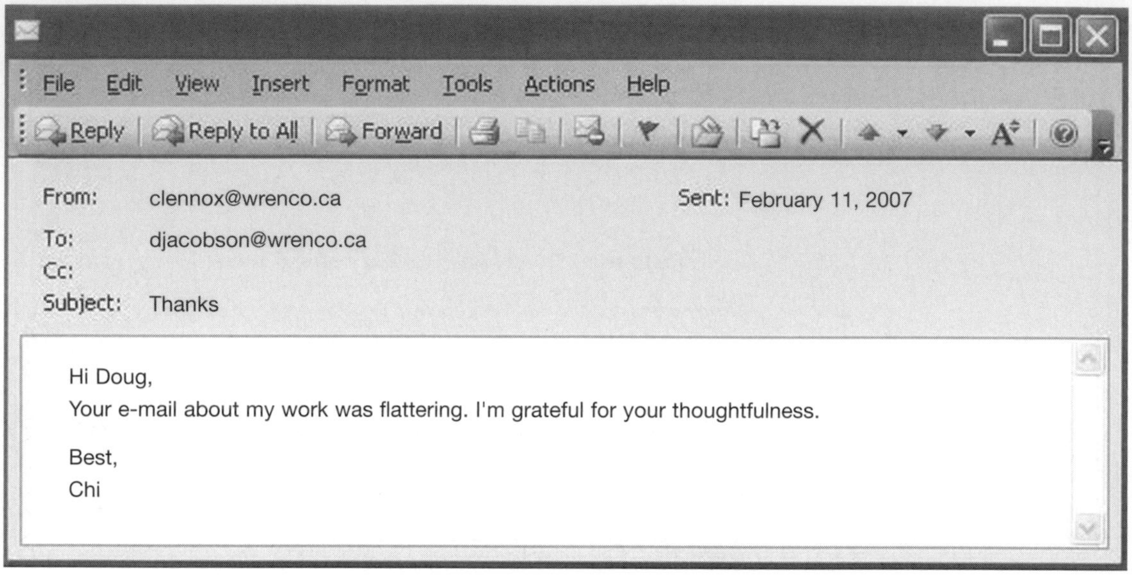

File Edit View Insert Format Tools Actions Help

Reply | Reply to All | Forward | 🖨 🗐 | 📧 | ▼ | 📂 | 📇 ✕ | ▲ ▾ ▾ ▾ Aᶜ | ⓘ

From: clennox@wrenco.ca   Sent: February 11, 2007

To: djacobson@wrenco.ca

Cc:

Subject: Thanks

Hi Doug,
Your e-mail about my work was flattering. I'm grateful for your thoughtfulness.

Best,
Chi

understand what a crushing blow it is; in the case of a death, praise the deceased in a personal way; offer assistance without going into excessive detail; and end on a reassuring, forward-looking note. Sympathy messages such as the one in Figure 4.17 are usually handwritten on notepaper or a card to express the personal nature of the message.

Figure 4.17 ▶ Card Expressing Condolences

Dear Gayle,

We were very sad to hear about your husband's passing away. Bill's kindness and friendliness endeared him to all who knew him. We'll miss him.

Although words hardly express how we feel, we want you to know that your friends here on the 16th floor extend their deepest sympathy to you and your family. If there's anything we can do to help out over the next while, just call us or send us an e-mail.

We hope you find strength in your family and friends, and in your memories of your many happy years together with Bill.

Take care,
Your friends on the 16th floor

CONCLUSION

In this chapter you learned to write e-mails, memos, and letters that respond favourably to information requests, orders, and customer claims. You also learned to write effective responses to these letters. Finally, you learned how to write recommendation and goodwill messages. The important decision in all of these cases is which channel to use. Sometimes this choice will be obvious, while at other times your decision will be guided by company practice and by your analysis of the audience. Virtually all of these routine letters use the direct strategy. They open immediately with the main idea followed by details and explanations. In the next chapter you will learn to use the indirect strategy in writing persuasive business messages.

Chapter Review

As a way of studying the material in this chapter, imagine you are at a job interview for your dream entry-level job after college or university. You've prepared answers for all the classic interview questions, but to your surprise, your interviewer also asks a number of questions based on routine business writing. How would you answer the following six questions?

1. Most of our employees communicate via e-mail at least 25 times per day. What do you think are the advantages and disadvantages to writing these e-mails in a standard way?
2. Managers in this company sometimes receive complaints from employees who say they're getting "unintelligible" e-mails. In your opinion, what makes for a well-written e-mail message?
3. Our customer service department, which you'll be working with closely, sometimes receives customer complaints about e-mails that are not customer-friendly. What do you think might be causing these complaints?
4. Until fairly recently everyone at this company above the managerial level (i.e., managers, directors, VPs, CEO) had a personal BlackBerry. We've recently decided that only VPs and the CEO should have access to a BlackBerry. Do you have any idea why we might have made this decision?
5. At our company we promise our customers a written response to any complaint or claim they may communicate to us. What should a response to such a complaint or claim look like, in your opinion?
6. Overall, whether it's in e-mail or letter format, what would you say are the top three or four qualities in any routine written business communication?

Problems

1. Lydia Juneau and Nicki Morrison work together in the Human Resources department at EnCana, the Calgary-based energy company. Lydia has recently been promoted to department manager, while Nicki is a human resources consultant. As a result of the booming energy sector, EnCana has announced a major hiring initiative outside of Alberta, using print ads, Internet ads, and consultants in key cities like Toronto, Montreal, Vancouver, and Halifax. Both Lydia and Nicki have been asked to sit on a committee that will coordinate the interview process for the expected thousands of applicants

applying for the hundred or so jobs available. In a meeting of the committee, Lydia, who was chairing the meeting, proposed that as a result of the expected increase in hours required of the Human Resources department, three more human resources consultants should be hired, bringing the total in the department to six. Nicki was unhappy about Lydia's proposal because in her estimation the existing three human resources consultants could handle the extra work. Nicki didn't voice her disagreement with Lydia's proposal in the committee meeting. However, as soon as the meeting was over, she sat down at her desk and wrote the following in an e-mail: "I think you should know that some managers are making suggestions that will negatively impact our jobs. The suggestion is that we should hire three more HR consultants, when it's been clear since the summer that we're being under-utilized as it is. I think this is a move to eventually push us out of the department. How can we voice our disagreement about this issue?" Nicki sent the e-mail to her two human resources consultant colleagues, and cc'd the e-mail to Lydia's boss, the VP of Human Resources, and to 14 other colleagues and friends in the company. She didn't send it to Lydia. It didn't take long for Lydia to hear about the e-mail chain. In fact, she heard about it in an anxious voice-mail message from her boss. What is the problem here and how could it be avoided in future?

<www.encana.com>

2. Before the VP of Human Resources in the above problem got around to calling Lydia, Lydia had already taken matters into her own hands. Her assistant, Kay, had told her that an e-mail was circulating, authored by Nicki, in which Nicki claimed that the whole point of hiring three new HR consultants was to eventually get rid of the existing consultants. Furthermore, according to Kay, Nicki's e-mail also questioned whether Lydia was the right person to be the director of the department. Lydia didn't ask Kay to track down a copy of the e-mail, but she did ask her to whom Nicki had sent the e-mail. Kay replied, "Well, she sent it to the VP, to Bill and Deb [the other two HR consultants] and to practically everyone else in the department." Lydia decided that she had to nip this situation in the bud. She slammed shut the door to her office and sat down at her desk. Then she composed an e-mail that in part said, "Despite what you've heard from some people, my qualifications to run this department are strong and I don't feel the need to explain myself. Furthermore, the decisions of the Hiring Initiative Committee were agreed to by all members of that committee, so I fail to see how any member of that committee can now turn around and claim not to have been heard in the meeting. In future, if there are any issues in regards to decisions made by the managers of this department, I'd ask you to come and see me first before sending e-mails to each other that contain untrue information." Lydia sent this e-mail to her boss, the VP, as well as to each person in the HR department, even those who had not been included in Nicki's original e-mail. Obviously, when these people got Lydia's e-mail, they were quite confused. Is there any way of justifying Lydia's actions and decisions? If not, what should she have done instead?

3. A week after the inter-office scandal described in the above problems had died down, the work of the Hiring Initiative Committee began in earnest. Lydia sent an e-mail to the hiring consultants across Canada asking for some information on how the process was unfolding. First to reply was Chris Atkins, the consultant hired in Halifax. Chris's e-mail to Lydia and the committee looked like this:

Hi Lydia,

In response to your request for information last week, you'll be happy to hear that I've been quite successful in putting together a highly qualified pool of candidates which I'm now ready to pass onto you. Here's a summary of my work to date. First off, for the project management positions I have the following candidates: Rob Neary, Rand Dupre, Heather Jax, Chris Mackinley, Sal Khafir, and Del Grey. All six of these candidates are eminently qualified as you can see from their résumés, which I've cut and pasted below. For the production engineer positions, five candidates have come through the door in the past week that I'd like to send on to you. They include Bryce Morrison, Margaret Penny, Steve Wong, Don Morgan, and Moe Kawano. Their résumés are also cut and pasted below. Finally, for the communications specialist positions you're looking to fill, I've got three possible candidates, all with strong credentials: Shannon Gough, Isabel Connor, and Mary Intah. I don't have their résumés yet, but I'll send them to you as soon as I can. I hope that the information in this e-mail was helpful, and I'm happy to send anything else you think you might need. In case the names listed above are not plentiful enough, I've also developed a file of second-tier candidates who could do in a pinch, depending on your needs. I'm happy to send their names and résumés if you like.

Regards,

Chris

Chris's e-mail, with all the résumés cut and pasted below the message, runs to about 20 screens. Some of the résumés are missing names and addresses, so it's impossible to tell which résumé belongs to which person. Lydia and the committee are frustrated by what they see as a lack of professionalism on Chris's part. At the same time, a pretty tight deadline is approaching for when interviews have to begin. Lydia has come close to writing Chris an e-mail asking him to format his e-mails in a more sensible way, but she didn't press the send button because she thought her e-mail might be taken as hostile criticism. After the scandal with Nicki's e-mail, Lydia doesn't want to be seen as causing any problems. What's wrong with the above situation?

4. The interview process at EnCana is progressing smoothly, although it's been incredibly busy. More than 50 candidates across the country have been pre-screened using telephone interviews, and 30 of them have been flown to Calgary for in-person follow-up interviews. There will be at least 70 more in-person interviews in the next six weeks. The pressure is starting to show on the faces of the Hiring Initiative Committee. Bob Lockhart, a marketing manager who's sitting on the committee and who's been put in charge of communications, has a bit of a problem on his hands. One of the

second-tier candidates mentioned by the Halifax consultant has been calling EnCana daily for the past three weeks demanding to speak to "someone in HR." Apparently, this candidate was "promised" by the Halifax consultant that he'd be flown to Calgary and interviewed for one of the project manager positions. Bob has been taking this person's phone calls and trying to explain the situation, but now, the candidate has sent an e-mail to the board of directors, the CEO, and all the VPs. His e-mail makes the following claims: "I'd like you to explain to me what sort of a business you're running? I'm approached by an HR consultant in Halifax, I send him my résumé, he calls me back and tells me that I'll be interviewed by EnCana in the next three to four weeks. It's now seven weeks later and I haven't heard a peep, despite my almost daily phone calls to EnCana. I'd like an explanation of your hiring decision in my case, at which point I will weigh whether or not to take legal action and to alert the media." The CEO has contacted Lydia and asked her to find a solution to the problem. What is this solution? Is it as simple as writing a claim response e-mail to this candidate? If not, what else can be done?

5. You are Brian Cahill, the manager of APA Petroleum Engineering Inc.'s St. John's, Newfoundland, office. Recently, an ex-employee of the company, Josh Mahone, has been in touch with you about providing a reference. Josh is sending a package to a consultant in Halifax who is doing local hiring for energy giant EnCana in Calgary. Brian waits a couple of days before replying to Josh's voice mail. It's been five years since Josh worked for Brian, and he's not quite sure what to do. Josh joined the company straight out of Memorial University with his engineering degree. He was the ideal employee for his first year with the company, undertaking all his responsibilities in an effective way, and volunteering for extra duties at a number of points along the way. Unfortunately, for the last three years of his time with APA, Josh's performance deteriorated. He still did his job well, but he began to call in sick at least once every two weeks. He also began to walk in once shifts had already begun and to leave early on a number of occasions. Brian remembers asking Josh if something was wrong at home, but Josh was evasive, saying that everything was okay. At the end of his voice mail, Josh said something about "recent hard times" and his need for "this job to work out." Brian infers from this that Josh has possibly been unemployed between his time at APA and today. He'd like to do something for Josh but at the same time as a business man, he also has a reputation to uphold—in fact he's good friends with a number of EnCana engineers back home in Calgary. What kind of a recommendation letter should Brian write for Josh?
<www.apa-inc.com>

Grammar/Style Review 4

In this review, you will be practising identifying preposition mistakes. There are five mistakes in total. For a brief explanation of this grammar problem, please read the explanation on page 327. Besides completing the exercise below, be sure to be on the lookout for preposition mistakes in your own writing.

To: All Staff

From: Susan Schneider

Re: Christmas Party

Hi everyone,

This e-mail is to inform everyone on details of this year's Christmas Party.

Upon this time of year, the company feels that it's an excellent idea all employees to get together socially outside of work.

Therefore, I'm happy to announce that this year's Christmas Party will be held in the second Friday of December, the 10th. We have booked the restaurant at the Hotel Eldorado.

Please RSVP to me on the very latest by November 30.

Sincerely,

Susan

Business Communication Lab 4

The article by Katherine Macklem at the beginning of this chapter looks at what one company, Pfizer Canada, is doing to eliminate a problem we might call e-mail addiction. E-mail addiction is the process by which employees become so caught up in checking their e-mail that they don't do as much work as they should. Imagine that you are the regional manager for an insurance company. In your office, there are roughly 120 employees, each of whom sits in a cubicle. From anecdotal evidence, as well as from your own observation, you know that your employees are spending too much time writing and answering e-mails. You'd like to propose a system like the Pfizer system, in which employees would be required to check their e-mail only three times per day: in the morning on arrival at work, just before lunch, and half an hour before they leave work around 5:00 p.m. Before you can institute this change as a policy, you need to secure your divisional manager's blessing. Write an action request e-mail to your divisional manager, Bev Cho, asking for her approval for your new policy. Feel free to quote and cite the *Maclean's* article in your e-mail.

CHAPTER 5

Persuasive Business Messages

The Invisible Salesman

BY IAN PORTSMOUTH, *PROFIT*, NOVEMBER 2005

RALPH GOODALE IS finally talking productivity. It's a brave step for a federal finance minister who is nearing an election, because in many minds higher productivity results in job cuts—hardly the foundation of a successful political campaign.

Of course, boosting productivity can also mean injecting our products and services with more value, thus making them more competitive. But no matter how it's defined, productivity improvements are meaningless if the product doesn't get sold (preferably at good margins). As it happens, we're running out of people to do the selling.

Toronto-based Merrithew Corp. is one company that's hamstrung by a shortage of good salespeople. Although it's a successful manufacturer in a hot niche—Pilates equipment and accessories—Merrithew struggles to fill its sales openings. For example, just 55 people responded over a two-month period to Merrithew's recent posting of a sales job on the massive Workopolis website. Meantime, openings for an event manager and lowly admin clerk pulled in more than 300 and 350 resumes, respectively.

At *Profit*'s recent GrowthCamp, the No. 1 complaint of the hot 50 CEOs in attendance was the dearth of qualified salespeople at reasonable prices. The consensus: young people don't have the motivation for a sales career, while the old pros want big base salaries but don't want to pound the pavement in search of clientele.

Statistics on the sales-pro shortage don't exist, perhaps because no one is measuring it. Harvey Copeman, president of the Canadian Professional Sales Association, hasn't heard of any research into the issue, but he's positive there's a problem. "We hear it from our members day in and day out," he says. "I don't think it's a figment of anyone's imagination."

Ironically, business might be to blame for the shortage. It has pressed government and academia to develop the workforce's technical skills; they've responded by building research parks and funnelling more money into science and engineering education. Liberal arts programs have suffered—even if they teach essential sales skills such as communication, persuasion and problem-solving with fuzzy logic.

Also, businesses over the past two decades have placed increased emphasis on marketing, often at the expense of sales. Thus fewer people have developed the critical sales skills and experience that so many companies crave today. Educators aren't helping, either. "People get to business school, and they're taught everything except how to generate revenue," says Colleen Francis, an Ottawa-based sales consultant. "They come out of school and see sales as a necessary evil."

Perhaps the sales function needs to do some rebranding of its own, beginning with what salespeople are called. "Client-decision facilitator" doesn't have much of a ring to it, but it does convey the increasingly consultative role of salespeople in a world of proliferating choice. (It doesn't conjure up images of Herb Tarlek, either.)

Whatever is causing the sales shortage, we need to fix it as baby boomers begin to leave the ankle-deep pool of skilled, experienced salespeople. If Ralph Goodale wants to be brave and prudent, he'll add solving the sales shortage to his productivity platform.

DIAGNOSING THE PROBLEM

Knowing how to communicate is one thing, but as the article above describes, it may not be enough. While the Canadian economy needs people who can write clearly and concisely using routine e-mails, letters, and memos—all the things we've discussed in the preceding chapters—there's obviously more at stake in the world of business. The ability to communicate persuasively, which is a special kind of communication, is also a hot commodity in today's workplace.

If we read Portsmouth's article about persuasive communication carefully, we can find all sorts of problems. He uses the problem of productivity in Canada as an introduction to the larger issue of persuasive communication by arguing that there's no point in trying to raise our productivity unless we also raise our ability to sell products. Portsmouth then moves on to a more specific problem, the lack of qualified salespeople in the country. He uses the example of a Toronto-based company as well as a group of top CEOs who both say the same thing: there are not enough good salespeople to go around right now. Another problem Portsmouth highlights is the fact that this lack of persuasive communicators is hard to measure. No one really knows how widespread the problem is, though everyone agrees there is a problem. A fourth problem the article describes is that for the most part, Canada's postsecondary educational institutions don't seem to be helping the situation because they're not teaching people how to sell. Finally, Portsmouth argues that part of the problem may lie with business owners because instead of making sales careers enticing propositions, they continue to be seen as a tacky or not-professional job category by many young people entering the workforce.

Portsmouth ends his article by giving some advice to the government: do something about the sales shortage. Let's turn Portsmouth's advice to the government into your next in-class activity, by asking some specific questions.

in-class
activity 5

WORKING IN SMALL groups of three to four, students will discuss the various problems outlined above and rank them by their importance. Then students will propose some solutions to the problems, beginning with the most important problem and working toward the least pressing problem. What will appropriate solutions to these problems look like and consist of? Why did your group choose these solutions? What might the consequences of your solutions be? Report back to the class within 20 minutes.

Now that you've presented your solution to the rest of the class, you're ready to discover some best practices in persuasive business message writing that could help solve the problem you've just examined. At the end of this chapter, you will be presented with some more problems that you may be asked to analyze, evaluate, and explain.

WHAT IS A PERSUASIVE BUSINESS MESSAGE?

The ability to persuade is an important life skill. When you try to persuade someone, you are using arguments and discussion to change an individual's beliefs or actions. Persuasion is an integral component of any business that sells goods or services, as we learned above in Ian Portsmouth's article. In this business sense, persuasion is the ability to motivate a potential customer to buy something that he or she may or may not have been interested in buying before you spoke or wrote to him or her. Persuasion happens all the time, in all kinds of businesses. The waiter who suggests a particular wine that is more expensive than you had planned on—but whose description of the wine's flavours and how well it can be paired with the dinner you've chosen manages to change your mind—has persuaded you. The sales associate at a clothing store who suggests that because the items you've just tried on are so well priced you should just buy all three of them—because they look so good on you—is using persuasion. Similarly, the magazine that sends you monthly reminders that your subscription is about to lapse—and how terrible this would be because you'd lose out on all kinds of bonuses like discounts in restaurants—is being persuasive.

In your personal life, you've had to be persuasive to convert others to your views or to motivate them to do what you want. You've written cover letters for jobs, you've asked co-workers to switch or cover shifts for you, and you've asked your parents for money for clothes and other expenses. In each case, the outcome of your persuasive efforts has depended largely on three criteria: the reasonableness of your request, your level of credibility, and your ability to make your request attractive to the receiver. In this chapter you will learn a number of techniques and strategies to help you use these three criteria successfully in any persuasive effort.

Successful persuasion always depends on successful audience analysis. When you think that your listener or reader is going to agree with your request, you can start directly with the main idea. But when the receiver is likely to resist, don't reveal the purpose too quickly. Ideas that require persuasion benefit from a slow approach that includes ample preparation. You must gain attention and move to logical reasons supporting your request. This indirect pattern is effective when you must persuade people to grant you favours, accept your recommendations, make adjustments in your favour, or grant your claims.

The same is true for sales messages. Instead of making a sales pitch immediately, smart business communicators prepare a foundation by developing credibility and tying their requests to benefits for the receiver. For example, a seasoned sales rep gains credibility by making numerous visits to potential clients before making a sales pitch. Wouldn't you be more likely to purchase equipment from someone you've talked to three times rather than someone you've just met? In persuasive messages other than sales messages, you must know precisely what you want the receiver to think or do. You must also anticipate what appeals to make or "buttons to push" to motivate action. Achieving these goals in written business messages requires special attention to the initial steps in the process. Similarly, oral business messages can be persuasive, and we'll look at those in later chapters.

HOW TO WRITE PERSUASIVE BUSINESS MESSAGES

Although you will be taught a writing plan for persuasive business messages below, it's important to understand that unlike routine messages, which follow the same pattern each time they're written, persuasive messages vary widely depending on the circumstances of the persuasion. In some cases you need to be gentle and lead readers by the hand toward what you want them to do, while at other times it makes more sense to be brisk and authoritative.

For example, a team leader meeting his team for the first time and who knows that the work the team has to do is heavy, and due within a short time frame, may decide to hold his first meeting in a delegating style. He spends a few minutes on introductions for those team members who don't know each other, and then he "gets down to business," dividing the work among the team members, giving each member a deadline, and reminding them all that he's available at any time if they need help. In another circumstance, with less pressure and a less pressing deadline, the first meeting might be largely discussion-based. All the team members will have their input heard and noted. Out of this discussion, a consensus is achieved about what needs to get done and when and by whom. Neither of these two kinds of persuasive meeting is more correct than the other, but one of them is more correct for one situation, while the other is more correct for the other situation.

Best Practices in Persuasive Message Planning

Persuasive situations vary so widely that there isn't a one-size-fits-all strategy that works each time you need to be persuasive. You wouldn't, for example, use the same techniques in asking for a raise from a stern boss as you would in persuading a friend to go to a movie that you want to see. Because of these variables, it makes sense to keep the following suggestions in mind each time you need to be persuasive:

- **Decide whether your persuasion will create problems for your audience.** If your views make trouble for the audience, think of ways to include the receivers in your recommendation if possible. Whatever your strategy, be tactful and display empathy.
- **Don't offer new ideas, instructions, or recommendations for change until your audience is ready for them.** Receivers are threatened by anything that upsets their values or interests. The greater the change you suggest, the more slowly you should proceed.
- **Choose a persuasive strategy that supports your credibility.** If you have great credibility with your audience, you can proceed directly. If not, you might want to establish that credibility first. *Given* credibility results from position or reputation, such as that of the boss of an organization or a highly regarded scientist. *Acquired* credibility is earned. To acquire credibility, successful persuaders often identify themselves, early in the message, with the goals and interests of the audience (*As a small business owner myself ...*). Another way to acquire credibility is to mention evidence or ideas that support the audience's existing views (*We agree that small business owners need more government assistance*). Finally, you can acquire credibility by citing authorities who rate highly with your audience (*Richard Love, recently named Small Businessperson of the Year, supports this proposal*). These methods of acquiring credibility are also known as appeals. Appeals can be to emotion (rarely in business except in advertising and marketing), to authority, or to logic.
- **In most cases, present both sides of the argument.** You might think that you would be most successful by revealing only one side of an issue—your side, of course. But persuasion doesn't work that way. You'll be more successful—particularly if the audience is unfriendly or uncertain—by disclosing *all* sides of an argument. This approach suggests that you are objective. It also helps the receiver remember your view by showing the pros and cons in relation to one another.

- **Win respect by making your opinion or recommendation clear.** Although you should be truthful in presenting both sides of an argument, don't be shy in supporting your conclusions or final proposals. You will, naturally, have definite views and should persuade your audience to accept them. The two-sided strategy is a means to an end, but it does not mean compromising your argument.
- **Place your strongest points strategically.** Some experts argue that if your audience is deeply concerned with your subject, you can afford to begin with your weakest points. Because of its commitment, the audience will stay with you until you reach the strongest points at the end of your argument. For an unmotivated audience, begin with your strongest points to get them interested. Other experts feel that a supportive audience should receive the main ideas or recommendations immediately, to avoid wasting time. Whichever position you choose, don't bury your recommendation, strongest facts, or main idea in the middle of your argument.
- **Recognize that information alone doesn't cause persuasion to happen.** Companies have pumped huge sums into advertising and public relations campaigns that provided facts alone. Such efforts often fail because learning something new (that is, increasing the knowledge of the audience) is rarely an effective way to change attitudes. Researchers have found that presentations of facts alone may strengthen opinions—but primarily for people who already agree with the persuader. The added information reassures them and provides ammunition for defending themselves in discussions with others.

Writing a Persuasive Business Message

Keeping in mind the three-part writing process described earlier in this book, remember that each time you're about to write a persuasive message, you should give some thought to analyzing your purpose for writing, adapting your message to your audience's needs, and researching and organizing your message. With regard to your purpose, it's safe to say that the purpose of any written persuasive business message is to convert the receiver to your ideas or to motivate that receiver to some form of action, such as purchasing a product.

To adapt your persuasive message to your audience's needs, keep some basic questions top of mind. For example, how can I tie my request to a goal or key need of the receiver, such as a goal for money, comfort, confidence, friends, or peace of mind? Second, can my request be seen to solve a problem the receiver may have, or to achieve a personal or work-related objective, or does my request somehow make life easier for my receiver? Finally, put yourself in the receiver's shoes and be able to answer questions like "Why should I?", "What's in it for me?", and "What's in it for you?"

Once you've analyzed the purpose of your message and adapted it to the audience, you're ready to begin composing the message. A tried and tested method for organizing indirect persuasive messages is described below.

Writing Plan for Indirect Persuasive Message

This chapter covers six different types of common persuasive message, each with its own special details. However, almost any persuasive message can be written using the following basic plan:

- Gain attention in the opening
- Build interest in the body
- Reduce resistance in the body

- Motivate action in the closing

Summarized in Figure 5.1, this plan appears to contain separate steps, but successful persuasive messages actually blend these steps into a seamless whole. For example, the sequence of the components may change depending on the situation and the emphasis. A number of persuasive direct-mail messages will reduce resistance before they build interest. Regardless of where they are placed, the key elements in persuasive requests are always present.

Gain attention. To grab attention, the opening statement in a persuasive request should be brief, relevant, and engaging. When only mild persuasion is necessary, the opener can be low-key and factual. If, however, your request is substantial and you anticipate strong resistance, provide a thoughtful, provocative opening. The following examples suggest possibilities.

- **Problem description.** In a recommendation to hire temporary employees: *Last month Legal Division staff members were forced to work 120 overtime hours, costing us $6000 and causing considerable employee unhappiness.* With this opener you've presented a capsule of the problem your proposal will help solve.
- **Unexpected statement.** In a memo to encourage employees to attend an optional sensitivity seminar: *Men and women draw the line at decidedly different places in identifying what behaviour constitutes sexual harassment.* Note how this opener gets readers thinking immediately.
- **Reader benefit.** In a proposal offering writing workshops to an organization: *For every letter or memo your employees can avoid writing, your organization saves $78.50.* Companies are always looking for ways to cut costs, and this opener promises significant savings.
- **Compliment.** In a letter inviting a business executive to speak: *Because our members admire your success and value your managerial expertise, they want you to be our speaker.* In offering praise or compliments, however, be careful to avoid obvious flattery.
- **Related fact.** In a memo encouraging employees to start car-pooling: *A car pool is defined as two or more persons who travel to work in one car at least once a week.* An interesting, relevant, and perhaps unknown fact sets the scene for the interest-building section that follows.
- **Stimulating question.** In a plea for funds to support environmental causes: *What do Sum 41, the maple leaf, and hockey have in common?* Readers will be curious to find the answer to this intriguing question.

Figure 5.1 ▶ Components of a Persuasive Message

Gaining Attention	Building Interest	Reducing Resistance	Motivating Action
Summary of problem	Facts, figures	Anticipate objections	Describe specific request
Unexpected statement	Expert opinion	Offer counterarguments	Sound confident
Reader benefit	Examples	Play What if? scenarios	Make action easy to take
Compliment	Specific details	Establish credibility	Offer incentive
Related fact	Direct benefits	Demonstrate competence	Don't provide excuses
Stimulating question	Indirect benefits	Show value of proposal	Repeat main benefit

Build interest. After capturing attention, a persuasive request must retain that attention and convince the audience that the request is reasonable. To justify your request, be prepared to invest in a few paragraphs of explanation. Persuasive requests are likely to be longer than direct requests because the audience must be convinced rather than simply instructed. You can build interest and conviction through the use of the following:

- Facts, statistics
- Expert opinion
- Direct benefits
- Examples
- Specific details
- Indirect benefits

Showing how your request can benefit the audience directly or indirectly is a key factor in persuasion. A *direct benefit* can be a tax write-off for a contribution. An *indirect benefit* comes from feeling good about helping others who will benefit from the gift. Nearly all charities rely in large part on indirect benefits—the self-lessness of givers—to promote their causes.

Reduce resistance. One of the biggest mistakes in persuasive requests is the failure to anticipate and offset audience resistance. How will the receiver object to your request? In brainstorming for clues, try "What if?" scenarios. For each "What if?" scenario, you need a counterargument.

Unless you anticipate resistance, you give the receiver an easy opportunity to dismiss your request. Countering this resistance is important, but you must do it with finesse. You can minimize objections by presenting your counterarguments in sentences that emphasize benefits. However, don't spend too much time on counterarguments, thus making them overly important. Finally, avoid bringing up objections that may never have occurred to the receiver in the first place.

Another factor that reduces resistance is credibility. Receivers are less resistant if your request is reasonable and if you are believable. When the receiver does not know you, you may have to establish your expertise, refer to your credentials, or demonstrate your competence. Even when you are known, you may have to establish your knowledge in a given area. Some charities establish their credibility by displaying on their stationery the names of famous people who serve on their boards. The credibility of speakers making presentations is usually outlined by someone who introduces them.

Motivate action. After gaining attention, building interest, and reducing resistance, you'll want to inspire the receiver to act. This is where your planning pays dividends. Knowing exactly what action you favour before you start to write enables you to point your arguments toward this important final paragraph. Here you will make your recommendation as specifically and confidently as possible—without seeming pushy. Compare the following closings for a persuasive memo recommending training seminars in communication skills.

Too General

We are certain we can develop a series of training sessions that will improve the communication skills of your employees.

Too Timid

If you agree that our training proposal has merit, perhaps we could begin the series in June.

Too Pushy

Because we're convinced that you will want to begin improving the skills of your employees immediately, we've scheduled your series to begin in June.

Effective

You will see decided improvement in the communication skills of your employees. Please call me at (613) 439-2201 by May 1 to give your approval so that training sessions may start in June, as we discussed.

Note how the last opening suggests a specific and easy-to-follow action.

Being Persuasive but Ethical

Business communicators may be tempted to make their persuasion even more forceful by fudging on the facts, exaggerating a point, omitting something crucial, or providing deceptive emphasis. A persuader is effective only when he or she is believable. If receivers suspect that they are being manipulated or misled, or if they find any part of the argument untruthful, the total argument fails. Persuaders can also fall into traps of logic without even being aware of it. Avoid the common logical fallacies of circular reasoning, begging the question, and post hoc (after, thus, because).

Persuasion becomes unethical when facts are distorted, overlooked, or manipulated with an intention to deceive. Of course, persuaders naturally want to put forth their strongest case. But that argument must be based on truth, objectivity, and fairness.

In prompting ethical and truthful persuasion, two factors act as powerful motivators. The first is the desire to preserve your reputation and credibility. Once lost, a good name is difficult to regain. An equally important force prompting ethical behaviour, though, is your opinion of yourself.

COMMON PERSUASIVE BUSINESS MESSAGES

While we've said earlier that persuasive messages vary widely depending on the circumstance, it is possible to narrow down these circumstances into six or so persuasive situations that occur regularly in many businesses. The models below can be adapted by you to work in almost any business situation you may find yourself in that requires persuasion.

Favour/Action Request

Persuading someone to do something that largely benefits you is not easy. Fortunately, many individuals and companies are willing to grant requests for time, money, information, special privileges, and cooperation. They grant these favours for a variety of reasons. They may just happen to be interested in your project, or they may see goodwill potential for themselves. Often, though, they comply because they see that others will benefit from the request. Professionals sometimes feel obligated to contribute their time or expertise to "pay their dues."

You may find that you have few direct benefits to offer in your persuasion. Instead, you'll focus on indirect benefits, as the writer does in Figure 5.2. In asking a professor to speak before a meeting of human resource managers, the writer has little to offer as a direct benefit other than an invitation to attend a dinner and the possibility of collecting further research data. But indirectly, the writer offers enticements such as an enthusiastic audience and a chance to help others in the profession. This persuasive request appeals primarily to the reader's desire to serve the profession —although a receptive audience and an opportunity to talk about one's work have a certain ego appeal as well. Together, these appeals—professional, egoistic, altruistic—make a persuasive argument rich and effective.

Adjustment Claim/Complaint Message

Persuasive adjustment letters make claims about damaged products, mistaken billing, inaccurate shipments, warranty problems, return policies, insurance mix-ups, faulty merchandise, and so on. Generally, the direct pattern is best for requesting straightforward adjustments (see Chapter 4). When you feel your request is justified and will be granted, the direct strategy is most efficient. But if a past request has been refused or ignored or if you anticipate reluctance, then the indirect pattern is appropriate.

In a sense, a claim letter is a complaint letter. Someone is complaining about something that went wrong. Some complaint letters just vent anger; the writers are mad, and they want to tell someone about it. But if the goal is to change something (and why bother to write except to motivate change?), then persuasion is necessary. Effective adjustment letters make a reasonable claim, present a logical case with clear facts, and adopt a moderate tone. Anger and emotion are not effective persuaders.

Strive for logical development in an adjustment letter. You'll want to open with sincere praise, an objective statement of the problem, a point of agreement, or a quick review of what you have done to resolve the problem. Then you can explain precisely what happened or why your claim is legitimate. Don't provide a blow-by-blow chronology of details; just hit the highlights. Be sure to enclose copies of relevant invoices, shipping orders, warranties, and payments. And close with a clear statement of what you want done: refund, replacement, credit to your account, or other action. Be sure to think through the possibilities and make your request reasonable.

The tone of the letter is important. You should never suggest that the receiver intentionally deceived you or intentionally created the problem. Rather, appeal to the receiver's sense of responsibility and pride in its good name. Calmly express your disappointment in view of your high expectations of the product and of the company. Communicating your feelings, without bitterness, is often your strongest appeal.

Observe how the claim letter shown in Figure 5.3 illustrates the preceding suggestions. When AMS Limitée bought new enhanced telephones, it discovered that they would not work when the fluorescent lights were on. The company's attempt to return the telephones had been refused by the retailer. Notice that the opening statement gains attention with a compliment about the product. The second paragraph builds interest by describing the problem without animosity or harsh words. The letter reduces resistance by suggesting the responsibility of the manufacturer while stressing the disappointment of the writer. The final paragraph motivates action by stating exactly what action should be taken.

Internal Suggestion

Within an organization the indirect strategy is useful when persuasion is needed in presenting new ideas to management or to colleagues. It's also useful in requesting action from employees and in securing compliance with altered procedures. Whenever resistance is anticipated, a sound foundation of reasoning should precede the main idea. This foundation prevents the idea from being rejected prematurely.

Figure 5.2 ▶ Persuasive Favour Request

Before

Provides easy excuse for refusal

Sounds writer-centred instead of reader-centred

Closes negatively and fails to tell how to respond

Dear Dr. Kasdorf:

Although your research, teaching, and consulting must keep you extremely busy, we hope that your schedule will allow you to be the featured speaker at the Canadian Association of Human Resource Managers' regional conference in Vancouver on March 23.

We are particularly interested in the article that appeared in the *Harvard Business Review*. A number of our members indicated that your topic, "Cost/Benefit Analysis for Human Resources," is something we should learn more about.

We have no funds to pay you, but we would like to invite you and your spouse to be our guests at the banquet following the day's sessions. We hope that you will be able to speak before our group.

Sincerely,

After

Canadian Association of Human Resource Managers
196 West 4th Avenue
Vancouver, BC V6R 3T4
(604) 543-8922

January 4, 2007

Professor Beverly J. Kasdorf
University College of the Cariboo
200 Mountain Way
Kamloops, BC V1L 2R4

Dear Dr. Kasdorf:

Cost/benefit analysis applied to human resources is a unique concept. Your recent article on that topic in the *Harvard Business Review* ignited a lively discussion at the last meeting of the Vancouver chapter of the Canadian Association of Human Resource Managers.

Many of the managers in our group are experiencing the changes you describe. Functions in the personnel area are now being expanded to include a wide range of salary, benefit, and training programs. These new programs can be very expensive. Our members are fascinated by your cost/benefit analysis that sets up a formal comparison of the costs to design, develop, and implement a program idea against the costs the idea saves or avoids.

The members of our association have asked me to invite you to be the featured speaker March 23, when we hold our annual conference in Vancouver. About 150 human resource specialists will attend the all-day conference at the Parkland Hotel. We would like you to speak at 2 p.m. on the topic of "Applying Cost/Benefit Analysis in Human Resources Today."

Although an honorarium is not provided, we can offer you an opportunity to help human resource managers apply your theories in solving some of their most perplexing problems. You will also meet managers who might be able to supply you with data for future research into personnel functions. In addition, the conference includes two other sessions and a banquet, to which you and a guest are invited.

Please call me at (604) 543-8922 to allow me to add your name to the program as the featured speaker before the Canadian Association of Human Resource Managers on March 23.

Respectfully,

Joanne North

Joanne North
Executive Assistant

Gains attention of reader by appealing to her interests

Builds interest by persuading reader that her expertise is valued

Makes direct request

Reduces resistance by softening negative aspects of request with reader benefits

Motivates specific action confidently

Figure 5.3 ▶ Persuasive Claim

Figure 5.3 ▶ Persuasive Claim

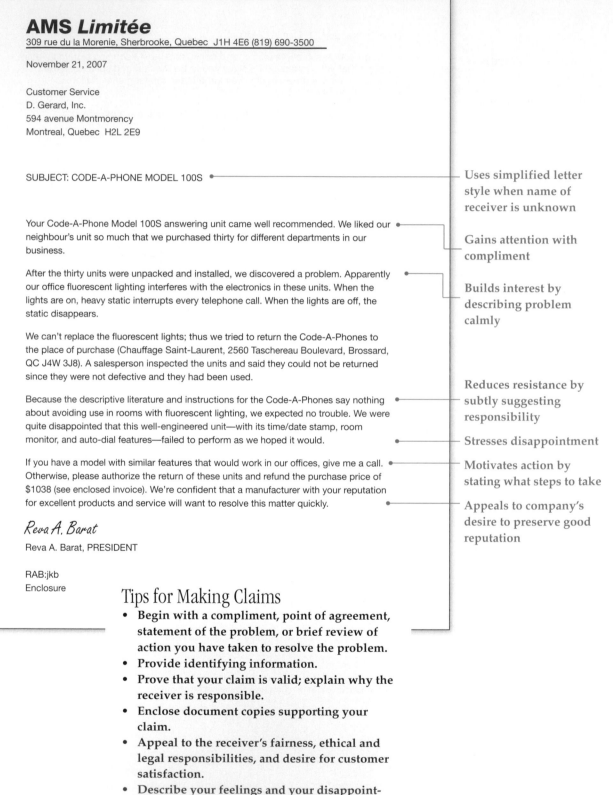

AMS *Limitée*
309 rue du la Morenie, Sherbrooke, Quebec J1H 4E6 (819) 690-3500

November 21, 2007

Customer Service
D. Gerard, Inc.
594 avenue Montmorency
Montreal, Quebec H2L 2E9

SUBJECT: CODE-A-PHONE MODEL 100S ●————————————— **Uses simplified letter style when name of receiver is unknown**

Your Code-A-Phone Model 100S answering unit came well recommended. We liked our ● —— **Gains attention with compliment**
neighbour's unit so much that we purchased thirty for different departments in our
business.

After the thirty units were unpacked and installed, we discovered a problem. Apparently ● —— **Builds interest by describing problem calmly**
our office fluorescent lighting interferes with the electronics in these units. When the
lights are on, heavy static interrupts every telephone call. When the lights are off, the
static disappears.

We can't replace the fluorescent lights; thus we tried to return the Code-A-Phones to
the place of purchase (Chauffage Saint-Laurent, 2560 Taschereau Boulevard, Brossard,
QC J4W 3J8). A salesperson inspected the units and said they could not be returned
since they were not defective and they had been used.

Because the descriptive literature and instructions for the Code-A-Phones say nothing ● —— **Reduces resistance by subtly suggesting responsibility**
about avoiding use in rooms with fluorescent lighting, we expected no trouble. We were
quite disappointed that this well-engineered unit—with its time/date stamp, room
monitor, and auto-dial features—failed to perform as we hoped it would. ● —— **Stresses disappointment**

If you have a model with similar features that would work in our offices, give me a call. ● —— **Motivates action by stating what steps to take**
Otherwise, please authorize the return of these units and refund the purchase price of
$1038 (see enclosed invoice). We're confident that a manufacturer with your reputation
for excellent products and service will want to resolve this matter quickly. ● —— **Appeals to company's desire to preserve good reputation**

Reva A. Barat

Reva A. Barat, PRESIDENT

RAB:jkb
Enclosure

Tips for Making Claims

- **Begin with a compliment, point of agreement, statement of the problem, or brief review of action you have taken to resolve the problem.**
- **Provide identifying information.**
- **Prove that your claim is valid; explain why the receiver is responsible.**
- **Enclose document copies supporting your claim.**
- **Appeal to the receiver's fairness, ethical and legal responsibilities, and desire for customer satisfaction.**
- **Describe your feelings and your disappointment.**
- **Avoid sounding angry, emotional, or irrational.**
- **Close by telling exactly what you want done.**

You should expect new ideas to meet with resistance. It doesn't matter whether the ideas are moving downward as orders from management, moving upward as suggestions to management, or moving laterally between co-workers. Resistance to change is natural. When asked to perform differently or to try something new, some individuals resist because they fear failure. Others resist because they feel threatened—the proposed changes may encroach on their status or threaten their security. Some people resist new ideas because they don't understand a proposed idea or are cautious of the person making the proposal.

Whatever the motivation, resistance to new ideas and altered procedures should be expected. You can prepare for this resistance by anticipating objections, offering counterarguments, and emphasizing benefits. Don't assume that the advantages of a new idea are obvious and therefore may go unmentioned. Use concrete examples and familiar illustrations in presenting arguments.

In the e-mail shown in Figure 5.4, Megan Wong, supervisor, argues for the purchase of a new scanner and software. She expects the director to resist this request because the budget is already overextended. Megan's memo follows the writing plan for a persuasive request. It gains attention by describing a costly problem in which Megan knows the reader is interested. To convince the director of the need for these purchases, Megan builds interest by explaining the background and providing a possible solution to the problem. Because Megan knows that the director values brevity, she tries to focus on the main points. To further improve readability, Megan begins every paragraph with a topic sentence.

After reviewing background information and the cause of the problem, Megan brings up the request for a new scanning system. She reduces resistance by discussing the benefits to the reader and the company (eliminating 40 percent of overtime and reducing turnaround time). Megan also anticipates objections (outsourcing as an alternative) but counters this possible objection by pointing out that outsourcing is expensive, slow, and insecure. In the closing, Megan motivates action by asking for authorization to go ahead and for providing support documentation to speed the request. She also includes end-dating, which prompts the director to act by a certain date.

Sales Message

Direct marketing in Canada is an $8.48-billion industry.[1] This figure includes all sales letters, packets, brochures, and catalogues sent directly to consumers. The professionals who specialize in direct mail marketing have made a science of analyzing a market, developing an appropriate mailing list, studying the product, preparing a comprehensive presentation that appeals to the needs of the target audience, and motivating the reader to act. This carefully orchestrated presentation typically concludes with a sales letter accompanied by a brochure, a sales list, illustrations of the product, testimonials, and so forth.

Although the sales letters of large organizations are usually written by professional copywriters, many smaller companies cannot afford such specialized services. Entrepreneurs and employees of smaller businesses may be called on to write their own sales messages. This is the reality Ian Portsmouth is describing in his article at the beginning of the chapter. For example, one recent graduate started a graphic design firm and immediately had to write a convincing letter offering her services. Another graduate went to work for a small company that installs security systems. Because of his recent diploma (other employees were unsure of their skills), he was asked to draft a sales letter outlining specific benefits for residential customers. Selling is part of almost all businesses.

Figure 5.4 ▶ Persuasive Suggestion

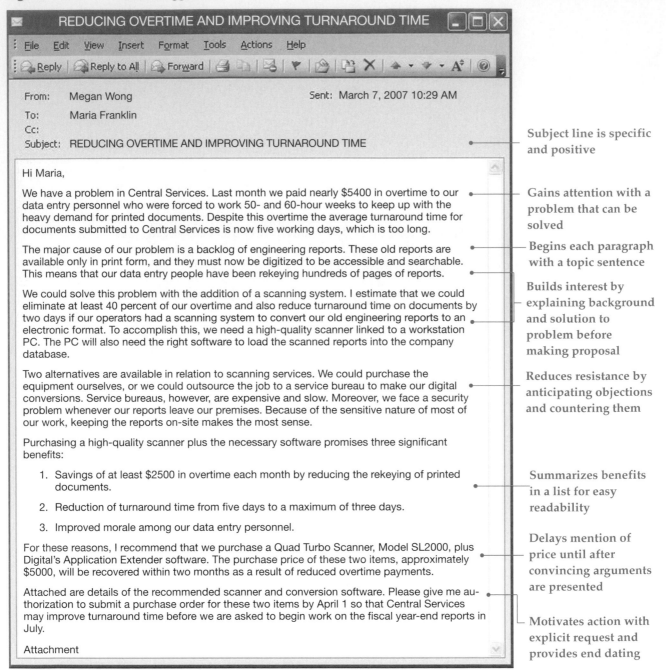

REDUCING OVERTIME AND IMPROVING TURNAROUND TIME

File   Edit   View   Insert   Format   Tools   Actions   Help

Reply | Reply to All | Forward

From: Megan Wong   Sent: March 7, 2007 10:29 AM
To: Maria Franklin
Cc:
Subject: REDUCING OVERTIME AND IMPROVING TURNAROUND TIME

Hi Maria,

We have a problem in Central Services. Last month we paid nearly $5400 in overtime to our data entry personnel who were forced to work 50- and 60-hour weeks to keep up with the heavy demand for printed documents. Despite this overtime the average turnaround time for documents submitted to Central Services is now five working days, which is too long.

The major cause of our problem is a backlog of engineering reports. These old reports are available only in print form, and they must now be digitized to be accessible and searchable. This means that our data entry people have been rekeying hundreds of pages of reports.

We could solve this problem with the addition of a scanning system. I estimate that we could eliminate at least 40 percent of our overtime and also reduce turnaround time on documents by two days if our operators had a scanning system to convert our old engineering reports to an electronic format. To accomplish this, we need a high-quality scanner linked to a workstation PC. The PC will also need the right software to load the scanned reports into the company database.

Two alternatives are available in relation to scanning services. We could purchase the equipment ourselves, or we could outsource the job to a service bureau to make our digital conversions. Service bureaus, however, are expensive and slow. Moreover, we face a security problem whenever our reports leave our premises. Because of the sensitive nature of most of our work, keeping the reports on-site makes the most sense.

Purchasing a high-quality scanner plus the necessary software promises three significant benefits:

1. Savings of at least $2500 in overtime each month by reducing the rekeying of printed documents.

2. Reduction of turnaround time from five days to a maximum of three days.

3. Improved morale among our data entry personnel.

For these reasons, I recommend that we purchase a Quad Turbo Scanner, Model SL2000, plus Digital's Application Extender software. The purchase price of these two items, approximately $5000, will be recovered within two months as a result of reduced overtime payments.

Attached are details of the recommended scanner and conversion software. Please give me authorization to submit a purchase order for these two items by April 1 so that Central Services may improve turnaround time before we are asked to begin work on the fiscal year-end reports in July.

Attachment

Subject line is specific and positive

Gains attention with a problem that can be solved

Begins each paragraph with a topic sentence

Builds interest by explaining background and solution to problem before making proposal

Reduces resistance by anticipating objections and countering them

Summarizes benefits in a list for easy readability

Delays mention of price until after convincing arguments are presented

Motivates action with explicit request and provides end dating

From a broader perspective, nearly every letter we write is a form of sales. We sell our ideas, our organizations, and ourselves. Learning the techniques of sales writing will help you be more effective in any communication that requires persuasion and promotion. Moreover, recognizing the techniques of selling will enable you to respond to such techniques more rationally. You will be a better-educated consumer of ideas, products, and services if you understand how sales appeals are made.

Analyzing the Product and the Reader

Before writing a sales letter, it's wise to study the product and the target audience so that you can emphasize features with reader appeal.

Know your product. To sell a product effectively, learn as much as possible about how it was created, including its design, its parts, and the process of production and distribution. Study its performance, including ease of use, efficiency, durability, and applications. Consider warranties, service, price, and special appeals. Know your own product but also that of your competitor. In this way, you can emphasize your product's strengths against the weaknesses of the competitor's products.

Know the culture. If a product is being developed and marketed for consumers in different cultures, learn as much as possible about the targeted cultures. Although companies would like to use the same products and advertising campaigns as they push into global markets, most find that using a single approach for every local market falls flat. They may think globally, but they must execute locally. In producing and selling frozen yogurt to the world, Canadian company Yogen Früz makes learning about the host country's culture a priority. For example, at the grand opening of its first franchise in Guatemala, a country with a strong religious tradition, the company ensured that a priest was on hand to bless the proceedings.[2]

Knowing the audience and adapting your message to it is important for any communication. But it's especially true for sales letters. That's why the most effective sales letters are sent to targeted audiences. Mailing lists for selected groups can be purchased or compiled. For example, the manufacturer of computer supplies would find an appropriate audience for its products in the mailing list of subscribers to a computer magazine.

Target the audience. By using a selected mailing list, a sales letter writer is able to make certain assumptions about the readers. Readers may be expected to have similar interests, abilities, needs, income, and so forth. The sales letter can be adapted to appeal directly to this selected group. In working with a less specific audience, the letter writer can make only general assumptions and must use a catch-all approach, hoping to find some appeal that motivates the reader.

The following writing plan for a sales letter attempts to overcome anticipated reader resistance by creating a desire for the product and by motivating the reader to act.

Writing Plan for a Sales Letter

- **Gain attention** in the opening by standing out from the competition.
- **Build interest** in the body by emphasizing a central selling point and appealing to the reader's needs.
- **Reduce resistance** in the body by creating a desire for the product and introducing price strategically.

Gaining the Reader's Attention by Standing Out from the Competition

Gaining the attention of the reader is essential in unsolicited or uninvited sales letters. In solicited sales letters, individuals have requested information; thus, attention-getting devices are less important. Provocative messages or unusual formats may be used to attract attention in unsolicited sales letters. These devices may be found within the body of a letter or in place of the inside address.

OFFER	*Your free calculator is just the beginning!*
PRODUCT FEATURE	*Your vacations—this year and in the future—can be more rewarding thanks to an exciting new book from* Canadian Geographic.
INSIDE-ADDRESS OPENING	*We Wonder, Mrs. Crain, If You Would Like to Know How to Retire in Style with Mutual Funds.*
STARTLING STATEMENT	*Extinction is forever. That's why we need your help in preserving many of the world's endangered species.*
STORY	*On a beautiful late spring afternoon, 25 years ago, two young men graduated from the same college. They were very much alike, these two young men.... Recently, these men returned to their college for their 25th reunion. They were still very much alike.... But there was a difference. One of the men was manager of a small department of [a manufacturing company]. The other was its president.*

Other effective openings include a bargain, a proverb, a solution to a problem, a quotation from a famous person, an anecdote, and a question.

Building Interest by Appealing to the Reader and Emphasizing Central Selling Points

Persuasive appeals generally fall into two broad groups: emotional appeals and rational appeals. Emotional appeals are those associated with the senses; they include how we feel, see, taste, smell, and hear. Strategies that arouse anger, fear, pride, love, and satisfaction are emotional.

Rational strategies are those associated with reason and intellect; they appeal to the mind. Rational appeals include references to making money, saving money, increasing efficiency, and making the best use of resources. Generally, use rational appeals when a product is expensive, long lasting, or important to health and security. Use emotional appeals when a product is inexpensive, short-lived, or nonessential.

Banks selling chequing and savings services frequently use rational appeals. They emphasize saving money in chequing fees, earning interest on accounts, receiving free personalized cheques, and saving time in opening the account. In contrast, a travel operator selling a student tour to Mexico uses an emotional strategy by describing the "sun, fun, and partying" to be enjoyed. Many successful selling campaigns combine appeals, emphasizing perhaps a rational appeal while also including an emotional appeal in a subordinated position.

Although a product may have a number of features, concentrate on just one or two of those features. Don't bewilder the reader with too much information. Analyze the reader's needs and tailor your appeal directly to the reader. The brochure selling the student tour to Mexico emphasized two points:

1. We see to it that you have a great time. Let's face it. By the end of the term, you've earned your vacation. The books and jobs and stress can all be shelved for a while.

2. We keep our trips affordable. Mazatlan 1A is again the lowest-priced adventure trip offered in Canada.

The writer analyzed the student audience and elected to concentrate on two appeals: an emotional appeal to the senses (having a good time) and a rational appeal to saving money (paying a low price).

Reducing Resistance by Creating a Desire for the Product and Introducing Price Strategically

In convincing readers to purchase a product or service, you may use a number of techniques:

- **Reader benefit.** Discuss product features from the reader's point of view. Show how the reader will benefit from the product:
  You'll be able to extend your summer swim season by using our new solar pool cover.
- **Concrete language.** Use concrete words instead of general or abstract language:
  Our Mexican tour provides more than just a party. Maybe you've never set eyes on a giant saguaro cactus ... or parasailed high above the Pacific Ocean ... or watched a majestic golden sunset from your own private island.
- **Objective language.** Avoid language that sounds unreasonable. Overstatements using words like *fantastic, without fail, foolproof, amazing, astounding,* and so forth do not ring true. Overblown language and preposterous claims may cause readers to reject the entire sales message.
- **Product confidence.** Build confidence in your product or service by assuring customer satisfaction. You can do this by offering a free trial, money-back guarantee, free sample, or warranty. Another way to build confidence is to associate your product with respected references or authorities:
  Our concept of economical group travel has been accepted and sponsored by three major airlines. In addition, our program has been featured in Maclean's, *the* Vancouver Sun, The Globe and Mail, *and the* National Post.
- **Testimonials.** The statements of satisfied customers are effective in creating a desire for the product or service:
  A student returning from one of our cruises last year said, "I've just been to paradise."

If product price is a significant sales feature, use it early in your sales letter. Otherwise, don't mention price until after you have created the reader's desire for the product. Some sales letters include no mention of price; instead, an enclosed order form shows the price. Other techniques for de-emphasizing price include the following:

- **Show the price in small units.** For instance, instead of stating the total cost of a year's subscription, state the magazine's price when calculated per issue. Or describe insurance premiums by their cost per day.
- **Show how the reader is saving money by purchasing the product.** In selling solar heating units, for example, explain how much the reader will save on heating bills.
- **Compare your prices with those of competitors.** Describe the savings to be realized when your product is purchased.
- **Make your price a bargain.** For instance, point out that the special introductory offer is one-third off the regular price. Or say that the price includes a special discount if the reader acts immediately.
- **Associate the price with reader benefits.** Note, for example, that for as little as $3 a month, you'll enjoy emergency road and towing protection, emergency trip-interruption protection, and nine other benefits.

Motivating Action by Stimulating the Reader to Buy

The closing of a sales letter has one very important goal: stimulating the reader to act.

- **Make the action clear.** Use specific language to say exactly what is to be done: *Submit your request at our website.*

Press/Media Release

News (media) releases announce information about your company: new products, new managers, new facilities, participation in community projects, awards given or received, joint ventures, donations, or seminars and demonstrations. Naturally, you hope that this news will be published and provide good publicity for your company. But this kind of largely self-serving information is not always appealing to magazine and newspaper editors or to TV producers. To get them to read beyond the first sentence, try these suggestions:

- Open with an attention-getting lead or a summary of the important facts.
- Include answers to the five Ws and one H (who, what, when, where, why, and how) in the article—but not all in the first sentence!
- Appeal to the audience of the target media. Emphasize reader benefits written in the style of the focus publication or newscast.
- Present the most important information early, followed by supporting information. Don't put your best ideas last because they may be chopped off or ignored.
- Make the release visually appealing. Limit the text to one or two double-spaced pages with attractive formatting.
- Look and sound credible—no typos, no imaginative spelling or punctuation, no factual errors.

The most important ingredient of a press release, of course, is *news*. Articles that merely plug products end up in the recycling bin.

Cover Letter

To accompany a résumé, you'll need a persuasive letter of application (also called a cover letter). The cover letter has three purposes: introducing the résumé, highlighting your strengths that will be of benefit to the reader, and gaining an interview. In many ways your cover letter is a sales letter; it sells your talents and tries to beat the competition.

Human resources professionals disagree on how long to make the cover letter. Many prefer short letters with no more than four paragraphs; instead of concentrating on the letter, these readers focus on the résumé. Others desire longer letters that supply more information, thus giving them a better opportunity to evaluate a candidate's qualifications. The latter group argues that hiring and training new employees is expensive and time-consuming; therefore, they welcome extra data to guide them in making the best choice the first time. Follow your judgment in writing a brief or a longer cover letter. If you feel, for example, that you need space to explain in more detail what you can do for a prospective employer, do so.

Gaining Attention in the Opening

The first step in gaining the interest of your reader is addressing that individual by name. Rather than sending your letter to the "Human Resources Department," try to identify the name of the appropriate individual. Make it a rule to call the orga-

Figure 5.5 ▶
Sales Letter

Doug Hervey
128 Featherstone Place
Okotoks, AB
T5G 3M3

KEEP UP TO DATE WITH EVENTS THAT IMPACT YOU AND YOUR FAMILY

Dear Doug Hervey,

POLITICS   We know you're busy these days with family and work, and we also know that just as you've become busier than ever the possibilities for entertainment have multiplied. Now you can choose from downloading music, listening to satellite radio, blogging and reading online, not to mention the traditional pastimes like going to the movies or playing sports.

CULTURE   So why are we writing to you today? In a busy world in which it's hard to know who's got the right information, it pays to take time to relax and get up to speed with current events. That's where we come in. As Canada's preeminent general interest/current events magazine, *New World* offers in-depth analysis that the newspapers and TV, radio, and online news can't come close to. And now, we're offering this experience for just **$50 a year** - more than 50% off the newsstand price. Delivered right to your door every week.

ANALYSIS   It's easier than ever to become a *New World* subscriber. Simply fill out the attached card and mail it to us (we've covered the postage for you), call our toll-free subscription hotline at 1-888-555-4616, or log onto our website at www.newworldmag.ca. This offer expires on November 30, 2007, so don't delay!

Sincerely,

Rita Carnevale

Rita Carnevale
Subscription Manager

P.S. Only *New World* subscribers get to read the popular columns by Peter Sussman and Marianne Macklin - they're not available at our website. Subscribe today!

nization for the correct spelling and the complete address. This personal touch distinguishes your letter and demonstrates your serious interest.

How you open your cover letter depends largely on whether the application is solicited or unsolicited. If an employment position has been announced and applicants are being solicited, you can use a direct approach. If you do not know whether a position is open and you are prospecting for a job, use an indirect approach. Whether direct or indirect, the opening should attract the attention of the reader. Strive for openings that are more imaginative than "Please consider this letter an application for the position of ..." or "I would like to apply for...."

Figure 5.6 ▶
Press/Media Release via
Website

Attention Entertainment Editors:

Mike Myers to Host The 2007 Genie Awards on Global TV

—**International movie star and comedian returns home for Canada's Film Awards**—

TORONTO, Feb. 1 /CNW/—International movie star and comedian Mike Myers has been selected to host The 2007 Genie Awards, Canada's Film Awards, it was announced today by broadcaster Global and the Academy of Canadian Television and Film. Global and the Academy will broadcast The 2007 Genie Awards on Sunday, March 23 from 8pm to 10pm ET on Global TV. The half-hour before the ceremony, Global will air a special edition of Entertainment Tonight Canada from the "red carpet" featuring interviews of celebrities by host Cheryl Hickey.

[Attention Media: Photos for The 2007 Genie Awards can be downloaded at www.globaltv.com.]

Named one of "The Most Powerful Canadians in Hollywood" in 2006 by the *National Post*, Myers is one of the world's most recognized stars, thanks to his multi-platform career as an actor and comedian. Myers joins an esteemed list of homegrown, international stars who have hosted The Genie Awards since Global TV began airing the awards telecast in 2005, including Kiefer Sutherland, Rachel McAdams, and Martin Short.

"Canadian movies are shagalicious," said Myers, lapsing into Austin Powers vocabulary. "It doesn't matter whether they're in French, or about Chinese immigrants in Vancouver or angst-driven teenagers in rural Nova Scotia, they speak about the place I come from. I can't wait to get this show started!"

Myers will host the two-hour awards broadcast featuring guest appearances by Canadian entertainment luminaries including Paul Gross, Shirley Douglas, Graham Greene, Hayden Christensen and Dan Aykroyd. Additional guest presenters will be announced soon.

"Mike's famous all over the place, but he's going to feel most at home in front of a hometown Toronto audience," said Ted Arnopolous, Global TV's Director of Programming. "I have no doubt that hundreds of thousands of Canadians will tune in to see what mayhem Mike can concoct onstage at the Elgin Theatre. He appeals to a wide cross-section of our audience: young, middle-aged, and older adults. They all love him!"

For further information on Global TV and The 2007 Genie Awards broadcast, please contact Tony Duree at (416) 332-4596 or tduree@globaltv.com. For information about The Academy of Canadian Television and Film, please contact Laura Taborelli at 416 555-2366 or laura.taborelli@acta.ca.[3]

Openings for solicited jobs. Here are some of the best techniques to open a cover letter for a job that has been announced:

- **Refer to the name of an employee in the company.** Remember that employers always hope to hire known quantities rather than complete strangers:

  Mitchell Sims, a member of your Customer Service Department, told me that IntriPlex is seeking an experienced customer service representative. The attached summary of my qualifications demonstrates my preparation for this position.

  At the suggestion of Ms. Jennifer Larson of your Human Resources Department, I submit my qualifications for the position of staffing coordinator.

- **Refer to the source of your information precisely.** If you are answering an advertisement, include the exact position advertised and the name and date of the publication. For large organizations it's also wise to mention the section of the newspaper where the ad appeared:

    Your advertisement in Section C-3 of the June 1 Daily News *for an accounting administrator greatly appeals to me. With my accounting training and computer experience, I believe I could serve Quad Graphics well.*

    The September 10 issue of The Globe and Mail *reports that you are seeking a mature, organized, and reliable administrative assistant with excellent communication skills.*

    Susan Butler, placement director at Durham College, told me that DataTech has an opening for a technical writer with knowledge of Web design and graphics.

- **Refer to the job title and describe how your qualifications fit the requirements.** Personnel directors are looking for a match between an applicant's credentials and the job needs:

    Will an honours graduate with a degree in recreation and two years of part-time experience organizing social activities for a convalescent hospital qualify for your position of activity director?

    Because of my specialized training in computerized accounting at the University of Regina, I feel confident that I have the qualifications you described in your advertisement for a cost accountant trainee.

Openings for unsolicited jobs. If you are unsure whether a position actually exists, you may wish to use a more persuasive opening. Since your goal is to convince this person to read on, try one of the following techniques:

- **Demonstrate interest in and knowledge of the reader's business.** Show the personnel director that you have done your research and that this organization is more than a mere name to you:

    Since Signa HealthNet, Inc., is organizing a new information management team for its recently established group insurance division, could you use the services of a well-trained information systems graduate who seeks to become a professional systems analyst?

- **Show how your special talents and background will benefit the company.** Human Resources staff need to be convinced that you can do something for them:

    Could your rapidly expanding publications division use the services of an editorial assistant who offers exceptional language skills, an honours degree from the University of Prince Edward Island, and two years' experience in producing a campus literary publication?

In applying for an advertised job, Nancy Sullivan James wrote the solicited cover letter shown in Figure 5.7. Notice that her opening identifies the position and the newspaper completely so that the reader knows exactly what advertisement Nancy means.

Building Interest in the Body

Once you have captured the attention of the reader, you can use the body of the letter to build interest and reduce resistance. Keep in mind that your résumé emphasizes what you have *done*; your application letter stresses what you *can do* for the employer.

Figure 5.7 ▶ Solicited Cover Letter

Creates own stationery

Nancy Sullivan James

8011 Davies Road NW, Edmonton, AB T6E 4Z6

May 23, 2007

Ms. Kesha M. Scott
Manager, Human Resources
Premier Enterprises
57 Bedford Drive NE
Calgary, AB T3K 1L2

Addresses proper person by name and title

Dear Ms. Scott:

Your advertisement for an assistant product manager, appearing May 22 in Section C of the *Calgary Herald,* immediately caught my attention because my education and training closely parallel your needs. According to your advertisement, the job includes "assisting in the coordination of a wide range of marketing programs as well as analyzing sales results and tracking marketing budgets."

Identifies specific ad and job title

Relates writer's experiences to job requirements

A recent internship at Ventana Corporation introduced me to similar tasks. I assisted the marketing manager in analyzing the promotion, budget, and overall sales success of two products Ventana was evaluating.

Discusses experience

Complementing this hands-on experience is my intensive course work in marketing and management. Proficiency in computer spreadsheets and databases, plus my practical experience, has given me the kind of marketing and computing training that Premier demands in a product manager.

Discusses schooling

Refers reader to résumé

I would like to discuss my qualifications with you and answer any questions you have about my enclosed résumé. The best way to reach me is to call my cell phone at (403) 343-2910 during business hours. I look forward to putting my skills to work for Premier Enterprises.

Asks for interview and repeats main qualifications

Sincerely,

Nancy Sullivan James

Nancy Sullivan James

Enclosure

Your first goal is to relate your remarks to a specific position. If you are responding to an advertisement, you'll want to explain how your preparation and experience fill the stated requirements. If you are prospecting for a job, you may not know the exact requirements. Your employment research and knowledge of your field, however, should give you a reasonably good idea of what is expected for this position. It's also important to emphasize reader benefits. In other words, you should describe your strong points in relation to the needs of the employer. In one employment survey many HR professionals expressed the same view: "I want you to tell me what you can do for my organization. This is much more important to me than telling me what courses you took in college or what 'duties' you performed on your previous jobs."[4]

Instead of "I have completed courses in business communication, report writing, and technical writing," try this: "Courses in business communication, report writing, and technical writing have helped me develop the research and writing skills required of your technical writers." Choose your strongest qualifications and show how they fit the targeted job. And remember, students with little experience are better off spotlighting their education and its practical applications, as this candidate did: "Because you seek an architect's apprentice with proven ability, I submit a drawing of mine that won second place in the Canadore College drafting contest last year."

In the body of your letter, you'll also want to discuss relevant personal traits. Employers are looking for candidates who, among other things, are team players, take responsibility, show initiative, and learn easily. Notice how the following paragraph uses action verbs to paint a picture of a promising candidate:

> *In addition to developing technical and academic skills at Grant MacEwan College, I have gained interpersonal, leadership, and organizational skills. As vice president of the business students' organization, I helped organize and supervise two successful fundraising events. These activities involved conceptualizing the tasks, motivating others to help, scheduling work sessions, and coordinating the efforts of 35 diverse students in reaching our goal. I enjoyed my success with these activities and look forward to applying such experience in your management trainee program.*

Finally, in this section or the next, you should refer the reader to your résumé. Do so directly or as part of another statement, as shown here:

> *Please refer to the attached résumé for additional information regarding my education, experience, and references.*

> *As you will notice from my résumé, I will graduate in June with an applied bachelors degree in financial services.*

Motivating Action in the Closing

After presenting your case, you should conclude with a spur to action. This is where you ask for an interview. If you live in a distant city, you may request an employment application or an opportunity to be interviewed by the organization's nearest representative. However, never ask for the job. To do so would be presumptuous and naive. In requesting an interview, suggest reader benefits or review your strongest points. Sound sincere and appreciative. Remember to make it easy for the reader to agree by supplying your telephone number and the best times to call you. And keep in mind that some personnel directors prefer that you take the initiative to call them. Here are possible endings:

> *I hope this brief description of my qualifications and the additional information in my résumé indicate to you my genuine desire to put my skills in accounting to work for you. Please call me at (604) 655-4455 before 10 a.m. or after 3 p.m. to arrange an interview.*

> *To add to your staff an industrious, well-trained administrative assistant with proven word processing and communication skills, call me at (705) 555-5555 to arrange an interview. I can meet with you at any time convenient to your schedule.*

> *Next week, after you have examined the attached résumé, I will call you to discuss the possibility of arranging an interview.*

Final Tips

As you revise your letter of application, notice how many sentences begin with *I*. Although it's impossible to talk about yourself without using *I*, you can reduce "I" domination with this writing technique. Make activities and outcomes, and not yourself, the subjects of sentences. For example, rather than "I took classes in business communication and computer applications," say "Classes in business communication and computer applications prepared me to...." Instead of "I enjoyed helping customers," say "Helping customers was a real pleasure."

CONCLUSION

The ability to persuade is a powerful and versatile communication tool. In this chapter you learned to apply the indirect strategy in writing favour/action requests, claim and complaint letters, persuasive internal suggestions, sales letters, press/media releases, and cover letters. The techniques suggested here will be useful in many other contexts beyond the writing of these business documents. You will find that logical organization of arguments is also extremely effective in expressing ideas orally or any time you must overcome resistance to change.

Not all business messages are strictly persuasive. Occasionally, you must deny requests and deliver bad news. In the next chapter you will learn to use the indirect strategy in conveying negative news.

Chapter Review

As a way of studying the material in this chapter, imagine you are at a job interview for your dream entry-level job after college or university. You've prepared answers for all the classic interview questions, but to your surprise, your interviewer also asks a number of questions based on persuasive business writing. How would you answer the following six questions?

1. Tell us about a time when you tried to persuade someone or a group of people and it backfired on you because you hadn't thought about your audience sufficiently. What would you do differently if you could persuade them again?
2. At our company it's a rule of thumb that sales reps "lay a good foundation" before they try to close a sale. What do you think is involved in laying a good foundation when trying to persuade someone?
3. If you are successful in this interview and are hired, you will participate in a two-week training period on sales and persuasive techniques. While we like to teach our "formula," we also want our employees to be ready for any situation. What kinds of planning strategies do you think could make you successful in any persuasive situation?
4. Can you give us some examples of when persuasion in a sales situation might go too far and stray into unethical practice?
5. Our sales reps do a mix of in-person and written sales calls. Specifically on the topic of written persuasive messages, what do you think are the main ingredients of a successful message? Would you rank these ingredients in importance or are they equally important?
6. Sometimes our sales reps work closely with our marketing staff in producing marketing material, including media releases and brochures. How much do you know about media releases?

Problems

1. Each year the Canadian Home Builders' Association organizes a meeting of its membership from across Canada. At this meeting, a number of high-profile speakers are invited to address the membership of the CHBA on top-

ics of importance to the industry. Last year, the CHBA invited the minister of housing to speak on government plans in the housing area for the next five years. The association is searching for another series of high-profile guest speakers for the 2007 conference to be held in Victoria. As the communications and events coordinator for the CHBA, it's your responsibility to coordinate speakers for the annual meeting as well as all logistical and travel arrangements. Your boss, Sid Charles, the president of the CHBA, has suggested that a high-profile architect from the Lower Mainland would be a good guest speaker. This person would be able to address issues such as the condo-building boom currently taking place in Vancouver and the Lower Mainland. After doing some preliminary research, you decide that the well-known Vancouver architect Bing Thom would make a great guest speaker. He's working at the cutting edge of architecture, he's designed numerous high-profile projects in British Columbia, and his firm is working on a number of interesting international projects as well. As you sit down to write a letter inviting Mr. Thom to speak to the CHBA, you're confident your request will meet with his approval: after all, the CHBA is a prestigious national organization, many of whose members have been or may be clients of Mr. Thom's. Why wouldn't he want to speak to such an audience? Furthermore, there's really no downside to your request, especially because not only will Mr. Thom be able to network with possible clients, but he'll also be paid a $5000 honorarium (the CHBA's maximum budget for a speaker) for his time—which will be no more than two hours. What might a request letter to Mr. Thom look like if it's written using the above audience analysis? What's unresolved about the audience analysis in the scenario? What might a request letter look like if it's based on a better analysis of its audience? <www.chba.ca> <www.bingthomarchitects.com>

2. The book publishing industry is roughly divided in two: there are the large publishers like Penguin and Random House mostly headquartered in Toronto and the smaller independent publishers that are found across the country. One of these independent publishers is Goose Lane Editions of Fredericton, New Brunswick. Goose Lane has been in business for over 25 years, and part of why it's managed to be successful in the face of stiff competition from large publishers is that it has become the leader in a particular publishing niche: audiobooks. Goose Lane, through its BTC Audiobooks subsidiary, is the leading publisher of audiobooks based on Canadian fiction. The production of an audiobook is a multi-step process: a book has to be scripted into an audiobook, the script must be rehearsed, an actor must be hired to read the script, the script must be recorded, the resulting compact disk must be packaged, and only then is it shipped to booksellers across the country. A lot of things can go wrong in such a complicated process, and unfortunately, something just has. The shipment of BTC's latest hit title, an audiobook version of best-selling author Margaret Atwood's novel *The Blind Assassin*, has arrived in Fredericton damaged. Of the 2500 audiobook cases, roughly 75 percent are dented so badly that the booksellers will not accept them. As the production manager at Goose Lane/BTC, it's your job to figure out who is responsible for the damage and to fix the problem. You quickly rule out FedEx, the shipping company, because none of the cardboard boxes in which the audiobooks were shipped are damaged—it's just the audiobooks inside that are dented. It's obvious that the problem lies with Friesens, the Altona, Manitoba-based printer and specialty packager Goose Lane/BTC has been using for over a decade. You've got a bit of a dilemma on your hands: the Atwood audiobook is going to be your bestseller this year—you're counting

on it for cash flow over the next six to twelve months. At the same time, Friesens has been your printer for over a decade and you have an excellent working relationship with the company. Still, a complaint has to be lodged, and quickly. As the production manager, what will you do to ensure that a complaint is lodged quickly that gets results?

<www.gooselane.com/btc/index.htm> <www.friesens.com>

3. As one of a number of group marketing representatives for Co-operators General Insurance Company, headquartered in Guelph, Ontario, your job is to increase the business of Co-operators in specific niche markets. Your specific role is to work on academic sales—in other words, sales of various kinds of insurance to universities and colleges, both for their employees and for the alumni. You've been doing the job for three years and enjoy it a lot. Lately, however, one sore point has arisen. Co-operators recently purchased Black-Berry PDAs for each of its 45 group marketing reps across Canada. While the "gift" was couched in positive language—it would aid communication, it would be easier to be in touch, etc.—the reality is that you feel as if you're working 24 hours a day seven days a week. The BlackBerry has become addictive, and once you start answering and sending e-mails after business hours, it's hard to stop. Sitting in your dentist's office one evening, you come across the January 30, 2006, issue of *Maclean's* magazine. In this issue you read the story by Katherine Macklem that is reprinted at the beginning of Chapter 4 of this textbook. The story explains how a large Canadian pharmaceutical company, Pfizer Canada, has recently adopted a policy that discourages employees from using communications technologies between 6 p.m. and 6 a.m. You think you've found a solution to your problem! All you have to do is write a suggestion e-mail to your boss, the vice president of Group Sales and Business Development, and she'll surely institute a similar policy at Co-operators. As you start planning the e-mail in your head, one problem keeps coming up: Cathy, the VP, loves her BlackBerry. She thinks it's the best thing since sliced bread for Co-operators. How are you going to convince someone who doesn't want to be convinced?

<www.cooperators.ca>

4. Glen Arbour is "Halifax's premium public golf course." Located north of the city, the golf course was also Nova Scotia's first residential golf community, a popular development trend that is spreading to many communities across Canada. The idea is to build homes and condominiums next to a golf course so that homeowners can have amenities like quiet, country-style living, right next to golf facilities that include the course, a club, and a restaurant. The homes at Glen Arbour are built by Nova Scotia's leading residential developer, Greater Homes. In its first phase, the condominiums at Glen Arbour sold out in record time. Now, Greater Homes is launching a second phase of higher-priced freehold homes and condominiums. While it always takes out advertisements in local newspapers like the *Daily News*, Greater Homes is hoping to market its new development more selectively. So it's entered into a partnership with the golf course by which each time someone comes to play golf, he or she is asked, when making the reservation, whether it would be okay to add that person's name to the golf club's mailing list. Over a period of two years, the golf course has collected over 1200 names and addresses. Greater Homes has purchased the list from the golf course and is in the process of putting together a sales package to mail out to prospective home buyers. The centrepiece of this package is a sales letter that will try to persuade golf course customers to purchase a home in the second phase of home

development at Glen Arbour. A trial batch of 50 sales packages went out in the mail last week, and already three complaints have been lodged via e-mail and telephone. One woman summed up the complaints when she said, "When I told the golf course it was okay to put me on its mailing list, I had no idea I would be receiving information from other companies. I want to play golf, not buy a condo. Leave me alone!" Obviously, the sales letter has to be re-tooled. What's the problem here and how can it be fixed?
<www.greaterhomes.ca> <www.glenarbour.com>

5. The fine-dining scene in Vancouver is ever-changing. Because of the large number of tourists who visit the city annually, as well as the passion of many Vancouver residents for eating out regularly, the city's restaurants have blossomed over the past ten years. It's now possible to enjoy various Asian cuisines, as well as French, Italian, and Mexican, among other international cuisines, in a number of highly praised restaurants. *Vancouver Magazine*, which follows the city's evolving restaurant scene, recently went so far as to claim that Vancouver was the best place "west of Chicago" for fine dining. Charles Abbes is no stranger to the Vancouver restaurant scene. His well-known restaurant Deborah's represented a milestone in the evolution of the restaurant scene in Vancouver. Operating between 1985 and 1989 in the basement of a heritage West End house, the restaurant earned the praises of all the restaurant critics in the city, as well as a number of kudos from critics in such esteemed publications as the *Los Angeles Times* and the *New York Times* (in a feature on Expo 86). Sadly, Deborah's had a controversial end. At the height of his fame, chef and owner Abbes was discredited when it surfaced that he had not paid any taxes during the five years of Deborah's successful operations. He paid a hefty fine to Revenue Canada and more or less disappeared from Vancouver, opening up a small restaurant in his native Tunisia. More than 15 years later, Abbes has returned to Vancouver and is about to launch a new fine-dining establishment that he's calling Tunis, after the city of his birth. Abbes thinks the time is right to launch Vancouver's first Middle Eastern-inspired fine-dining restaurant. He's managed to convince popular chef Billy Ramsay at competing restaurant Eau to work for him. He's secured a five-year lease in a fashionable Yaletown location. And he's added a number of extra touches: an exclusive cigar lounge (sure to be popular with visiting Americans) and a Saturday-morning exclusive cooking school. Now all Abbes has to do is get the people of Vancouver back on his side. To do this, he hires a publicist to draft a media release and to field interview requests. As the publicist, you're happy to take on this high-profile client, but you also foresee a couple of problems. What might these problems be and how might you get around them in a media release?
<www.vanmag.com>

∷ *Grammar/Style Review 5*

In this review, you will be practising identifying article mistakes. There are five mistakes in total. For a brief explanation of this grammar problem, please read the explanation on page 327. Besides completing the exercise below, be sure to be on the lookout for article mistakes in your own writing.

To: prochefort@aventis.ca

From: sli@aventis.ca

Re: Sales conference in June

Hi Pierre,

A couple of people I know at Biovail and Novopharm have used Pillar & Post Inn in Niagara-on-the-Lake and they say it's the good hotel. Personally, I think the things got out of hand at last year's conference, and anything that will save us money makes sense. If you like, I'd be happy to find out cost for using the Pillar. I think we want to show the reps good time but at the same time not go overboard. Let me know.

Best,

Steve

Business Communication Lab 5

As a recent graduate of a college business program, you come across the issue of *Profit* magazine in which Ian Portsmouth's article is published. You find the article a little bit ironic, because you've applied for at least five sales jobs and not been hired for one. Your guess is that your lack of experience is against you. It's hard to get experience, though, when no one will give you a chance. You re-read Portsmouth's article and an idea hits you. Harvey Copeman of the CPSA is quoted in the article as saying that he hasn't heard about any research into the issue of a skilled salesperson shortage. Could this be an opportunity for you? One of your elective courses at college was a course in Business Research and Report Writing. Maybe you could convince Mr. Copeman to hire you as a consultant to do some research for the CPSA ... Using your skills as a persuasive business message writer, write Mr. Copeman an e-mail or a letter in which you pitch him your idea. <www.cpsa.com>

CHAPTER 6

Negative Business Messages

"It became a really hard decision"

BY LISA SCHMIDT, *CALGARY HERALD*, JULY 31, 2005, E2

WHEN ALKARIM SUNDERJI arrives in Calgary later this month, it will be a homecoming with mixed feelings.

There will be family and old friends to see, favourite restaurants to visit and Flames hockey starting in the fall.

But he and his wife, Merge Gupta-Sunderji, will also be leaving a happy life behind in Toronto, where they've been for the past three years.

One of the hundreds of Imperial Oil employees relocating to Calgary as the firm shifts its headquarters to the west, the couple admits the decision to return was much harder than it would seem.

"Part of us is being uprooted, part of us is happy to be back," says Merge.

It was an average work day for Alkarim Sunderji, who was checking his e-mail after a meeting when the message arrived from public affairs saying that the company was relocating.

Every year there had been a rumour Imperial was pulling up stakes to head west, or the western office was being moved back. Was it a joke, he and colleagues wondered?

The reality started to sink in when he left work, passing through television camera crews and photographers gathered outside the office.

By 8 p.m. the calls started coming in from excited family and friends back in Calgary.

But two hours later as he dialed the cellphone number of his wife, who was travelling on business in New York, he was apprehensive.

Did she want to hear the good news or bad news first, he ventured. The bad, she said.

He decided to give her the good instead.

"You know that vacation home we want to buy in the Caribbean? It just got easier," he told her.

Merge didn't find anything funny about the bombshell. Self-employed as a professional speaker and management-training consultant, she had slowly built a roster of clients over the past three years.

"My first thought was I did all that for nothing," she says, admitting she was very angry and declared she wasn't leaving Toronto.

"I've come a long way since then."

The move takes the couple back to where they started, when both worked in the oilpatch after graduating from university where they met.

"Calgary is my home, the Flames are my team," says Sunderji, 42, who was born in Tanzania and immigrated to Canada in 1975 with his parents, who still live in the city.

Merge, 39, was born in India and travelled because of her father's job with the United Nations. Her family has been in Calgary since 1981 and she worked as a manager for Shell Canada until 2002.

By October, Sunderji knew that his job would be transferred, but it wouldn't be until January that he had to make the decision.

When the couple went on a holiday, he brought along a list of pros and cons of the move.

"I'm an accountant so I do stuff like that," said Alkarim.

Sunderji loved his job, but there was Merge's business to consider. Would clients, who cover travel expenses, pay for the extra time and distance? Could she take more time on the road?

"If it wasn't for me, it would have been slam dunk, but I'm the reason why it became a really hard decision," says Merge.

The other problem: Calgary was home, but they had fallen in love with Toronto with its multi-cultural neighbourhoods and nightlife.

It was only three years ago the couple moved to the city after Sunderji was promoted to his current position in the controller's office, where he accounts for movement of oil and gas.

Taking the advice of a colleague, they started house-hunting for a place that was "double the price, half the size" of their Calgary home. Stay in the city, he suggested, spend more money and avoid the frustrating commute.

"He told us to suck it up and get the mortgage," said Merge. "It was the best advice I ever had."

Near Yonge and Eglinton, they found a charming two and a half storey brick home now on the market for $724,000, a block from a subway line. Within three blocks, the avid diners counted 75 restaurants and Merge declared she would never cook again.

For their return to Calgary, they wanted a similar lifestyle and narrowed their choices to a few inner city neighbourhoods, quickly settling on a condominium in Kensington where Sunderji can still walk to work or use transit.

It was a complete change from the home they once owned in Calgary.

"We've gone the other way. We used to live in suburbia, the estate-size lot and house," Merge says of their sprawling 2,700 square foot home in Foothills Estates.

"I think we did that because that was what everybody did."

In early July, they flew out to close the deal, arranging for a few renovations before the moving trucks arrive in the middle of August.

In breaking the news to clients, Merge says she was pleasantly surprised. Most of the larger firms weren't concerned, and she plans to expand her business on the west coast.

Sunderji's last day is in mid-August, helping pack up his office before flying out to Calgary with Merge and the couple's two cats on the 18th.

But they leave behind one tie to Toronto: a condo just a couple of blocks on the other side of Yonge, which they will rent out for now but eventually may use as a base for Merge's business.

"It's the right decision. I'm a huge believer in that things happen for a reason," says Merge.

"There's something waiting there in Calgary, I just don't know what it is yet."

DIAGNOSING THE PROBLEM

It may not seem like a bad-news story on the surface—Merge Gupta-Sunderji and her husband, Alkarim, seem to have it all: a new condominium in Calgary, a well-paying job in the booming oil patch of Alberta, an income-producing piece of real estate in Toronto, and a possible Caribbean vacation home—but if we read carefully between the lines of the above article, we can see that there were three instances in which this couple experienced negative business-related news. First, Alkarim received an e-mail from Imperial Oil's public affairs department announcing a historic move. The largest oil company in Canada had decided to uproot its entire headquarters—500 employees and their families—by moving its head office to Calgary. So the first problem we encounter in this story is how to spin possible bad news into good news so that you get your employees onside.

Next, Alkarim had some personal bad news to convey. He had to decide how to break the news to his wife that Imperial Oil was moving to Calgary. What's more, he needed to persuade her that he wanted to be part of the move, even though she had a thriving business of her own in Toronto. This is a second problem. How do we deliver bad news on a personal level to people in our lives?

Finally, there's one more piece of business-related bad news in this story. Merge had a solid client base she had spent three years nurturing. Now she was going to have to let her clients know that she was moving almost 3000 kilometres away. How would they react? Would they still use her consulting services? Obviously, Merge had a bit of a problem on her hands as she sat down to craft the bad-news message to her clients. In groups, put yourself in Merge and Alkarim's shoes in the next in-class activity ...

in class
activity 6

WORKING IN SMALL groups of three to four, students will discuss a number of solutions to each of the three problems discussed above and rank the solutions by their effectiveness. Why did your group choose these solutions? What might the consequences of these solutions be? Once you've considered these questions, choose one of the solutions the group has proposed and create that letter/e-mail/memo. Report back to the class within 20 minutes.

Now that you've presented your solution to the rest of the class, you're ready to discover some best practices in negative business message writing that will help you if you ever find yourself in the shoes of the couple in the article above, or in any other number of negative business situations. At the end of this chapter, you will be presented with more problems that you may be asked to analyze, evaluate, and explain.

WHY WE WRITE NEGATIVE BUSINESS MESSAGES

In all businesses, things occasionally go wrong and unpleasant but necessary things happen. Prices go up, profits go down, goods are not delivered, a product fails to perform as expected, service is poor, clients are incorrectly invoiced, or customers are misunderstood. All businesses offering products or services must sometimes deal with situations that cause unhappiness to customers and to employees. Whenever possible, these problems should be dealt with immediately and personally. One study found that a majority of business professionals resolve problems in the following manner. First, they call the individual involved, and they describe the problem and apologize. Next, they explain why the problem occurred, what they are doing to resolve it, and how they will prevent it from happening again. Finally, they follow up with an e-mail or letter that documents the phone call and promotes goodwill.[1]

There are a number of reasons why we have to communicate negative news at work, but the most important are these:

- **Acceptance.** Make sure the reader understands and *accepts* the bad news. The indirect pattern helps in achieving this objective.
- **Positive image.** Promote and maintain a good image of yourself and your organization. Realizing this goal assumes that you will act ethically.
- **Message clarity.** Make the message so clear that additional correspondence is unnecessary.
- **Protection.** Avoid creating legal liability or responsibility for you or your organization.

These are ambitious goals, and we're not always successful in achieving them all. The strategies you're about to learn, however, give business communicators tested methods for conveying disappointing news sensitively and safely. With experience, you'll be able to vary these patterns and adapt them to your organization's specific writing tasks.

Dealing with problems immediately is very important in resolving conflict and retaining goodwill. In today's climate of service-based business, unhappy clients and customers will shop elsewhere, so it's important to keep them happy. Letters are generally too slow for problems that demand immediate attention, so these days e-mail or phone calls are the preferred way of conveying bad news. Written negative messages via letter are still important when other forms of contact are impossible, to establish a record of the incident, to formally confirm follow-up procedures, and to promote good relations.

A bad-news follow-up e-mail is shown in Figure 6.1. Consultant Robert Buch found himself in the embarrassing position of explaining why he had given out the name of his client to a salesperson. The client, Data.com, Inc., had hired his firm, Buch Consulting Services, to help find an appropriate service for outsourcing its payroll functions. Without realizing it, Buch had mentioned to a potential vendor (Payroll Services, Inc.) that his client was considering hiring an outside service to handle its payroll. An overeager salesperson from Payroll Services immediately called on Data.com, thus angering the client. The client had hired the consultant to avoid this very kind of intrusion. Data.com did not want to be hounded by vendors selling their payroll services.

When he learned of the problem, the first thing Buch did was call his client to explain and apologize. But he also followed up with the e-mail in Figure 6.1. The e-mail not only confirms the telephone conversation but also adds an extra touch of formality. It sends the nonverbal message that the matter is being taken seriously and that it is important enough to warrant an e-mail, which can be printed and stored as evidence of the settling of the problem.

HOW TO WRITE NEGATIVE BUSINESS MESSAGES

Breaking bad news is a fact of life for nearly every business communicator. In all businesses, things occasionally go wrong. Because bad news disappoints, irritates, and sometimes angers the receiver, such messages must be written carefully. The bad feelings associated with disappointing news can generally be reduced if the reader knows the reasons for the rejection and the bad news is revealed with sensitivity. You've probably heard people say, "It wasn't so much the bad news that I resented. It was the way I was told!"

As we said in the previous chapter when discussing persuasive messages, in the real world, it's not always clear what "plan" to follow when confronted with a bad-news situation that requires communication. For example, sometimes bad news is routine. A telecommunications company regularly informs its customers that telephone service rates are increasing. While this is bad news, it's not terribly unexpected bad news, and so it should be written differently than truly bad news such as when an employee is terminated suddenly. For this reason, it's important to once again analyze your audience before writing any negative business communication: is it going to be so disappointed or angry upon receiving the bad news that it will take further action, or is it going to shrug its shoulders in a gesture that says "What else is new?" or "It's that time of year again"?

Generally, when conveying bad news in writing, you have two choices: you can do so in an indirect way or a direct way. Many business writers prefer to use

Figure 6.1 ▶ Bad-News Follow-Up Message

(Labels at left margin of email figure:)

Opens with agreement and apology

Explains what caused problem and how it was resolved

Promises to prevent recurrence

Closes with forward look

File Edit View Insert Format Tools Actions Help

Reply Reply to All Forward

From: rbuch@buchconsulting.com   Sent: October 23, 2007

To: nvanier@buchconsulting.com
Cc:
Subject: Payroll

Dear Noelle:

You have every right to expect complete confidentiality in your transactions with an independent consultant. As I explained in yesterday's telephone call, I am very distressed that you were called by a salesperson from Payroll Services, Inc. This should not have happened, and I apologize to you again for inadvertently mentioning your company's name in a conversation with a potential vendor, Payroll Services, Inc.

All clients of Buch Consulting are assured that their dealings with our firm are held in the strictest confidence. Because your company's payroll needs are so individual and because you have so many contract workers, I was forced to explain how your employees differed from those of other companies. The name of your company, however, should never have been mentioned. I can assure you that it will not happen again. I have informed Payroll Services that it had no authorization to call you directly and its actions have forced me to reconsider using its services for my future clients.

A number of other payroll services offer excellent programs. I'm sure we can find the perfect partner to enable you to outsource your payroll responsibilities, thus allowing your company to focus its financial and human resources on its core business. I look forward to our next appointment when you may choose from a number of excellent payroll outsourcing firms.

Sincerely,

Robert Buch
Senior Consultant

Tips for Resolving Problems and Following Up

- **Whenever possible, call or see the individual involved. Don't e-mail instead.**
- **Describe the problem and apologize.**
- **Explain why the problem occurred.**
- **Explain what you are doing to resolve it.**
- **Explain how it will not happen again.**
- **Follow up with a letter that documents the personal message.**
- **Look forward to positive future relations.**

the indirect pattern in delivering negative messages. The indirect strategy buries the bad news instead of putting it front and centre. It is especially appealing to relationship-oriented writers. They care about how a message will affect its receiver. Some of the common examples of situations in which you might choose to write an indirect negative message include refusing routine requests, declining invitations, and delivering negative news to employees and customers.

The direct strategy, on the other hand, which you learned to apply in earlier chapters, frontloads the main idea, even when it's bad news. This direct strategy appeals to efficiency-oriented writers who don't want to waste time with efforts to soften the effects of bad news.[2] So the marketing department at the telecommunications company knows that it's once-yearly or bi-yearly messages about price increases are fairly routine and bound not to anger customers; therefore, it chooses the direct strategy for its negative message.

Avoiding Legal Problems When Writing Negative Messages

Whichever strategy you use—and both will be spelled out below—it's important first to consider the language you will use in such a sensitive message. You must always avoid exposing yourself and your employer to legal liability in writing negative messages. Although we can't always anticipate the consequences of our words, we should be alert to three causes of legal difficulties: abusive language, careless language, and the "good-guy syndrome."

Abusive language. Calling people names (such as *deadbeat, crook,* or *quack*) can get you into trouble. *Defamation* is the legal term for any false statement that harms an individual's reputation. When the abusive language is written, it's called *libel*; when spoken, it's *slander.*

To be actionable (likely to result in a lawsuit), abusive language must be false, damaging to one's good name, and "published"—that is, spoken within the presence of others or written. Thus, if you were alone with Jane Doe and accused her of accepting bribes and selling company secrets to competitors, she couldn't sue because the defamation wasn't published. Her reputation was not damaged. But if anyone heard the words or if they were written, you might be legally liable.

Today you may be prosecuted if you send a harassing or libellous message by e-mail or on a computer bulletin board. Such electronic transmission is considered to be "published." Moreover, a company may incur liability for messages sent through its computer system by employees. That's why many companies are increasing their monitoring of both outgoing and internal messages. "Off-the-cuff, casual e-mail conversations among employees are exactly the type of messages that tend to trigger lawsuits and arm litigators with damaging evidence," says e-mail guru Nancy Flynn.[3] Instant messaging adds another danger for companies. Its use continues to increase, and it's largely an unmonitored channel.[4]

Careless language. As the marketplace becomes increasingly litigious, we must be certain that our words communicate only what we intend. First, be careful in making statements that are potentially damaging or that could be misinterpreted. Be wary of explanations that convey more information than you intend. Second, be careful about what documents you save. Lawyers may demand, in pursuing a lawsuit, all company files pertaining to a case. Even documents marked "Confidential" or "Personal" may be used.

Remember, too, that e-mail messages are especially risky. You may think that a mere tap of the *Delete* key makes a file disappear; however, messages continue to exist on backup storage devices in the files of the sender and the recipient.

The good-guy syndrome. Most of us hate to have to reveal bad news—that is, to be the bad guy. To make ourselves look better, to make the receiver feel better, and to maintain good relations, we are tempted to make statements that are legally dangerous.

Business communicators act as agents of their organizations. Their words, decisions, and opinions are assumed to represent those of the organization. If you want to communicate your personal feelings or opinions, use your home computer or write on plain paper (rather than company letterhead) and sign your name without title or affiliation. Volunteering extra information can lead to trouble. Thus, avoid supplying data that could be misused, and avoid making promises that can't be fulfilled. Don't admit or imply responsibility for conditions that caused damage or injury. Even apologies ("We're sorry that a faulty bottle cap caused damage to your carpet") may suggest liability.

In this chapter we'll make specific suggestions for avoiding legal liability in writing responses to claim letters, credit letters, and personnel documents. You may find that in the most critical areas (such as collection letters or hiring/firing messages) your organization provides language guidelines and form letters approved by legal counsel. As the business environment becomes more perilous, we must not only be sensitive to receivers but also keenly aware of risks to ourselves and to the organizations we represent.

Writing Plan for Indirect Negative Messages

When sending a bad-news message that will upset or irritate the receiver, many business communicators use the indirect pattern. Revealing bad news indirectly shows sensitivity to your reader. Whereas good news can be announced quickly, bad news generally should be revealed gradually. By preparing the reader, you soften the impact. A blunt announcement of disappointing news might cause the receiver to stop reading and toss the message aside.

The indirect pattern enables you to keep the reader's attention until you have been able to explain the reasons for the bad news. The most important part of a bad-news letter is the explanation, which you'll learn about shortly. The indirect plan consists of four main parts:

- Buffer opening
- Reasons given first in the body
- Bad news following in the body
- Pleasant closing

Buffering the Opening

A buffer is a device that reduces shock or pain. To buffer the pain of bad news, begin your letter with a neutral but meaningful statement that makes the reader continue reading. The buffer should be relevant and concise. Although it should avoid revealing the bad news immediately, it should not convey a false impression that good news follows. It should provide a natural transition to the explanation that follows. The individual situation, of course, will help determine what you should put in the buffer. Here are some possibilities for opening bad-news messages:

- **Best news.** Start with the part of the message that represents the best news. For example, in a memo that announces a new service along with a cutback in mailroom hours, you might write, "To ensure that your correspondence goes out with the last pickup, we're starting a new messenger pickup service at 2:30 p.m. daily beginning June 1."

- **Compliment.** Praise the receiver's accomplishments, organization, or efforts, but do so with honesty and sincerity. For instance, in a letter declining an invitation to speak, you could write, "I admire the United Way for its fundraising projects in our community. I am honoured that you asked me to speak Friday, November 5."

- **Appreciation.** Convey thanks to the reader for doing business, for sending something, for showing confidence in your organization, for expressing feelings, or simply for providing feedback. In a letter responding to a complaint about poor service, you might say, "Thank you for telling us about your experience at our hotel and for giving us a chance to look into the situation." Avoid thanking the reader, however, for something you are about to refuse.

- **Agreement.** Make a relevant statement with which both reader and receiver can agree. A letter that rejects a loan application might read "We both realize how much your business has been affected by the U.S. ban on Canadian beef in the past few years."

- **Facts.** Provide objective information that introduces the bad news. For example, in a memo announcing cutbacks in the hours of the employees' cafeteria, you might say, "During the past five years the number of employees eating breakfast in our cafeteria has dropped from 32 percent to 12 percent."

- **Understanding.** Show that you care about the reader. In announcing a product defect, the writer can still manage to express concern for the customer: "We know you expect superior performance from all the products you purchase from OfficeCity. That's why we're writing personally about the Excell printer cartridges you recently ordered."

- **Apology.** A study of letters responding to customer complaints revealed that 67 percent carried an apology of some sort.[5] If you do apologize, do it early, briefly, and sincerely. For example, a manufacturer of ice cream might respond to a customer's complaint with "We're genuinely sorry that you were disappointed with the price of the ice cream you recently purchased from one of our vendors. Your opinion is important to us, and we appreciate your giving us the opportunity to look into the problem you describe."

Presenting the Reasons

The most important part of a bad-news message is the section that explains why a negative decision is necessary. Without sound reasons for denying a request or refusing a claim, a letter will fail, no matter how cleverly it is organized or written. As part of your planning before writing, you analyzed the problem and decided to refuse a request for specific reasons. Before disclosing the bad news, try to explain those reasons. Providing an explanation reduces feelings of ill will and improves the chances that the reader will accept the bad news.

- **Being cautious in explaining.** If the reasons are not confidential or legally questionable, you can be specific: "Growers supplied us with a limited number of patio roses, and our demand this year was twice that of last year." In refusing a speaking engagement, tell why the date is impossible: "On January 17 we have a board of directors meeting that I must attend."

- **Citing reader benefits.** Readers are more open to bad news if in some way, even indirectly, it may help them. Readers also accept bad news better if they recognize that someone or something else benefits, such as other workers or the environment: "Although we would like to consider your application, we prefer to fill managerial positions from within." Avoid trying to show reader benefits, though, if they appear insincere: "To improve our service to you, we're increasing our brokerage fees."

- **Explaining company policy.** Readers resent blanket policy statements prohibiting something: "Company policy prevents us from making cash refunds" or "Proposals may be accepted from local companies only" or "Company policy requires us to promote from within." Instead of hiding behind company policy, gently explain why the policy makes sense: "We prefer to promote from within because it rewards the loyalty of our employees. In addition, we've found that people familiar with our organization make the quickest contribution to our team effort." By offering explanations, you demonstrate that you care about your readers and are treating them as important individuals.
- **Choosing positive words.** Because the words you use can affect a reader's response, choose carefully. Remember that the objective of the indirect pattern is to hold the reader's attention until you've had a chance to explain the reasons justifying the bad news. To keep the reader in a receptive mood, avoid expressions that might cause the reader to tune out. Be sensitive to negative words such as *claim, error, failure, fault, impossible, mistaken, misunderstand, never, regret, unwilling, unfortunately,* and *violate.*
- **Showing that the matter was treated seriously and fairly.** In explaining reasons, demonstrate to the reader that you take the matter seriously, have investigated carefully, and are making an unbiased decision. Customers are more accepting of disappointing news when they feel that their requests have been heard and that they have been treated fairly. Avoid deflecting responsibility, known as passing the buck, or blaming others within your organization. Such unprofessional behaviour makes the reader lose faith in you and your company.

Cushioning the Bad News

Although you can't prevent the disappointment that bad news brings, you can reduce the pain somewhat by breaking the news sensitively. Be especially considerate when the reader will suffer personally from the bad news. A number of thoughtful techniques can lessen the impact.

- **Positioning the bad news.** Instead of spotlighting it, enclose the bad news between other sentences, perhaps among your reasons. Try not to let the refusal begin or end a paragraph—the reader's eye will linger on these high-visibility spots. Another technique that reduces shock is putting a painful idea in a subordinate clause: "Although another candidate was hired, we appreciate your interest in our organization and wish you every success in your job search." Subordinate clauses often begin with words such as *although, as, because, if,* and *since.*
- **Using the passive voice.** Passive-voice verbs enable you to describe an action without connecting the action to a specific person. Whereas the active voice focuses attention on a person ("We don't give cash refunds"), the passive voice highlights the action ("Cash refunds are not given because ..."). Use the passive voice for the bad news. In some instances you can combine passive-voice verbs and a subordinate clause: "Although ice cream vendors cannot be required to lower their prices, we are happy to pass along your comments for their consideration."
- **Accentuating the positive.** As you learned earlier, messages are far more effective when you describe what you can do instead of what you can't do. Rather than "We will no longer accept requests for product changes after June 1," try a more positive appeal: "We are accepting requests for product changes until June 1."

- **Implying the refusal.** It's sometimes possible to avoid a direct statement of refusal. Often, your reasons and explanations leave no doubt that a request has been denied. Explicit refusals may be unnecessary and at times cruel. In this refusal to contribute to a charity, for example, the writer never actually says no: "Because we will soon be moving into new offices, all our funds are earmarked for moving and furnishings. We hope that next year we'll be able to support your worthwhile charity." This implied refusal is effective even though the bad news is not stated. The danger of an implied refusal, of course, is that it can be so subtle that the reader misses it. Be certain that you make the bad news clear, thus preventing the need for further correspondence.
- **Suggesting a compromise or an alternative.** A refusal is not so harsh—for the sender or the receiver—if a suitable compromise, substitute, or alternative is available. In denying permission to a class to visit a research facility, for instance, this writer softens the bad news by proposing an alternative: "Although class tours of the entire research facility are not given due to safety and security reasons, we do offer tours of parts of the facility during our open house in the fall."

You can further reduce the impact of the bad news by refusing to dwell on it. Present it briefly (or imply it), and move on to your closing.

Closing Pleasantly

After explaining the bad news sensitively, close the message with a pleasant statement that promotes goodwill. The closing should be personalized and may include a forward look, an alternative, good wishes, special offers, resale information, or an off-the-subject remark.

- **Forward look.** Anticipate future relations or business. A letter that refuses a contract proposal might read: "Thank you for your bid. We look forward to working with your talented staff when future projects demand your special expertise."
- **Alternative.** If an alternative exists, end your letter with follow-through advice. For example, in a letter rejecting a customer's demand for replacement of landscaping plants, you might say, "We will be happy to give you a free inspection and consultation. Please call 746-8112 to arrange a date for a visit."
- **Good wishes.** A letter rejecting a job candidate might read: "We appreciate your interest in our company. Good luck in your search to find the perfect match between your skills and job requirements."
- **Special offers.** When customers complain—primarily about food products or small consumer items—companies often send coupons, samples, or gifts to restore confidence and to promote future business. In response to a customer's complaint about a frozen dinner, you could write, "Thank you for your loyalty and for sharing in our efforts to make Green Valley frozen entrees the best they can be. We appreciate your input so much that we'd like to buy you dinner. We've enclosed a coupon to cover the cost of your next entree."
- **Resale or sales promotion.** When the bad news is not devastating or personal, references to resale information or promotion may be appropriate: "The laptops you ordered are unusually popular because they have more plug-ins for peripheral devices than any other laptop in their price range. To help you locate additional accessories for these computers, we invite you to visit our

website at < . . . > where our online catalogue provides a huge selection of peripheral devices such as stereo speakers, printers, personal digital assistants, and digital pagers."

Writing Direct Negative Messages

In the direct pattern, the components of an indirect negative message are switched around and one is deleted. A writing plan for the direct pattern consists of three parts:

- Bad news in the opening
- Reasons given in the body
- Pleasant closing

This pattern is more effective than the indirect pattern in situations such as the following:

- **When the receiver may overlook the bad news.** With the crush of mail today, many readers skim messages, looking only at the opening. If they don't find substantive material, they may discard the message. Rate increases, changes in service, new policy requirements—these critical messages may require boldness to ensure attention.
- **When organization policy suggests directness.** Some companies expect all internal messages and announcements—even bad news—to be straightforward and presented without frills.
- **When the receiver prefers directness.** Busy managers may prefer directness. Such shorter messages enable the reader to get in the proper frame of mind immediately. If you suspect that the reader prefers that the facts be presented straightaway, use the direct pattern.
- **When firmness is necessary.** Messages that must demonstrate determination and strength should not use delaying techniques. For example, the last in a series of collection letters that seek payment of overdue accounts may require a direct opener.
- **When the bad news is not damaging.** If the bad news is insignificant (such as a small increase in cost) and doesn't personally affect the receiver, the direct strategy certainly makes sense.
- **When the receiver's goodwill is not an issue.** Rarely, a business may have to send a message rejecting a customer's business. For instance, a chain of bargain retail stores sent letters to two sisters announcing that their business was no longer welcome. The sisters had a history of returning items and making complaints about service.[6]

COMMON NEGATIVE BUSINESS MESSAGES

While we've said earlier that negative business messages can vary depending on the circumstance, it is possible to narrow down these circumstances into three main categories of negative situations that occur regularly in many businesses. The models below can be adapted by you to work in almost any business situation you may find yourself in that requires breaking bad news.

Refusing Requests

Every business communicator will occasionally have to say no to a request. Depending on how you think the receiver will react to your refusal, you can use the direct or the indirect pattern. If you have any doubt, use the indirect pattern.

Most of us prefer to be let down gently when we're being refused something we want. That's why the reasons-before-refusal pattern works well when you must turn down requests for favours, money, information, action, and so forth.

Refusing requests from outside an organization. Requests for contributions to charity are common. Many large and small companies receive requests for contributions of money, time, equipment, and support. Although the causes may be worthy, resources are usually limited. In a letter from Forest Financial Services, shown in Figure 6.2, the company must refuse a request for a donation to a charity. Following the indirect strategy, the letter begins with a buffer acknowledging the request. It also praises the good work of the charity and uses those words as a transition to the second paragraph. In the second paragraph, the writer explains why the company cannot donate, using a gentle refusal, thereby making it unnecessary to be blunter in stating the denial. In the letter shown in Figure 6.2, the writer felt a connection to the charity. Thus, he wanted to provide a full explanation.

Refusing internal requests. Just as managers must refuse requests from outsiders, they must also occasionally refuse requests from employees. More rarely, employees will refuse requests from managers. For example, in the article you read at the beginning of this chapter, what would have happened if Alkarim and Merge had decided not to move to Calgary? Alkarim would have had to write an e-mail or make a phone call to his supervisor refusing the request for transfer to Calgary. In Figure 6.3, you see the first draft and revision of a message responding to a request from a key manager, Mark Stevenson. He wants permission to attend a conference. However, he can't attend the conference because the timing is bad; he must be present at budget planning meetings scheduled for the same two weeks. Normally, this matter would be discussed in person. But Mark has been travelling among branch offices, and he just hasn't been in the office recently.

The vice president's first inclination was to send a quick memo, as shown in Figure 6.3, and "tell it like it is." In revising, the vice president realized that this message was going to hurt and that it had possible danger areas. Moreover, the memo misses a chance to give Mark positive feedback. An improved version of the memo starts with a buffer that delivers honest praise. By the way, don't be stingy with compliments; they cost you nothing. The buffer also includes the date of the meeting, used strategically to connect the reasons that follow. You will recall from Chapter 3 that repetition of a key idea is an effective transitional device to provide smooth flow between components of a message.

The middle paragraph provides reasons for the refusal. Notice that they focus on positive elements: Mark is the specialist; the company relies on his expertise; and everyone will benefit if he passes up the conference. In this section it becomes obvious that the request will be refused. The writer is not forced to say, "No, you may not attend." Although the refusal is implied, the reader gets the message.

The closing suggests a qualified alternative ("if our workloads permit, we'll try to send you then"). It also ends positively with gratitude for Mark's contributions to the organization and with another compliment ("you're a valuable player"). Notice that the improved version focuses on explanations and praise rather than on refusals and apologies.

The success of this message depends on attention to the entire writing process, not just on using a buffer or scattering a few compliments throughout.

Declining invitations. When we must decline an invitation to speak or attend a program, we generally try to provide a response that says more than "I can't" or "I don't want to." Unless the reasons are confidential or business secrets, try to

PREWRITING

Analyze: The purpose of this letter is to reject the request for a monetary donation without causing bad will.

Anticipate: The reader is proud of his or her organization and the good work it pursues.

Adapt: The writer should strive to cushion the bad news and explain why it is necessary.

WRITING

Research: Collect information about the receiver's organization as well as reasons for the refusal.

Organize: Use the indirect strategy. Begin with complimentary comments, present reasons, reveal the bad news gently, and close pleasantly.

Compose: Write the message and consider keeping a copy to serve as a form letter.

REVISING

Revise: Be sure that the tone of the message is positive and that it suggests that the matter was taken seriously.

Proofread: Check the receiver's name and address to be sure they are accurate. Check the letter's format.

Evaluate: Will this message retain the goodwill of the receiver despite its bad news?

Figure 6.2 ▶ Refusing Donation Request

FOREST FINANCIAL SERVICES
3410 Oxford Road
London, ON N5V 2Z7
519.593.4400
www.forestfinancial.com

November 14, 2007

Mr. Alan Gee, Chair
Oxford-Wellington County Chapter
National Reye's Syndrome Foundation
RR # 2
Kerwood, ON N0M 2B0

Dear Mr. Gee:

Opens with praise and compliments —

We appreciate your letter describing the good work your Oxford-Wellington County chapter of the National Reye's Syndrome Foundation is doing in preventing and treating this serious affliction. Your organization is to be commended for its significant achievements resulting from the efforts of dedicated members.

— *Doesn't say yes or no*

Transitions with repetition of key idea (good work) —

Supporting the good work of your organization and others, although unrelated to our business, is a luxury we have enjoyed in past years. Because of sales declines and organizational downsizing, we're forced to take a much harder look at funding requests that we receive this year. We feel that we must focus our charitable contributions on areas that relate directly to our business.

— *Explains sales decline and cutback in gifts*

Reveals refusal without actually stating it

We're hopeful that the worst days are behind us and that we'll be able to renew our support for worthwhile projects like yours next year.

— *Closes graciously with forward look*

Sincerely,

Paul Rosenberg

Paul Rosenberg
Vice President

Figure 6.3 ▶   Refusing an Internal Request

Before

DATE: July 2, 2007

TO: Mark Stevenson
        Manager, Telecommunications

FROM: Ann Wells-Freed   AWF
        VP, Management Information Systems

SUBJECT: CONFERENCE REQUEST

We can't allow you to attend the conference in September, Mark. Perhaps you didn't know that budget planning meetings are scheduled for that month.

Your expertise is needed here to help keep our telecommunications network on schedule. Without you, the entire system—which is shaky at best—might fall apart. I'm sorry to have to refuse your request to attend the conference. I know this is small thanks for the fine work you have done for us. Please accept our humble apologies.

In the spring I'm sure your work schedule will be lighter, and we can release you to attend a conference at that time.

→ Announces the bad news too quickly and painfully

→ Gives reasons, but includes a dangerous statement

→ Makes a promise that might be difficult to keep

After

DATE: July 2, 2007

TO: Mark Stevenson
        Manager, Telecommunications

FROM: Ann Wells-Freed   AWF
        VP, Management Information Systems

SUBJECT: REQUEST TO ATTEND SEPTEMBER CONFERENCE

The Management Council and I are extremely pleased with the leadership you have provided in setting up live video transmission to our regional offices. Because of your genuine professional commitment, Mark, I can understand your desire to attend the conference of the Telecommunication Specialists of North America September 23 to 28 in Kelowna.

The last two weeks in September have been set aside for budget planning. As you and I know, we've only scratched the surface of our teleconferencing projects for the next five years. Since you are the specialist and we rely heavily on your expertise, we need you here for those planning sessions.

If you're able to attend a similar conference in the spring and if our workloads permit, we'll try to send you then. You're a valuable player, Mark, and I'm grateful you're on our MIS team.

Transition: Uses date to move smoothly from buffer to reasons

Bad news: Implies refusal

Closing: Contains realistic alternative, praise, and appreciation

Buffer: Includes sincere praise

Reasons: Tells why refusal is necessary

explain them. Because responses to invitations are often taken personally, make a special effort to soften the refusal.

In the letter shown in Figure 6.4, an accountant must say no to the invitation from a friend's son to speak before the young man's college business club. The refusal is embedded in a long paragraph and de-emphasized in a subordinate clause ("Although your invitation must be declined"). The reader naturally concentrates on the main clause that follows. In this case that main clause contains an alternative that draws attention away from the refusal. Notice that the tone of a refusal is warm, upbeat, and positive. This refusal starts with conviviality and compliments.

Figure 6.4 ▶ Refusing an Invitation

Opens cordially with praise

Focuses attention on alternative

Reduces impact of refusal by placing it in subordinate clause

Ends positively with compliments and offer of assistance

GALLAGHER, BRACIO, CASAGRANDE, L.L.P.
Certified Public Accountants
942 Savin Boulevard
Toronto, ON M4P 2A9
(416) 435-9800

E-mail: cpa@gbcllp.com   www.gbcllp.com

April 14, 2007

Mr. Tyler Simpson
4208 Eastern Avenue
Toronto, ON M5A 1H5

Dear Tyler:

News of your leadership position in your campus student association fills me with delight and pride. Your father must be proud also of your educational and extracurricular achievements.

You honour me by asking me to speak to your group in the spring about codes of ethics in the accounting field. Because our firm has not yet adopted such a code, we have been investigating the codes developed by other accounting firms. I am decidedly not an expert in this area, but I have met others who are. Although your invitation must be declined, I would like to recommend Dr. Carolyn S. Marshall, who is a member of the ethics subcommittee of the Institute of Internal Auditors. Dr. Marshall is a professor who often addresses groups on the subject of ethics in accounting. I spoke with her about your club, and she indicated that she would be happy to consider your invitation.

It's good to learn that you are guiding your organization toward such constructive and timely program topics. Please call Dr. Marshall at (416) 389-2210 if you would like to arrange for her to address your club.

Sincerely,

Joan F. Gallagher
Joan F. Gallagher, CPA

JFG:mhr

Customer Bad News

Businesses must occasionally respond to disappointed customers. In Chapter 4 you learned to use the direct strategy in granting claims and making adjustments because these were essentially good-news messages. But in some situations you have little good news to share. Sometimes your company is at fault, in which case an apology is generally in order. Other times the problem is with product orders you can't fill, poor service you can't take back, claims you must refuse, credit that you must deny, or money you must collect. In the case of Merge Sanderji described in the article at the beginning of this chapter, the bad news for her customers is that she's moving her business more than halfway across the country. Messages with bad news for customers generally follow the same pattern as other negative messages. Customer letters, though, differ in one major way: they usually include resale or sales promotion emphasis.

Handling order problems. Not all customer orders can be filled as received. Suppliers may be able to send only part of an order or none at all. Substitutions may be necessary, or the delivery date may be delayed. Suppliers may suspect that all or part of the order is a mistake; the customer may actually want something else. In writing to customers about problem orders, it's generally wise to use the direct pattern if the message has some good-news elements. But when the message is disappointing, the indirect pattern is more appropriate.

Let's say you represent Live and Learn Toys, a large West Coast toy manufacturer, and you're scrambling for business in a slow year. A big customer, Child Land, calls in August and asks you to hold a block of your best-selling toy, the Space Station. Like most vendors, you require a deposit on large orders. September rolls around, and you still haven't received any money from Child Land. You must now write a tactful letter asking for the deposit—or else you will release the toy to other buyers. The problem, of course, is delivering the bad news without losing the customer's order and goodwill. Another challenge is making sure the reader understands the bad news. An effective letter, found in Figure 6.5, might begin with a positive statement that also reveals the facts.

Handling problems with service. Another category of customer complaint is a complaint about service. Service encompasses many things, but for most customers, it comes down to the level of courtesy and cooperation demonstrated by the employees of the company being dealt with. Consider the following example.

Figure 6.5 ▶   Order-Related Negative Message via E-Mail

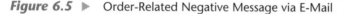

File   Edit   View   Insert   Format   Tools   Actions   Help

Reply   Reply to All   Forward

From: nlockson@lltoys.ca   Sent: March 6, 2007

To: ronzelli218@hotmail.com

Cc:

Subject: Your Space Stations Order

Dear Mr. Ronzelli:

You were smart to reserve a block of 500 Space Stations, which we have been holding for you since August. As the holidays approach, the demand for all our learning toys, including Space Station, is rapidly increasing.

Toy stores from St. John's to Victoria are asking us to ship these Space Stations. One reason the Space Station is moving out of our warehouses so quickly is its assortment of gizmos that children love, including a land rover vehicle, a shuttle craft, a hovercraft, astronauts, and even a robotic arm. As soon as we receive your deposit of $4000, we'll have this popular item on its way to your stores. Without a deposit by September 20, though, we must release this block to other retailers.

Please send us your cheque immediately. You can begin showing this fascinating Live and Learn toy in your stores by November 1.

Sincerely,

Nick Lockson

for Live and Learn Toys

Each year banks send their customers T5 slips, which show how much investment income customers have accrued in the previous year. This information is often important because it helps individuals decide whether or how much to contribute to an RRSP to avoid having to pay tax.

Josh Stein has not received his T5 from Great North Bank yet, and it's February 27. He's worried that he won't have enough time to do his taxes and put some money into an RRSP if necessary. (The RRSP deadline is March 1.) He calls Great North's customer service line to ask where his slip is. After all, all his other slips have arrived weeks ago. He sees no reason why Great North's slips should be so late. Once he gets through to a live customer service representative, he makes his complaint: "It's two days before RRSP cut-off and I still haven't received a T5 slip from you. Can you tell me why not?" The customer service rep gives Josh the answer he's been instructed to give: "T5 slips were mailed out beginning on February 10. Due to circumstances beyond our control, not everyone across Canada will have received their slip before March 1. Unfortunately, we can't request a duplicate slip until after March 1." At this point Josh is quite angry. "So what you're telling me," he says, "is that even though you screwed up by not getting me my slip on time, there's nothing you can do about it until *after* the RRSP cut-off date!" "It looks that way, sir. In fact, you're the first person to call with this problem," is the rep's response. "Frankly, I don't care if I'm the first or the four-hundred-and-fiftieth," Josh says. "If you can't get my slip, then I'd like you to find out the amount on the slip. If I have the amount, at least I can do my taxes and figure out my situation." "I'm sorry," the customer service rep replies, "but I don't have access to that information. But you can figure it out yourself by adding up all your interest accrued in your accounts over the past 12 months."

The conversation continues for another few minutes. Josh is exasperated because he doesn't understand how his financial institution, which is bound by law to provide him with a T5 slip, can be so cavalier about the fact that he doesn't have his slip yet. On the other hand, the customer service rep may not understand what all the fuss is about. Josh ends the phone call by telling the rep that he has not been helpful and that he intends to write a letter to the bank about the poor service he's received. In what Josh takes as a final bit of bad customer service, the rep encourages him to write the letter!

Taking time out of his busy schedule, Josh sits down the next day and composes a complaint letter to the president of Great North Bank. He ends his letter by suggesting that the bank mail T5 slips out by February 1, so that they reach customers in plenty of time. He finds the mailing address online and mails the letter on March 1. Two weeks later, he receives a phone call from the VP of Customer Relations at Great North. This person thanks Josh for taking the time to send his letter. He tells him that he understands the problems Josh has experienced, and that he appreciates the suggestion about moving up the date of T5 mailing. He says that he can't commit to such a recommendation without further discussion with staff in his department, but that he promises to look into it and keep Josh up to date via e-mail of any progress with his recommendation.

In essence, what the VP of Customer Relations has managed to do in his negative news phone call is four things: he's acknowledged Josh's complaint, he's personalized the response both by phoning instead of writing and by remarking on the "trouble" Josh has been through, he's resolved the problem following company policy (i.e., he's suggested that he and his fellow employees will investigate Josh's recommendation, not that they will adopt it), and he's promised to follow up.[7] Notice that although the VP's phone call contained bad news (i.e., Josh's recommendation wasn't being adopted), it sounded upbeat and positive.

Although best practices in customer service stipulate that the phone is used instead of writing whenever possible, sometimes the sheer volume of complaints makes it unfeasible for customers to be reached by phone. In such cases, letters are usually sent instead. Figure 6.6 shows what the VP's phone call might look like if it were a letter instead.

Denying claims. Customers occasionally want something they're not entitled to or that you can't grant. They may misunderstand warranties or make unreasonable demands. Because these customers are often unhappy with a product or service, they are emotionally involved. Letters that say no to emotionally involved receivers will probably be your most challenging communication task.

Fortunately, the reasons-before-refusal plan helps you be empathic and artful in breaking bad news. Obviously, in denial letters you'll need to adopt the proper tone. Don't blame customers, even if they are at fault. Avoid *you* statements that sound preachy ("You would have known that cash refunds are impossible if you had read your contract"). Use neutral, objective language to explain why the claim must be refused. Consider offering resale information to rebuild the customer's confidence in your products or organization. In Figure 6.7 the writer denies a customer's claim for the difference between the price the customer paid for speakers and the

Figure 6.6 ▶ Service-Related Negative Message via E-Mail

File Edit View Insert Format Tools Actions Help

Reply | Reply to All | Forward

From: b.beattie@gnb.ca   Sent: March 6, 2007
To: josteinman@gmail.com
Cc:
Subject: Your T5 Suggestion

Dear Mr. Stein,

I would like to thank you for taking the time to send your letter dated March 1, 2007. It is helpful for us to understand what our customers' needs are.

I've read your letter and I want to tell you that I understand the problem you've experienced with your T5 slip. Furthermore, I appreciate the suggestion made in your letter about moving up the date of our annual T5 mailing. While I am not able to commit firmly to such a recommendation without further discussion with staff in my department, I promise to seriously look into it.

In the meantime, if you'd be so good as to send me an e-mail at b.beattie@gnb.ca, I can promise to keep you up to date via e-mail of any progress on your suggestion.

Yours truly,

Brian Beattie
VP, Customer Relations

price he saw advertised locally (which would have resulted in a cash refund of $151). While the catalogue service does match any advertised lower price, the price-matching policy applies only to exact models. This claim must be rejected because the advertisement the customer submitted showed a different, older speaker model.

The letter to Matthew Tyson opens with a buffer that agrees with a statement in the customer's letter. It repeats the key idea of product confidence as a transition to the second paragraph. Next comes an explanation of the price-matching policy. The writer does not assume that the customer is trying to pull a fast one. Nor does he suggest that the customer is a dummy who didn't read or understand the price-matching policy. The safest path is a neutral explanation of the policy along with precise distinctions between the customer's speakers and the older ones. The writer also gets a chance to resell the customer's speakers and demonstrate what a quality product they are. By the end of the third paragraph, it's evident to the reader that his claim is unjustified.

Figure 6.7 ▶ Denying a Claim

Combines agreement with resale

Explains price-matching policy and how reader's purchase is different from lower-priced model

Without actually saying no, shows why reader's claim can't be honoured

Builds reader's confidence in wisdom of purchase

Continues resale; looks forward to future business

---

c·e·l·e·s·t·i·a·l
c a t a l o g u e   s a l e s

479 Pleasant Street, Truro, NS B2N 5J9 • phone (902) 455-2100 •
fax (902) 435-3260 • http://www.celestial.ca

February 19, 2007

Mr. Matthew R. Tyson
177 Beech Avenue
Toronto, ON M4E 3K4

Dear Mr. Tyson:

You're right, Mr. Tyson. We do take pride in selling the finest products at rock-bottom prices. The Boze speakers you purchased last month are premier concert hall speakers. They're the only ones we present in our catalogue because they're the best. — **Buffer**

We have such confidence in our products and prices that we offer the price-matching policy you mention in your letter of February 15. That policy guarantees a refund of the price difference if you see one of your purchases offered at a lower price for 30 days after your purchase. To qualify for that refund, customers are asked to send us an advertisement or verifiable proof of the product price and model. As our catalogue states, this price-matching policy applies only to exact models with Canadian warranties. — **Reasons**

Our Boze AM-5 II speakers sell for $749. You sent us a local advertisement showing a price of $598 for Boze speakers. This advertisement, however, describes an earlier version, the Boze AM-4 model. The AM-5 speakers you received have a wider dynamic range and smoother frequency response than the AM-4 model. Naturally, the improved model you purchased costs a little more than the older AM-4 model that the local advertisement describes. Your speakers have a new three-chamber bass module that virtually eliminates harmonic distortion. Finally, your speakers are 20 percent more compact than the AM-4 model. — **Implied refusal**

You bought the finest compact speakers on the market, Mr. Tyson. If you haven't installed them yet, you may be interested in ceiling mounts, shown in the enclosed catalogue on page 48. For the most up-to-date prices and product information, please see our online catalogue at our prize-winning website. We value your business and invite your continued comparison shopping. — **Positive closing**

Sincerely yours,

Rick Thalman

Rick K. Thalman
Customer Service

mmt
Enclosure

Refusing credit. As much as companies want business, they can extend credit only when payment is likely to follow. Credit applications, from individuals or from businesses, are generally approved or disapproved on the basis of the applicant's credit history. This record is supplied by a credit-reporting agency, such as Equifax. After reviewing the applicant's record, a credit manager applies the organization's guidelines and approves or disapproves the application.

If you must deny credit to prospective customers, you have four goals in conveying the refusal:

- Avoiding language that causes hard feelings
- Retaining customers on a cash basis
- Preparing for possible future credit without raising false expectations
- Avoiding disclosures that could cause a lawsuit

Because credit applicants are likely to continue to do business with an organization even if they are denied credit, you'll want to do everything possible to encourage that patronage. Thus, keep the refusal respectful, sensitive, and upbeat. A letter to a customer denying her credit application might look like the one in Figure 6.8 below.

To avoid possible litigation, some organizations give no explanation of the reasons for the refusal. Instead, they provide the name of the credit-reporting agency and suggest that inquiries be directed to it. In Figure 6.8, notice the use of the passive voice ("credit cannot be extended") and a long sentence to de-emphasize the bad news. Also, notice how the cordial close looks forward to the possibility of future reapplication. Some businesses do provide reasons explaining credit denials ("Credit cannot be granted because your firm's current and long-term credit

Figure 6.8 ▶
Credit Refusal via Letter

Dear Ms. Love,

We genuinely appreciate your application of January 12 for a Fashion Express credit account.

After receiving a report of your current credit record from Equifax, it is apparent that credit cannot be extended at this time. To learn more about your record, you may call an Equifax credit counsellor at 1-800-356-0922.

Thanks, Ms. Love, for the confidence you've shown in Fashion Express. We invite you to continue shopping at our stores, and we look forward to your reapplication in the future.

Sincerely,

Roxanne Charles

Roxanne Charles

Credit Manager, Fashion Express

obligations are nearly twice as great as your firm's total assets"). They may also provide alternatives, such as deferred billing or cash discounts. When the letter denies a credit application that accompanies an order, the message may contain resale information. The writer tries to convert the order from credit to cash.

Whatever form the bad-news letter takes, it's a good idea to have the message reviewed by legal counsel because of the litigation landmines awaiting unwary communicators in this area.

Collection letters. One of the most important processes in business is the collection process. Collection is usually a two-step process an organization takes to ensure that its unpaid invoices are paid. The first phase in the collection process is usually the sending of a short reminder letter or e-mail that lets the client or customer know that his or her invoice is outstanding. Most often, this first message is written following the indirect pattern. Best practices stipulate that a copy of the outstanding invoice should be attached to this short reminder message, in case the client has misplaced the original.

Knowing how to write a direct negative message becomes useful in the second step in the collection process. If the client or customer with the outstanding invoice does not reply in a timely manner to the short reminder message described above, it is time to write a direct bad-news message demanding payment. The main objective of a bad-news collection letter is to receive payment, but at the same time to make sure that the goodwill of the client or customer is retained. According to CreditGuru.com, a website that offers advice on the collection process, the main features of a well-written collection letter are a reminder of the dates of the invoice, a reminder of the total amount outstanding, a request for immediate payment or payment by a specified date, a request for the payment to be sent by the quickest means (e.g., courier), and finally, a sense of urgency coupled with an unapologetic and a non-threatening tone.[8] Figure 6.9 shows a typical example of such a letter.

Bad News in Organizations

A tactful tone and a reasons-first approach help preserve friendly relations with customers. These same techniques are useful when delivering bad news within organizations. Interpersonal bad news might involve telling the boss that something went wrong or confronting an employee about poor performance. Organizational bad news might involve declining profits, lost contracts, harmful lawsuits, public relations controversies, and changes in policy. Whether you use a direct or an indirect pattern in delivering that news depends primarily on the anticipated reaction of the audience. Generally, bad news is better received when reasons are given first. Within organizations, you may find yourself giving bad news in person or in writing.

Giving bad news personally. Whether you are an employee or a supervisor, you may have the unhappy responsibility of delivering bad news. First, decide whether the negative information is newsworthy. For example, trivial, non-criminal mistakes or one-time bad behaviours are best left alone. But fraudulent travel claims, consistent hostile behaviour, or failing projects must be reported.[9] For example, you might have to tell the boss that the team's computer crashed with all its important files. As a team leader or supervisor, you might be required to confront an underperforming employee. If you know that the news will upset the

Figure 6.9 ▶ Collection Letter

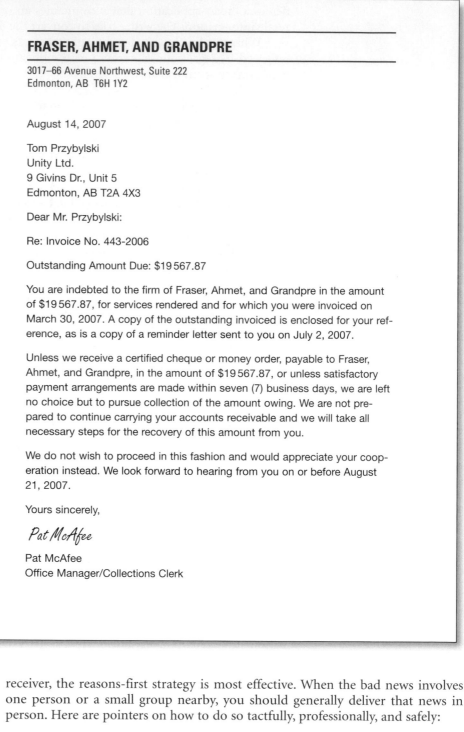

FRASER, AHMET, AND GRANDPRE

3017–66 Avenue Northwest, Suite 222
Edmonton, AB T6H 1Y2

August 14, 2007

Tom Przybylski
Unity Ltd.
9 Givins Dr., Unit 5
Edmonton, AB T2A 4X3

Dear Mr. Przybylski:

Re: Invoice No. 443-2006

Outstanding Amount Due: $19 567.87

You are indebted to the firm of Fraser, Ahmet, and Grandpre in the amount of $19 567.87, for services rendered and for which you were invoiced on March 30, 2007. A copy of the outstanding invoiced is enclosed for your reference, as is a copy of a reminder letter sent to you on July 2, 2007.

Unless we receive a certified cheque or money order, payable to Fraser, Ahmet, and Grandpre, in the amount of $19 567.87, or unless satisfactory payment arrangements are made within seven (7) business days, we are left no choice but to pursue collection of the amount owing. We are not prepared to continue carrying your accounts receivable and we will take all necessary steps for the recovery of this amount from you.

We do not wish to proceed in this fashion and would appreciate your cooperation instead. We look forward to hearing from you on or before August 21, 2007.

Yours sincerely,

Pat McAfee

Pat McAfee
Office Manager/Collections Clerk

receiver, the reasons-first strategy is most effective. When the bad news involves one person or a small group nearby, you should generally deliver that news in person. Here are pointers on how to do so tactfully, professionally, and safely:

- **Gather all the information.** Cool down and have all the facts before marching in on the boss or confronting someone. Remember that every story has two sides.
- **Prepare and rehearse.** Outline what you plan to say so that you are confident, coherent, and dispassionate.

- **Explain: past, present, future.** If you are telling the boss about a problem such as the computer crash, explain what caused the crash, the current situation, and how and when you plan to fix it.
- **Consider taking a partner.** If you fear a "shoot the messenger" reaction, especially from your boss, bring a colleague with you. Each person should have a consistent and credible part in the presentation. If possible, take advantage of your organization's internal resources. To lend credibility to your view, call on auditors, inspectors, or human resources experts.
- **Think about timing.** Don't deliver bad news when someone is already stressed or grumpy. Experts also advise against giving bad news on Friday afternoon when people have the weekend to dwell on it.
- **Be patient with the reaction.** Give the receiver time to vent, think, recover, and act wisely.[10]

Delivering workplace bad news. Many of the same techniques used to deliver bad news personally are useful when organizations face a crisis or must deliver bad news in the workplace. Smart organizations involved in a crisis prefer to communicate the news openly to employees, customers, and stockholders. This was the case in the Imperial Oil corporate move from Toronto to Calgary. A crisis might involve serious performance problems, a major relocation, massive layoffs, a management shakeup, or public controversy. Instead of letting rumours distort the truth, smart organizations explain their side of the story honestly and early. Morale can be destroyed when employees learn of major events affecting their jobs through the grapevine or from news accounts—rather than from management.

When routine bad news must be delivered to employees, management may want to deliver the news personally. But with large groups this is generally impossible. Instead, organizations deliver bad news through hard-copy memos. Organizations are experimenting with other delivery channels such as e-mail, videos, webcasts, and voice mail. Still, hard-copy memos seem to function most effectively because they are more formal and make a permanent record.

The draft of the memo shown in Figure 6.10 announces a substantial increase in the cost of employee health care benefits. However, the memo suffers from many problems. It announces jolting news bluntly in the first sentence. Worse, it offers little or no explanation for the steep increase in costs. It also sounds insincere ("We did everything possible ...") and arbitrary. In a final miscue, the writer fails to give credit to the company for absorbing previous health cost increases.

The revision of this bad-news memo uses the indirect pattern and improves the tone considerably. Notice that it opens with a relevant, upbeat buffer regarding health care—but says nothing about increasing costs. For a smooth transition, the second paragraph begins with a key idea from the opening ("comprehensive package"). The reasons section discusses rising costs with explanations and figures. The bad news ("you will be paying $119 a month") is clearly presented but embedded within the paragraph. Throughout, the writer strives to show the fairness of the company's position. The ending, which does not refer to the bad news, emphasizes how much the company is paying and what a wise investment it is. Notice that the entire memo demonstrates a kinder, gentler approach than that shown in the first draft. Of prime importance in breaking bad news to employees is providing clear, convincing reasons that explain the decision.

Saying no to job applicants. Being refused a job is one of life's major rejections. The blow is intensified by tactless letters ("Unfortunately, you were not among the candidates selected for ...").

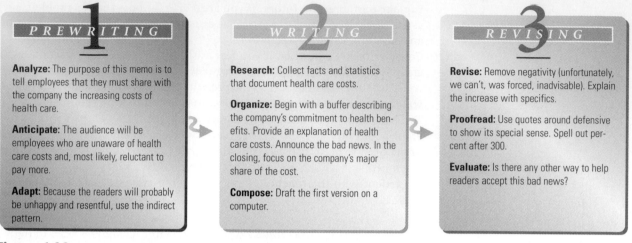

PREWRITING

Analyze: The purpose of this memo is to tell employees that they must share with the company the increasing costs of health care.

Anticipate: The audience will be employees who are unaware of health care costs and, most likely, reluctant to pay more.

Adapt: Because the readers will probably be unhappy and resentful, use the indirect pattern.

WRITING

Research: Collect facts and statistics that document health care costs.

Organize: Begin with a buffer describing the company's commitment to health benefits. Provide an explanation of health care costs. Announce the bad news. In the closing, focus on the company's major share of the cost.

Compose: Draft the first version on a computer.

REVISING

Revise: Remove negativity (unfortunately, we can't, was forced, inadvisable). Explain the increase with specifics.

Proofread: Use quotes around defensive to show its special sense. Spell out percent after 300.

Evaluate: Is there any other way to help readers accept this bad news?

Figure 6.10 ▶ Announcing Bad News to Employees

Before

Beginning January 1 your monthly payment for supplementary health care benefits will be increased to $119 (up from $52 last year). → Hits readers with bad news without any preparation

Every year supplementary health care costs go up. Although we considered dropping other benefits, Midland decided that the best plan was to keep the present comprehensive package. Unfortunately, we cant do that unless we pass along some of the extra cost to you. Last year the company was forced to absorb the total increase in health care premiums. However, such a plan this year is inadvisable. → Offers no explanation

We did everything possible to avoid the sharp increase in costs to you this year. A rate schedule describing the increases in payments for your family and dependants is enclosed. → Fails to take credit for absorbing previous increases

After

DATE:	October 2, 2007
TO:	Fellow Employees
FROM:	Lawrence R. Romero, President *LRR*
SUBJECT:	MAINTAINING QUALITY HEALTH CARE

Begins with positive buffer ——

Supplementary health care programs have always been an important part of our commitment to employees at Midland, Inc. We're proud that our total benefits package continues to rank among the best in the country.

Offers reasons explaining why costs are rising ——

Such a comprehensive package does not come cheaply. In the last decade supplementary health care costs alone have risen over 300 percent. We're told that several factors fuel the cost spiral: inflation, technology improvements, increased cost of outpatient services, and "defensive" medicine practised by doctors to prevent lawsuits.

Reveals bad news clearly but embeds it in paragraph ——

Just two years ago our monthly health care cost for each employee was $515. It rose to $569 last year. We were able to absorb that jump without increasing your contribution. But this year's hike to $639 forces us to ask you to share the increase. To maintain your current health care benefits, you will be paying $119 a month. The enclosed rate schedule describes the costs for families and dependants.

Ends positively by stressing the company's major share of the costs ——

Midland continues to pay the major portion of your health care program ($520 each month). We think it's a wise investment.

Enclosure

You can reduce the receiver's disappointment somewhat by using the indirect pattern—with one important variation. In the reasons section it's wise to be vague in explaining why the candidate was not selected. First, giving concrete reasons may be painful to the receiver ("Your grade point average of 2.7 was low compared with GPAs of other candidates"). Second, and more important, providing extra information may prove fatal in a lawsuit. Hiring and firing decisions generate considerable litigation today. To avoid charges of discrimination or wrongful actions, legal advisers warn organizations to keep employment rejection letters general, simple, and short. Figure 6.11, in which a job search professional or "headhunter" responds to a client, provides an example of such a rejection letter.

CONCLUSION

In this chapter you learned to write follow-up bad-news messages as well as to apply the indirect and direct strategies in refusing requests, denying claims, and delivering bad news to employees and customers. Now that you have completed your instruction in writing shorter business documents such as e-mails, letters, and memos, you're ready to learn about writing longer business documents like plans, proposals, and reports. Chapter 7 introduces routine reports and proposals and then Chapter 8 looks at more formal plans, proposals, and reports.

Figure 6.11 ▶ Employment Rejection via E-Mail

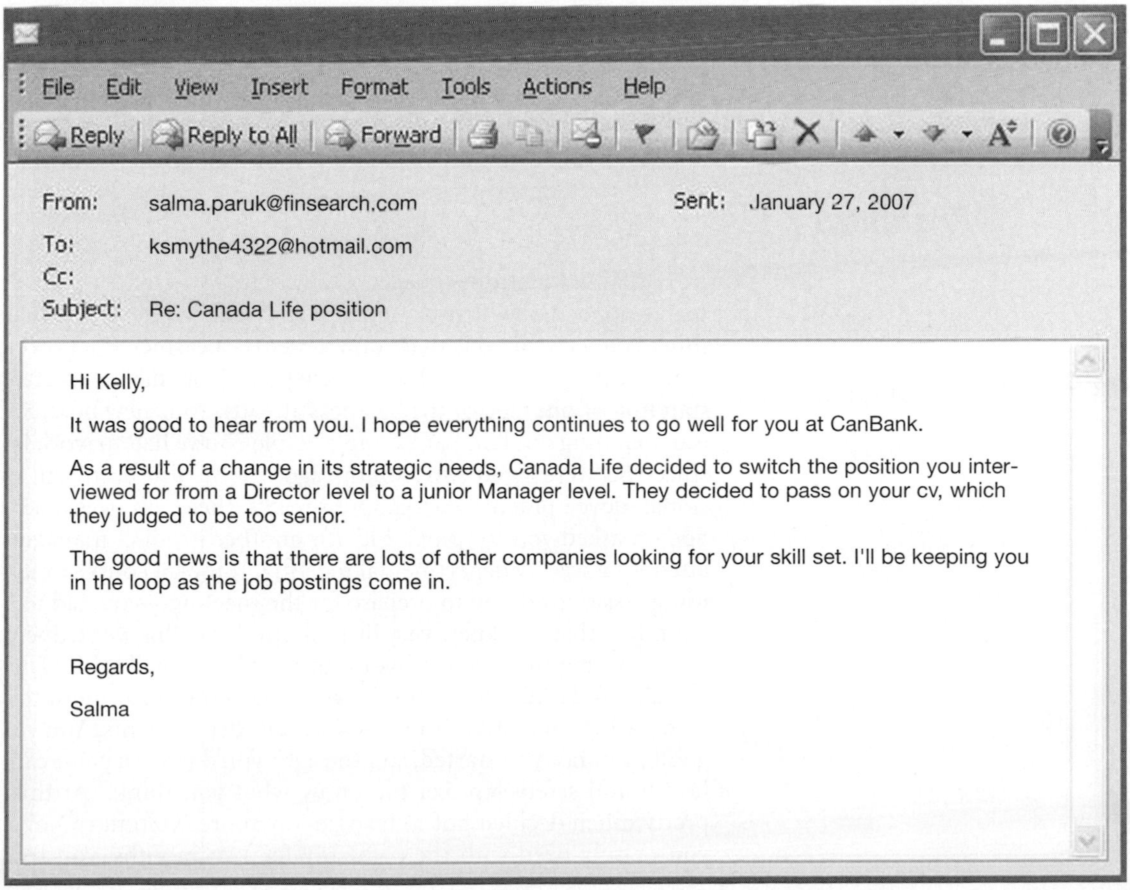

File Edit View Insert Format Tools Actions Help

Reply | Reply to All | Forward

From: salma.paruk@finsearch.com Sent: January 27, 2007

To: ksmythe4322@hotmail.com

Cc:

Subject: Re: Canada Life position

Hi Kelly,

It was good to hear from you. I hope everything continues to go well for you at CanBank.

As a result of a change in its strategic needs, Canada Life decided to switch the position you interviewed for from a Director level to a junior Manager level. They decided to pass on your cv, which they judged to be too senior.

The good news is that there are lots of other companies looking for your skill set. I'll be keeping you in the loop as the job postings come in.

Regards,

Salma

:: *Chapter Review*

As a way of studying the material in this chapter, imagine you are at a job interview for your dream entry-level job after college or university. You've prepared answers for all the classic interview questions, but to your surprise, your interviewer also asks a number of questions based on bad-news business writing. How would you answer the following six questions?

1. In this position you'll be communicating with clients regularly, and the news you'll have to give them won't always be positive. Besides just communicating bad news, what else should your e-mail or phone call convey?

2. Your answer to question 1 made a lot of sense. So you know what negative messages should do, but can you also tell us what these messages should stay away from?

3. We find there are generally two ways to communicate bad news: either directly or indirectly. What's the main difference between the two, and can you imagine a situation you might be in with a customer or a fellow employee in which you might have to use the direct method?

4. When responding to customer complaints, we train our staff to use an indirect method of delivering bad news. Why do you think we train our staff this way?

5. As a financial institution, much of our business involves various forms of credit: credit cards, loans, lines of credit, mortgages, etc. If a client doesn't meet our requirements for credit, how do you think we should communicate with that person?

6. As a team leader in the retail credit group, you will be in charge of up to 15 customer service representatives. Can you foresee a situation in which you'd have to deliver bad news to one of your representatives? How would you approach the conversation?

:: *Problems*

1. After graduating from college, you were lucky to land an entry-level product manager position with a national grocery chain. One of the main reasons you think you were hired is that you worked as a cashier at a grocery store for six years during high school and college, so you have a pretty good understanding of one side of the business already. Your new boss, Spence Stafford, is demanding but fair. For example, while you've had to work late most nights since you were hired two months ago, you've also been sent on two professional development workshops already (held on weekends). Last week, Spence asked you to "pinch hit" for another product manager who couldn't attend the weekly departmental meeting. It took a couple of late-night cramming sessions for you to prepare for the meeting—you had to learn all about a product that you knew very little about. Early this week, Spence sent you an e-mail asking for another favour. In part, his e-mail said, "The company has a health and safety committee that meets about once a month, and there has to be a representative from each of the departments. You've done a really good job since you started, so I thought you'd make a good candidate for our health and safety rep. Let me know what you think." At this point, you've pretty much decided not to take on any more "voluntary" jobs. Even though you've only been with the company for two months, you feel as though in

that time you've proven yourself to be a strong employee who goes over and above the call of duty (and the job description). At the same time, you have a sneaking suspicion that Spence might be testing you with his health and safety committee offer. After mulling it over, you decide to refuse Spence's request. What should your refusal look and sound like? Why?

2. As a marketing intern in the credit department at Great North Bank, you've been assigned the following task: you've been provided with a list of telephone numbers, and you've been asked to call the people on the list. The purpose of your call is to encourage these people to apply for the Great North Bank Basic Visa Card. Your call is following up on a letter they will have received in the mail in the past week and a half. Cold calling is not your favourite aspect of marketing, but you're determined to make a good impression during your internship, so you give it your best. It takes you four days to get through the 200 or so people on your list. Of the 200 calls made, you got voice mail in 99 cases. The other 101 cases were split as follows: 38 people said they were busy and couldn't talk, 37 people said they weren't interested, and interestingly, 26 people were downright angry and demanded to know why such a rude letter had been sent to them. Of course, being an intern, you didn't really have an answer to their question. After your calls are done, you talk to your internship supervisor about what you found out. "Bob," you say, "of the 200 names on the list you gave me to call, did you know that about 12 percent were incredibly angry, specifically about the letter they were sent?" "What do you mean, angry?" Bob asks. "I guess I mean they were angry at the bank because of something about the letter that was sent... Can I see a copy of the letter?" Bob pulls up a file on his computer. You read the following very short letter on Great North stationery:

Dear Potential Credit Card Customer, We are afraid that you did not qualify for the Great North "Plus Visa Card" you recently applied for. Oftentimes, the reason for disqualification is an insufficient income level, or a problematic past credit history. We are happy, however, to offer you the chance to apply for our "Basic Visa Card." An application form is attached and we'd appreciate it if you would complete the form and send it to us at your earliest convenience. Sincerely, Credit Department, Great North Bank.

"Well, you know, Bob," you say to your supervisor, "I think I can see why I'm having some trouble on the phone with potential customers."

What is your analysis of the problem and what do you recommend to Bob as a way of fixing the situation?

3. You are the owner of a company named RS Creations Inc. located in New Delhi, India. RS Creations makes clothing (women's, men's, and children's) that is sold in chain stores in North America and Europe. Because India is so far away from both Europe and North America, the major cost involved in your business is shipping. Shipping also happens to be your main headache. The process of shipping a container of clothing from your factory to a retailer's distribution centre (say in Montreal) is as follows: You pack a shipping container at your factory. It is transported via truck to Bombay, which takes at least a day. The shipping container is then transferred to a ship that is bound for a large container port in the Persian Gulf (say in Qatar). Once

in Qatar, your container full of clothing is transferred from the Bombay ship to a much larger ocean tanker that is sailing for Halifax, then Montreal. In total, the shipment takes between 9 and 14 days. Because retail clothing is such a time-sensitive business, you have to make sure your shipments arrive on time. Otherwise, the retailers will refuse to pay you the full amount of the shipment. And what's worse, they may decide to subcontract their clothing manufacturing to another company next time, possibly in China, which is much easier to ship from. In essence, for your clothes to make it to Montreal on time, all the components of the journey have to work well. There's no room for error. Of course, errors have occurred. Once the truck from Delhi to Bombay died and your shipment didn't make it onto the ship bound for Qatar. Another time, your shipment arrived from Bombay on time in Qatar, but the ocean tanker had already left for North America. Most recently, a large shipment (ten containers) of summer clothing for Zap!, a major North American retailer, has been held up in Bombay by a port workers' strike. If the strike lasts more than two days, you will miss your shipment date in Montreal, and because of the size of this particular shipment, you may be forced to let go half of your employees as a cost-cutting measure in order to "swallow" the lost revenue. Perhaps knowing ahead of time for once that the shipment might not make it on time, you can convince the people at Zap! to reconsider their policy of non-payment for late shipments...

4. Zap!, the North American clothing chain, has a straightforward "Customer Satisfaction" policy. Any article of clothing bought in a Zap! store can be returned or exchanged within 30 days of purchase, as long as an original receipt is provided. In today's competitive retail climate, it's important for retailers to have simple, customer-friendly policies such as this. Sometimes, however, even this generous policy is not enough to satisfy demanding customers. For example, earlier this week, a customer walked into the Zap! store you manage in suburban Winnipeg. She didn't join the line of people waiting to make a purchase. Instead, she walked up to the side of the counter and asked loudly, "Can I talk to a manager, please?" Since you happened to be standing there, you cheerfully responded, "Yes, you can. I'm the manager. What can I do for you?" The customer said she wanted a refund on a pair of jeans she had purchased. Even though you would usually ask a customer to join the line, you could see this woman was agitated, so you decided to make an exception. "Sure," you said to her, "I can do that for you. I'll just need your receipt." The customer looked at you with raised eyebrows as if to say, "Excuse me?" You repeated your request: "I'll need the receipt." To make a long story short, the customer did not have a receipt, and she claimed to have bought the jeans just before Christmas, which was six weeks ago. Following company policy, you have to deny this customer's claim. How would you go about this in the situation described above (i.e., in front of a number of other employees and customers)? Imagine the customer then leaves the store angrily and writes a scathing complaint letter to Zap!'s president in Montreal. The president asks her manager of Customer Service to respond to the woman's letter. Here are the president's instructions: "Deny the claim nicely, and make sure you back up what our manager in Winnipeg said and did. Okay?"

5. The Moose Grille is a chain of family dining restaurants located in several Canadian cities, including Niagara Falls and Banff. The company has been successful in the past through a combination of efficient and courteous service, good prices for good food, and a particular blend of kitschy Canadiana (maple leafs, beavers, etc.). Tourists tend to flock to the restaurants, and

there's also a steady stream of teenagers who like to hang out at "the Moose." One of the Moose's main suppliers is the multinational company Tafco, with Canadian headquarters in London, Ontario. Tafco supplies restaurants across North America with virtually everything they need for their operations: staff uniforms, food supplies, cleaning supplies, furniture, etc. The Moose Grille chain has been a customer of Tafco's since its founding five years ago. There haven't been any problems in the relationship yet, but a recent downturn in tourism (especially from the United States) has begun to affect the bottom line at the Moose. The chain has decided to close one of its underperforming Vancouver locations and has let go of its "head chefs" at all 15 locations. The plan is to make do with sous chefs instead. Another casualty of the downturn in tourism has been the Moose's ability to pay its suppliers on time. This week represents the third month in a row that the Moose is more than 30 days past paying its Tafco invoices (which are payable in 30 days). In total the Moose owes Tafco $148 766.20. As the Tafco sales rep responsible for the Moose account, you have let things slide until now (the Moose isn't the only client suffering because of the tourism slump), but you've been instructed by your director not to let things slide any further. You've been specifically told to use the Tafco collection template to start the collection process with the Moose account. The problem is, the template is very blunt and its tone might anger customers to the point where they may decide to switch suppliers. Instead, you consider drafting your own response—which you'll show the director before sending it, of course.

Grammar/Style Review 6

In this review, you will be practising identifying wordiness mistakes. There are at least five mistakes in total. For a brief explanation of this style problem, please read the explanation on page 328. Besides completing the exercise below, be sure to be on the lookout for wordiness mistakes in your own writing.

To: mmarino@mesfin.ca

From: tsmith@mesfin.ca

Re: Cancelling meeting

Hi Maria,

I'd like to suggest that this week's team meeting be cancelled. Due to a scheduling mix-up and due to the fact that I feel we haven't had the necessary time needed to prepare, I think it would be better if we re-scheduled the meeting.

I wanted you to know about this early, because I know you've been preparing a presentation about new CRM software for us. Let's talk at the end of the week in a few days and we can decide when to re-schedule.

Regards,

Ted

Business Communication Lab 6

Using the skills you've learned in this chapter, assume the role of the manager of Public Affairs at Imperial Oil. As described in the article at the beginning of this chapter, an e-mail went out to all staff of Imperial Oil at its Toronto head-quarters informing everyone that the company was moving to Calgary. You've already decided not to try to frame this as a totally "good news story" because you know that the grapevine says that a lot of people are unhappy about the prospect of moving to Calgary. Instead you decide to draft a bad-news e-mail to employees, but one that won't sound negative at all. Draft the e-mail you think Alkarim Sunderji might have received in the *Calgary Herald* story.

Writing Longer Business Documents: Reports, Proposals, Plans

CHAPTER 7

Routine Reports and Proposals

Whitecaps set sights on 2009 debut for stadium

Best-case scenario detailed for 16,000-seat facility

BY DAN STINSON, *VANCOUVER SUN*, FEBRUARY 17, 2006, G8

THE BEST-CASE SCENARIO for Whitecaps Waterfront Stadium to be fully constructed and operational is the spring of 2009, Whitecaps president John Rocha said Thursday as the soccer club discussed a progress report on the planned 16,000-seat facility.

Rocha said the Whitecaps will submit a development permit application to Vancouver city council this May, adding that the permit and rezoning process is expected to take between 12 and 18 months.

"We hope to have the development permit approved in the fall of 2007," Rocha said. "We can then proceed on construction of the stadium, which we estimate will take between 18 months and two years. Ideally, the stadium will be up and ready for use sometime in the spring of 2009."

The Whitecaps announced last October their plans to build the stadium over a seven-hectare parcel of rail lands east of the Waterfront Seabus terminal in Vancouver's Gastown area. The cost of the project is estimated at $65 million, which includes land acquisition costs of about $17 million.

The Whitecaps' initial plans are to construct a 16,000-seat stadium, but the facility can be expanded to as many as 30,000 seats with the addition of two upper decks.

Rocha said 31 companies in the Greater Vancouver area have put down $1,000 deposits on suites in the planned stadium, adding that 30–35 suites are scheduled to be built in the facility.

Current stadium plans feature a three-sided horseshoe shape that's open on the north side to Burrard Inlet, two grandstand seating areas of about 6,500 seats each, and a 3,000-seat end zone area.

DIAGNOSING THE PROBLEM

As with the article from Chapter 6 about a couple's move from Toronto to Calgary along with Imperial Oil, the above article about the Whitecaps' new stadium doesn't seem to be about any obvious problems, on the surface at least. But if we look carefully at the language of the article, we discover a small problem, or at least a challenge. The phrase "best-case scenario" is the key. Usually, this is a phrase we use when we're trying to put a positive spin on what is more than likely bad news. For example, "The best-case scenario is that the marketing project will get done early next week, but it's more likely to be finished late next week." In other words, "best-case scenario" is the kind of phrase we use when we want to cushion and lessen bad news, as we learned in Chapter 6. The word "ideally," which is used by the president of the soccer club later in the article, performs the same task—it's a synonym for "best-case scenario" that puts a positive spin on negative or not-obviously positive news. So what is the bad news that's being cushioned in the press conference?

It seems that what the Whitecaps soccer club is trying to achieve by holding a press conference is to put a positive spin on what is otherwise not terribly good news: it doesn't really know when its stadium will be finished, and, what's more important, the process seems to be taking longer than the club had anticipated. Notice the reason the club gives for holding its press conference: it is going to discuss a progress report.

Normally, progress reports are internal documents we write for our supervisors at work—they don't get released to the media and featured on the front page of a major newspaper. But, if we think about it, what is it about the phrase "progress report" that might put a positive spin on what is a not-so-positive situation and get the media interested in the story? Frankly, it's the word "progress" itself. There's an implication that whatever the report might contain—in this case news that a development permit application will be submitted to the city of Vancouver in a few months' time—progress is being made. In other words, however small the progress, it is progress, and that must be positive.

Using what you know from reading the article and the analysis of the article provided above, complete the following in-class activity...

in class
activity 7

WORKING IN SMALL groups of three to four, students will discuss the analysis of the problem provided above in order to decide whether it accurately represents the situation described in the article. Then students will consider the Whitecaps' progress report as a problem in itself. What should the report contain? How should it be formatted? What should be highlighted and what should be downplayed? Report back to the class within 20 minutes.

Now that you've presented your solution to the rest of the class, you're ready to discover more information on the basics of writing routine business reports and proposals. At the end of this chapter, you will be presented with some more problems that you may be asked to analyze, evaluate, and explain.

WHAT IS A ROUTINE BUSINESS REPORT?

Good report writers are good at simplifying facts so that anyone can understand them. Collecting information and organizing it clearly and simply into meaningful reports are skills that all successful businesspeople today require. In this age of information, reports play a significant role in helping decision makers solve problems. You can learn to write good reports by examining basic techniques and by analyzing appropriate models.

Because of their abundance and diversity, business reports are difficult to define. They may range from informal e-mail trip reports to formal 200-page financial forecasts. Reports may be presented orally in front of a group using PowerPoint, while many reports appear as e-mails, memos, and letters. Still others consist primarily of numerical data, such as tax reports or profit-and-loss statements. Although reports vary in length, content, format, organization, and level of formality, they all have one common purpose: they are systematic attempts to answer business questions and solve business problems. In this chapter we'll concentrate on informal reports. These reports tend to be short (under ten pages); use e-mail, memo, or letter format; and are personal in tone.

Most reports can be classified into two functional categories: information reports and analytical reports. Reports that present data without analysis or recommendations are primarily informational. Although writers collect and organize facts, they are not expected to analyze the facts for readers. A trip report describing an employee's visit to a conference, for example, simply presents information. Other reports that present information without analysis involve routine operations, compliance with regulations, and company policies and procedures.

Reports that provide analysis and conclusions as well as data are analytical. If requested, writers also supply recommendations. Analysis is the process of breaking down a problem into its parts in order to understand it better and solve it (for example, each time you write an outline, as shown in Figure 3.4 on page 55, you are analyzing a problem). Analytical reports attempt to persuade readers to act or change their opinions. For example, a recommendation report that compares several potential locations for an employee fitness club might recommend one site, but not until after it has analyzed and discussed the alternatives. This analysis should persuade readers to accept the writer's choice.

WHAT DO ROUTINE BUSINESS REPORTS LOOK LIKE?

How should a report look? The following four formats are frequently used.

- **Letter format** is appropriate for informal reports prepared by one organization for another. These reports are much like letters except that they are more carefully organized, using headings and lists where appropriate.
- **E-mail and memo format** is common for informal reports written for circulation within an organization. These internal reports follow the conventions of e-mails and memos that you learned in Chapter 4—with the addition of headings.
- **Manuscript format** is used for longer, more complicated, and more formal reports. Printed on plain paper, with a cover, title page, executive summary, and table of contents, these reports carefully follow a pattern that is described in detail in Chapters 8 and 9. A sophisticated use of major headings (first level), subheadings (second level), and sub-subheadings (third level) characterizes this format.
- **Prepared forms or templates** are useful in reporting routine activities such as accident reports or merchandise inventories. Standardized headings or fields on these forms (which today are often in digital format) save time for the writer. Forms also make similar information easy to locate.

Today's reports and other business documents are far more sophisticated than typewritten documents of the past. Using a computer, you know how easy it is to make your documents look as if they were professionally printed. In fact, many business reports such as corporate annual reports are not typed; they are designed. As a report writer, you have a wide selection of fonts and formats from which to choose, plus a number of word processing capabilities to fashion attractive documents.

When it comes to the organization of your informal report, you have two choices. Like correspondence discussed earlier in this book, reports may be organized directly or indirectly. The choice rests on the content of your report and the expectations of your audience.

- The **direct pattern** is the most common organizational pattern for business reports. In an informational business report such as a trip report, the report opens with a short introduction, followed by the facts, and finally a summary. Figure 7.2, later in the chapter, shows such a direct-pattern information report. Notice that because it is an e-mail, the writer has dispensed with headings for her three sections. Many businesspeople prefer the direct pattern because it gives them the results of the report immediately. An analytical report may also be organized directly, especially when readers are supportive and familiar with the topic. In an analytical business report such as a recommendation report, the report opens with a short introduction, followed by the conclusions and recommendations, then the facts and findings, and finally the analysis and discussion. Figure 7.4, later in the chapter, shows a direct-pattern analytical report.
- The **indirect pattern** is also used when writing business reports. Information reports are never indirect, but analytical reports may be. The difference between direct and indirect analytical reports is simply the placement of the conclusions and recommendations. In an indirect-pattern report, the introduction comes first, followed by the facts and findings, the analysis and discussion, and only then by the conclusions and recommendations. This pattern is helpful when readers are unfamiliar with the problem. It's also useful when readers must be persuaded or when they may be disappointed, skeptical, or hostile toward the report's findings. A side benefit of the indirect pattern is that it reads like a novel or movie, building "suspense" toward a climax, which is resolved in the conclusions and recommendations.

Figure 7.1 summarizes the questions you should ask yourself about your audience before writing your report, as well as your choices for structuring your informal business report.

HOW TO PLAN AN INFORMAL REPORT

Your natural tendency in preparing a report may be to sit down and begin writing immediately. If you follow this urge, however, you will very likely have to rewrite or even start again. Reports require planning, beginning with defining the project and gathering data. The following guidelines will help you plan your project.

Defining the Project

Begin the process of report writing by defining your project. This definition should include a statement of purpose. Ask yourself: Am I writing this report to inform, to analyze, to solve a problem, or to persuade? The answer to this question should be a clear, accurate statement identifying your purpose. In informal reports the statement of purpose may be only one sentence; that sentence usually becomes part of the introduction. Notice how the following introductory statement describes the purpose of the report:

This report presents information regarding professional development activities coordinated and supervised by the Human Resources Department between the first of the year and the present.

Figure 7.1 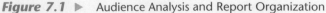 Audience Analysis and Report Organization

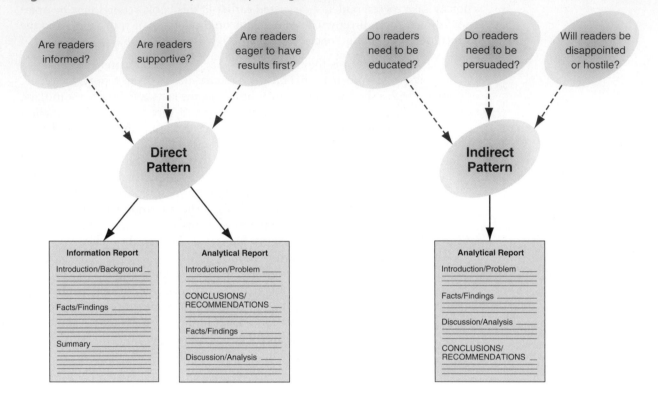

After writing a statement of purpose, analyze who will read your report. If your report is intended for your immediate supervisors and they are supportive of your project, you need not include extensive details, historical development, definition of terms, or persuasion. Other readers, however, may require background information and persuasive strategies.

The expected audience for your report influences your writing style, research method, vocabulary, areas of emphasis, and communication strategy. Remember, too, that your audience may consist of more than one set of readers. Reports are often distributed to secondary readers who may need more details than the primary reader.

Gathering Data

A good report is based on solid, accurate, verifiable facts. Typical sources of factual information for informal reports include company records, observation, surveys, questionnaires, and inventories, interviews, and research.

Company records. Many business-related reports begin with an analysis of company records and files. From these records you can observe past performance and methods used to solve previous problems. You can collect pertinent facts that will help determine a course of action.

Observation. Another logical source of data for many problems lies in personal observation and experience. For example, if you were writing a report on the need for additional computer equipment, you might observe how much the current equipment is being used and for what purpose.

Surveys, questionnaires, and inventories. Primary data from groups of people can be collected most efficiently and economically by using surveys, questionnaires, and inventories. For example, if you were part of a committee investigating the success of a campus recycling program, you might begin by using a questionnaire to survey use of the program by students and faculty. You might also do some informal telephoning to see if departments on campus know about the program and are using it.

Interviews. Talking with individuals directly concerned with the problem produces excellent primary information. For example, in the article above, the Whitecaps may have been able to claim at their press conference that they hoped the development permit would be approved in 2007, based on a discussion with someone in the city of Vancouver's planning department. Interviews also allow for one-on-one communication, thus giving you an opportunity to explain your questions and ideas in eliciting the most accurate information.

Electronic and other research. In doing secondary research information for reports, you would probably be interested in finding examples from other organizations that shed light on the problem identified in your report. You might also check out your competitors to see what they are currently doing and what they have done in the past. An extensive source of current and historical information is available electronically through online library databases and other online resources. From a home, office, or library computer you can obtain access to vast amounts of information provided by governments, newspapers, magazines, and companies from all over the world. For informal reports, the most usable data will probably be found in periodicals and online resources. Chapter 8 contains more detailed suggestions about online research.

Developing an Appropriate Writing Style

Like other business messages, reports can range from informal to formal, depending on their purpose, audience, and setting. Research reports from consultants to their clients tend to be rather formal. Such reports must project an impression of objectivity, authority, and impartiality. But a report to your boss describing a trip to a conference (as in Figure 7.2) would probably have informal elements.

In this chapter we are most concerned with an informal writing style. Your informal reports will probably be written for familiar audiences and involve non-controversial topics. You may use first-person pronouns (*I, we, me, my, us, our*) and contractions (*I'm, we'll*). You'll emphasize active-voice verbs and strive for shorter sentences using familiar words.

Using Headings Effectively

Headings are helpful to both the report reader and the writer. For the reader they serve as an outline of the text, highlighting major ideas and categories. They also act as guides for locating facts and pointing the way through the text. Moreover, headings provide resting points for the mind and for the eye, breaking up large chunks of text into manageable and inviting segments. For the writer, headings force organization of the data into meaningful blocks.

You may choose functional or talking headings. Functional headings (such as *Introduction, Discussion of Findings,* and *Summary*) help the writer outline a report; they are used in the progress report shown in Figure 7.3. But talking headings (such as *Students Perplexed by Shortage of Parking* or *Short-Term Parking*

Solutions) provide more information to the reader. Many of the examples in this chapter use functional headings for the purpose of instruction. To provide even greater clarity, you can make headings both functional and descriptive, such as *Recommendations: Shuttle and New Structures*. Whether your headings are talking or functional, keep them brief and clear. Here are general tips on displaying headings effectively:

- **Consistency.** The cardinal rule of headings is that they should be consistent. In other words, don't use informational headings in three of four cases and a talking heading in the fourth case. Or don't use bolded headings for 80 percent of your report and underlined headings for the other 20 percent.
- **Strive for parallel construction.** Use balanced expressions such as Visible Costs and Invisible Costs rather than Visible Costs and Costs That Don't Show.
- **Use only short first- and second-level headings.** Many short business reports contain only one or two levels of headings. For such reports use first-level headings (centred, bolded) and/or second-level headings (flush left, bolded).
- **Capitalize and underline carefully.** Most writers use all capital letters (without underlines) for main titles, such as the report, chapter, and unit titles. For first- and second-level headings, they capitalize only the first letter of main words. For additional emphasis, they use a bold font.
- **Keep headings short but clear.** Try to make your headings brief (no more than eight words) but understandable. Experiment with headings that concisely tell who, what, when, where, and why.
- **Don't enclose headings in quotation marks.** Quotation marks are appropriate only for marking quoted words or words used in a special sense, such as slang. They are unnecessary in headings.
- **Don't use headings as antecedents for pronouns such as** *this, that, these,* **and** *those.* For example, when the heading reads *Laser Printers*, don't begin the next sentence with *These are often used with desktop publishing software.*

Being Objective

Reports are convincing only when the facts are believable and the writer is credible. You can build credibility in a number of ways:

- **Present both sides of an issue.** Even if you favour one possibility, discuss both sides and show through logical reasoning why your position is superior. Remain impartial, letting the facts prove your point.
- **Separate fact from opinion.** Suppose a supervisor wrote, "Our department works harder and gets less credit than any other department in the company." This opinion is difficult to prove, and it damages the credibility of the writer. A more convincing statement might be "Our productivity has increased six percent over the past year, and I'm proud of the extra effort my employees are making." After you've made a claim or presented an important statement in a report, ask yourself: Is this a verifiable fact? If the answer is no, rephrase your statement to make it sound more reasonable.
- **Be sensitive and moderate in your choice of language.** Don't exaggerate. Instead of saying "Most people think...", it might be more accurate to say "Some people think...." Obviously, avoid using labels and slanted expressions. Calling someone an *idiot*, a *techie*, or an *elitist* demonstrates bias. If readers suspect that a writer is prejudiced, they may discount the entire argument.
- **Cite sources.** Tell your readers where the information came from by using lead-ins to your quotations and paraphrases, and by citing your sources. If

you don't do so, you are probably guilty of plagiarism, which is discussed in more detail in Chapter 8. For example, in a report that reads, "In a recent *Vancouver Province* article, Blake Spence, Director of Transportation, argues that the Sky Train must be expanded to cope with the influx of tourists expected during the 2010 Olympics (A17)," "Blake Spence ... argues that" is the lead-in, and "(A17)" is the page reference. Together these two elements are a citation.

SIX COMMON ROUTINE BUSINESS REPORTS

You are about to examine six types of informal report frequently written in business. In some instances the types overlap; distinctions are not always clear-cut. For example, it's sometimes difficult to distinguish between a justification report and a feasibility report. Similarly, an information report may be the same thing as a summary report in some circumstances. Individual situations, goals, and needs may make one report take on some characteristics of a different type of report. Still, these common types, presented here in a brief overview, are helpful to beginning writers. The reports will be illustrated and discussed in more detail below.

- **Information reports.** Reports that collect and organize information are informative or investigative. They may record routine activities such as daily, weekly, and monthly reports of sales or profits. They may investigate options, performance, or equipment. Although they provide information, they do not analyze that information.
- **Progress reports.** Progress reports monitor the headway of unusual or non-routine activities. For example, progress reports would keep management informed about a committee's preparations for a trade show 14 months from now. As we saw in the *Vancouver Sun* article above, such reports usually try to answer three questions: Is the project on schedule? Are corrective measures needed? What activities are next?
- **Justification/recommendation reports.** Recommendation and justification reports are similar to information reports in that they present information. However, they offer analysis in addition to data. They attempt to solve problems by evaluating options and offering recommendations. Usually these reports revolve around a significant company decision.
- **Feasibility reports.** When a company or organization must decide whether to proceed with a plan of action based on a previously accepted recommendation, it may require a feasibility report that establishes how possible the plan is. For example, a company has decided to redesign its website, but how feasible is it to have the redesign accomplished in six months' time? A feasibility report would examine the practicality of implementing the recommendation or proposal.
- **Summary reports.** A summary condenses the primary ideas, conclusions, and recommendations of a longer report or publication. Employees may be asked to write summaries of technical or research reports. Students may be asked to write summaries of periodical articles or books to sharpen their writing skills.
- **Minutes of meetings.** A final type of informal report is "the minutes" of a meeting. This is a record of the proceedings and action points of a meeting. Although informal business meetings today take place without minutes being recorded, many companies, organizations, clubs, committees, and boards still require minutes to be recorded. The person delegated to take notes at a

meeting usually turns them into the minutes, distributes them to the participants after the meeting, asks for revisions, and then files the report. You'll find more information on meetings in Chapter 11.

Information Reports

Writers of information reports provide information without drawing conclusions or making recommendations. Some information reports are highly standardized, such as police reports, hospital admittance reports, accident reports, monthly sales reports, or statistical reports on government program use. Many of these are fill-in reports using prepared forms or templates for recurring data and situations. Other information reports, such as conference reports, are more personalized, as illustrated below in Figure 7.2. They often include these sections:

Introduction. The introduction to an information report may be called *Introduction* or *Background.* In this section do the following: explain why you are writing, describe what methods and sources were used to gather information and why they are credible, provide any special background information that may be necessary, give the purpose of the report, if known, and offer a preview of your findings. You'll notice in Figure 7.2 that not all five of these criteria are met, nor is a heading included, because it is a short informal information report. However, if you were writing an information report for a client in letter format, you would use the heading "Introduction" and try to fit in all five criteria.

Findings. The findings section of a report may also be called *Observations*, *Facts*, *Results*, or *Discussion.* Important points to consider in this section are organization and display. Consider one of these methods of organization: chronological, alphabetical, topical, or most to least important. You'll notice that in Figure 7.2, the writer uses a chronological method of organization.

To display the findings effectively, number paragraphs, underline or boldface keywords, or use other graphic highlighting methods such as bullets. Be sure that words used as headings are parallel in structure. If the findings require elaboration, either include this discussion with each segment of the findings or place it in a separate section entitled *Discussion.*

Summary. A summary section is optional. If it is included, use it to summarize your findings objectively and impartially. The information report shown in Figure 7.2 summarizes the facts laid out in bullet format by looking for commonalities (networking opportunities) and putting these facts into perspective (all Expo events led to exposure for Nancy's company). In addition, the significance of the facts is explained (Nancy may have found some new products for her company to sell in Canada).

Notice how easy this information report is to read. Short paragraphs, ample use of graphic highlighting, white space, and concise writing all contribute to improved readability.

Progress Reports

Progress reports, like the one you learned about in the article about the Vancouver Whitecaps soccer club, describe the progress being made in both routine and non-routine projects. Most progress reports include these four parts:

- The purpose and nature of the project
- A complete summary of the work already completed

Figure 7.2 ▶ Information Report—E-Mail Format

Software Expo 07 Report

File Edit View Insert Format Tools Actions Help

Reply | Reply to All | Forward

From: Nancy Pinto <npinto@softsolutions.ca>   Sent: June 30, 2007

To: Mitch Freeman <mfreeman@softsolutions.ca>

Cc:

Subject: Software Expo 07 Report

Hi Mr. Freeman,

As requested, here's a brief trip report describing the details of my recent time spent at Software Expo 07 in San Francisco.

I arrived in San Francisco on June 18 and, after lunch, began attending expo activities:

- Microsoft Seminar—info on expected launch of Windows 07 (June 18 pm)

- Breakfast Meeting—Jerry Schwartz of AccPac (June 19 am)

- Industry Roundtable on the Future of Accounting Software—useful networking opportunity (June 19 am)

- Lunch Meeting—Lisa O'Toole of Microsoft (June 19 pm)

- Software Fair—useful networking opportunity (June 19 pm)

- Dinner Meeting—Tom Nzobugu and Bill McKay of SAS (June 19 pm)

In essence, Software Expo continues to be a great networking opportunity. It's important for our company to have a presence at this high-profile show, especially because of the competitive nature of our business. I made a number of useful contacts, and I think I've located two hot new software products without current licensing or sales and distribution agreements in Canada.

Regards,

Nancy

- A thorough description of work currently in progress, including personnel, methods, and obstacles, as well as attempts to remedy obstacles
- A forecast of future activities in relation to the scheduled completion date, including recommendations and requests

Progress reports are increasingly important in the business world—for example, they are mentioned frequently in job descriptions—partly because of the nature of the business world. Many businesses today run on a project management basis. Project management is a workplace innovation of the past decade in which "modern management techniques" such as "directing and coordinating human and material resources throughout a project's life" are used to "achieve project objectives."[1] One of the main tools of successfully run projects is progress reports. Therefore, knowing how to write them is a valuable asset for a business school graduate.

In Figure 7.3 Maria Robinson explains the construction of a realty company branch office. She begins with a statement summarizing the construction progress in relation to the expected completion date. She then updates the reader with a brief recap of past progress. She emphasizes the present status of construction and concludes by describing the next steps to be taken.

Justification/Recommendation Reports

Some business communicators use progress reports to do more than merely report progress. These reports can also be used to offer ideas and suggest possibilities. Let's say you are reporting on the progress of redesigning the company website. You might suggest a different way to handle customer responses. Instead of making an official recommendation, which might be rejected, you can lay the foundation for a change within your progress report. Progress reports can also be used to build the image of a dedicated, conscientious employee.

Both managers and employees must occasionally write reports that justify or recommend something, such as buying equipment, changing a procedure, hiring an employee, consolidating departments, or investing funds. Large organizations sometimes prescribe how these reports should be organized; they use forms with conventional headings. At other times, such reports are not standardized. For example, an employee takes it upon himself to write a report suggesting improvements in telephone customer service because he feels strongly enough about it. When you are free to select an organizational plan yourself, however, let your audience and topic determine your choice of direct or indirect structure.

For non-sensitive topics and recommendations that will be agreeable to readers, you can organize directly according to the following sequence:

- In the introduction identify the problem or need briefly.
- Announce the recommendation, solution, or action concisely and with action verbs.
- Discuss pros, cons, and costs. Explain more fully the benefits of the recommendation or steps to be taken to solve the problem.
- Conclude with a summary specifying the recommendation and action to be taken.

Justin Brown applied the preceding process in writing the recommendation report shown in Figure 7.4. Justin is operations manager in charge of a fleet of trucks for a large parcel delivery company in Richmond, B.C. When he heard about a new Goodyear smart tire with an electronic chip, Justin thought his company should give the new tire a try. His recommendation report begins with a short introduction to the problem followed by his two recommendations. Then he explains the product and how it would benefit his company. He concludes by highlighting his recommendation and specifying the action to be taken.

Feasibility Reports

Feasibility reports examine the practicality and advisability of following a course of action. They answer this question: Will this plan or proposal work? Feasibility reports are typically internal reports written to advise on matters such as consolidating departments, offering a wellness program to employees, or hiring an outside firm to handle a company's accounting or computing operations. These reports may also be written by consultants called in to investigate a problem. The

Figure 7.3 ▶ Progress Report

CONSTRUCTION PROGRESS OF MISSISSAUGA BRANCH OFFICE

File Edit View Insert Format Tools Actions Help

Reply | Reply to All | Forward

From: Maria Robinson <mrobinson@prealty.ca>   Sent: April 20, 2007
To: Dorothy Prevatt <dprevatt@prealty.ca>
Cc:
Subject: CONSTRUCTION PROGRESS OF MISSISSAUGA BRANCH OFFICE

Dear Ms. Prevatt,

Construction of Prevatt Realty's Mississauga branch office has entered Phase 3. Although we are one week behind the contractor's original schedule, the building should be ready for occupancy August 15.

Past Progress

Phase 1 involved development of the architect's plans; this process was completed February 5. Phase 2 involved submission of the plans for local building permit approval. The plans were then given to four contractors for estimates. The lowest bidder was Holst Brothers Contractors. This firm began construction on March 25.

Present Status

Phase 3 includes initial construction procedures. The following steps have been completed as of April 20:

1. Demolition of existing building 273 Lakeshore Boulevard
2. Excavation of foundation footings for the building and for the surrounding wall
3. Installation of steel reinforcing rods in building pad and wall
4. Pouring of concrete foundation

The contractor indicated that he was one week behind schedule for the following reasons:

1. The building inspectors required additional steel reinforcement not shown on the architect's blueprints.
2. The excavation of the footings required more time than the contractor anticipated because the Number 4 footings were all below grade.

Future Schedule

Despite some time lost in Phase 3, we are substantially on target for the completion of this office building by August 1. Phase 4 includes framing, drywalling, and plumbing.

Introduces report with a summary

Describes completed work concisely

Itemizes current activities

Projects future activities

Tips for Writing Progress Reports

- Identify the purpose and the nature of the project immediately.
- Supply background information only if the reader must be educated.
- Describe the work completed.
- Discuss the work in progress, including personnel, activities, methods, and locations.
- Identify problems and possible remedies.
- Consider future activities.
- Close by giving the expected date of completion.

Figure 7.4 ▶ Justification/Recommendation Report—Memo Format

Applies memo format for short informal internal report

Presents recommendations immediately

Justifies recommendation by explaining product and benefits

Explains recommendation in more detail

Introduces problem briefly

Enumerates items for maximum impact and readability

Specifies action to be taken

Interoffice Memo    **Pacific Trucking, Inc.**

DATE: July 19, 2007
TO: Bill Montgomery, Vice President
FROM: Justin Brown, Operations Manager   𝒥ℬ
SUBJECT: Pilot Testing Smart Tires

Next to fuel, truck tires are our biggest operating cost. Last year we spent $211 000 replacing and retreading tires for 495 trucks. This year the costs will be greater because prices have jumped at least 12 percent and because we've increased our fleet to 550 trucks. Truck tires are an additional burden since they require labour-intensive paperwork to track their warranties, wear, and retread histories. To reduce our long-term costs and to improve our tire tracking system, I recommend that we do the following:

- Purchase 24 Goodyear smart tires.
- Begin a one-year pilot test on four trucks.

How Smart Tires Work

Smart tires have an embedded computer chip that monitors wear, performance, and durability. The chip also creates an electronic fingerprint for positive identification of a tire. By passing a hand-held sensor next to the tire, we can learn where and when a tire was made (for warranty and other information), how much tread it had originally, and its serial number.

How Smart Tires Could Benefit Us

Although smart tires are initially more expensive than other tires, they could help us improve our operations and save us money in four ways:

1. **Retreads.** Goodyear believes that the wear data is so accurate that we should be able to retread every tire three times, instead of our current two times. If that's true, in one year we could save at least $27 000 in new tire costs.
2. **Safety.** Accurate and accessible wear data should reduce the danger of blowouts and flat tires. Last year, drivers reported six blowouts.
3. **Record keeping and maintenance.** Smart tires could reduce our maintenance costs considerably. Currently, we use an electric branding iron to mark serial numbers on new tires. Our biggest headache is manually reading those serial numbers, decoding them, and maintaining records to meet safety regulations. Reading such data electronically could save us thousands of dollars in labour.
4. **Theft protection.** The chip can be used to monitor each tire as it leaves or enters the warehouse or yard, thus discouraging theft.

Summary and Action

Specifically, I recommend that you do the following:
- Authorize the special purchase of 24 Goodyear smart tires at $450 each, plus one electronic sensor at $1 200.
- Approve a one-year pilot test in our Lower Mainland territory that equips four trucks with smart tires and tracks their performance.

Tips for Memo Reports

- **Use memo format for most short (ten or fewer pages) informal reports within an organization.**
- **Leave side margins of 2.5 to 3 cm.**
- **Sign your initials on the FROM line.**
- **Use an informal, conversational style.**
- **For a receptive audience, put recommendations first.**
- **For an unreceptive audience, put recommendations last.**

focus in these reports is on the decision: stopping or proceeding with the proposal. Since your role is not to persuade the reader to accept the decision, you'll want to present the decision immediately. In writing feasibility reports, consider this plan:

- Announce your decision immediately.
- Describe the background and problem necessitating the proposal.
- Discuss the benefits of the proposal.
- Describe any problems that may result.
- Calculate the costs associated with the proposal, if appropriate.
- Show the time frame necessary for implementation of the proposal.

Elizabeth Webb, customer service manager for a large insurance company in London, Ontario, wrote the feasibility report shown in Figure 7.5. Because her company had been losing customer service reps (CSRs) after they were trained, she talked with the vice president about the problem. He didn't want her to take time away from her job to investigate what other companies were doing to retain their CSRs. Instead, he suggested that they hire a consultant to investigate what other companies were doing to keep their CSRs. The vice president then wanted to know whether the consultant's plan was feasible. Although Elizabeth's report is only one page long, it provides all the necessary information: background, benefits, problems, costs, and time frame.

Summary Reports

In today's knowledge economy, information is what drives organizations. Information is important because without it, business decisions cannot be made. Because there is a huge amount of information available today on any given topic (e.g., the millions of pages of Web material), people who make decisions don't always have the time to read and review all the information on a particular problem, issue, or topic. Therefore, decision makers need the essential elements of an issue or problem presented in a short, logical, easy-to-understand format that helps them quickly grasp what's vital.

Any time you take what someone else has written or said and reduce it to a concise, accurate, and faithful version of the original—in your own words—you are summarizing. A well-written summary report does three things: it provides all the important points from the original without introducing new material; it has a clear structure that often reflects the structure of the original material; and it is independent of the original, meaning the reader of the summary can glean all essential information in the original without having to refer to it.

The ability to summarize well is a valuable skill for a number of reasons. Businesspeople are under pressure today to make decisions based on more information than ever before. Someone who can summarize that information into its key parts is way ahead of someone who cannot. Second, summarizing is a key communication task in many businesses today. For example, a financial adviser must be able to summarize reports on mutual funds and stocks so that her client can understand what's truly important. Third, the ability to summarize makes you a better writer. As you learn to pick apart the structure of articles, reports, and essays written by professional writers such as journalists, for example, you can introduce their tricks of the trade into your own writing. Finally, as part of writing the more complex reports discussed in Chapter 8 and 9, you will have to write executive summaries of your own work. Why not learn how to do this by summarizing other people's writing first?

There are four steps to writing an effective summary:

- **Read the material carefully for understanding.** Ideally, you will read the original three times. The first time you read to understand the topic. The second

Figure 7.5 ▶   Feasibility Report—E-Mail Format

Outlines organization of report →

Reveals decision immediately →

Describes problem and background →

Evaluates positive and negative aspects of proposal objectively →

Presents costs and schedule; omits unnecessary summary →

FEASIBILITY OF PROGRESSION SCHEDULE FOR CSRs

File   Edit   View   Insert   Format   Tools   Actions   Help

Reply | Reply to All | Forward

From: Elizabeth W. Webb <ewebb@bmc.ca>   Sent: November 11, 2007
To: Shawn Clay-Taylor <sclaytaylor@bmc.ca>
Cc:
Subject: FEASIBILITY OF PROGRESSION SCHEDULE FOR CSRs

Hi Shawn

The plan calling for a progression schedule for our customer service representatives is workable, and I think it could be fully implemented by April 1. This report discusses the background, benefits, problems, costs, and time frame involved in executing the plan.

Background: Training and Advancement Problems for CSRs. Because of the many insurance policies and agents we service, new customer service representatives require eight weeks of intensive training. Even after this thorough introduction, CSRs are overwhelmed. They take about eight more months before feeling competent on the job. Once they reach their potential, they often look for other positions in the company because they see few advancement possibilities in customer service. These problems were submitted to an outside consultant, who suggested a CSR progression schedule.

Benefits of Plan: Career Progression and Incremental Training. The proposed plan sets up a schedule of career progression, including these levels: (1) CSR trainee, (2) CSR Level I, (3) CSR Level II, (4) CSR Level III, (5) Senior CSR, and (6) CSR supervisor. This program, which includes salary increments with each step, provides a career ladder and incentives for increased levels of expertise and achievement. The plan also facilitates training. Instead of overloading a new trainee with an initial eight-week training program, we would train CSRs slowly with a combination of classroom and on-the-job experiences. Each level requires additional training and expertise.

Problems of Plan: Difficulty in Writing Job Descriptions and Initial Confusion. One of the biggest problems will be distinguishing the job duties at each level. However, I believe that, with the help of our consultant, we can sort out the tasks and expertise required at each level. Another problem will be determining appropriate salary differentials. Attached is a tentative schedule showing proposed wages at each level. We expect to encounter confusion and frustration in implementing this program at first, particularly in placing our current CSRs within the structure.

Costs. Implementing the progression schedule involves two direct costs. The first is the salary of a trainer, at about $40 000 a year. The second cost derives from increased salaries of upper-level CSRs, shown on the attached schedule. I believe, however, that the costs involved are within the estimates planned for this project.

Time Frame. Developing job descriptions should take us about three weeks. Preparing a training program will require another three weeks. Once the program is started, I expect a breaking-in period of at least three months. By April 1 the progression schedule will be fully implemented and showing positive results in improved CSR training, service, and retention.

Attachment

time you read with a pen, pencil, or highlighter in hand and you underline the main points (usually no more than three in an article-length piece). Finally, you should read again and underline or flag connections, patterns such as lists, contradictions, and similarities. These are often the sites of main points.

- **Lay out the structure of your summary.** This step is easy to accomplish. You simply write the main points you've underlined in the first step in a list. For example, the person summarizing the *Toronto Star* article in Figure 7.6 has identified three main points (MP), three contradictions (C), and two patterns (P). To lay out the structure of his summary, he would simply write:

  1. The federal government's retail debt program is costly, is unsustainable, and should be phased out.
  2. There are three reasons why sales of Canada Savings Bonds are falling: lower interest rates, aggressive competition from banks, and more choices for investors.
  3. The Canada Savings Bonds program is costly because marketing is expensive, the transaction costs are high, and there's little accountability to taxpayers.

- **Write a first draft.** In this step, you take your list from the step before (which uses the original author's exact language in many parts) and convert it into your own words. Our summary writer might write something like this:

  As requested, I've researched the topic of current opinion on the value of Canada Savings Bonds.

  The most useful article I found was by Ellen Roseman of the Toronto Star. *In her article called, "Report queries value of Canada Savings Bonds" (Sept. 15, 2004), Roseman makes 1 main point and supports her point with 2 types of evidence.*

    - *Roseman's main point is that the CSB program is too expensive, does not pay for itself, and it should be eliminated. She bases her argument on an analysis of a report published by the consulting firm Cap Gemini Ernst & Young on January 31, which is now available on the ministry of finance's website.*
    - *The first argument Roseman uses to support her main point is that sales of CSBs has been falling steadily. This decline in sales is due to low interest rates, strong competition from the banking sector, and a wide choice of competing products for consumers.*
    - *The second argument Roseman makes to support her main point are that costs are up at the same time as sales are down. She attributes these costs to 3 main factors: the high cost of marketing the bonds, the high cost of transactions, and a lack of accountability on the part of the people who run the program and whose expenses appear to be out of control.*

  I appreciated the opportunity to provide this summary. If there's anything else you need, please let me know.

  Sincerely,

  Brent Bingley

- **Proofread and revise.** The final step of writing a summary, like any written document, is to proofread for grammar, spelling, punctuation, and style mistakes and to rewrite where necessary. In the example above, *the* summary writer found a number of mistakes in his draft. He judged the phrase the *topic of current opinion on* to be wordy and rewrote it as *current opinion on*. He likewise found the word *called* to be wordy and deleted it. There are three instances where he should have written a number as a word instead of in numerical format. He also found a parallelism problem and changed *it should* to *should*. The phrase *ministry of finance* was spelled incorrectly, without capitals. Finally, two subject-verb agreement errors resulted in a change in verb tense to *have* from *has* and to *is* from *are*.

A final proofread and revised version of this descriptive summary report appears in Figure 7.7.

Figure 7.6 ▶
Article for Summary

Report queries value of Canada Savings Bonds

Ellen Roseman

Just before the Labour Day weekend, the federal government released a disturbing assessment of the Canada Savings Bond program.

Three-and-a-half million Canadians own the savings bonds, first offered in 1946. They are seen as secure and easily cashable.

But, according to consulting firm Cap Gemini Ernst & Young, the federal government's retail debt program is costly, unsustainable and should be phased out.

Finance Minister Ralph Goodale responded by saying he wouldn't make any changes at this time. The 2004-2005 sales campaign would go on as planned next month.

But I guarantee you'll think twice about the program's value if you read the Cap Gemini report.

You'll find it on the Internet at the finance department's website, www.fin.gc.ca. Make sure you search for the 164-page appendices, which I found far more interesting than the summarized 36-page final report.

Cap Gemini finished its work on Jan. 31, but the release was delayed until after the June 28 federal election.

"This certainly cuts into Paul Martin's image as a deficit fighter in the 1990s," says freedom-of-information activist Ken Rubin, who pushed for the report's publication (and is challenging the parts that were omitted).

Let's start with the Canada Investment and Savings Agency, set up in 1995 as a special operating agency within the finance department.

Its mandate was to reverse the declining trend in the holding of federal securities by individual investors.

At the time, the CSB campaign had $3.5 billion in gross sales. Today, sales are still stuck in the range of $2.8 billion to $3.5 billion a year.

The relaunch did not reverse the declining trend. And the addition of new products, such as the less cashable Canada Premium Bond designed for registered plans, simply cannibalized sales of regular savings bonds.

"The $2.2 billion drop in sales from 1998-1999 to 1999-2000 has not been recovered," Cap Gemini said.

"Management was not successful in meeting its targets, demonstrating an inability to predict the sales. The targets were lowered from 2000 onward, indicating that the program is no longer aiming to grow or even retain the stock."

Why are sales falling? You can name a few reasons without having to think too hard:

★ Lower interest rates. Recent savings bonds yielded 1.25 per cent in the first year, while the premium bonds yielded 2 per cent in the first year — less than what you could earn with a premium savings account.

★ Aggressive competition from banks. They currently pay 3.25 per cent on a five-year guaranteed investment certificate, compared with 2.79 per cent on an escalating-rate premium bond held for five years. And bank customers can get a bonus of a quarter to half a per cent above the posted GIC rate if they haggle.

★ More choices for investors, who are buying Government of Canada bonds through mutual funds or directly from investment dealers. These provide higher returns, though prices fluctuate.

When former finance minister and now Prime Minister Paul Martin set up the agency, the federal debt was high and rising and interest rates had moved sharply higher.

Today, with seven budget surpluses in a row, the government has less need to sustain a broad investor base.

"There is an insurance value in keeping this channel open," the finance department said in a release this month.

But consider the following when analyzing the costs and benefits of Canada Savings Bonds.

First damning argument: Marketing is expensive. The Canada Investment and Savings Agency's costs fell by only 1 per cent from 1997-1998 to 2002-2003. What was saved on media advertising was offset by higher commissions and bonuses paid to the sales force.

Second damning argument: Savings bonds sold through employers are used as savings accounts. This means high transaction costs, as investors redeem often and in small amounts. Sales and redemptions were equal in 2003, cancelling out the value of this distribution channel.

Third damning argument: There's little accountability to taxpayers. The agency's operations were not reviewed after five years, as dictated by its charter document. And the chief executive has kept her job for eight years, despite declining sales and market share.

I asked Goodale's office about the review of the retail debt program. It hasn't started yet, I was told yesterday, despite the fact the report has been in hand since the beginning of the year.

Exactly how much money is being lost on the marketing of Canada Savings Bonds? Even Cap Gemini couldn't figure that one out.

"The business plans and financial statements do not provide stakeholders with sufficient information to understand the objectives, performance or overall subsidy provided by government," the report concluded. Read it and weep.

Figure 7.7 ▶ Summary Report—E-Mail Format

✉ CSB Summary You Requested   ⊟ ☐ ⊠

File   Edit   View   Insert   Format   Tools   Actions   Help

Reply | Reply to All | Forward | ...

From:	Brent Bingley <bingleb@bmc.ca>	Sent: May 9, 2007
To:	John Swiderski <swidersj@bmc.ca>	
Cc:		
Subject:	CSB Summary You Requested	

Dear John,

As requested, I've researched current opinion on the value of Canada Savings Bonds.

The most useful article I found was by Ellen Roseman of the *Toronto Star*. In her article, "Report queries value of Canada Savings Bonds" (Sept. 15, 2004), Roseman makes one main point and supports her point with two types of evidence.

- Roseman's main point is that the CSB program is too expensive, does not pay for itself, and should be eliminated. She bases her argument on an analysis of a report published by the consulting firm Cap Gemini Ernst & Young on January 31, which is now available on the Ministry of Finance's website.

- The first argument Roseman uses to support her main point is that sales of CSBs have been falling steadily. This decline in sales is due to low interest rates, strong competition from the banking sector, and a wide choice of competing products for consumers.

- The second argument Roseman makes to support her main point is that costs are up at the same time as sales are down. She attributes these costs to three main factors: the high cost of marketing the bonds, the high cost of transactions, and a lack of accountability on the part of the people who run the program and whose expenses appear to be out of control.

I appreciated the opportunity to provide this summary. If there's anything else you need, please let me know.

Sincerely,

Brent

Minutes of Meetings

Minutes provide a summary of the proceedings of meetings. Formal, traditional minutes, illustrated in Figure 7.8, are written for large groups and legislative bodies. If you are the secretary of a meeting, you'll want to write minutes that do the following:

- Provide the name of the group, as well as the date, time, and place of the meeting.
- Identify the names of attendees and absentees, if appropriate.
- Describe the disposition of previous minutes.
- Record old business, new business, announcements, and reports.

- Include the precise wording of motions; record the vote and action taken.
- Conclude with the name and signature of the person recording the minutes.

Notice in Figure 7.8 that secretary Carol Allen tries to summarize discussions rather than capture every comment. However, when a motion is made, she records it verbatim. She also shows in parentheses the name of the individual making the motion and the person who seconded it. By using all capital letters for "MOTION" and "PASSED," she makes these important items stand out for easy reference.

Figure 7.8 ▶ Minutes of Meeting—Report Format

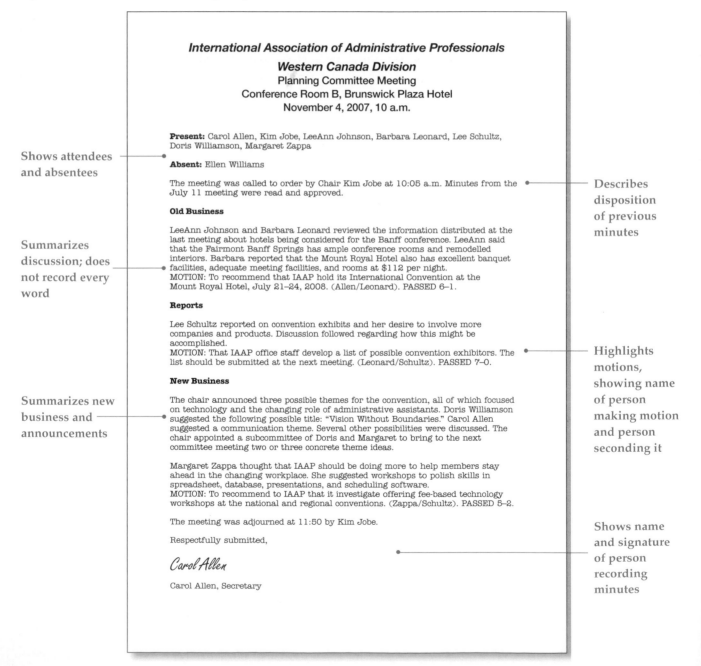

Shows attendees and absentees

Summarizes discussion; does not record every word

Summarizes new business and announcements

Describes disposition of previous minutes

Highlights motions, showing name of person making motion and person seconding it

Shows name and signature of person recording minutes

International Association of Administrative Professionals

Western Canada Division
Planning Committee Meeting
Conference Room B, Brunswick Plaza Hotel
November 4, 2007, 10 a.m.

Present: Carol Allen, Kim Jobe, LeeAnn Johnson, Barbara Leonard, Lee Schultz, Doris Williamson, Margaret Zappa

Absent: Ellen Williams

The meeting was called to order by Chair Kim Jobe at 10:05 a.m. Minutes from the July 11 meeting were read and approved.

Old Business

LeeAnn Johnson and Barbara Leonard reviewed the information distributed at the last meeting about hotels being considered for the Banff conference. LeeAnn said that the Fairmont Banff Springs has ample conference rooms and remodelled interiors. Barbara reported that the Mount Royal Hotel also has excellent banquet facilities, adequate meeting facilities, and rooms at $112 per night.
MOTION: To recommend that IAAP hold its International Convention at the Mount Royal Hotel, July 21–24, 2008. (Allen/Leonard). PASSED 6–1.

Reports

Lee Schultz reported on convention exhibits and her desire to involve more companies and products. Discussion followed regarding how this might be accomplished.
MOTION: That IAAP office staff develop a list of possible convention exhibitors. The list should be submitted at the next meeting. (Leonard/Schultz). PASSED 7–0.

New Business

The chair announced three possible themes for the convention, all of which focused on technology and the changing role of administrative assistants. Doris Williamson suggested the following possible title: "Vision Without Boundaries." Carol Allen suggested a communication theme. Several other possibilities were discussed. The chair appointed a subcommittee of Doris and Margaret to bring to the next committee meeting two or three concrete theme ideas.

Margaret Zappa thought that IAAP should be doing more to help members stay ahead in the changing workplace. She suggested workshops to polish skills in spreadsheet, database, presentations, and scheduling software.
MOTION: To recommend to IAAP that it investigate offering fee-based technology workshops at the national and regional conventions. (Zappa/Schultz). PASSED 5–2.

The meeting was adjourned at 11:50 by Kim Jobe.

Respectfully submitted,

Carol Allen

Carol Allen, Secretary

Informal minutes are usually shorter and easier to read than formal minutes. For example, in most business meetings you'll attend, motions aren't passed. Rather, action items are decided upon, and a person or team of people is assigned responsibility for that action item. Therefore, a more informal minutes report, such as the one in Figure 7.9, would be formatted with three categories: summary of topics discussed, summary of decisions reached, and action items (showing the action item, the person responsible, and the due date).

ROUTINE BUSINESS PROPOSALS

Proposals are persuasive offers to solve problems, provide services, or sell equipment or other products. Let's say that the City of Fredericton wants to upgrade the computers and software in its human resources department. If it knows exactly

Figure 7.9 ▶ Minutes of Meeting—Informal Report

Meeting Minutes
Promotions/Events Team, CFTV Montreal
July 3, 2007 1:00 pm - 2:00 pm

Present: Melodee Macpherson, Francine Theriault, Ali Hamid

Regrets: Bill Todd

Main topics discussed

The meeting covered two main topics: our upcoming Back-to-School promotion in cooperation with a number of West Island schools, and the state of our partnership with the Montreal Film Festival.

Decisions reached

The team feels it is on schedule with all tasks undertaken for the Back-to-School promotion. Melodee pointed out that one potential trouble spot is that activist organization Free Schools (which campaigns against commercial encroachment in public schools) has heard about the promotion and may be formulating a protest of some sort. The team decided to renew its participation with the Montreal Film Festival as media sponsor.

Actions items

Melodee: Will contact Free Schools and attempt to arrange a meeting in order to forestall negative publicity around the Back-to-School promotion. Deadline: July 10, 2007

Francine: Will contact Thierry at MFF to confirm participation as media sponsor. Deadline: July 5, 2007

Next meeting

July 10, 2007
1:00 pm
Conference room

what it wants, it would prepare a request for proposal (RFP) specifying its requirements. It then publicizes the RFP, and companies interested in bidding on the job submit proposals. RFPs are traditionally publicized in newspapers, but increasingly on special websites, such as <www.merx.com>, which is the best-known Canadian site.

Both large and small companies, organizations, and agencies are increasingly likely to use RFPs to solicit competitive bids on their projects. This enables them to compare "apples to apples." That is, they can compare the prices different companies would charge for completing the same project. RFPs also work for companies in situations where needs are not clear. An RFP can be issued stating broad expectations and goals within which bidding companies offer innovative solutions and price quotes. In most cases, a proposal also acts as a legal statement of work from which a contract for services is developed.

Many companies earn a sizable portion of their income from sales resulting from proposals. It's important to realize that not all proposals are solicited, in other words published in the newspaper or on websites. Unsolicited proposals are also important business documents. For example, if I'm a consultant who specializes in coaching and team-building skills, I can send an unsolicited proposal to a large organization like a bank, offering my services.

Whether they are solicited or unsolicited, the ability to write effective proposals is especially important today. In writing proposals, the most important thing to remember is that they are sales presentations. They must be persuasive, not merely mechanical descriptions of what you can do. You may recall from Chapter 5 that effective persuasive sales messages build interest by emphasizing benefits for the reader, reduce resistance by detailing your expertise and accomplishments, and motivate action by making it easy for the reader to understand and respond.

Proposals may be routine or formal; they differ primarily in length and format. Routine proposals are often presented in letter format. Sometimes called letter proposals, they contain six principal parts: introduction, background, proposal, staffing, budget, and authorization. The informal letter proposal shown in Figure 7.10 illustrates all six parts of a letter proposal. This proposal is addressed to a Calgary dentist who wants to improve patient satisfaction.

Introduction. Most proposals begin by explaining briefly the reasons for the proposal and by highlighting the writer's qualifications. To make your introduction more persuasive, use persuasive techniques to gain the reader's attention. One proposal expert suggests these possibilities:

- Hint at extraordinary results with details to be revealed shortly.
- Promise low costs or speedy results.
- Mention a remarkable resource (well-known authority, new computer program, well-trained staff) available exclusively to you.
- Identify a serious problem (worry item) and promise a solution, to be explained later.
- Specify a key issue or benefit that you feel is the heart of the proposal.[2]

For example, Dana Swensen, in the introduction of the proposal shown in Figure 7.10, focused on a key benefit. In this proposal to conduct a patient satisfaction survey, Dana thought that the client, Dr. Larocque, would be most interested in specific recommendations for improving service to her patients. But Dana didn't hit on this benefit until after the first draft had been written. Indeed, it's often a good idea to put off writing the introduction to a proposal until after you

Plan, schedule. In the plan section itself, you should discuss your proposal for solving the problem. In some proposals this is tricky because you want to disclose enough of your plan to secure the contract without giving away so much information that your services aren't needed. Without specifics, though, your proposal has little chance, so you must decide how much to reveal. Explain what you propose to do and how it will benefit the reader. Remember, too, that a proposal is a sales presentation. Sell your methods, product, and "deliverables"—items that will be left with the client. In this section some writers specify how the project will be managed, how its progress will be audited, and what milestones along the way will indicate the project is progressing as planned. Most writers also include a schedule of activities or a timetable showing when events take place.

Staffing. The staffing section of a proposal describes the credentials and expertise of the project leaders and the company as a whole. A well-written staffing section describes the capabilities of the whole company. Although the example in Figure 7.10 does not do so, staffing sections often list other high-profile jobs that have been undertaken by the company, as a way of building interest and reducing resistance. For example, before she mentioned Dr. Miller and Dr. Malau, Dana Swensen could have said, "Among our well-known clients are Husky Energy and the Calgary Board of Education."

This section may also identify the size and qualifications of the support staff, along with other resources such as computer facilities and special programs for analyzing statistics. In longer proposals, résumés of key people may be provided. The staffing or personnel section is a good place to endorse and promote your staff.

Budget. A central item in most proposals is the budget, a list of project costs. You need to prepare this section carefully because it represents a contract; you can't raise the price later, even if your costs increase. You can—and should—protect yourself with a deadline for acceptance. In the budget section some writers itemize hours and costs; others present a total sum only. A proposal to install a complex computer system might, for example, contain a detailed line-by-line budget.

In the proposal shown in Figure 7.10, Dana Swensen felt that she needed to justify the budget for her firm's patient satisfaction survey, so she itemized the costs. But the budget included for a proposal to conduct a one-day seminar to improve employee communication skills might be a lump sum only. Your analysis of the project will help you decide what kind of budget to prepare.

Authorization. Informal proposals often close with a request for approval or authorization. In addition, the closing should remind the reader of key benefits and motivate action. It might also include a deadline date beyond which the offer is invalid. At some companies, such as Hewlett-Packard, authorization to proceed is not part of the proposal. Instead, it is usually discussed after the customer has received the proposal. In this way the customer and the sales account manager are able to negotiate terms before a formal agreement is drawn.

Formal Proposals

Formal proposals, which we won't cover in this book, differ from routine proposals not in style but in size and format. Formal proposals respond to big projects and may range from 5 to 200 or more pages. To facilitate comprehension and reference, they are organized into many parts. In addition to the six basic parts just described, formal proposals contain some or all of the following additional parts: copy of the RFP, letter of transmittal, abstract and/or executive summary, title page, table of contents, figures, and appendix.

Well-written proposals win contracts and business for companies and individuals. In fact, many companies, especially those that are run on a consulting model, depend entirely on proposals to generate their income. Companies such as Microsoft, Hewlett-Packard, and IBM employ staffs of people that do nothing but prepare proposals to compete for new business. For more information about industry standards and resources, visit the website of the Association of Proposal Management Professionals <www.apmp.org>.

CONCLUSION

This chapter presented seven types of routine business reports: information reports, progress reports, justification/recommendation reports, feasibility reports, summaries, minutes of meetings, and routine proposals. Information reports generally provide data only. But justification/recommendation reports as well as feasibility reports and sometimes summary reports are more analytical in that they also evaluate the information, draw conclusions, and make recommendations. Proposals are offers to solve problems, provide services, or sell equipment or goods. Both small and large businesses today write proposals to generate income. Informal proposals may be as short as two pages; formal proposals may be 200 pages or more. Regardless of the size, proposals contain standard parts that must be developed persuasively.

This chapter also discussed four formats for reports. Letter format is used for reports sent outside an organization; memo format is used for internal reports. More formal reports are formatted on plain paper with a manuscript design, while routine reports may be formatted on prepared forms or using digital templates. All of the examples in this chapter are considered relatively informal. Longer, more formal reports are necessary for major investigations and research. These reports, along with suggestions for research methods, are presented in Chapters 8 and 9.

Chapter Review

As a way of studying the material in this chapter, imagine you are at a job interview for your dream entry-level job after college or university. You've prepared answers for all the classic interview questions, but to your surprise, your interviewer also asks a number of questions based on report and proposal writing. How would you answer the following six questions?

1. Our business is information-driven, which means that everyone on staff writes reports on a weekly basis. We find, however, that because of how frequently we have to write reports, few of us sit back to consider best practices in report writing. So in your opinion, what's the point of writing a report? What is the essence of a report's function?

2. The reports we write and present here obviously have various functions, as you've suggested in your previous answer. Do you have any thoughts on what these different reports should look like? And how do we know when to choose one "look" over another?

3. Despite the fact that report writing becomes pretty routine once you've worked for us for a while, we'd like to know what you learned in your business communications course about what goes into the planning of a well-written report.

4. One of the reasons we wanted to interview you was that you seemed to know a lot about different kinds of reports, which is refreshing. Considering that you'll be joining our sales department, what kinds of routine reports do you think you might be writing, and in what circumstances?

5. You mentioned progress reports in your previous answer. We actually have a computerized template for progress reports, so you don't have to write them from scratch. But you will have to provide us with personalized conference and sales-visit reports. What do you think these should look like?

6. Sometimes we solicit new business through the RFP process. Can you tell us what you understand to be the main differences between routine reports and routine proposals?

∷ *Problems*

1. You are the head of Purchasing in the IT department at Kilpatrick and Sons, a leading engineering company located in Moncton, New Brunswick. Kilpatrick and Sons provides engineering services to a wide range of industries, including consumer products (e.g., food, cosmetics), pharmaceuticals, and printing among others. Companies often hire Kilpatrick and Sons when they're trying to create more seamless automated systems (e.g., warehousing, delivery). To increase its business, Kilpatrick and Sons employs a team of sales representatives whose job it is to identify new business opportunities, make contact with potential clients, give proposal presentations, and close the sale. These potential clients can be from anywhere in Canada and the eastern United States, which is why trip and conference reporting are an important part of the sales representative position at Kilpatrick and Sons. Recently, the director of Sales e-mailed the VP of the IT department asking whether he had heard of any trip-reporting software that might make the job of typing trip reports from scratch less onerous on her sales reps. The VP wrote back saying that he'd look into it and have a report for her within a week. (Sales is considered the most important department at the company, and it's usual for other departments to want to please people in sales.) In turn, the VP of IT (your boss) has asked you to "find any information you can" on trip or conference or sales-call reporting software and to have a report in his in-box by Friday, which is three days away. While he hasn't explicitly asked you for a recommendation or for your opinion (he clearly only asked for information), in the course of your research, you start to question the wisdom of spending money on report software. Research a few of the leading trip/conference/sales-call report software products and decide how you'll respond to your boss.

2. Two weeks after your e-mail to the VP of IT at Kilpatrick and Sons, you hear through the grapevine that the company is going to be purchasing PDAs (specifically, BlackBerrys) for all of its sales representatives. Loaded onto the PDAs will be one of the three trip/conference/sales-call report software packages you described in your information report to the VP of IT. As the head of Purchasing, it's your job to procure both the PDAs and the new reporting software (unfortunately, they're not manufactured or sold by the same companies). You've been given two weeks, which is a tight deadline. So far, you've been in touch with two PDA retailers (Rogers Wireless in Moncton and DownEast in Amherst, Nova Scotia) and you've also received a quote from a retailer you deal with regularly <www.tigerdirect.ca>. Both of the local retailers are within a few dollars of each other for the PDAs themselves. There

is a substantial difference, however, in the price of their various service plans, and it's taking you some time to pull together a fair comparison based on similar criteria. On top of sorting out the PDAs, you have to get a quote on the trip report software the director of Sales has chosen, and it's taking you some time. Your e-mails to the company that sells the software in the Atlantic Region have not yet been answered. Then your boss, the VP of IT, sends you a stern e-mail asking for an "immediate progress report" on the project. It's only three days into your two-week window on the project, and already your boss is breathing down your neck. How will you make your progress report sound fair and balanced, yet positive?

3. It has been a month since sales reps at Kilpatrick and Sons have been using their new BlackBerrys with reporting software loaded on them. The director of Sales has invited the VP of IT and the head of Purchasing to her monthly sales meeting to listen to feedback from the sales reps. A day before the meeting, an e-mail goes out to all meeting attendees, including the following agenda: 1. Introductions; 2. Summary reports from the field; 3. Discussion of pros/cons of BlackBerry and report software; 4. Other business. At the meeting, the director of Sales warmly welcomes you and your boss and introduces you to her team as "the person responsible for our lovely new BlackBerrys." The five sales reps (representing the following territories: New Brunswick, Halifax, the rest of Nova Scotia, Newfoundland, New England) then give short anecdotal reports about interesting things that have happened in the past four weeks. For example, Bud McLaughlin from the New England territory mentions that he's close to closing a deal with Ben & Jerry's ice cream of Vermont. The largest chunk of the meeting is taken up with a lively discussion about the pros and cons of the new technological gadgets. Three of the five sales reps think the BlackBerry is wonderful, although none of them has started to use the new reporting software yet. They all admit to writing their reports "the old-fashioned way." The director of Sales says (to no one in particular), "It sounds like we'll have to set up some training for you guys on the reporting software." The other two reps claim the BlackBerry is hard to turn off, and that it's forcing them to take their job with them everywhere and "all the time." These two reps have tried to use the reporting software, but for whatever reason—they're not clear—it hasn't worked for them yet. So they've had double the work as they've gone back to the older method of reporting even though they took the time to input information and data into the reporting template on their PDA. It sounds more or less like the sales reps are frustrated about having to take time out to learn new technology, and they're not clear on how to do this. The director of Sales looks meaningfully at your boss, the VP of IT, who says, "I think your idea of training is a good one. Let me look into it. I'll get back to you by tomorrow." You can't help roll your eyes a little, since you know it will fall to you to "look into" the possibility of training, and you know that figuring it out in one day will be impossible. You don't say this, though. What you do say, instead, is "Why don't you let me look into that, Craig?" The meeting ends but not before the director of Sales says, "We don't usually send out minutes when it's just us [by which she means her sales team] but why don't I send around an e-mail just so we can keep track of what we decided today." What will the director of Sales' minutes report look like?

4. Who offers training on the use of BlackBerrys, on short notice, in Atlantic Canada? Luckily, Internet search engines rarely disappoint. Right after the meeting discussed in problem 3, you return to your office and type "blackberry

training Canada" into your search engine. One of the results of your search is a link to St. John's, Newfoundland-based Consilient, which appears to be one of Canada's leading providers of BlackBerry training. Unfortunately, you can't find an e-mail address on the site, only a phone number. Because it's nearly 5:00 p.m. your time (and coming up to 5:30 p.m. in St. John's), you get voice mail at the main switchboard instead of a live person. You leave a message anyway, asking to speak to someone in charge of BlackBerry training. The next day, you receive a phone call from Dale McVie from Consilient. You explain the situation to McVie and end by asking him whether he can e-mail or fax you a brief proposal for providing training onsite (in Moncton) to the five-person sales staff of Kilpatrick and Sons, along with the director of Sales and the VP of IT. McVie is not exactly polite about your request for a proposal. He says that the standard way that Consilient contracts for training is at $125 per student plus the price of air-fare and accommodation, with a minimum of ten students. You explain to McVie that your boss is a little old-fashioned and that he prefers to see things written down in proposal format before making a decision. McVie says he has to talk to his boss about it, and that he'll call you right back. Fifteen minutes later you get a call from McVie who says he'll "put something together" and e-mail it to you by tomorrow. You thank him and send a quick e-mail to your boss letting him know that you'll be receiving a proposal from Canada's "leading BlackBerry training company" tomorrow. Using information you find at <www.consilient.com>, what sort of proposal will McVie put together, considering that the seven people attending the training at Kilpatrick and Sons don't meet the minimum ten participants required?

5. Not surprisingly, once word gets out around Kilpatrick and Sons that the sales reps have BlackBerrys, talk around the cafeteria starts to revolve around how soon everyone else in the company will get a BlackBerry. Soon enough, you receive an e-mail from the VP of IT asking you to stop by his office when you have a minute. You stop by his office after lunch. He asks you to have a seat. "What do you think the pros and cons are of BlackBerrys?" he asks. Startled by the direct nature of his request, you rattle off a few clichéd ideas (e.g., one pro is the ability to be at work anywhere, anytime; a con is the inability to leave work anywhere, anytime). Your boss looks at you in that way he sometimes has and says sharply, "This isn't a joke. We're getting pressure from management to look into getting BlackBerrys for all managers and training staff. This could be huge." "What do you want me to do?" you wisely ask, knowing that the only reason you were asked to your boss's office must have to do with a purchasing decision. "Well, you remember the report you wrote a while back when the sales reps wanted BlackBerrys? I kind of need you to do the same thing, but on a larger scale. This time, give me your opinion on it, not just the specs. Can we afford BlackBerrys for all our managers and all our training staff? Do they need BlackBerrys? Why or why not?" You've been at Kilpatrick and Sons long enough to know a make-work project when you see one. It's obvious in this situation that the company wants to go down the PDA road in a big way, and it wants the IT "folks" to give the decision their blessing. "When do you need the report by?" You realize, even as you ask the question, what the answer will be. "Well, they're pretty hot to trot on this one. Do you think you can do it by Tuesday?" (It's Thursday afternoon at this point.) "No problem," you say, getting up out of the comfortable chair. "So a basic recommendation report, right?" you ask, just to make sure

nothing else is required. "Yeah, that's right. It should sound impartial. Make sure it sounds impartial." There are ten managers at Kilpatrick and Sons and five full-time trainers. What will your recommendation report look like?

Grammar/Style Review 7

In this review, you will be practising identifying precision mistakes. There are at least five mistakes in total. For a brief explanation of this style problem, please read the explanation on page 329. Besides completing the exercise below, be sure to be on the lookout for precision mistakes in your own writing.

To: m.muller@vmedia.ca

From: m.engle@vmedia.ca

Re: Potential client?

Hi Mike,

I was reading in the Sun yesterday and saw a story on the Whitecaps' plan to build a

new soccer stadium downtown. I checked out the Whitecaps' website after reading

the article, and found that it could use some work. For example, if you go to the Photo

Reel section that has pictures from the stadium press conference, everyone of them

looks so static! There are no captions and it takes awhile to figure out how to navigate

the site. I'm not sure what you intend on doing about new business, but I would rec-

ommend you to send them a proposal.

Cheers,

May

Business Communication Lab 7

As the president of the Vancouver Whitecaps soccer club, you are playing a high-stakes public relations game with politicians, the media, and the public on a daily basis. Your dream of a new stadium is popular, but increasingly one that has vocal detractors. Your recent press conference to discuss a progress report on the construction of the stadium attracted fewer media outlets than you had expected. After discussing the situation with your VP of Marketing and Sales, you decide to re-evaluate your strategy of selling the stadium. To do this, you first have to understand public opinion on the issue—something you've not been so good at until this point. You ask the club's marketing assistant to do a "quick search of the main media outlets" to see what they've "had to say about the stadium." You hope that by understanding opposition to the stadium, you can better strategize for the next phase of the project. As the club's marketing assistant, do some quick research using the websites of the three main local newspapers: *The Vancouver Sun*, *The Province*, and *The Georgia Straight*. Find three articles that provide a good picture of the range of opinion on the stadium. Write a summary report via e-mail to the president about what you've found out.

CHAPTER 8

Formal Report Planning, Research, and Illustration

How not to write a research report

BY DUNCAN STEWART, *NATIONAL POST*, SEPTEMBER 1, 2005, FP9

MY MAIN JOB as a research analyst at Orion Securities is to write research. My two biggest challenges to doing that job are both tied around the word "quotidian."

It is a lovely word, derived from French, and Latin before that, and it simply means "daily." If I walked my dog only once a day, I would a) have a quotidian task and b) need new carpets. Those things that we do every day, but not numerous times a day, fit the definition. Anything done with that frequency will, over time, probably become dull or humdrum, which is why quotidian usually has a pejorative air about it, like its synonyms: "routine," "commonplace" or "mundane."

And it can be pernicious. In my old job as a portfolio manager, and in my new job writing sell-side research, I have come to the realization that I spend most of my time doing stuff that is merely quotidian. In between attending meetings, checking for news, previewing and participating and analyzing conference calls and on and on, I work 10–12 hour days—of which I spend, if I am not careful, only 5–10 minutes doing creative thinking.

I am writing, in addition to this column, my first research report. It is tremendous fun, but one of my real challenges is excluding what I might call the quotidian details. In this era, when every company is probably already covered by at least a handful of analysts (or more than 40 in the case of Cognos) there isn't much that hasn't already been said.

As I am drafting my first report, I replayed the most recent quarterly conference call. Every minute or so I shouted "aha!" and jotted something down as I hauled another nugget of information from the Webcast. Then I kicked myself sharply as I realized that just because I can write something down doesn't mean I should. Let alone type it into some seven-kilogram doorstop report.

Sell-side analysts sometimes seem to act like we get paid by the word. We cram our reports full of details that show we were on the call, hadn't fallen asleep and haven't given ourselves carpal tunnel syndrome from typing—yet. As market and sector freaks, we tend to regard every bit of minutiae as fascinating. As a former consumer of that information, I need to remember that the buy-side pays for insight, not stenography.

That reporting of the mundane, that battle against the quotidian, works against me writing useful research. Every day I try to remind myself what I should be doing. And I keep a specific example in mind:

Earlier this summer, a tech company that I'd rather not name announced revenues, earnings and guidance well below Street expectations, and was duly given a 25% haircut. As one would expect, there were a number of causes for the shortfall, but a big chunk of it came from having one of their divisions see revenues fall from $7-million to $3-million in a single quarter.

The earnings and margin effects were even more significant, and while there were other divisions that underperformed too, people who bought and sold this stock would have loved to have known about the potential weakness before it happened.

It wasn't exactly hidden. The contract that represented the shortfall was on the company Web site, as was the customer's name, and product. It was the largest contract in the division's history. It was a new product introduction, and so the customer had been ordering components in advance, but had manufacturing problems with other parts of the system, and didn't need to order more inventory from the tech company.

It took me three seconds (with hindsight) to find a dozen Web sites where potential users of this product were wildly complaining it was late. The tech company shortfall was perfectly obvious to anyone who looked.

This isn't a story where I look smart. My clients didn't benefit, except for a decent post-mortem on why their shares were worth less than before. So now, I fight a battle between just slipping into the daily routine, and trying to do some actual thinking.

DIAGNOSING THE PROBLEM

Duncan Stewart's slightly tongue-in-cheek article contains an important lesson for student and professional business communicators. In the first three paragraphs of his article, he describes how routine can get in the way of creativity. It happens in two ways, according to Stewart. First, because research is part of Stewart's daily job, it has become routine—or at least he has come to see it as routine instead of creative. For some of us meetings are routine, for others teaching is routine, while for still others talking to customers on the phone becomes routine. Every job has its routine aspects. What Stewart is unhappy about in this article is the fact that research—which should, by its very nature, be creative—has become routine instead.

The second way in which routine has stifled creativity in Stewart's job is through the sheer repetitiveness of the tasks he undertakes. He reads, he goes to meetings, and he prepares for and analyzes what happens at those meetings and on conference calls. As we learn toward the end of the article, when he describes an example of how he missed a very important piece of information about a company, it is this sense of routine events that cannot be escaped that caused Stewart not to be able to see the information he needed to see.

So if we were to sum it up, we could say that Stewart's article describes a specific case related to financial services (notice examples of financial service jargon such as "sell-side" and "buy-side") in which a business communicator has become frustrated by the routine ("quotidian") aspects of what he feels makes up business research, when what he would really like to be able to do is to think creatively—"outside the box," to use a contemporary phrase—in order to find meaningful research that hasn't "already been said," as Stewart notes. In other words, real business research provides its readers with "insight," not just information for information's sake.

This may sound like a tall order. After all, how many of us can claim to speak or write insightfully, and not just competently or well? Still, Stewart is onto something here. When it comes to formal research reports, which we'll be looking at in this chapter, we owe it to ourselves and to our audience as business communicators to break the habit of routine that we are so used to. For example, in Stewart's case, breaking out of routine means not taking what he reads in newspapers, on business databases and sites, or what he hears in management conference calls as the whole truth. The truth is also available in some surprising places, such as the websites he discovered in which potential users of the technology in question had posted complaints about the product's lateness.

in-class
activity 8

WORKING IN SMALL groups of three to four, students will imagine they have been assigned a research report in which they must compare the efficiency of their college or university's customer service to the level of customer service at competitor institutions. Taking Duncan Stewart's advice to think outside the box of routine research, what innovative research methods can students think of to solve this research problem? What should the resulting formal research report contain and what is better left out? Report back to the class within 20 minutes.

Now that you've presented your solution to the rest of the class, you're ready to discover more information on the basics of writing formal business reports. At the end of this chapter, you will be presented with some more problems that you may be asked to analyze, evaluate, and explain.

WHAT MAKES A REPORT FORMAL?

Formal reports, whether they offer only information or whether (what's more likely) they also analyze that information and make recommendations, typically have three characteristics: formal tone, traditional structure, and considerable length. Formal research reports in business serve an important function. They provide management with vital data for decision making. This chapter considers the process of writing a formal report: preparing to write, and researching, generating, documenting, organizing, and illustrating data; the next chapter considers the format of how formal reports are presented.

As you learned in Chapter 3, writing business documents involves a process: prewriting, writing, and revising. Because formal business reports are the longest documents you will write in your business communications course, we have expanded the three-step process into seven specific steps. Each time you need to write a formal business report, follow these seven steps to ensure quality and consistency:

- **Step 1:** Analyze the problem and purpose.
- **Step 2:** Anticipate the audience and issues.
- **Step 3:** Prepare a work plan.
- **Step 4:** Implement your research strategy.
- **Step 5:** Organize, analyze, interpret, and illustrate the data.
- **Step 6:** Compose the first draft.
- **Step 7:** Revise, proofread, and evaluate.

How much time you spend on each step depends on your report task. A complex analytical report—for example, one in which you are comparing a number of options based on research—demands a comprehensive work plan, extensive research, and careful data analysis.

To illustrate the planning stages of a report (Steps 1 to 3), we'll watch Diane Camas develop a report she's preparing for her boss, Mike Rivers, at Mycon Pharmaceutical Laboratories. Mike asked Diane to investigate the problem of transportation for sales representatives. Currently, some Mycon reps visit customers (mostly doctors and hospitals) using company-leased cars. A few reps drive their own cars, receiving reimbursements for use. In three months Mycon's leasing agreement for 14 cars expires, and Mike is considering a major change. Diane's task is to investigate the choices and report her findings to Mike.

Analyzing the Problem and Purpose

The first step in writing a report is understanding the problem or assignment clearly. For complex reports it's wise to prepare a written problem statement. In analyzing her report task, Diane had many questions. Is the problem that Mycon is spending too much money on leased cars? Does Mycon wish to invest in owning a fleet of cars? Is Mike unhappy with the paperwork involved in reimbursing sales reps when they use their own cars? Does he suspect that reps are submitting inflated mileage figures? Before starting research for the report, Diane talked with Mike to define the problem. She learned several dimensions of the situation and wrote the following statement to clarify the problem—both for herself and for Mike.

> PROBLEM STATEMENT: *The leases on all company cars will be expiring in three months. Mycon must decide whether to renew them or develop a new policy regarding transportation for sales reps. Expenses and paperwork for employee-owned cars seem excessive.*

Diane further defined the problem by writing a specific question that she would try to answer in her report:

> PROBLEM QUESTION: *What plan should Mycon follow in providing transportation for its sales reps?*

Now Diane was ready to concentrate on the purpose of the report. Again, she had questions. Exactly what did Mike expect? Did he want a comparison of costs for buying cars and leasing cars? Should she conduct research to pinpoint exact reimbursement costs when employees drive their own cars? Did he want her to do all the legwork, present her findings in a report, and let him make a decision? Or did he want her to evaluate the choices and recommend a course of action? After talking with Mike, Diane was ready to write a simple purpose statement for this assignment.

> SIMPLE STATEMENT OF PURPOSE: *To recommend a plan that provides sales reps with cars to be used in their calls.*

Preparing a written purpose statement is a good idea because it defines the focus of a report and provides a standard that keeps the project on target. In writing useful purpose statements, choose active verbs telling what you intend to do: *analyze, choose, investigate, compare, justify, evaluate, explain, establish, determine,* and so on. Notice that Diane's statement begins with the active verb *recommend.*

Some reports require only a simple statement of purpose: to investigate expanded teller hours, to select a manager from among four candidates, to describe the position of accounts supervisor. Many assignments, though, demand additional focus to guide the project. An expanded statement of purpose considers three additional factors:

- **Scope.** What issues or elements will be investigated? To determine the scope, Diane brainstormed with Mike and others to pin down her task. She learned that Mycon currently had enough capital to consider purchasing a fleet of cars outright. Mike also told her that employee satisfaction was almost as important as cost-effectiveness. Moreover, he disclosed his suspicion that employee-owned cars were costing Mycon more than leased cars. Diane had many issues to sort out in setting the boundaries of her report.

- **Significance.** Why is the topic worth investigating at this time? Some topics, after initial examination, turn out to be less important than originally thought. Others involve problems that cannot be solved, making a study useless. For Diane and Mike the problem had significance because Mycon's leasing agreement would expire shortly and decisions had to be made about a new policy for transportation of sales reps.
- **Limitations.** What conditions affect the generalizations and utility of a report's findings? In Diane's case her conclusions and recommendations might apply only to reps in her Edmonton sales district. Her findings would probably not be reliable for reps in Rimouski, Windsor, or Brandon. Another limitation for Diane is time. She must complete the report in four weeks, thus restricting the thoroughness of her research.

Diane decided to expand her statement of purpose to define the scope, significance, and limitations of the report.

EXPANDED STATEMENT OF PURPOSE: *The purpose of this report is to recommend a plan that provides sales reps with cars to be used in their calls. The report will compare costs for three plans: outright ownership, leasing, and compensation for employee-owned cars. It will also measure employee reaction to each plan. The report is significant because Mycon's current leasing agreement expires April 1 and an improved plan could reduce costs and paperwork. The study is limited to costs for sales reps in the Edmonton district.*

After preparing a statement of purpose, Diane checked it with Mike Rivers to be sure she was on target.

Anticipating the Audience and Issues

After defining the purpose of a report, a writer must think carefully about who will read it. Concentrating solely on a primary reader is a major mistake. Although one individual may have solicited the report, others within the organization may eventually read it, including upper management and people in other departments. A report to an outside client may first be read by someone who is familiar with the problem and then be distributed to others less familiar with the topic. Moreover, candid statements to one audience may be offensive to another audience. Diane could make a major blunder, for instance, if she mentioned Mike's suspicion that sales reps were padding their mileage statements. If the report were made public—as it probably would be to explain a new policy—the sales reps could feel insulted that their integrity was questioned.

As Diane considered her primary and secondary readers, she asked herself these questions:

- What do my readers need to know about this topic?
- What do they already know?
- What is their education level?
- How will they react to this information?
- Which sources will they trust?
- How can I make this information readable, believable, and memorable?

Answers to these questions help writers determine how much background material to include, how much detail to add, whether to include jargon, what method of organization and presentation to follow, and what tone to use.

In the planning stages a report writer must also break the major investigative problem into subproblems. This process, sometimes called factoring, identifies issues to be investigated or possible solutions to the main problem. In this case Mycon must figure out the best way to transport sales reps. Each possible "solution" or issue that Diane considers becomes a factor or subproblem to be investigated. Diane came up with three tentative solutions to provide transportation to sales reps: purchase cars outright, lease cars, or compensate employees for using their own cars. These three factors form the outline of Diane's study.

Diane continued to factor these main points into the following subproblems for investigation:

What plan should Mycon use to transport its sales reps?

I. Should Mycon purchase cars outright?
    A. How much capital would be required?
    B. How much would it cost to insure, operate, and maintain company-owned cars?
    C. Do employees prefer using company-owned cars?

II. Should Mycon lease cars?
    A. What is the best lease price available?
    B. How much would it cost to insure, operate, and maintain leased cars?
    C. Do employees prefer using leased cars?

III. Should Mycon compensate employees for using their own cars?
    A. How much has it cost in the past to operate employee-owned cars?
    B. How much paperwork is involved in reporting expenses?
    C. Do employees prefer being compensated for using their own cars?

Each subproblem would probably be further factored into additional subproblems. These issues may be phrased as questions, as Diane's are, or as statements. In factoring a complex problem, prepare an outline showing the initial problem and its breakdown into subproblems. Make sure your divisions are consistent (don't mix issues), exclusive (don't overlap categories), and complete (don't skip significant issues).

Preparing a Work Plan

After analyzing the problem, anticipating the audience, and factoring the problem, you're ready to prepare a work plan. A good work plan includes the following:

- Statement of the problem (based on key background/contextual information)
- Statement of the purpose including scope, significance, and limitations
- Research strategy including description of the sources and methods of collecting data
- Tentative outline that factors the problem into manageable chunks
- Work schedule

Preparing a plan forces you to evaluate your resources, set priorities, outline a course of action, and establish a time schedule. Such a plan keeps you on schedule and also gives management a means of measuring your progress.

A work plan gives a complete picture of a project. Because the usefulness and quality of any report rest primarily on its data, you'll want to allocate plenty of time to locate sources of information. For firsthand information you might interview people, prepare a survey, or even conduct a scientific experiment. For secondary information you'll probably search printed materials such as books and magazines as well as electronic materials on the Internet and Web. Your work plan describes how you expect to generate or collect data. Since data collection is a major part of report writing, the next section of this chapter treats the topic more fully.

Figure 8.1 (page 202) shows a complete work plan for a proposal to Lee Jeans. This work plan is particularly useful because it outlines the issues to be investigated. Notice that considerable thought and discussion—and even some preliminary research—are necessary to be able to develop a useful work plan.

Although this tentative outline guides investigation, it does not determine the content or order of the final report. You may, for example, study five possible solutions to a problem. If two prove to be useless, your report may discuss only the three winners. Moreover, you will organize the report to accomplish your goal and satisfy the audience. Remember that a busy executive who is familiar with a topic may prefer to read the conclusions and recommendations before a discussion of the findings. If the report is authorized by someone, be sure to review the work plan with that individual (your manager, client, or professor, for example) before proceeding with the project.

BUSINESS RESEARCH USING SECONDARY DATA

Step 4 in the report writing process, which is a vital part of producing a quality research report, is gathering data or research. Because a report is only as good as its data, the remainder of this chapter describes finding, documenting, and illustrating data. As you analyze a report's purpose and audience, you'll assess the kinds of data needed to support your argument or explain your topic. Do you need statistics, background data, expert opinions, group opinions, or organizational data?

Data fall into two broad categories: primary and secondary. Primary data result from firsthand experience and observation. Secondary data come from reading what others have experienced and observed. Secondary data are easier and cheaper to develop than primary data, which might involve interviewing large groups or sending out questionnaires.

We're going to discuss secondary data first because that's where nearly every research project should begin. Often, something has already been written about your topic. Reviewing secondary sources can save time and effort and prevent you from "reinventing the wheel." Most secondary material is available either in print or electronically.

Print Resources

Although we're seeing a steady movement away from print to electronic data, print sources are still the most visible part of nearly all libraries. Much information is available only in print, and you may want to use some of the following print resources.

By the way, if you are an infrequent library user, begin your research by talking with a reference librarian about your project. These librarians won't do your research for you, but they will steer you in the right direction. Many libraries help you understand their computer, cataloguing, and retrieval systems by providing advice, brochures, handouts, and workshops.

Books. Although quickly outdated, books provide excellent historical, in-depth data on subjects. Books can be located through computer-based library catalogues. Your college or university will have its own library catalogue, which can be accessed from the institution's website. Tutorials on how to use the catalogue are usually offered either online or at the library.

Figure 8.1 ▶   Work Plan for a Formal Report

Tips for Preparing a Work Plan
- Start early; allow plenty of time for brainstorming and preliminary research.
- Describe the problem motivating the report.
- Write a purpose statement that includes the report's scope, significance, and limitations.
- Describe the research strategy including data collection sources and methods.
- Divide the major problem into subproblems stated as questions to be answered.
- Develop a realistic work schedule citing dates for completion of major tasks.
- Review the work plan with whoever authorized the report.

Defines purpose, scope, limits, and significance of report

Statement of Problem

Many women between the ages of 22 and 35 have trouble finding jeans that fit. Lee Jeans hopes to remedy that situation with its One True Fit line. We want to demonstrate to Lee that we can create a word-of-mouth campaign that will help it reach its target audience.

Statement of Purpose

The purpose of this report is to secure an advertising contract from Lee Jeans. We will examine published accounts about the jeans industry and Lee Jeans in particular. In addition, we will examine published results of Lee's current marketing strategy. We will conduct focus groups of women in our company to generate campaign strategies for our pilot study of 100 BzzAgents. The report will persuade Lee Jeans that word-of-mouth advertising is an effective strategy to reach women in this demographic group and that BzzAgent is the right company to hire. The report is significant because an advertising contract with Lee Jeans would help our company grow significantly in size and stature.

Describes primary and secondary data

Research Strategy (Sources and Methods of Data Collection)

We will gather information about Lee Jeans and the product line by examining published marketing data and conducting focus group surveys of our employees. In addition, we will gather data about the added value of word-of-mouth advertising by examining published accounts and interpreting data from previous marketing campaigns, particularly those with similar age groups. Finally, we will conduct a pilot study of 100 BzzAgents in the target demographic.

Tentative Outline

I. How effectively has Lee Jeans marketed to the target population (women, ages 22 to   35)?
    A. Historically, who has typically bought Lee Jeans products? How often? Where?
    B. How effective are the current marketing strategies for the One True Fit line?
II. Is this product a good fit for our marketing strategy and our company?
    A. What do our staff members and our sample survey of BzzAgents say about this   product?
    B. How well does our pool of BzzAgents correspond to the target demography in terms of age and geographic distribution?
III. Why should Lee Jeans engage BzzAgent to advertise its One True Fit line?
    A. What are the benefits of word of mouth in general and for this demographic in   particular?
    B. What previous campaigns have we engaged in that demonstrate our company's credibility?
    C. What are our marketing strategies, and how well did they work in the pilot study?

Factors problem into manageable chunks

Estimates time needed to complete report tasks

Work Schedule

Investigate Lee Jeans and the One True Fit line's current marketing strategy	July 15–25
Test product using focus groups	July 15–22
Create campaign materials for BzzAgents	July 18–31
Run a pilot test with a selected pool of 100 BzzAgents	August 1–21
Evaluate and interpret findings	August 22–25
Compose draft of report	August 26–28
Revise draft	August 28–30
Submit final report	September 1

Periodicals. Magazines, pamphlets, and journals are called *periodicals* because of their recurrent or periodic publication. Journals, by the way, are compilations of scholarly articles. Articles in journals and other periodicals will be extremely useful to you because they are concise, limited in scope, current, and can supplement information in books.

Electronic Databases

As a writer of business reports today, you will probably begin your secondary research with electronic resources. Most writers turn to them first because they are fast, cheap, and easy to use. This means that you can conduct detailed searches without ever leaving your office, home, or dorm room. Today databases are almost solely available in online format. CD-ROM and paper-based databases have been replaced by this more easy-to-update and storage-capable format. Online databases, as anyone who has stepped inside a library in the past five years knows, have become the staple of secondary research.

A database is a collection of information stored electronically so that it is accessible by computer and is digitally searchable. Databases provide both bibliographic (titles of documents and brief abstracts) and full-text documents. Most researchers today, however, prefer full-text documents. Databases contain a rich array of magazine, newspaper, and journal articles, as well as newsletters, business reports, company profiles, government data, reviews, and directories. Provided with this textbook is access to InfoTrac, a Web-centred database that is growing rapidly. Web-based documents are enriched with charts, graphs, bold and italic fonts, colour, and pictures. Other well-known databases you may have access to through your college or university library include E-stat from Statistics Canada, and various databases from the largest commercial database providers such as ABI Inform, Lexis Nexis, Proquest, and Thomson-Gale.

Developing a search strategy and narrowing your search can save time. As you develop your strategy, think about the time frame for your search, the language of publication, and the types of materials you will need. One of the advantages of databases is the ability to focus a search easily. In addition, don't constrain yourself to English-language articles only; some websites offer translation services, and some of these services are free.

Although well stocked and well organized, specialized commercial databases are indeed expensive to use. This is why as a student you're at a great advantage. A part of your tuition fees goes to purchasing subscriptions to these online databases, which many private companies find too expensive to subscribe to themselves. Many databases involve steep learning curves, which is why it's important to sign up for a tutorial session as soon as possible that will familiarize you with how to search online databases. The search tips below will also be helpful.

The World Wide Web

After e-mail, the most-used function of the Internet is the World Wide Web.[1] According to the federal government, Canadians surf the Internet more than any other people in the world.[2] To a business researcher, the Web offers a wide range of organizational and commercial information. You can expect to find such items as product and service facts, public relations material, mission statements, staff directories, press releases, current company news, government information, selected article reprints, collaborative scientific project reports, and employment information.

Although a wealth of information is available, finding what you need can be frustrating and time-consuming. The constantly changing contents of the Web and its lack of organization make it more problematic for research than searching commercial databases such as InfoTrac. Moreover, Web content is uneven and often the quality is questionable.

The problem of gathering information is complicated by the fact that the total amount of information on the Web grows daily at a rate of over 7 million pages.[3] In addition, what is now being called the "deep" or "invisible" Web is 400 to 500 times larger than that of the "surface" Web, which is the part of the Web indexed by the most familiar search tools, such as Google.[4] Thus, to succeed in your search for information and answers, you need to understand the search tools. You also need to understand how to evaluate the information you find.

Search tools. Finding what you are looking for on the Web is hopeless without powerful, specialized search tools, such as Google, AskJeeves, and Yahoo! These search tools can be divided into three types: subject directories, search engines, and search engine partners. Early in the history of the Internet, search tools usually were classified in only one category. Today, larger tools such as Yahoo! are actually search engines and subject directories combined. Subject directories fall into two categories—commercial ones (e.g., Yahoo!) and academic ones (e.g., Infomine). Organized into subject categories, these directories contain a collection of links to Internet resources submitted by site creators or evaluators. The best are excellent; the worst can be misleading or out of date.

Search engines and search engine partners, sometimes referred to as second-generation search tools, are gaining popularity and becoming more sophisticated. Search engines such as Google use automated software "spiders" that crawl through the Web at regular intervals to collect and index the information from each location visited. Search engine partners, such as AskJeeves, use natural language-processing technology to enable you to ask questions to gather information. Both tools will help you search for specific information.

Even though search engines such as Google boast about the numbers of items they have indexed (e.g., close to 6 billion),[5] no single search engine or directory can come close to indexing all the pages on the Internet. In fact, according to the NEC Research Institute, these engines index less than 16 percent of the surface Web, or what we commonly call the World Wide Web, and only about 0.03 percent of the total pages available on the surface and invisible Webs combined.[6]

The invisible Web is considerably different from the surface Web. Some researchers claim that it has 500 times more data than the surface Web.[7] Much of that information is dynamic and changing constantly (e.g., data in job banks, flight information, geographical and company information), and some is accessible only through paid subscription sites such as Hoover's. Other information such as that contained in many government databases is free, but often it too is not easily accessed. To help you search for data on both the visible and invisible Webs, consider using the search tools listed in Figure 8.2.

Internet search tips and techniques. To conduct a thorough search for information you need, build a (re)search strategy by understanding the tools available.

- **Use two or three search tools.** Begin by conducting a topic search. Use a subject directory such as Yahoo! or the BUBL link at <http://bubl.ac.uk/link/>. Once you have narrowed your topic, switch to a search engine or search engine partner.
- **Understand case-sensitivity.** Generally use lowercase for your searches, unless you are searching for a term that is usually written in upper and lowercase, such as a person's name.

Figure 8.2 ▶ Visible and Invisible Web Search Tools

Visible Web Search Engines	Size and Type	Key Features
Google <www.google.com> <www.google.ca>	Nearly 6 billion pages— over 4 billion fully indexed	Relevance ranking Advanced search options
Yahoo! Search <search.yahoo.com> <ca.yahoo.com>	Over 3 billion pages fully indexed	Relevance ranking Advanced search options (includes options for different languages)
MSN Search <search.msn.com>	Over 3 billion pages fully indexed	Advanced search options (including international search sites)
Teoma <www.teoma.com>	Over 1 billion pages fully indexed and 1 billion partially indexed	Subject-specific rankings Advanced search options (ten languages) "Refine" feature—suggests topics to explore after initial search
AskJeeves <www.askjeeves.com>	Over 1 billion pages fully indexed and 1 billion partially indexed	Natural language questions Relies on Teoma.com's technology Binoculars tool (preview search results)
Infospace <www.infospace.com>	N/A; relies on other search engines for data	Metasearch technology: searches Google, FAST, Yahoo!, About, AskJeeves, FindWhat, LookSmart, Inktomi
Vivisimo <http://vivisimo.com>	Slightly less than 1 billion pages indexed	Metasearch function clusters results into categories Advanced search options and help
LookSmart <search.looksmart.com>	Over 2.3 billion pages indexed	Primarily a human-compiled directory Articles tab provides access to thousands of periodicals Uses textual analysis of hyperlinks, Web page popularity, and user feedback
HotBot <www.hotbot.com>	N/A; relies on other search engines for data	Quick check of three major search engine databases (Google, Yahoo!, AskJeeves/Teoma) Advanced search options and help
Open Directory Project <http://dmoz.org>	Over 3 billion pages indexed	Comprehensive human-edited directory (59 000 + editors)

INVISIBLE OR DEEP WEB

InfoMine <http://infomine.ucr.edu>	Directory of nearly 120 000 sites, grouped into nine indexed and annotated categories for scholarly research
About <http://www.about.com>	Directory that organizes content from over 1 million sites with commentary from chosen experts
Librarian's Index to the Internet <http://lii.org/>	Directory of 14 000 well-chosen and annotated sites of use for academic research
CompletePlanet <http://www.completeplanet.com/>	Directory with over 70 000 searchable databases and specialty search engines

- **Use nouns as search words and up to six or eight words in a query.** The right keywords—and more of them—can narrow the search effectively.
- **Combine keywords into phrases.** Phrases, marked by the use of quotation marks (e.g., "business ethics") will limit results to specific matches.
- **Omit articles and prepositions.** These are known as "stop words," and they do not add value to a search. Instead of *request for proposal*, use *proposal request*.

- **Use wild cards.** Most search engines support wild cards, such as asterisks. For example, the search term *cent** will retrieve *cents*, while *cent*** will retrieve both *centre* and *center*.
- **Know your search tool.** When connecting to a search service for the first time, always read the description of its service, including its FAQs (Frequently Asked Questions), Help, and How to Search sections. Often there are special features (e.g., News Category on AskJeeves) that can speed up the search process.
- **Learn basic Boolean search strategies.** You can save yourself a lot of time and frustration by narrowing your search with the following Boolean operators:

AND	Identifies only documents containing all of the specified words: ***employee AND productivity AND morale***
OR	Identifies documents containing at least one of the specified words: ***employee OR productivity OR morale***
NOT	Excludes documents containing the specified word: ***employee productivity NOT morale***
NEAR	Finds documents containing target words or phrases within a specified distance, for instance, within ten words: ***employee NEAR productivity***

- **Bookmark the best.** To keep track of your favourite Internet sites, save them as bookmarks or favourites.
- **Keep trying.** If a search produces no results, check your spelling. If you are using Boolean operators, check the syntax of your queries. Try synonyms and variations on words. Try to be less specific in your search term. If your search produces too many hits, try to be more specific. Think of words that uniquely identify what you're looking for. Use as many relevant keywords as possible.
- **Repeat your search a week later.** For the best results, return to your search a couple of days or a week later. The same keywords will probably produce additional results. That's because millions of new pages are being added to the Web every day.

Remember, subject directories and search engines vary in their contents, features, selectivity, accuracy, and retrieval technologies. Only through clever cyber-searching can you uncover the jewels hidden on the Internet.

Evaluating Web sources. Most of us using the Web have a tendency to assume that any information turned up via a search engine has somehow been evaluated as part of a valid selection process.[8] Wrong! The truth is that the Internet is rampant with unreliable sites that reside side by side with reputable sites. Anyone with a computer and an Internet connection can publish anything on the Web. Unlike library-based research, information at many sites has not undergone the editing or scrutiny of scholarly publication procedures. The information we read in journals and most reputable magazines is reviewed, authenticated, and evaluated. That's why we have learned to trust these sources as valid and authoritative. But information on the Web is much less reliable. Some sites exist to distribute propaganda; others want to sell you something. To use the Web meaningfully, you must scrutinize what you find. Here are specific questions to ask as you examine a site.

- **Currency.** What is the date of the Web page? When was it last updated? Is some of the information obviously out of date? If the information is time-sensitive and the site has not been updated recently, the site is probably not reliable.

- **Authority.** Who publishes or sponsors this Web page? What makes the presenter an authority? Is a contact address available for the presenter? Learn to be skeptical about data and assertions from individuals whose credentials are not verifiable.
- **Content.** Is the purpose of the page to entertain, inform, convince, or sell? How would you classify this page (e.g., news, personal, advocacy, reference)? Who is the intended audience, based on content, tone, and style? Can you judge the overall value of the content compared with the other resources on this topic? Web presenters with a slanted point of view cannot be counted on for objective data.
- **Accuracy.** Do the facts that are presented seem reliable to you? Do you find errors in spelling, grammar, or usage? Do you see any evidence of bias? Are footnotes provided? If you find numerous errors and if facts are not referenced, you should be alerted that the data may be questionable.

BUSINESS RESEARCH USING PRIMARY DATA

Up to this point, we've been talking about secondary data. You should begin nearly every business report assignment by evaluating the available secondary data. However, you'll probably need primary data to provide a complete picture for your audience. Business reports that solve specific current problems typically rely on primary, firsthand data. Providing answers to business problems often means generating primary data through surveys, interviews, observation, or experimentation.

Surveys

Surveys collect data from groups of people. When companies develop new products, for example, they often survey consumers to learn their needs. The advantages of surveys are that they gather data economically and efficiently. Mailed surveys reach big groups nearby or at great distances. Moreover, people responding to mailed surveys have time to consider their answers, thus improving the accuracy of the data.

Mailed, e-mailed, or web-based questionnaires, of course, have disadvantages. Most of us rank them with junk mail, so response rates may be no higher than 15 percent. Furthermore, those who do respond may not represent an accurate sample of the overall population, thus invalidating generalizations from the group. A final problem with surveys has to do with truthfulness. Some respondents exaggerate their incomes or distort other facts, thus causing the results to be unreliable. Nevertheless, surveys may be the best way to generate data for business and student reports. In preparing print or electronic surveys, consider these pointers:

- **Explain why the survey is necessary.** In a cover letter or an opening paragraph, describe the need for the survey. Suggest how someone or something other than you will benefit. If appropriate, offer to send recipients a copy of the findings.
- **Consider incentives.** If the survey is long, persuasive techniques may be necessary. Response rates can be increased by offering money, coupons, gift certificates, free books, or other gifts.
- **Limit the number of questions.** Resist the temptation to ask for too much. Request only information you will use. Don't, for example, include demographic questions (income, gender, age, and so forth) unless the information is necessary to evaluate responses.

- **Use questions that produce quantifiable answers.** Check-off, multiple-choice, yes-no, and scale (or rank-order) questions (illustrated in Figure 8.3) provide quantifiable data that are easily tabulated. Responses to open-ended questions ("What should the bookstore do about plastic bags?") reveal interesting, but difficult-to-quantify, perceptions.[9] To obtain workable data, give interviewees a list of possible responses (as shown in items 5–8 of Figure 8.3). For scale and multiple-choice questions, try to present all the possible answer choices. To be safe, add an "Other" or "Don't know" category in case the choices seem insufficient to the respondent. Many surveys use scale questions because they capture degrees of feelings. Typical scale headings are "agree strongly," "agree somewhat," "neutral," "disagree somewhat," and "disagree strongly."

- **Avoid leading or ambiguous questions.** The wording of a question can dramatically affect responses to it. Because words have different meanings for different people, you must strive to use objective language and pilot test your questions with typical respondents. Stay away from questions that suggest an answer ("Don't you agree that the salaries of CEOs are obscenely high?"). Instead, ask neutral questions ("Do CEOs earn too much, too little, or about the right amount?"). Also avoid queries that really ask two or more things ("Should the salaries of CEOs be reduced or regulated by government legislation?"). Instead, break them into separate questions ("Should the salaries of CEOs be regulated by government legislation? Should the salaries of CEOs be reduced by government legislation?").

- **Select the survey population carefully.** Many surveys question a small group of people (a sample) and project the findings to a larger population. To be able to generalize from a survey, you need to make the sample as large as possible. In addition, you need to determine whether the sample is like the larger population. For important surveys you will want to consult books on or experts in sampling techniques.

- **Make it easy for respondents to return the survey.** These days, the easiest way to communicate is via e-mail. Therefore, unless you know your intended survey group will have time to devote to filling out a paper-based survey, you should design your survey so that it can be answered online and returned to you online. Web-based services such as Zoomerang will let you design online surveys for free, with some limitations.

- **Conduct a pilot study.** Try the questionnaire with a small group so that you can remedy any problems. For example, in the survey shown in Figure 8.3, a pilot study revealed that female students generally favoured cloth book bags and were willing to pay for them. Male students opposed purchasing cloth bags. By adding a gender category, researchers could verify this finding. The pilot study also revealed the need to ensure an appropriate representation of male and female students in the survey.

Interviews

Some of the best report information, particularly on topics about which little has been written, comes from individuals. These individuals are usually experts or veterans in their fields. Consider both in-house and outside experts for business reports. Tapping these sources will call for in-person, telephone, or online interviews. To elicit the most useful data, try these techniques:

- **Locate an expert.** Ask managers and individuals working in an area whom they consider to be most knowledgeable in their areas. Check membership lists of professional organizations, and consult articles about the topic or

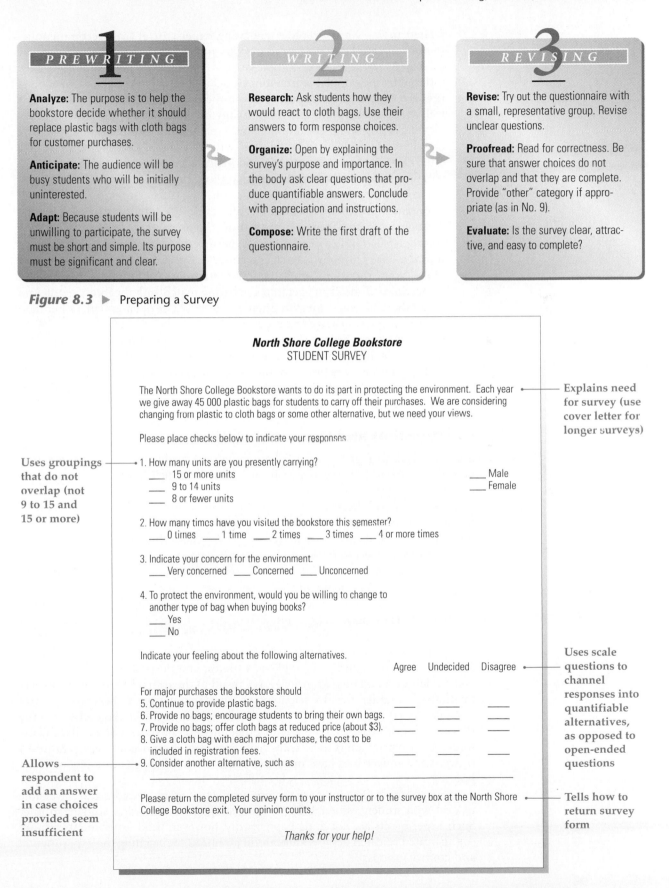

1

PREWRITING

Analyze: The purpose is to help the bookstore decide whether it should replace plastic bags with cloth bags for customer purchases.

Anticipate: The audience will be busy students who will be initially uninterested.

Adapt: Because students will be unwilling to participate, the survey must be short and simple. Its purpose must be significant and clear.

2

WRITING

Research: Ask students how they would react to cloth bags. Use their answers to form response choices.

Organize: Open by explaining the survey's purpose and importance. In the body ask clear questions that produce quantifiable answers. Conclude with appreciation and instructions.

Compose: Write the first draft of the questionnaire.

3

REVISING

Revise: Try out the questionnaire with a small, representative group. Revise unclear questions.

Proofread: Read for correctness. Be sure that answer choices do not overlap and that they are complete. Provide "other" category if appropriate (as in No. 9).

Evaluate: Is the survey clear, attractive, and easy to complete?

Figure 8.3 ▶ Preparing a Survey

North Shore College Bookstore
STUDENT SURVEY

The North Shore College Bookstore wants to do its part in protecting the environment. Each year we give away 45 000 plastic bags for students to carry off their purchases. We are considering changing from plastic to cloth bags or some other alternative, but we need your views.

Explains need for survey (use cover letter for longer surveys)

Please place checks below to indicate your responses

Uses groupings that do not overlap (not 9 to 15 and 15 or more)

1. How many units are you presently carrying?
   ____ 15 or more units
   ____ 9 to 14 units
   ____ 8 or fewer units

   ____ Male
   ____ Female

2. How many times have you visited the bookstore this semester?
   ____ 0 times ____ 1 time ____ 2 times ____ 3 times ____ 4 or more times

3. Indicate your concern for the environment.
   ____ Very concerned ____ Concerned ____ Unconcerned

4. To protect the environment, would you be willing to change to another type of bag when buying books?
   ____ Yes
   ____ No

Indicate your feeling about the following alternatives.

	Agree	Undecided	Disagree
For major purchases the bookstore should			
5. Continue to provide plastic bags.	____	____	____
6. Provide no bags; encourage students to bring their own bags.	____	____	____
7. Provide no bags; offer cloth bags at reduced price (about $3).	____	____	____
8. Give a cloth bag with each major purchase, the cost to be included in registration fees.	____	____	____

Uses scale questions to channel responses into quantifiable alternatives, as opposed to open-ended questions

Allows respondent to add an answer in case choices provided seem insufficient

9. Consider another alternative, such as

_____

Please return the completed survey form to your instructor or to the survey box at the North Shore College Bookstore exit. Your opinion counts.

Tells how to return survey form

Thanks for your help!

related topics. Most people enjoy being experts or at least recommending them. You could also post an inquiry to an Internet *newsgroup*. An easy way to search newsgroups in a topic area is through the browse groups now indexed by the popular search tool Google <http://groups.google.com>.

- **Prepare for the interview.** Learn about the individual you're interviewing as well as the background and terminology of the topic. Let's say you're interviewing a corporate communication expert about producing an in-house newsletter. You ought to be familiar with terms like *font* and software like QuarkXpress, Adobe Pagemaker, and Ventura Publisher. In addition, be prepared by making a list of questions that pinpoint your focus on the topic. Ask the interviewee if you may record the talk.
- **Maintain a professional attitude.** Call before the interview to confirm the arrangements and then arrive on time. Be prepared to take notes if your recorder fails (and remember to ask permission beforehand if you want to record). Use your body language to convey respect.
- **Make your questions objective and friendly.** Adopt a courteous and respectful attitude. Don't get into a debating match with the interviewee. And remember that you're there to listen, not to talk! Use open-ended, rather than yes-or-no, questions to draw experts out.
- **Watch the time.** Tell interviewees in advance how much time you expect to need for the interview. Don't overstay your appointment.
- **End graciously.** Conclude the interview with a general question, such as "Is there anything you'd like to add?" Express your appreciation, and ask permission to telephone later if you need to verify points.

Observation and Experimentation

Some kinds of primary data can be obtained only through firsthand observation and investigation. As Duncan Stewart argued in his article at the beginning of the chapter, good data don't always come from traditional methods (like surveys and interviews). If you determine that the questions you have require observational data, then you need to plan the observations carefully. One of the most important questions is to ask what or whom you're observing and how often those observations are necessary to provide reliable data.

When you observe, plan ahead. Arrive early enough to introduce yourself and set up whatever equipment you think is necessary. Make sure that you've received permission beforehand, particularly if you are recording. In addition, take notes, not only of the events or actions but also of the settings. Changes in environment often have an effect on actions.

Experimentation produces data suggesting causes and effects. Informal experimentation might be as simple as a pretest and posttest in a college course. Did students expand their knowledge as a result of the course? More formal experimentation is undertaken by scientists and professional researchers who control variables to test their effects. For example, think back to the in-class activity at the beginning of this chapter. One way to gauge the level of success of a college's customer service program is to actually visit its customer service delivery area (most colleges and universities have one) and observe what happens in a day or in an hour.

For example, how long are the line-ups? How many employees are available to deal with student issues? What is the average wait-time for a student in line? Such experiments are not done haphazardly, however. Valid experiments require sophisticated research designs and careful attention to matching the experimental and control groups.

ILLUSTRATING BUSINESS DATA

After collecting information, you need to consider how best to present it. If your report contains complex data and numbers, you may want to consider using graphics such as tables and charts. These graphics clarify data, create visual interest, and make numerical data meaningful. By simplifying complex ideas and emphasizing key data, well-constructed graphics make key information easier to remember. However, the same data can be shown in many different forms, for example, in a chart, table, or graph. That's why you need to recognize how to match the appropriate graphics with your objective and incorporate it into your report.

Matching Graphics and Objectives

In developing the best graphics, you must first decide what data you want to highlight. Chances are you will have many points you would like to show in a table or chart. But which graphics are most appropriate for your objectives? Tables? Bar charts? Pie graphs? Line charts? Flow charts? Organization charts? Pictures? Figure 8.4 summarizes appropriate uses for each type of graphic. The following text discusses each visual in more detail.

Tables. Probably the most frequently used graphic in reports is the table. Because a table presents quantitative or verbal information in systematic columns and rows, it can clarify large quantities of data in small spaces. You may have made rough tables to help you organize the raw data collected from literature, questionnaires, or interviews. In preparing tables for your readers or listeners, though, you'll need to pay more attention to clarity and emphasis. Here are tips for making good tables.

- Provide clear headings for the rows and columns.
- Identify the units in which figures are given (percentages, dollars, units per worker hour, and so forth) in the table title, in the column or row head, with the first item in a column, or in a note at the bottom.
- Provide titles and labels at the top of the table.
- Arrange items in a logical order (alphabetical, chronological, geographical, highest to lowest) depending on what you need to emphasize.
- Use *N/A* (not available) for missing data.
- Make long tables easier to read by shading alternate lines or by leaving a blank line after groups of five.
- Place tables as close as possible to the place where they are mentioned in the text.

Bar charts. Although they lack the precision of tables, bar charts enable you to make emphatic visual comparisons. Bar charts can be used to compare related items, illustrate changes in data over time, and show segments as part of a whole.

Many techniques for constructing tables also hold true for bar charts. Here are a few additional tips:

- Keep the length of each bar and segment proportional.
- Include a total figure in the middle of a bar or at its end if the figure helps the reader and does not clutter the chart.
- Start dollar or percentage amounts at zero.
- Avoid showing too much information, thus producing clutter and confusion.

Figure 8.4 ▶ Matching Graphics to Objectives

Graphics		Objective
Table	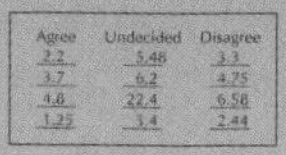	To show exact figures and values
Bar chart		To compare one item with others
Line chart	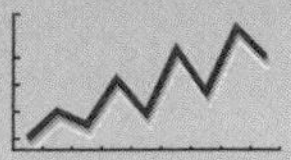	To demonstrate changes in quantitative data over time
Pie graph		To visualize a whole unit and the proportions of its components
Flow chart	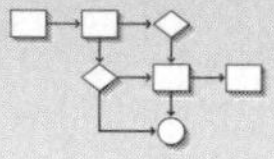	To display a process or procedure
Organization chart	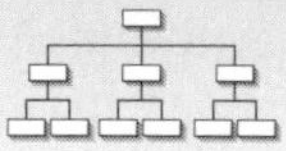	To define a hierarchy of elements
Photograph, map, illustration		To create authenticity, to spotlight a location, and to show an item in use

Selecting an appropriate graphic form depends on the purpose that it serves.

- Place the first bar at some distance (usually half the amount of space between bars) from the y axis.

Line charts. The major advantage of line charts is that they show changes over time, thus indicating trends. The vertical axis is typically the dependent variable, and the horizontal axis the independent one. Simple line charts show just one variable. Multiple-line charts combine several variables. Segmented line charts, also called surface charts, illustrate how the components of a whole change over time.
  Here are tips for preparing a line chart:

- Begin with a grid divided into squares.
- Arrange the time component (usually years) horizontally across the bottom; arrange values for the other variable vertically.
- Draw small dots at the intersections to indicate each value at a given year.
- Connect the dots and add colour if desired.
- To prepare a segmented (surface) chart, plot the first value (say, video income) across the bottom; add the next item (say, motion picture income) to the first figures for every increment; for the third item (say, theme park income) add its value to the total of the first two items. The top line indicates the total of the three values.

Pie graphs. Pie, or circle, graphs enable readers to see a whole and the proportion of its components, or wedges. Although less flexible than bar or line charts, pie graphs are useful in showing percentages. They are very effective for non-expert audiences. A wedge can be "exploded" or popped out for special emphasis.

For the most effective pie graphs, follow these suggestions:

- Begin at the 12 o'clock position, drawing the largest wedge first. (Computer software programs don't always observe this advice, but if you're drawing your own graphs, you can.)
- Include, if possible, the actual percentage or absolute value for each wedge.
- Use four to eight segments for best results; if necessary, group small portions into one wedge called "Other."
- Draw radii from the centre.
- Distinguish wedges with colour, shading, or crosshatching.
- Keep all the labels horizontal.

Many software programs help you prepare professional-looking graphs with a minimum of effort.

Flow charts. Procedures are simplified and clarified by diagramming them in a flow chart. Whether you need to describe the procedure for handling a customer's purchase order or outline steps in solving a problem, flow charts help the reader visualize the process. Traditional flow charts use the following symbols:

- Ovals to designate the beginning and end of a process
- Diamonds to denote decision points
- Rectangles to represent major activities or steps

Organization charts. Many large organizations are so complex that they need charts to show the chain of command, from the boss down to line managers and employees. Organization charts provide such information as who reports to whom, how many subordinates work for each manager (the span of control), and what channels of official communication exist. They may also illustrate a company's structure (by function, customer, or product, for example), the work being performed in each job, and the hierarchy of decision making.

Photographs, maps, and illustrations. Some business reports include photographs, maps, and illustrations to serve specific purposes. Photos, for example, add authenticity and provide a visual record. Maps enable report writers to depict activities or concentrations geographically, such as dots indicating sales reps in provinces across the country. Illustrations and diagrams are useful in indicating how an object looks or operates. With today's computer technology, photographs, maps, and illustrations can be scanned directly into business reports.

Incorporating Graphics into Reports

Used appropriately, graphics make reports more interesting and easier to understand. In putting graphics into your reports, follow these suggestions for best effects.

- **Evaluate the audience.** Evaluate the reader, the content, your schedule, and your budget (graphics take time and money to prepare) in deciding how many graphics to use. Six charts in an internal report to an executive may seem like overkill; but in a long technical report to outsiders, six may be too few.

- **Use restraint.** Don't overuse colour or decorations. Although colour can effectively distinguish bars or segments in charts, too much colour can be distracting and confusing. Remember, too, that colours themselves sometimes convey meaning: reds suggest deficits or negative values, blues suggest coolness, and yellow may suggest warning.
- **Be accurate and ethical.** Double-check all graphics for accuracy of figures and calculations. Be certain that your visuals aren't misleading—either accidentally or intentionally. Manipulation of a chart scale can make trends look steeper and more dramatic than they really are. Also, be sure to cite sources when you use someone else's facts.
- **Introduce a graphic meaningfully.** Refer to every graphic in the text, and place the graphic close to the point where it is mentioned. Most important, though, help the reader understand the significance of a graphic. You can do this by telling the reader what to look for or by summarizing the main point of a graphic. Don't assume the reader will automatically draw the same conclusions you reached from a set of data. Instead of "The findings are shown in Figure 3," tell the reader what to look for: "Two thirds of the responding employees, as shown in Figure 3, favour a flextime schedule." The best introductions for graphics interpret them for readers.
- **Choose an appropriate caption or title style.** Like reports, graphics may use "talking" titles or generic, descriptive titles. "Talking" titles are more persuasive; they tell the reader what to think. Descriptive titles describe the facts more objectively.

Talking Title
Average Annual Health Care Costs per Worker Rise Steeply as Workers Grow Older
Descriptive Title
Average Annual Health Care Costs per Worker as Shown by Age Groups

Judge the style you should use by your audience and your company's preferences. Regardless of the style, make the titles consistent and specific.

DOCUMENTING BUSINESS DATA

In writing business and other reports, you will often build on the ideas and words (and sometimes graphic illustrations) of others. In Western culture whenever you borrow the ideas of others, you must give credit to your information sources. This is called *documentation*.

As a careful writer, you should take pains to properly document report data for the following reasons:

- **To strengthen your argument.** Including good data from reputable sources will convince readers of your credibility and the logic of your reasoning.
- **To protect you from charges of plagiarism.** Acknowledging your sources keeps you honest. Plagiarism, which is illegal and unethical, is the act of using others' ideas without proper documentation.
- **To instruct the reader.** Citing references enables readers to pursue a topic further and make use of the information themselves.

Academic Documentation vs. Business Documentation

In the academic world documentation is critical. Especially in the humanities and sciences, students are taught to cite sources by using quotation marks, parenthetical citations, footnotes, and bibliographies. Academic term papers require full documentation to demonstrate that a student has become familiar with respected sources and can cite them properly in developing an argument. Giving credit to the author is extremely important. Students who plagiarize risk a failing grade in a class and even expulsion from school.

In the business world, however, documentation is often viewed differently. Business communicators on the job may find that much of what is written does not follow the standards they learned in school.[10] In many instances, individual authorship is unimportant. For example, employees may write for the signature of their bosses. The writer receives no credit. Similarly, team projects turn out documents written by many people, none of whom receives individual credit. Internal business reports, which often include chunks of information from previous reports, also fail to acknowledge sources or give credit. Even information from outside sources may lack proper documentation. Yet, if facts are questioned, business writers must be able to produce their source materials.

Although both internal and external business reports are not as heavily documented as school assignments or term papers, business communication students are well advised to learn proper documentation methods. Your instructor may use a commercial plagiarism detection service, which can cross-reference much of the information on the Web, looking for documents with similar phrasing. The result, an "originality report," will provide the instructor with a clear idea of whether you've been accurate and honest.

Plagiarism of words and phrases or ideas is a serious charge, which can lead to academic penalties or loss of a job. You can avoid charges of plagiarism as well as add clarity to your work by knowing what to document and developing good research habits.

Learning What to Document

When you write reports, especially in college or university, you are continually dealing with other people's ideas. You are expected to conduct research, synthesize ideas, and build on the work of others. But you are also expected to give proper credit for borrowed material. To avoid plagiarism, you must give credit whenever you use the following:

- Another person's ideas, opinions, examples, or theory
- Any facts, statistics, graphs, and illustrations that are not common knowledge
- Quotations of another person's actual spoken or written words
- Paraphrases of another person's spoken or written words[11]

Information that is common knowledge requires no documentation. For example, the statement "*The Globe and Mail* is a popular business newspaper" would require no citation. Statements that are not common knowledge, however, must be documented. For example, "*The Globe and Mail* is the largest daily newspaper in Canada" would require a citation because most people do not know this fact. Cite sources for proprietary information such as statistics organized and reported by a newspaper or magazine. Also use citations to document direct quotations and ideas that you summarize in your own words.

Developing Good Manual and Electronic Research Habits

Report writers who are gathering information have two methods available for recording the information they find. The time-honoured manual method of note-taking works well because information is recorded on separate cards, which can then be arranged in the order needed to develop a thesis or argument. Today, though, writers rely heavily on electronic researching. Traditional note-taking methods may seem antiquated and laborious in comparison. Let's explore both methods.

Manual note-taking. To make sure you know whose ideas you are using, train yourself to take excellent notes. If possible, know what you intend to find before you begin your research so that you won't waste time on unnecessary notes. Here are some pointers on taking good notes:

- Record all major ideas from various sources on separate note cards.
- Include all publication data along with precise quotations.
- Consider using one card colour for direct quotes and a different colour for your paraphrases and summaries.
- Put the original source material aside when you are summarizing or paraphrasing.

Electronic note-taking. Instead of recording facts on note cards, smart researchers today take advantage of electronic tools. Here are some pointers on taking good electronic notes:

- Begin your research by setting up a folder on your hard drive or on a storage device (zip disk, USB pen, etc.). Create subfolders for major topics, such as introduction, body, and closing.
- When you find facts on the Web or in electronic databases, highlight the material you want to record, copy it, and paste it into a document in an appropriate folder.
- Be sure to include all publication data.
- Consider archiving on a zip disk those Web pages or articles used in your research in case the data must be verified.

Developing Paraphrasing Skills

In writing reports and using the ideas of others, you will probably rely heavily on *paraphrasing*, which means restating an original passage in your own words and in your own style. To do a good job of paraphrasing, follow these steps:

- Read the original material intently to comprehend its full meaning.
- Write your own version without looking at the original.
- Do not repeat the grammatical structure of the original, and do not merely replace words with synonyms.
- Reread the original to be sure you covered the main points but did not borrow specific language.

To better understand the difference between plagiarizing and paraphrasing, study the following passages. Notice that the writer of the plagiarized version uses the same grammatical construction as the source and often merely replaces words with synonyms. Even the acceptable version, however, requires a reference to the source author.

SOURCE

The collapse in the cost of computing has made cellular communication economically viable. Worldwide, one in two new phone subscriptions is cellular. The digital revolution in telephony is most advanced in poorer countries because they have been able to skip an outdated technological step relying on land lines.

PLAGIARIZED VERSION

The drop in computing costs now makes cellular communication affordable around the world. In fact, one out of every two new phones is cellular. The digital revolution in cellular telephones is developing faster in poorer countries because they could skip an outdated technological process using land lines.

ACCEPTABLE PARAPHRASE

Cellular phone use around the world is increasing rapidly as a result of decreasing computing costs. Half of all new phones are now wireless. Poorer countries are experiencing the most rapid development because they can move straight to cellular without focusing on outdated technology using land lines (Henderson 44).

Knowing When and How to Quote

On occasion you will want to use the exact words of a source. But beware of overusing quotations. Documents that contain pages of spliced-together quotations suggest that writers have few ideas of their own. Wise writers and speakers use direct quotations for three purposes only:

- To provide objective background data and establish the severity of a problem as seen by experts
- To repeat identical phrasing because of its precision, clarity, or aptness
- To duplicate exact wording before criticizing

When you must use a long quotation, try to summarize and introduce it in your own words. Readers want to know the gist of a quotation before they tackle it. For example, to introduce a quotation discussing the shrinking staffs of large companies, you could precede it with your words: "In predicting employment trends, Charles Waller believes the corporation of the future will depend on a small core of full-time employees." To introduce quotations or paraphrases, use wording such as the following:

- According to Waller, . . .
- Waller argues that . . .
- In his recent study, Waller reported . . .

Use quotation marks to enclose exact quotations, as shown in the following: "The current image," says Charles Waller, "of a big glass-and-steel corporate headquarters on landscaped grounds directing a worldwide army of tens of thousands of employees may soon be a thing of the past."

Using Citation Formats

You can direct readers to your sources with parenthetical notes inserted into the text and with bibliographies. The most common citation formats are those presented by the Modern Language Association (MLA) and the American Psychological Association (APA).

CONCLUSION

In this chapter you learned that formal reports present well-organized information systematically. Formal reports are different than informal reports primarily because of their length, but also because of the level of formality in the presentation of the data, and because of the amount and complexity of the research required to solve the usually analytical problem. Because of the complexity inherent in formal research reports, the planning stages of the project are especially important. Planning steps include analyzing the problem and purpose as well as the audience, and then writing a detailed work plan that divides the main research problem into smaller subproblems.

The data for formal research reports may be collected from primary or secondary sources. An effective formal research report combines both kinds of data, and tries to be innovative at the same time. Innovation means not relying solely on standard research methods when there are more interesting alternatives available. Primary and secondary data are usually presented in a formal research report using some form of graphic. Graphics should only be used, however, if they clarify your data, create visual interest, and make statistical or numeral data meaningful.

All ideas borrowed from others must be documented. Understanding proper documentation formats begins by developing effective research habits, including manual and electronic note-taking and the ability to paraphrase.

Chapter Review

As a way of studying the material in this chapter, imagine you are at a job interview for your dream entry-level job after college or university. You've prepared answers for all the classic interview questions, but to your surprise, your interviewer also asks a number of questions based on formal report writing. How would you answer the following six questions?

1. As a team member in our research department, one of your main tasks will be writing team-based research reports. Your résumé indicates you've written such reports in prior jobs. Can you tell us the best practices you follow when approaching a report-writing project?
2. Our research department follows a pretty standard protocol when it comes to the planning stages of a report. We send our clients a work plan. Are you familiar with research report work plans, and if yes, what do you think they should include?
3. Tell us about some interesting secondary and primary research you had to do for a prior project. Which of the two did you find more beneficial?
4. Does your prior research experience include any surveying or interview or focus group work? If so, can you tell us which method you found more beneficial and why?
5. We find a number of our junior research report writers like to get carried away with producing computer-generated graphics to illustrate their reports. Do you know why we frown on this?
6. Can you tell us what you understand by the word "documentation"? We know you had to use it in college, but can you see the importance of documentation to a workplace like this one?

Problems

1. As the director of Business Development at Altria, a telecommunications provider, you've been busy the past year. Your business has been growing substantially, due to an increase in sales of cell phones and PDAs. As a result, you're finding your current customer service centres stretched in their capabilities. You'd like to open up at least one new customer service centre in

another part of Canada. Currently, there is only one call centre, located north of Toronto in Markham, Ontario. You've been given the green light by your boss, the VP of Business Development, to research up to three possible locations for a new call centre. Your boss, who even in good times is notoriously tight-fisted, has specified that your project manager should only do secondary research—"stuff that's already available out there." He's worried about the price of primary research. You ask your project manager to research and write a report ("four pages max!") in which she will identify three cities in Canada where Altria should build new customer service operations. Because Altria does not subscribe to any business research databases, the project manager has only the Internet and publicly accessible library resources available to her. On the day you assign her the task, you say to her, "I'm going to make it a little easier on you. I already know the boss has a few ideas about where the new centre should be opened. Don't waste your time. Just research Charlottetown, Moncton, and Ottawa." As the project manager, find secondary research that will enable you to recommend which of the three cities mentioned by the director would make the best home for a new Altria customer service centre. (Hint: a good place to start would be <**www.statcan.ca**>.)

2. Imagine the same situation as described in problem 1. Only this time, your boss has been given the exact opposite instructions. Instead of worrying about the price of primary research, the VP has instructed the director as follows: "Just make sure that we're not using the Internet to do this research. I want real data, from the horse's mouth so to speak. I don't care what it costs. I want to know for sure that our decision is the right one, and I think that's only going to happen through primary research." When the director meets with you to assign the task of locating research and compiling it into a report, he says, "Don't be tempted to look these places up on the Internet, or to use Statistics Canada research. Go right to the source. But because it'll probably cost some money—long-distance phone calls, conference calls, maybe a trip or two—why don't you put together a work plan for me first. Send it to me by Monday morning, okay?" This time, your task is a bit different: you don't have to actually find the primary research requested, but you have to identify exactly, in a work plan, what kind of primary research will be necessary and how this research will be done.

3. Imagine that the neighbourhood in which your college or university is located has a Business Improvement Association. The BIA's job is to help increase shopping traffic in the neighbourhood to boost the business of local retailers and merchants. Lately, the BIA in your area has noticed a disturbing trend: even though there's a major postsecondary institution located right in its midst, it seems that the thousands of students of the institution prefer not to spend their money in the neighbourhood. For example, instead of buying lunch at Dora's Schnitzel Haus, which is located a block away from the campus, they prefer to eat in the cafeteria. Instead of buying clothes at Harvey's Men's Department Store right across the street, they walk ten blocks away to the Mainland Mall. One day, the coordinator of the Marketing program at your institution receives a phone call from the president of the local BIA. The BIA would like students in the Marketing program to conduct research and write a report with recommendations about what can be done to increase traffic between the school and the local businesses. Using the example of your own college or university neighbourhood, what kind of primary and secondary research could you do to help solve the BIA's problem? (Hint: secondary research on spending habits of 18- to 25-year-olds might be useful to know.)

4. Using statistics you can find on the Internet (e.g., from Statistics Canada), design one graph for research problem 1 above and one for research problem 3 above. Make sure the graph follows best practices as described in this chapter. Hand in the original statistics along with your graphics.

5. Using quotations from secondary or primary research you've uncovered as part of answering research problems 1 and 3 above, write two paragraphs (one for each problem) in which you paraphrase from some already published research. Make sure your paraphrase follows best practices as described in this chapter. Provide a works cited reference for all the sources from which you quote. Hand in the original sources along with your paragraphs.

Grammar/Style Review 8

In this review, you will be practising identifying parallelism mistakes. There are at least three mistakes in total. For a brief explanation of this style problem, please read the explanation on page 329. Besides completing the exercise below, be sure to be on the lookout for parallelism mistakes in your own writing.

To: bflahiff@rgroup.ca

From: mmohammed@rgroup.ca

Re: Problems with our focus group

Hi Brenda,

As you know we've been conducting focus groups on nutrition, the 18–34 demographic's shopping habits, and fitness. Our session last night went well, but I wanted to alert you to some potential problems:

Mike thinks we need to hold another focus group because the responses last night were so-so

Going this route will put us over budget

Choosing not to do another focus group will undermine our research

When you have a minute, can we talk about these potential problems, potential solutions, and who will communicate with Mike. Thanks a lot.

Best,

Munir

Business Communication Lab 8

You were just hired by a small business consulting firm in your hometown to work as a sales representative/research coordinator. You were hired because of your diploma in business, which included courses in business communication. Your new boss is eager to expand the company's services from its current specialty of business tax advice and preparation into a full-service business consulting firm, including market research services. On your first day at work, this is what your boss says: "I've lined up two clients, one existing and one new, who are interested in buying some market research. I'll fill you in on the details tomorrow, but what I want you to do today is research best practices in research report writing. You told me about your report writing experience in college, but I want you to find out what's happening in the real world. What do research reports look like? Is there a best practices model we can follow?" You say: "No problem, I'll start right away." "Great," your new boss says, "and by the way, you might want to read this article from the *National Post* I saw recently. The writer has some interesting ideas about what makes for good research." He searches through a pile of paper on his desk and hands you a copy of the Duncan Stewart article from the beginning of the chapter. Write your boss a short e-mail with the results of your research into "real-world" business research reports. Make sure to list where you found your research in the e-mail.

CHAPTER 9

Formal Report Analysis, Interpretation, and Organization

Go big or stay small

BY REBECCA HARRIS, *MARKETING*, SEPTEMBER 27, 2004, 19–20

IF MARKET RESEARCHERS played a word-association game with the phrase "state of the industry," their answers might range from "exciting" to "evolving" to "depressed." With consolidation, changing technology and increased client demands topping the list of issues market researchers face today, all three answers might indeed be correct.

In Canada, the $442-million market research industry is undergoing unprecedented change. Global players have swallowed up smaller firms, the Internet has introduced new ways of conducting research, and shrinking budgets mean marketers want more service for less money. Add to that increased competition and the public's negative perception of market research, and it's clear the industry is in a state of flux....

Going global

Steve Levy, president of Ipsos-Reid Eastern Canada, notes that almost all of the major agencies in Canada are owned by—and in some cases have been bought and sold twice to—European conglomerates ...

"The industry landscape in Canada doesn't look anything like it did in 1985," says Levy. "And I would venture to guess that a number of the medium-size companies, which are few in number in Canada, would probably like to be acquired by someone." He cites three reasons: Multinational companies that are building global brands want global ad agencies, global consulting companies and global accounting firms; Canadian entrepreneurs reach an age where they want liquidity and want to sell; and those acquiring companies are public companies that, by their very mandate, have to grow.

The question is, will small, independent companies be able to survive globalization? According to Levy, smaller companies (five to eight people) in Canada will actually flourish. "There will be more of them, they'll be niche-oriented and specialist-based. The problem is the middle-size companies because they will get squeezed out. They won't be able to compete with the increasing number of very large companies and they don't have the global offerings."

Duncan McKie, president of Canadian-owned Pollara, doesn't buy the argument made by multinationals. "Some people would say consolidation gives you access to worldwide market intelligence, international norms and standards and blah, blah blah ... That's interesting and sometimes nice to know, but I don't know if it makes a great deal of difference when it comes down to deciding whether your business is doing well in Canada." He adds that consolidation is driven by the desire to save money as much as anything else. "It isn't methodologically an improvement to know what the customer service norms are in Germany."

The need for speed

On the technology front, a new way of conducting surveys arrived on the market research scene with much controversy. People watched it with both interest and suspicion, wondering if it would work as well as the old methodologies, whether there would be errors and disadvantages. "It was controversial for a while and some clients were reluctant to use it, but now people don't even think about it," says Barry

Watson, president and CEO of Toronto-based Environics Research Group.

He's talking, of course, about the first computer-assisted telephone interviewing developed 22 years ago. "Technological innovation has always been a very significant part of our industry and I think the Internet is just the latest one, although certainly one which is maybe more far-reaching than the others," he says.

Cost and speed are the key factors driving Internet usage. "The Internet makes market research cheaper and companies are delivering their data not on paper, not in research reports, but on portals on the Internet," says Levy. "As soon as you have the data, you can deliver it anywhere. We collect data from McDonald's in over 30 countries around the world. We deliver the country data specific to that country, but we also deliver all of the data from all of the countries to McDonald's (head office) in America."

While market research has certainly come a long way from pen-and-paper and door-to-door interviews, the Internet hasn't exactly made traditional methodologies obsolete. "People initially had perceptions that it would take over a lot more of the current methodologies, but it hasn't done that to the degree people thought it would," notes Joanne Tofani, president of the Canadian Survey Research Council. "It has opened up different ways of doing research and allowed us to get to more difficult-to-reach audiences."

Jean-Marc Léger, president of Montreal-based Leger Marketing, says using the Internet for research will increase, but it won't replace the phone interview or postal survey. "It's only a technique to join the population (of other methods)," he says. "But the most important thing is clients want more speed. People say 'I want my survey next week,' but if you want a good survey, you have to take time. The Internet gave us pressure to really deliver the results quickly."

More for less

Indeed, client demands are starting to sound like a fast-food restaurant motto: fast and cheap. But it's not just the hard data they're looking for. In addition to the numbers, marketers want insight into what it all means. There's an increasing desire by the client for agencies to be stronger in terms of interpretation, giving insight, advising them on what to do with the data. This is partly driven by the fact that marketers' in-house research departments are smaller than in the past.

"They're trying to extract costs from their businesses and often that means the first group to be downsized is the research department. Because it's not considered to be an investment...it's a bit of a luxury," adds McKie. He believes these cost reduction exercises are to blame for increased competition in the marketplace, meaning there are "too many people chasing too few dollars." According to McKie, downsizing created a glut of independent market researchers, who charge less than larger market research firms. In turn, clients now expect that they won't have to pay for additional services such as data analysis when they do turn to bigger firms.

"It's a pretty sad state of affairs," says McKie. "I think the whole business is depressed, frankly. (These)...high-volume, low-value companies...have pushed the value proposition down to the point where it's very difficult to suggest to anyone that they pay for interpretative or consultative services on top of simply data collection and statistical analysis." But, he says, "that will go away in 10 years because all those people will be collecting pensions or be in Florida."

Nikita Nanos, president of Ottawa-based SES Research, believes the market research industry is morphing into a "market intelligence" industry. "It's more than just someone in a call centre picking up the phone and dialling a number," he says. "It's companies providing integrated research services and high level detailed analysis, and they're really becoming strategic and advisory partners for companies."

His point echoes the belief of other researchers who say the value of market research is growing, not waning. As Watson notes, "I think marketing problems are not going away and market research is a significant part of the solution."

DIAGNOSING THE PROBLEM

Rebecca Harris details a number of problems, or changes, to the market research industry in Canada. First, she argues that globalization is adversely affecting some medium-sized firms that can no longer effectively compete with large firms that have offices around the world. Second, she shows how evolving technology, which has always been part of the market research industry, is now threatening to change it beyond recognition. The use of the Internet to conduct surveys, as opposed to telephone operators or mail-based surveys or in-person surveying, is seen as a threat to jobs. Finally, Harris notes that clients are starting to expect more research-based service for less money. In other words, not only do many clients want market research firms to find and collect the data, but they are also expecting them to package analysis and interpretation services—which were once considered valuable extra services—into the price.

Of the three problems Harris discusses, the last two are important for business communicators. If the Internet is here to stay as a research tool, then logically business communicators have to become adept at using this new technology as a primary research tool. It's not enough to be able to search for something in Google, as most of us do daily; now, it seems that knowing how to design and execute an online questionnaire, for example, is also a vital business communication tool.

Similarly, the final point in Harris's article deserves our attention. While obviously not all of us will end up as either in-house market researchers, employees of a market research firm, or freelance research consultants, it's important to understand the lesson that Harris's article teaches. There is an important difference between the skills of data collection and data analysis and interpretation. Both are important, both are different, and both are necessary when doing primary research. While it seems that less value is being placed by clients on analysis and interpretation (which are actually the more intellectually difficult parts of research), the truth is that for a research project to be successful, all the ingredients must be present.

Now that you understand some of the background of changes taking place in the market research industry, consider the following activity ...

in-class
activity 9

IMAGINE THAT YOUR team members work for a market research firm. You've recently been hired by a large clothing manufacturer. The company makes men's slacks (e.g., khakis), and its sales have been falling in the past five years. It wants to know why. You propose to carry out focus group interviews, survey no fewer than 1000 men across Canada, and deliver a research report back to the company within six weeks. To do your research, what methods will you use? How will technology be important in your work? Your proposal price included both data collection and analysis. How will you apportion your time to get the ambitious data collection finished and to provide effective analysis? Report back to the class in 20 minutes.

Now that you've presented your solution to the rest of the class, you're ready to discover more information on how to organize and analyze business research and how to format your research report. At the end of this chapter, you will be presented with some more problems that you may be asked to analyze, evaluate, and explain.

ANALYZING AND INTERPRETING BUSINESS DATA

Organizations need information to keep up with what's happening inside and outside of their firms. Rebecca Harris's article describes the market research industry that provides organizations with this information if they don't have their own in-house research department. Whether the data is collected in-house or by an outside company, it is usually presented to decision makers in the form of reports.

Three Methods of Analysis

Unprocessed data (for example, 1000 questionnaire responses from across Canada to the question: "What qualities do you find appealing about Clarkson pants?") become meaningful information only once they have been analyzed, which means they've been sorted, combined, and recombined in a variety of ways. For example, what do we find when we divide our 1000 questionnaires into age groups? Or what do we find when we divide our questionnaires by geographical region? Or what do we find when we divide our questionnaires by annual income of the respondent?

Just as Rebecca Harris's article above is clearly separated into three main sections (one for each change happening in the market research industry), so too will your analysis of any business research problem be separated. This is because you can't solve a problem without analyzing it, and analysis, at its simplest level, is the dividing of something into its parts in order to describe it better. If a pant manufacturer wants to understand her customers, one of the ways to divide them is by age, another is by income, and another is by region. There are other ways, of course, but these three are popular among market researchers.

Hopefully, you can see that a shortcut that professional researchers use to help them analyze data is to design their primary research so that it produces the separations, divisions, or classifications they're interested in. For example, if you want to know what men in their 50s and 60s think of Clarkson pants, as well as what teenagers think, you obviously need a question at the beginning of the survey that asks respondents to declare their age.

Analysis can be analyzed itself into three main categories, all of which are important for business research. The kind of analysis most of us are used to is known as *descriptive analysis*. Any time you are describing the parts of something, you are providing a descriptive analysis. For example, if you are describing the organizational hierarchy of Clarkson pants, from the board of directors, down through the CEO and her VPs, to the managers and their designers, cutters, sewers, sales people, and customer service representatives, you are providing a descriptive analysis of Clarkson pants. Sometimes a descriptive analysis seems so natural to us that we don't realize we're doing it. Earlier, we mentioned that Rebecca Harris's article is divided into three sections that prove her three main points: this was a descriptive analysis on our part of a magazine article—a description of how it is put together.

Another typical type of analysis, especially in business, is the *analysis of a process*. Any time you describe how an action such as sewing or selling, or how an event, such as a business presentation or meeting, happens, you are providing an analysis of a process. Process analysis is more complex than descriptive analysis because it has to be able to describe the parts or stages or steps of a process logically. For example, the making of the appointment happens before the sales call, which happens before the follow-up. Also, in process analysis, it's important to understand how the various parts of the process are related to each other (e.g., the follow-up takes place as a way to close the sale). This is not always true in descriptive analysis.

Finally, there is *analysis of cause and effect*, sometimes called causal analysis. One of the most common ways of analyzing a problem is to look for the reasons it took place. Often, as a researcher you are one step ahead if you already know some of the effects in the situation. For example, if Clarkson hires you to research what men think about its pants, the reason might be that the company's sales are down. In this situation, you understand one of the major effects already, and you've been hired to find the causes of this effect. Another example you're already familiar with is Rebecca Harris's article about market research. If you skim the article again, you'll see that the method of analysis she's chosen to employ is a causal analysis. Each of her three main sections is labelled with a cause such as globalization and technology. Then, in that section, she proceeds to describe what effects these causes have on the market research industry.

As a business researcher, you will probably use all three methods of analysis in any research report you have to write. As mentioned above, we aren't always able to discriminate between the three types of analysis because they come naturally to us. The trick, now that we've analyzed the three types for you, is to treat each method as a powerful tool that can be used to achieve results.

Tabulating Data for Interpretation

Sometimes analysis of a problem is sufficient for understanding. For example, Rebecca Harris's article with its cause-and-effect analysis gives us a useful explanation for the problem she describes. At other times (especially when primary data are involved) before you can achieve results in a research report, you have to add one more step. Besides analyzing your data—that is, describing it systematically either through its parts or by dividing it into causes and effects—you need to be able to explain the meaning of the data. The process by which we explain the meaning of something is known as *interpretation*.

A good way of thinking of how interpretation takes place is the idea of the "educated guess." In other words, when you interpret, you use common sense, information you already have, secondary research materials, and best practices in your field, to find the meaning in a set of data. There are some shortcuts seasoned researchers use to make their educated guesses more useful. They look for patterns in data, contradictions in data, and implications of data.

If the researcher looking at Clarkson pants analyzes his data by region and finds that in all five geographical regions of Canada, the same pattern of responses is apparent (e.g., men over the age of 50 have bought a pair of Clarkson pants in the past year), then an educated guess or interpretation can be made. Clarkson pants, the researcher may infer, are most popular among this age group. Furthermore, he may infer that marketing and design of Clarkson pants should be targeted toward this demographic.

Let's say the same researcher next analyzes his data by age group and finds that both the 16-to-24 and the 50-to-65 age groups rate Clarkson pants as "highly desirable." On the surface, this seems like a contradiction. In other words, both things can't be true because it doesn't make sense. How can older men and young men both like Clarkson pants? An educated guess or interpretation is that Clarkson pants, because they are a well-known Canadian brand that's been around for over 50 years, appeal to men who remember these pants as "what was fashionable and desirable" when they were young. And, what's more, Clarkson pants appeal to young men because of their "retro" or "nostalgic" appeal. Therefore, Clarkson can market its pants to two different age groups (in a slightly different way: one emphasizing the pants' tradition, the other their retro appeal).

Finally, the researcher analyzes his data by income level of respondent. Once again, he's slightly surprised to find that Clarkson pants are most popular among the highest income earners (over $100 000 per year) and the lowest income earners (less than $20 000 per year). The educated guess or interpretation in this case might be that middle-class and upper-middle-class teenagers who find Clarkson pants cool can afford to pay their premium price, as can wealthy retirees. The implication (which you can think of as a not-obvious connection between two things) the researcher makes is that the price of Clarkson pants should not be lowered (in fact it might be slightly increased) because both groups that can afford to pay for the pants rate them highly.

As a business researcher, your first step in interpreting raw data (for example, from a survey) is to tabulate it. A number of tabulating and statistical techniques can help you create order from the "chaos" of raw data. These techniques simplify, summarize, and classify large amounts of data into meaningful terms. From the condensed data you're more likely to be able to draw valid conclusions and make reasoned recommendations. The most helpful summarizing techniques include tables, statistical concepts (mean, median, and mode), correlations, and grids.

Tables. Numerical data from questionnaires or interviews are usually summarized and simplified in tables. Using systematic columns and rows, tables make quantitative information easier to comprehend. After assembling your data, you'll want to prepare preliminary tables to enable you to see what the information means.

Sometimes data become more meaningful when cross-tabulated. This process allows analysis of two or more variables together. By cross-tabulating the findings, you sometimes uncover data that may help answer your problem question or that may prompt you to explore other possibilities. Don't, however, undertake cross-tabulation unless it serves more than mere curiosity.

Tables also help you compare multiple data collected from questionnaires and surveys. Figure 9.1 shows, in raw form, responses to several survey items. To convert these data into a more usable form, you need to calculate percentages for each item. Then you can arrange the responses in some rational sequence, such as largest percentage to smallest.

Once the data are displayed in a table, you can more easily draw conclusions. As Figure 9.1 shows, Midland College students apparently are not interested in public transportation or shuttle buses from satellite lots. They want to park on campus, with restricted visitor parking; only half are willing to pay for new parking lots.

The three Ms: mean, median, mode. Tables help you organize data, and the three Ms help you describe it. These statistical terms—mean, median, and mode—are all occasionally used loosely to mean "average." To be safe, though, you should learn to apply these statistical terms precisely.

When people say *average*, they usually intend to indicate the *mean*, or arithmetic average. The *median* represents the midpoint in a group of figures arranged from lowest to highest (or vice versa).

The *mode* is simply the value that occurs most frequently. Although mode is infrequently used by researchers, knowing the mode is useful in some situations. To remember the meaning of *mode*, think about fashion; the most frequent response, the mode, is the most fashionable.

Mean, median, and mode figures are especially helpful when the range of values is also known. Range represents the span between the highest and lowest values. To calculate the range, you simply subtract the lowest figure from the

Figure 9.1 ▶   Converting Survey Data Into Finished Tables

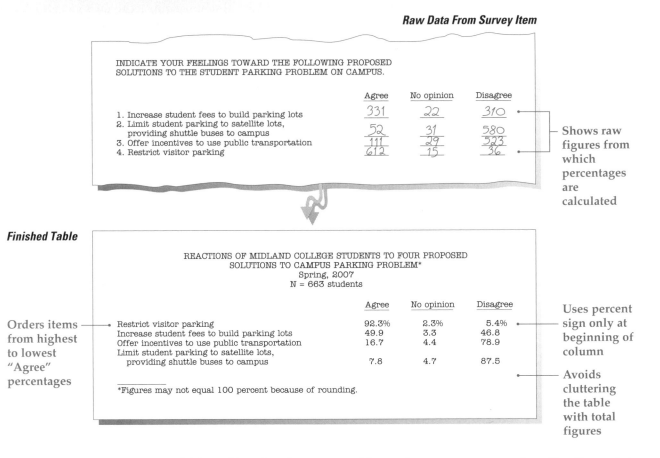

Tips for Converting Raw Data
- **Tabulate the responses on a copy of the survey form.**
- **Calculate percentages (divide the score for an item by the total for all responses to that item; for example, for item 1, divide 331 by 663).**
- **Round off figures to one decimal point or to whole numbers.**
- **Arrange items in a logical order, such as largest to smallest percentage.**
- **Prepare a table with a title that tells such things as who, what, when, where, and why.**
- **Include the total number of respondents.**

Raw Data From Survey Item

INDICATE YOUR FEELINGS TOWARD THE FOLLOWING PROPOSED
SOLUTIONS TO THE STUDENT PARKING PROBLEM ON CAMPUS.

	Agree	No opinion	Disagree
1. Increase student fees to build parking lots	331	22	310
2. Limit student parking to satellite lots, providing shuttle buses to campus	52	31	580
3. Offer incentives to use public transportation	111	29	523
4. Restrict visitor parking	612	15	36

Shows raw figures from which percentages are calculated

Finished Table

REACTIONS OF MIDLAND COLLEGE STUDENTS TO FOUR PROPOSED
SOLUTIONS TO CAMPUS PARKING PROBLEM*
Spring, 2007
N = 663 students

	Agree	No opinion	Disagree
Restrict visitor parking	92.3%	2.3%	5.4%
Increase student fees to build parking lots	49.9	3.3	46.8
Offer incentives to use public transportation	16.7	4.4	78.9
Limit student parking to satellite lots, providing shuttle buses to campus	7.8	4.7	87.5

*Figures may not equal 100 percent because of rounding.

Orders items from highest to lowest "Agree" percentages

Uses percent sign only at beginning of column

Avoids cluttering the table with total figures

highest. Knowing the range enables readers to put mean and median figures into perspective. This knowledge also prompts researchers to wonder why such a range exists, thus stimulating hunches and further investigation to solve problems.

Correlations. In tabulating and analyzing data, you may see relationships among two or more variables that help explain the findings. Intuition suggests correlations that may or may not prove to be accurate. Although one event may not be said to cause another, the business researcher who sees a correlation begins to ask why and how the two variables are related. In this way, apparent correlations stimulate investigation and present possible problem solutions to be explored.

In reporting correlations, you should avoid suggesting that a cause-and-effect relationship exists when none can be proved. Only sophisticated research methods can statistically prove correlations. Instead, present a correlation as a possible relationship. Cautious statements followed by explanations gain you credibility and allow readers to make their own decisions.

Grids. Another technique for analyzing raw data—especially verbal data—is the grid. Complex verbal information is transformed into concise, manageable data; readers can see immediately which points are supported and opposed.

Arranging data in a grid also works for projects such as feasibility studies that compare many variables. The popular magazine *Consumer Reports* often uses grids to show information; additionally, grids help classify employment data.

WRITING A CONCLUSION AND RECOMMENDATIONS

The most widely read portions of a report are the sections devoted to the conclusion and recommendations. In fact today in business, many people expect a report's conclusion and recommendations to be placed at the front, which is the opposite of where they are placed in traditional formal report organization. Knowledgeable readers go straight to the conclusion to see what the report writer thinks the data mean. Because the conclusion synthesizes and explains the findings, it represents the heart of a report. Your value in an organization rises considerably if you can draw conclusions that analyze information logically and show how the data answer questions and solve problems. As some of the people quoted in Harris's article above might say, this is the "value-added" part of the report.

Interpreting Data to Arrive at Conclusions

Any set of data can produce a variety of conclusions. Always bear in mind, though, that the audience for a report wants to know how these data relate to the problem being studied. What do the findings mean with regard to solving the original report problem?

For example, the Marriott Corporation recognized a serious problem among its employees. Conflicting home and work requirements seemed to be causing excessive employee turnover and decreased productivity. To learn the extent of the problem and to consider solutions, Marriott surveyed its staff.[1] It learned, among other things, that nearly 35 percent of its employees had children under age twelve, and 15 percent had children under age five. Other findings, shown in Figure 9.2, indicated that one-third of its staff with young children took time off because of child-care difficulties. Moreover, many current employees left previous jobs because of work and family conflicts. The survey also showed that managers did not consider child-care or family problems to be appropriate topics for discussion at work.

A sample of possible conclusions that could be drawn from these findings is shown in Figure 9.2. Notice that each conclusion relates to the initial report problem. Although only a few possible findings and conclusions are shown here, you can see that the conclusions try to explain the causes for the home/work conflict among employees. Many report writers would expand the conclusion section by explaining each item and citing supporting evidence. Even for simplified conclusions, such as those shown in Figure 9.2, you will want to number each item separately and use parallel construction (balanced sentence structure).

Although your goal is to remain objective, drawing conclusions naturally involves a degree of subjectivity. Your goals, background, and frame of reference all

Figure 9.2 ▶ Report Conclusions and Recommendations

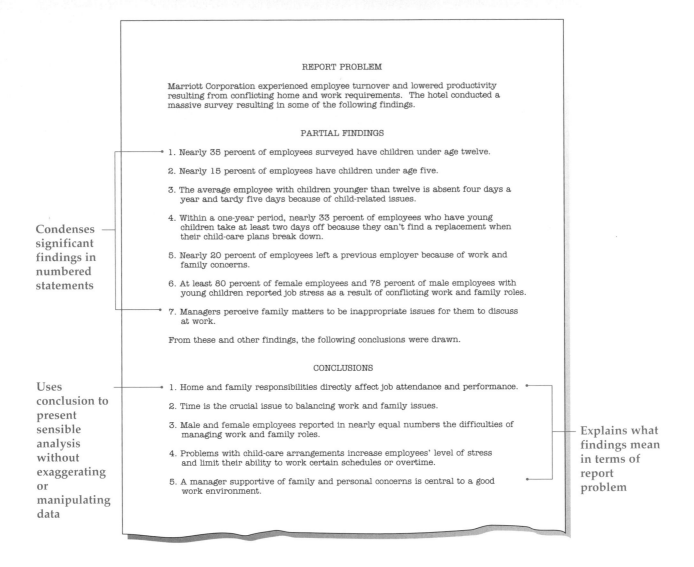

Tips for Writing Conclusions

- Interpret and summarize the findings; tell what they mean.
- Relate the conclusions to the report problem.
- Limit the conclusions to the data presented; do not introduce new material.
- Number the conclusions and present them in parallel form.
- Be objective; avoid exaggerating or manipulating the data.
- Use consistent criteria in evaluating options.

REPORT PROBLEM

Marriott Corporation experienced employee turnover and lowered productivity resulting from conflicting home and work requirements. The hotel conducted a massive survey resulting in some of the following findings.

PARTIAL FINDINGS

Condenses significant findings in numbered statements

1. Nearly 35 percent of employees surveyed have children under age twelve.
2. Nearly 15 percent of employees have children under age five.
3. The average employee with children younger than twelve is absent four days a year and tardy five days because of child-related issues.
4. Within a one-year period, nearly 33 percent of employees who have young children take at least two days off because they can't find a replacement when their child-care plans break down.
5. Nearly 20 percent of employees left a previous employer because of work and family concerns.
6. At least 80 percent of female employees and 78 percent of male employees with young children reported job stress as a result of conflicting work and family roles.
7. Managers perceive family matters to be inappropriate issues for them to discuss at work.

From these and other findings, the following conclusions were drawn.

CONCLUSIONS

Uses conclusion to present sensible analysis without exaggerating or manipulating data

1. Home and family responsibilities directly affect job attendance and performance.
2. Time is the crucial issue to balancing work and family issues.
3. Male and female employees reported in nearly equal numbers the difficulties of managing work and family roles.
4. Problems with child-care arrangements increase employees' level of stress and limit their ability to work certain schedules or overtime.
5. A manager supportive of family and personal concerns is central to a good work environment.

Explains what findings mean in terms of report problem

colour the inferences you make. Findings will be interpreted from the writer's perspective, but they should not be manipulated to achieve a preconceived purpose.

You can make your report conclusions more objective if you use consistent evaluation criteria. Let's say you are comparing computers for an office equipment purchase. If you evaluate each by the same criteria (such as price, specifications, service, and warranty), your conclusions are more likely to be bias-free.

You also need to avoid the temptation to sensationalize or exaggerate your findings or conclusions. Be careful of words like *many, most,* and *all.* Instead of

Figure 9.2 ▶ *Continued*

Tips for Writing Recommendations

- **Make specific suggestions for actions to solve the report problem.**
- **Prepare practical recommendations that will be agreeable to the audience.**
- **Avoid conditional words such as** *maybe* **and** *perhaps.*
- **Present each suggestion separately as a command beginning with a verb.**

- **Number the recommendations for improved readability.**
- **If requested, describe how the recommendations may be implemented.**
- **When possible, arrange the recommendations in an announced order, such as most important to least important.**

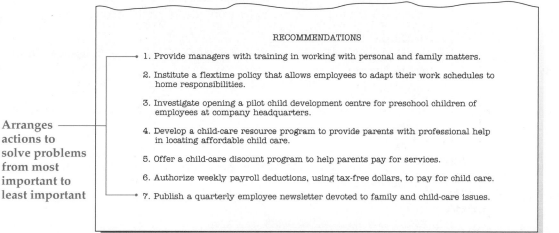

RECOMMENDATIONS

Arranges actions to solve problems from most important to least important

1. Provide managers with training in working with personal and family matters.
2. Institute a flextime policy that allows employees to adapt their work schedules to home responsibilities.
3. Investigate opening a pilot child development centre for preschool children of employees at company headquarters.
4. Develop a child-care resource program to provide parents with professional help in locating affordable child care.
5. Offer a child-care discount program to help parents pay for services.
6. Authorize weekly payroll deductions, using tax-free dollars, to pay for child care.
7. Publish a quarterly employee newsletter devoted to family and child-care issues.

many of the respondents felt..., you might more accurately write *some of the respondents....* Examine your motives before drawing conclusions. Don't let preconceptions or wishful thinking colour your reasoning.

Preparing Report Recommendations

Recommendations, unlike conclusions, make specific suggestions for actions that can solve the report problem. Typically, readers prefer specific recommendations. They want to know exactly how to implement the suggestions. The specificity of your recommendations depends on your authorization. What are you commissioned to do, and what does the reader expect? In the planning stages of your report project, you anticipate what the reader wants in the report. Your intuition and your knowledge of the audience indicate how far your recommendations should be developed.

In the recommendations section of the Marriott employee survey, shown in Figure 9.2, many of the suggestions are summarized. In the actual report each recommendation could have been backed up with specifics and ideas for implementing them. For example, the child-care resource recommendation would be explained: it provides parents with names of agencies and professionals who specialize in locating child care across the country.

A good report provides practical recommendations that are agreeable to the audience. In the Marriott survey, for example, report researchers knew that the company wanted to help employees cope with conflicts between family and work obligations. Thus, the report's conclusions and recommendations focused on ways to resolve the conflict. If Marriott's goal had been merely to reduce employee absenteeism and save money, the recommendations would have been quite different.

If possible, make each recommendation a command. Note in Figure 9.2 that each recommendation begins with a verb. This structure sounds forceful and confident and helps the reader comprehend the information quickly. Avoid words such as *maybe* and *perhaps*; they suggest conditional statements that reduce the strength of recommendations.

Experienced writers may combine recommendations and conclusions. And in short reports, writers may omit conclusions and move straight to recommendations. The important thing about recommendations, though, is that they include practical suggestions for solving the report problem.

Recommendations evolve from interpretation of the findings and conclusions. Consider the following examples from the Marriott survey:

FINDING
A majority of managers perceive family matters to be inappropriate issues for them to discuss at work.

CONCLUSION
Managers are neither willing nor trained to discuss family troubles that may cause employees to miss work.

RECOMMENDATION
Provide managers with training in recognizing and working with personal and family troubles that affect work.

FINDING
Within a one-year period, nearly 33 percent of employees who have young children take at least two days off because they can't find a replacement when their child-care plans break down.

CONCLUSION
Problems with child-care arrangements increase employees' level of stress and create absenteeism.

RECOMMENDATION
Develop a child-care resource program to provide parents with professional help in locating affordable child care.

ORGANIZING DATA IN THE REPORT

After collecting data, analyzing it, interpreting it to draw conclusions, and designing recommendations to solve the issues you've identified, you're ready to organize the parts of the report into a logical written and illustrated framework. Poorly organized reports lead to frustration. Readers will not understand, remember, or be persuaded. Wise writers know that reports rarely "just organize themselves." Instead, organization must be imposed on the data.

Informational reports, as you learned in Chapter 7, generally present data without interpretation. As summarized in Figure 9.3, informational reports are typically organized in three parts: introduction/background, facts/findings, and summary/conclusion. Analytical reports, which generally analyze data and draw conclusions, typically contain four parts: introduction/problem, facts/findings, discussion/analysis, and conclusions/recommendations. However, the parts in analytical reports do not always follow the same sequence. For readers who know about the project, are supportive, or are eager to learn the results quickly, the direct method is appropriate. Conclusions and recommendations, if requested, appear upfront. For readers who must be educated or persuaded, the indirect method works better. Conclusions/recommendations appear last, after the findings have been presented and analyzed.

Although every report is different, the overall organizational patterns described here typically hold true. The real challenge lies in organizing the facts/findings and discussion/analysis sections, providing reader cues, and maintaining consistency of headings.

Ordering Information Logically

Whether you're writing informational or analytical reports, the data you've collected must be structured coherently. Five common organizational methods are by time, importance, component, criteria, or convention. Notice that these methods are also methods of analysis—a way of breaking data down into manageable pieces. Regardless of the method you choose, be sure that it helps the reader understand the data. Reader comprehension, not writer convenience, should govern organization.

Time. Ordering data by time means establishing a chronology of events. Agendas, minutes of meetings, progress reports, and procedures are usually organized by time. Beware of overusing time chronologies, however. Although this method is easy and often mirrors the way data are collected, chronologies tend to be boring, repetitious, and lacking in emphasis. Readers can't always pick out what's important.

Importance. Organization by importance involves beginning with the most important item and proceeding to the least important—or vice versa. The Marriott report describing work/family conflicts might begin by discussing child care, if the writer considered it the most important issue. Using importance to structure findings involves a value judgment. The writer must decide what is most important, always keeping in mind the readers' priorities and expectations. Busy readers appreciate seeing important points first; they may skim or skip other points. On the other hand, building to a climax by moving from least important to most important enables the writer to focus attention at the end. Thus, the reader is more likely to remember the most important item. Of course, the writer also risks losing the attention of the reader along the way.

Component. Especially for informational reports, data may be organized by components such as location, geography, division, product, or part. Organization by components works best when the classifications already exist. For example, a

Figure 9.3 ▶ Organizing Informational and Analytical Reports

Informational Reports	Analytical Reports	
	Direct Pattern	**Indirect Pattern**
I. Introduction/background	I. Introduction/problem	I. Introduction/problem
II. Facts/findings	II. Conclusions/recommendations	II. Facts/findings
III. Summary/conclusion	III. Facts/findings	III. Discussion/analysis
	IV. Discussion/analysis	IV. Conclusions/recommendations

company trying to decide where to open up its next call centre may have asked its researchers to look into three Canadian cities: Ottawa, Moncton, and Charlottetown. Obviously, the organization of the findings in this report should follow these three geographical components.

Criteria. More sophisticated research-based reports establish criteria by which they judge data. This method helps writers (and readers) to treat topics consistently. Organizing a report around criteria helps readers make comparisons, instead of forcing them to search through the report for similar data. In the report discussed above, the criteria for choosing in which city to open up a call centre could be education of workforce, municipal corporate tax rate, and incentives offered by the city and province. In this case, the report findings could be organized by these three criteria (and each city/component would be discussed under each criteria). Alternatively, the report could be organized by component (the cities) and under each component you could describe what you found out about the three criteria (i.e., education, taxes, and incentives).

Convention. Many recurring reports are structured according to convention. That is, they follow a prescribed plan or template to which everyone in the company has access. For example, an organization divided into three major departments (Operations, Finance, and Production) may hold twice-yearly budget meetings at which the VP of each area must provide a budget report using a template. A good example of a real-world business research report written by convention is a stock analysis report. All the major stock brokerage firms have templates that their stock analysts use. While the components of these reports are similar across various competing firms (e.g., recommendation to buy, sell, or hold; highlights of past quarter performance; graphic representation of recent past performance; legal disclaimers), each firm has its own template, including its own logo, and recommendation vocabulary.

Providing Reader Cues

When you envision your report, you probably see a neat outline in your mind: major points, supported by subpoints and details. However, readers don't know the material as well as you; they did not get a chance to read your report work plan. To guide them through the data, you need to provide the equivalent of a map and road signs. For both formal and informal reports, devices such as introductions, transitions, and headings prevent readers from getting lost.

Introduction. The best way to point a reader in the right direction is to provide an introduction that does three things:

- Tells the purpose of the report
- Describes the significance of the topic
- Previews the main points and the order in which they will be developed

The following paragraph includes all three elements in introducing a report on computer security:

> *The purpose of this report is to examine the security of our current computer operations and present suggestions for improving security. Lax computer security could mean loss of information, loss of business, and damage to our equipment and systems. Because many former employees, released during recent downsizing efforts, know our systems, major changes must be made. To improve security, I will present*

three recommendations: (1) begin using smart cards that limit access to our computer system, (2) alter sign-on and log-off procedures, (3) move central computer operations to a more secure area.

This opener tells the purpose (examining computer security), describes its significance (loss of information and business, damage to equipment and systems), and outlines how the report is organized (three recommendations). Good openers in effect set up a contract with the reader. The writer promises to cover certain topics in a specified order. Readers expect the writer to fulfill the contract. They want the topics to be developed as promised—using the same wording and presented in the order mentioned. For example, if in your introduction you state that you will discuss the use of *smart cards*, don't change the heading for that section to *access cards*. Remember that the introduction provides a map to a report; switching the names on the map will ensure that readers get lost. To maintain consistency, delay writing the introduction until after you have completed the report. Long, complex reports may require introductions for each section.

Transitions. Expressions such as *on the contrary, at the same time,* and *however* show relationships and help reveal the logical flow of ideas in a report. These transitional expressions enable writers to tell readers where ideas are headed and how they relate. The following expressions enable you to show readers how you are developing your ideas.

> TO PRESENT ADDITIONAL THOUGHTS: additionally, again, also, moreover, furthermore
>
> TO SUGGEST CAUSE AND EFFECT: accordingly, as a result, consequently, therefore
>
> TO CONTRAST IDEAS: at the same time, but, however, on the contrary, though, yet
>
> TO SHOW TIME AND ORDER: after, before, first, finally, now, previously, then, to conclude
>
> TO CLARIFY POINTS: for example, for instance, in other words, that is, thus

In using these expressions, recognize that they don't have to sit at the head of a sentence. Listen to the rhythm of the sentence, and place the expression where a natural pause occurs. Used appropriately, transitional expressions serve readers as guides; misused or overused, they can be as distracting and frustrating as too many road signs on a highway.

Headings. Good headings are another structural cue that assist readers in comprehending the organization of a report. They highlight major ideas, allowing busy readers to see the big picture in a glance. Moreover, headings provide resting points for the mind and for the eye, breaking up large chunks of text into manageable and inviting segments.

Report writers may use functional or talking heads. Functional heads (for example, *Background, Findings, Personnel,* and *Production Costs*) describe functions or general topics. They show the outline of a report but provide little insight for readers. Functional headings are useful for routine reports. They're also appropriate for sensitive topics that might provoke emotional reactions. By keeping the headings general, experienced writers hope to minimize reader opposition or response to controversial subjects. Talking heads (for example, *Two Sides to Campus Parking Problem* or *Survey Shows Support for Parking Fees*) provide more information and interest. Unless carefully written, however, talking heads can fail to reveal the organization of a report. With some planning, though, headings can be both functional and talking, such as *Parking Recommendations: Shuttle and New Structures*. To create the most effective headings, follow a few basic guidelines:

- **Use appropriate heading levels.** The position and format of a heading indicate its level of importance and relationship to other points. Figure 9.4 both illustrates and discusses a commonly used heading format for business reports.
- **Capitalize and underline carefully.** Most writers use all capital letters (without underlines) for main titles, such as the report, chapter, and unit titles. For first- and second-level headings, they capitalize only the first letter of main words. For additional emphasis, they use a bold font, as shown in Figure 9.4.
- **Balance headings within levels.** All headings at a given level should be grammatically similar. For example, *Developing Product Teams* and *Presenting Plan to Management* are balanced, but *Development of Product Teams* and *Presenting Plan to Management* are not.
- **For short reports use first- or second-level headings.** Many business reports contain only one or two levels of headings. For such reports use first-level headings (centred, bolded) and/or second-level headings (flush left, bolded). See Figure 9.4.
- **Include at least one heading per report page.** Headings increase the readability and attractiveness of report pages. Use at least one per page to break up blocks of text.
- **Keep headings short but clear.** One-word headings are emphatic but not always clear. For example, the heading *Budget* does not adequately describe figures for a summer project involving student interns for an oil company in Alberta. Try to keep your headings brief (no more than eight words), but make sure they are understandable. Experiment with headings that concisely tell who, what, when, where, and why.

FORMATTING THE REPORT

A number of front and end items (e.g., executive summary, appendixes) make formal reports longer than routine reports. These items also enhance the professional tone of formal reports by serving multiple audiences. Formal reports may be read by many levels of managers, technical specialists, financial consultants, and clients, customers, or stockholders. Therefore, breaking a long, formal report into small segments makes its information more accessible and easier to understand for all readers. These segments are discussed below and also illustrated in the model report shown in Figure 9.5. This analytical research report studies the recycling program at West Coast College and makes recommendations for improving its operation.

Cover. Formal reports are usually enclosed in vinyl or heavy paper binders to protect the pages and to give a professional, finished appearance. Some companies have binders imprinted with their name and logo. The title of the report may appear through a cut-out window or may be applied with an adhesive label. Good stationery and office supply stores usually stock an assortment of report binders and labels.

Title page. A report title page, as illustrated in the Figure 9.5 model report (page 242), begins with the name of the report typed in uppercase letters (no underscore and no quotation marks). Next comes *Presented to* (or *Submitted to*) and the name,

Figure 9.4 ▷ Levels of Headings in Reports

5-cm top margin

REPORT, CHAPTER, AND PART TITLES

2 blank lines

The title of a report, chapter heading, or major part (such as CONTENTS or NOTES) should be centred in all caps. If the title requires more than one line, arrange it in an inverted triangle with the longest lines at the top. Begin the text a triple space (two blank lines) below the title, as shown here.

Places major headings in the centre

2 blank lines

First-Level Subheading

1 blank line

Capitalizes initial letters of main words

Headings indicating the first level of division are centred and bolded. Capitalize the first letter of each main word. Whether a report is single-spaced or double-spaced, most typists triple-space (leaving two blank lines) before and double-space (leaving one blank line) after a first-level subheading.

1 blank line

Every level of heading should be followed by some text. For example, we could not jump from "First-Level Subheading," shown above, to "Second-Level Subheading," shown below, without some discussion between.

Does not indent paragraphs because a blank line is left between paragraphs

Good writers strive to develop coherency and fluency by ending most sections with a lead-in that introduces the next section. The lead-in consists of a sentence or two announcing the next topic.

2 blank lines

Starts at left margin

Second-Level Subheading

Headings that divide topics introduced by first-level subheadings are bolded and begin at the left margin. Use a triple space above and a double space after a second-level subheading. If a report has only one level of heading, use either first- or second-level subheading style.

Always be sure to divide topics into two or more subheadings. If you have only one subheading, eliminate it and absorb the discussion under the previous major heading. Try to make all headings within a level grammatically equal. For example, all second-level headings might use verb forms (*Preparing*, *Organizing*, and *Composing*) or noun forms (*Preparation*, *Organization*, and *Composition*).

1 blank line

Makes heading part of paragraph

Third-Level Subheading. Because it is part of the paragraph that follows, a third-level subheading is also called a "paragraph subheading." Capitalize only the first word and proper nouns in the subheading. Bold the subheading and end it with a period. Begin typing the paragraph text immediately following the period, as shown here. Double-space before a paragraph subheading.

title, and organization of the individual receiving the report. Lower on the page is *Prepared by* (or *Submitted by*) and the author's name plus any necessary identification. The last item on the title page is the date of submission. All items after the title are typed in a combination of upper- and lowercase letters.

Letter or memo of transmittal. Generally written on organization stationery, a letter or memorandum of transmittal introduces a formal report. You will recall that letters are sent to outsiders and memos to insiders. A transmittal letter or memo follows the direct pattern and is usually less formal than the report itself (e.g., the letter or memo may use contractions and the first-person pronouns *I* and *we*). The transmittal letter or memo typically announces the topic of the report and tells how it was authorized; briefly describes the project; highlights the report's findings, conclusions, and recommendations, if the reader is expected to be supportive; and closes with appreciation for the assignment, instruction for the reader's follow-up actions, acknowledgment of help from others, or offers of assistance in answering questions. If a report is going to different readers, a special transmittal letter or memo should be prepared for each, anticipating what each reader needs to know in using the report.

Table of contents. The table of contents shows the headings in a report and their page numbers. It gives an overview of the report topics and helps readers locate them. You should wait to prepare the table of contents until after you've completed the report. For short reports you should include all headings. For longer reports you might want to list only first- and second-level headings. Leaders (spaced or unspaced dots) help guide the eye from the heading to the page number. Items may be indented in outline form or typed flush with the left margin.

List of figures. For reports with several figures or illustrations, you may wish to include a list of figures to help readers locate them. This list may appear on the same page as the table of contents, space permitting. For each figure or illustration, include a title and page number. Some writers distinguish between tables and all other illustrations, which are called figures. If you make this distinction, you should also prepare separate lists of tables and figures. Because the model report in Figure 9.5 has few illustrations, the writer labelled them all "figures," a method that simplifies numbering (page 244).

Executive summary. The purpose of an executive summary is to present an overview of a longer report to people who may not have time to read the entire document. Generally, an executive summary is prepared by the author who is writing about his or her own report. But occasionally you may be asked to write an executive summary of a published report or article written by someone else. In either case you will probably perform the following activities:

- **Summarize key points.** Your goal is to summarize the important points, including the purpose of the report; the problem addressed; and the findings, conclusions, and recommendations. You might also summarize the research methods, if they can be stated concisely.
- **Look for strategic words and sentences.** Read the completed report carefully. Pay special attention to first and last sentences of paragraphs, which often contain summary statements. Look for words that enumerate (*first, next, finally*) and words that express causation (*therefore, as a result*). Also look for words that signal essentials (*basically, central, leading, principal, major*) and words that contrast ideas (*however, consequently*).
- **Prepare an outline with headings.** At a minimum include headings for the purpose, findings, and conclusions/recommendations. What kernels of information would your reader want to know about these topics?
- **Fill in your outline.** Some writers use their computers to cut and paste important parts of the text. Then they condense with careful editing. Others find it most efficient to create new sentences as they prepare the executive summary.
- **Begin with the purpose.** The easiest way to begin an executive summary is with the words "The purpose of this report is to...." Experienced writers may be more creative.
- **Follow the report order.** Present all your information in the order in which it is found in the report.
- **Eliminate nonessential details**. Include only main points. Don't include anything not in the original report. Use minimal technical language.

- **Control the length.** An executive summary is usually no longer than 10 percent of the original document. Thus, a 100-page report might require a 10-page summary. A 10-page report might need only a 1-page summary—or no summary at all. The executive summary for a long report may also include graphics to adequately highlight main points.

To see a representative executive summary, look at the one in Figure 9.5 (page 245). Although it is only one page long, this executive summary includes headings to help the reader see the main divisions immediately. Let your organization's practices guide you in determining the length and form of an executive summary.

Introduction. Formal reports begin with an introduction that sets the scene and announces the subject. Because they contain many parts serving different purposes, formal reports have a degree of redundancy. The same information may be included in the letter of transmittal, summary, and introduction. To avoid sounding repetitious, try to present the data slightly differently. But don't skip the introduction because you've included some of its information elsewhere. You can't be sure that your reader saw the information earlier. A good report introduction typically covers the following elements, although not necessarily in this order:

- **Background.** Describe events leading up to the problem or need.
- **Problem or purpose.** Explain the report topic and specify the problem or need that motivated the report.
- **Significance.** Tell why the topic is important. You may wish to quote experts or cite newspapers, journals, books, and other secondary sources to establish the importance of the topic.
- **Scope.** Clarify the boundaries of the report, defining what will be included or excluded.
- **Organization.** Launch readers by giving them a road map that previews the structure of the report.

Beyond these minimal introductory elements, consider adding any of the following information that is relevant for your readers:

- **Authorization.** Identify who commissioned the report. If no letter of transmittal is included, also tell why, when, by whom, and to whom the report was written.
- **Literature review.** Summarize what other authors and researchers have published on this topic, especially for academic and scientific reports.
- **Sources and methods.** Describe your secondary sources (periodicals, books, databases). Also explain how you collected primary data, including survey size, sample design, and statistical programs used.
- **Definitions of key terms.** Define words that may be unfamiliar to the audience. Also define terms with special meanings, such as *small business* when it specifically means businesses with fewer than 30 employees.

Body. The principal section in a formal report is the body. It discusses, analyzes, interprets, and evaluates the research findings or solution to the initial problem. This is where you show the evidence that justifies your conclusions. Organize the body into main categories following your original outline or using one of the patterns described earlier (such as time, component, importance, criteria, or convention).

Although we refer to this section as the body, it doesn't carry that heading. Instead, it contains clear headings that explain each major section. Headings may be functional or talking. Functional heads (such as *Results of the Survey, Analysis of Findings,* or *Discussion*) help readers identify the purpose of the section but don't reveal what's in it. Such headings are useful for routine reports or for sensitive topics that may upset readers. Talking heads (e.g., *Recycling Habits of Campus Community*) are more informative and interesting, but they don't help readers see the organization of the report. The model report in Figure 9.5 uses functional heads for organizational sections requiring identification (*Introduction, Conclusions,* and *Recommendations*) and talking heads to divide the body.

Conclusions. This important section tells what the findings mean, particularly with regard to solving the original problem. Some writers prefer to intermix their conclusions with the analysis of the findings—instead of presenting the conclusions separately. Other writers place the conclusions before the body so that busy readers can examine the significant information immediately. Still others combine the conclusions and recommendations. Most writers, though, present the conclusions after the body because readers expect this structure. In long reports this section may include a summary of the findings. To improve comprehension, you may present the conclusions in a numbered or bulleted list.

Recommendations. When requested, you should submit recommendations that make precise suggestions for actions to solve the report problem. Recommendations are most helpful when they are practical and reasonable. Naturally, they should evolve from the findings and conclusions. Don't introduce new information in the conclusions or recommendations. As with conclusions, the position of recommendations is somewhat flexible. They may be combined with conclusions, or they may be presented before the body, especially when the audience is eager and supportive. Generally, though, in formal reports they come last.

Recommendations require an appropriate introductory sentence, such as "The findings and conclusions in this study support the following recommendations." When making many recommendations, number them and phrase each as a command, such as "Begin an employee fitness program with a workout room available five days a week." If appropriate, add information describing how to implement each recommendation. Some reports include a timetable describing the who, what, when, where, and how for putting each recommendation into operation.

Appendix. Incidental or supporting materials belong in appendixes at the end of a formal report. These materials are relevant to some readers but not to all. Appendixes may include survey forms, copies of other reports, tables of data, computer printouts, and related correspondence. If additional appendixes are necessary, they would be named *Appendix A, Appendix B,* and so forth.

Works cited, references, or bibliography. Readers look in the bibliography section to locate the sources of ideas mentioned in a report. Your method of report documentation determines how this section is developed. If you use the MLA referencing format, all citations would be listed alphabetically in the "Works Cited." If you use the APA format, your list would be called "References." Regardless of the format, you must include the author, title, publication, date of publication, page number, and other significant data for all ideas or quotations used in your report. For electronic references include the preceding information plus a description of the electronic address or path leading to the citation. Also include the date on which you located the electronic reference. To see electronic and other citations, examine the list of references at the end of Figure 9.5 (page 254).

Final Writing Tips

Formal reports involve considerable effort in all three phases of writing, beginning with analysis of the problem and anticipation of the audience. Researching the data, organizing it into a logical presentation, and composing the first draft make up the second phase of writing. Revising, proofreading, and evaluating are the third phase. Although everyone approaches the writing process somewhat differently, the following tips offer advice in problem areas faced by most formal report writers.

- **Allow sufficient time.** Develop a realistic timetable and stick to it.
- **Finish data collection.** Don't begin writing until you've collected all the data and drawn the primary conclusions. Starting too early often means back-tracking. For reports based on survey data, compile the tables and figures first.
- **Work from a good outline.** A clear outline provides the necessary order and direction.
- **Provide a proper writing environment.** You'll need a quiet spot where you can spread out your materials and work without interruption.
- **Use a computer.** Preparing a report on a computer enables you to keyboard quickly; revise easily; and check spelling, grammar, and synonyms readily.
- **Write rapidly; revise later.** Some experts advise writers to record their ideas quickly and save revision until after the first draft is completed.
- **Save difficult sections.** If some sections are harder to write than others, save them until you've developed confidence and rhythm working on easier topics.
- **Be consistent in verb tense.** Use past-tense verbs to describe completed action, use present-tense verbs to explain current actions, and use past-tense verbs when citing references.
- **Generally avoid *I* and *we* and write in the third person.** This formal style sometimes results in the overuse of passive-voice verbs so look for alternative constructions.
- **Let the first draft sit and return to it with the expectation of revising and improving it.**
- **Revise for clarity, coherence, and conciseness.** Make sure that your writing is so clear that a busy manager does not have to reread any part.
- **Proofread the final copy three times.** First, read a printed copy slowly for word meanings and content. Then read the copy again for spelling, punctuation, grammar, and other mechanical errors. Finally, scan the entire report to check its formatting and consistency.

Putting It All Together

Formal reports in business generally aim to study problems and recommend solutions. Alan Christopher, business senator to the Office of Associated Students (OAS) at West Coast College, was given a campus problem to study, resulting in the formal report shown in Figure 9.5.

The campus recycling program, under the direction of Cheryl Bryant and supported by the OAS, was not attracting the anticipated level of participation. As the campus recycling program began its second year of operation, Cheryl and the OAS wondered whether campus community members were sufficiently aware of the program. They also wondered how participation could be increased. Alan volunteered to investigate the problem because of his strong support for environmental causes. He also needed to conduct a research project for one of his business courses, and he had definite ideas for improving the campus OAS recycling program.

Figure 9.5 ▶   Model Formal Report with MLA Citation Style

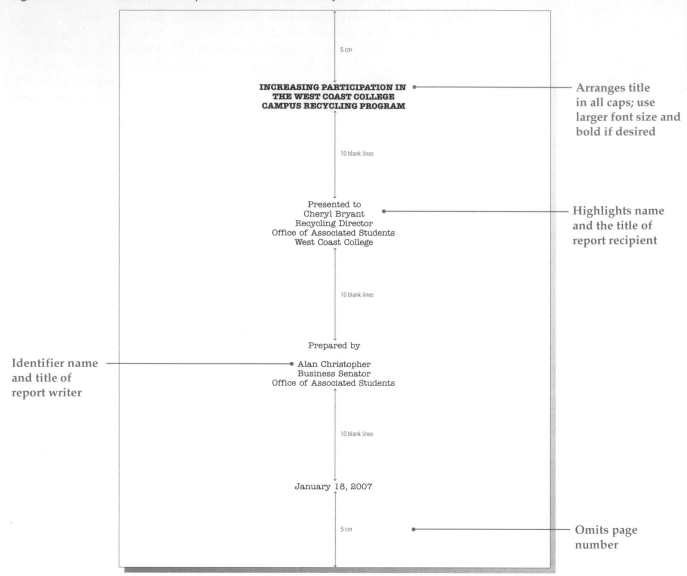

Identifier name
and title of
report writer

Arranges title
in all caps; use
larger font size and
bold if desired

Highlights name
and the title of
report recipient

Omits page
number

Alan arranges the title page so that the amount of space above the
title is equal to the space below the date. If a report is to be
bound on the left, move the left margin and centre point
approximately 0.5 cm to the right. Notice that no page number
appears on the title page, although it is counted as page i.

If you use scalable fonts, word processing capabilities, or a laser
printer to enhance your report and title page, be careful to avoid
anything unprofessional (such as too many type fonts, oversized
print, and inappropriate graphics).

Figure 9.5 ▶ *Continued*

Includes 3- to 4-cm top margin

MEMORANDUM

DATE: January 18, 2007

TO: Cheryl Bryant, Director, Recycling Program
Office of Associated Students

FROM: Alan Christopher, OAS Business Senator *AC*

SUBJECT: INCREASING PARTICIPATION IN WEST COAST COLLEGE'S
RECYCLING PROGRAM

Uses memo format for internal report

Here is the report you requested December 11 about the status of West Coast College's recycling program, along with recommendations for increasing its use. The study included both primary and secondary research. The primary study focused on a survey of members of the West Coast College campus community.

Announces report and gives broad overview of research conducted

Although the campus recycling program is progressing well, the information gathered shows that with some effort we should be able to increase participation and achieve our goal of setting an excellent example for both students and the local community. Recommendations for increasing campus participation in the program include educating potential users about the program and making recycling on campus easy.

Highlights report findings and recommendations

I am grateful to my business communication class for helping me develop a questionnaire, for pilot testing it, and for distributing it to the campus community. Their enthusiasm and support contributed greatly to the success of this OAS research project.

Acknowledges help of others

Establishes warm tone by using the name of the receiver, including first-person pronouns, and volunteering to help

Please call, Ms. Bryant, if I may provide additional information or answer questions. I would be happy, at your request, to implement some of the recommendations in this report by developing promotional materials for our recycling campaign.

Offers to answer questions and looks forward to follow-up actions

ii

Uses lowercase roman numeral to indicate second page

(continued)

Because this report is being submitted within his own organization, Alan uses a memorandum of transmittal. Formal organization reports submitted to outsiders would carry a letter of transmittal printed on company stationery.

The margins for the transmittal should be the same as for the report, about 3 cm on all sides. If a report is to be bound, add an extra 0.5 cm to the left margin.

Figure 9.5 ▶ *Continued*

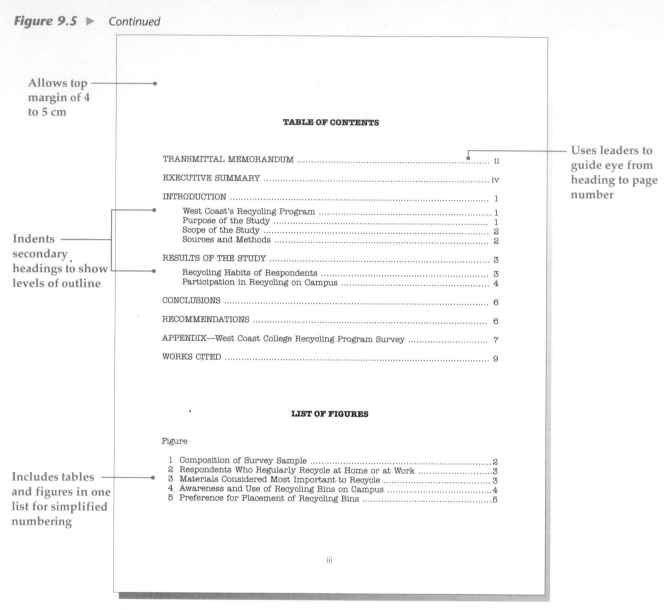

Allows top margin of 4 to 5 cm

TABLE OF CONTENTS

Uses leaders to guide eye from heading to page number

Indents secondary headings to show levels of outline

LIST OF FIGURES

Figure

Includes tables and figures in one list for simplified numbering

iii

Because Alan's table of contents and list of figures are small, he combines them on one page. Notice that he uses all caps for the titles of major report parts and a combination of upper- and lowercase letters for first-level headings. This duplicates the style within the report.

Advanced word processing capabilities enable you to generate a table of contents automatically, with leaders and accurate page numbering—no matter how many times you revise!

Figure 9.5 ▶ *Continued*

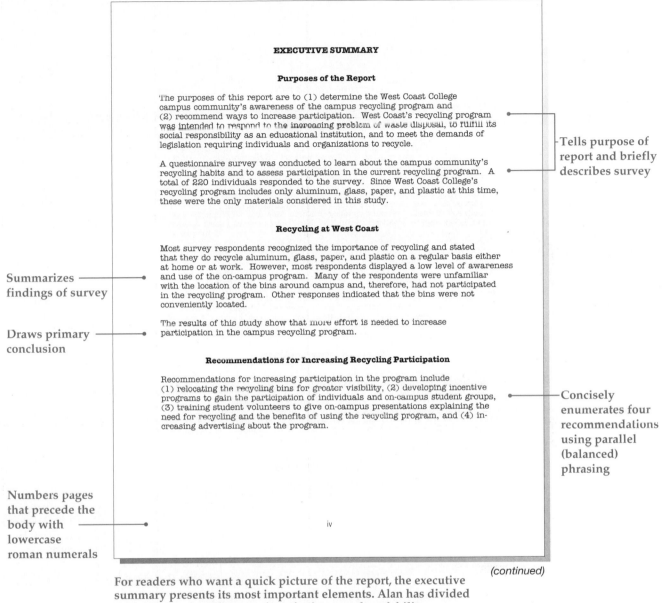

EXECUTIVE SUMMARY

Purposes of the Report

The purposes of this report are to (1) determine the West Coast College campus community's awareness of the campus recycling program and (2) recommend ways to increase participation. West Coast's recycling program was intended to respond to the increasing problem of waste disposal, to fulfill its social responsibility as an educational institution, and to meet the demands of legislation requiring individuals and organizations to recycle.

A questionnaire survey was conducted to learn about the campus community's recycling habits and to assess participation in the current recycling program. A total of 220 individuals responded to the survey. Since West Coast College's recycling program includes only aluminum, glass, paper, and plastic at this time, these were the only materials considered in this study.

Recycling at West Coast

Most survey respondents recognized the importance of recycling and stated that they do recycle aluminum, glass, paper, and plastic on a regular basis either at home or at work. However, most respondents displayed a low level of awareness and use of the on-campus program. Many of the respondents were unfamiliar with the location of the bins around campus and, therefore, had not participated in the recycling program. Other responses indicated that the bins were not conveniently located.

The results of this study show that more effort is needed to increase participation in the campus recycling program.

Recommendations for Increasing Recycling Participation

Recommendations for increasing participation in the program include (1) relocating the recycling bins for greater visibility, (2) developing incentive programs to gain the participation of individuals and on-campus student groups, (3) training student volunteers to give on-campus presentations explaining the need for recycling and the benefits of using the recycling program, and (4) increasing advertising about the program.

iv

Callouts:
- Tells purpose of report and briefly describes survey
- Summarizes findings of survey
- Draws primary conclusion
- Concisely enumerates four recommendations using parallel (balanced) phrasing
- Numbers pages that precede the body with lowercase roman numerals

(continued)

For readers who want a quick picture of the report, the executive summary presents its most important elements. Alan has divided the summary into three sections for increased readability.

Executive summaries generally contain little jargon or complex statistics; they condense what management needs to know about a problem and the study's findings about the problem. Report abstracts, sometimes written in place of summaries, tend to be more technical and are aimed at specialists rather than management.

Figure 9.5 ▶ *Continued*

Leaves 5-cm top margin on first page

Begins by establishing the significance of the problem

Builds credibility by documenting statistics with reference citations

Uses MLA referencing style

Describes background of problem

Includes centred page number on first and succeeding pages

Discusses conditions that prompted the need for study

ANALYSIS OF THE WEST COAST COLLEGE
CAMPUS RECYCLING PROGRAM

INTRODUCTION

North American society is often criticized as a "throw-away" one, and perhaps the criticism is accurate (Cahan 116). We discard 11 to 14 billion tonnes of waste each year, according to the Environmental Protection Agency. Of this sum, 180 million tonnes come from households and businesses, areas where recycling efforts could make a difference (Schneider 6). According to a survey conducted by Decima Research, 73 percent of North American companies have waste reduction programs ("Recycling to the Rescue" 23). Although some progress has been made, there is still a problem. For example, the annual volume of discarded plastic packaging in North America is 8 billion tonnes—enough to produce 118 million plastic park benches yearly (Joldine 111). Despite many recycling programs and initiatives, most of our trash finds its way to landfill sites. With an ever-increasing volume of waste, estimates show that 80 percent of North America's landfills will be full by the year 2010 (de Blanc 32).

To combat the growing waste disposal problem, some states and provinces are trying to pass legislation aimed at increasing recycling. Many North American communities have enacted regulations requiring residents to separate bottles, cans, and newspapers so that they may be recycled (Schneider 6). Other means considered to reduce waste include tax incentives, packaging mandates, and outright product bans (Holusha D2). All levels of government are trying both voluntary and mandatory means of reducing trash sent to landfills.

West Coast's Recycling Program

In order to do its part in reducing trash and to meet the requirements of legislation, West Coast College began operating a recycling program one year ago. Aluminum cans, glass, office and computer paper, and plastic containers are currently being recycled through this program. Recycling bins are located at various sites around campus, outside buildings, and in department and administrative offices to facilitate the collection of materials. The Office of Associated Students oversees the operation of the program. The program relies on promotions, advertisements, and word of mouth to encourage its use by the campus community.

Purpose of the Study

OAS had projected that participation in the recycling program would have increased to greater levels than it has thus far. Experts say that recycling

1

The first page of a report generally contains the title printed 5 cm from the top edge. Titles for major parts of a report (such as Introduction, Results, Conclusion, and so forth) are centred in all caps. First-level headings are bold and printed with upper- and lowercase letters. Second-level headings begin at the side. For illustration of heading formats, see Figure 9.4.

Notice that Alan's report is single-spaced. Many businesses prefer this space-saving format. However, some organizations prefer double-spacing, especially for preliminary drafts. Page numbers may be centred 2.5 cm from the top or bottom of the page or placed 2.5 cm from the upper right corner at the margin.

Figure 9.5 ▶ *Continued*

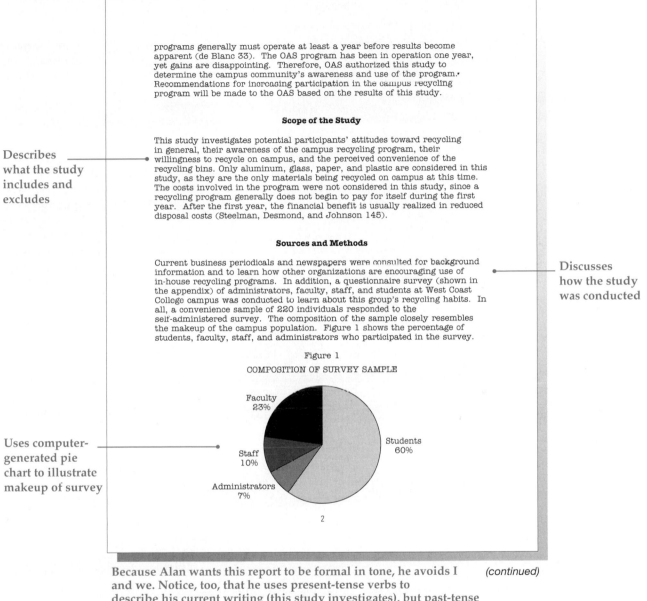

Describes what the study includes and excludes

Discusses how the study was conducted

Uses computer-generated pie chart to illustrate makeup of survey

Because Alan wants this report to be formal in tone, he avoids I and we. Notice, too, that he uses present-tense verbs to describe his current writing (this study investigates), but past-tense verbs to indicate research completed in the past (newspapers were consulted).

(continued)

If you use figures or tables, be sure to introduce them in the text. Although it's not always possible, try to place them close to the spot where they are first mentioned. If necessary to save space, you can print the title of a figure at its side.

Figure 9.5 ▶   *Continued*

RESULTS OF THE STUDY ●————————————————Introduces body
of report with
The findings of the study will be presented in two categories: recycling habits   functional heading
of the respondents and participation in the West Coast College recycling
program.

Recycling Habits of Respondents

A major finding of the survey reveals that most respondents are willing to
recycle even when not required to do so. Data tabulation shows that 72
percent of the respondents live in an area where neither the city nor the
region requires separation of trash. Yet 80 percent of these individuals
Interprets and ●————indicated that they recycle aluminum on a regular basis at home or at work,
discuss results   while another 55 percent said that they recycle paper on a regular basis.
of survey   Although the percentages are somewhat smaller, many of the respondents
also regularly recycle glass (46 percent) and plastic (45 percent). These
results, summarized in Figure 2, clearly show that campus respondents are ●————Introduces figure
accustomed to recycling the four major materials targeted for the West Coast   as part of another
College recycling program.   statement

Figure 2
————————————————Summarizes
RESPONDENTS WHO REGULARLY ●   findings of survey
RECYCLE AT HOME OR AT WORK   question in table

Material	Percentage
Aluminum	80%
Paper	55
Glass	46
Plastic	45

Respondents were asked to rank the importance of recycling the materials
collected in the West Coast program. Figure 3 shows that they felt aluminum
was most important, although most respondents also ranked the other
materials (glass, paper, and plastic) as either "extremely important" or
"somewhat important" to recycle. Respondents were also asked what
materials they actually recycled most frequently, and aluminum again ranked
first.

Figure 3
MATERIALS CONSIDERED MOST IMPORTANT TO RECYCLE

Presents bar ●———
chart for visual
comparison of
responses to
survey question

3

Alan selects the most important survey findings to
interpret and discuss for readers. Notice that he continues
to use present-tense verbs (the survey reveals and these
results clearly show) to
discuss the current report.

Because he has few tables and charts, Alan labels them all
as Fi gures." Notice that he numbers them consecutively,
and places the label above each figure. Report writers
with
a great many tables, charts, and illustrations may prefer to
label and number them separately. Tables are labelled as
such; everything else is generally called a figure. When
tables and figures are labelled separately, tables may be

Figure 9.5 ▶ *Continued*

Adds personal interpretation

When asked how likely they would be to go out of their way to deposit an item in a recycling bin, 29 percent of the respondents said "very likely," and 55 percent said "somewhat likely." Thus, respondents showed a willingness—at least on paper—to recycle even if it means making a special effort to locate a recycling bin.

Participation in Recycling on Campus

For any recycling program to be successful, participants must be aware of the location of recycling centres and must be trained to use them (de Blanc 33). Another important ingredient in thriving programs is convenience to users. If recycling centres are difficult for users to reach, these centres will be unsuccessful. To collect data on these topics, the survey included questions assessing awareness and use of the current bins. The survey also investigated reasons for not participating and the perceived convenience of current bin locations.

Introduces more findings and relates them to the report's purpose

Student Awareness and Use of Bins

Two of the most significant questions in the survey asked whether respondents were aware of the OAS recycling bins on campus and whether they had used the bins. Responses to both questions were disappointing, as Figure 4 illustrates.

Figure 4

AWARENESS AND USE OF RECYCLING BINS ON CAMPUS

Arranges responses from highest to lowest with "unaware" category placed last

Location	Awareness of bins at this location	Use of bins at this location
Cafeteria	38%	21%
Bookstore	29	12
Administration building	28	12
Computer labs	16	11
Library	15	7
Student union	9	5
Classrooms	8	6
Department and administrative offices	6	3
Athletic centre	5	3
Unaware of any bins; have not used any bins	20	7

Only 38 percent of the respondents, as shown in Figure 4, were aware of the bins located outside the cafeteria. Even fewer were aware of the bins outside the bookstore (29 percent) and outside the administration building (28 percent). Equally dissatisfying, only 21 percent of the respondents had used the most visible recycling bins outside the cafeteria.

Clarifies and emphasizes meaning of findings

4

(continued)

In discussing the results of the survey, Alan highlights those that have significance for the purpose of the report.

As you type a report, avoid orphans and widows (ending a page with the first line of a paragraph or carrying a single line of a paragraph to a new page). Strive to start and end pages with at least two lines of a paragraph, even if a slightly larger bottom margin results.

Figure 9.5 ▶ *Continued*

Other recycling bin locations were even less familiar to the survey respondents and, of course, were little used. These responses plainly show that the majority of the respondents in the West Coast campus community have a low awareness of the recycling program and an even lower record of participation.

Reasons for Not Participating

Respondents offered several reasons for not participating in the campus recycling program. Forty-five percent said that the bins are not convenient to use. Thirty percent said that they did not know where the bins were located. Another 25 percent said that they are not in the habit of recycling. Although many reasons for not participating were listed, the primary one appears to centre on convenience of bin locations.

Location of Recycling Bins

When asked specifically how they would rate the location of the bins currently in use, only 13 percent of the respondents felt that the bins were extremely convenient. Another 35 percent rated the locations as somewhat convenient. Over half the respondents felt that the locations of the bins were either somewhat inconvenient or extremely inconvenient. Recycling bins are currently located outside nearly all the major campus rooms or buildings, but respondents clearly considered these locations inconvenient or inadequate.

In indicating where they would like recycling bins placed (see Figure 5), 42 percent of the respondents felt that the most convenient locations would be inside the cafeteria. Placing more recycling bins near the student union seemed most convenient to another 33 percent of those questioned, while 15 percent stated that they would like to see the bins placed near the vending machines. Ten percent of the individuals responding to the survey did not seem to think that the locations of the bins would matter to them.

Figure 5

PREFERENCE FOR PLACEMENT OF RECYCLING BINS

Inside the cafeteria	42%
More in student union	33
Near vending machines	15
Does not matter	10

5

—Discusses results of other survey questions not represented in tables or charts

Clarifies results of another survey question with textual discussion accompanied by table

After completing a discussion of the survey results, Alan lists on the next page what he considers the five most important conclusions to be drawn from this survey. Some writers combine the conclusions and recommendations, particularly when they are interrelated. Alan separated them in his study because the survey findings were quite distinct from the recommendations he would make based on them.

Figure 9.5 ▶ *Continued*

CONCLUSIONS

Based on the findings of the recycling survey of members of the West Coast College campus community, the following conclusions are drawn:

1. Most members of the campus community are already recycling at home or at work without being required to do so.

2. Over half of the respondents recycle aluminum and paper on a regular basis; most recycle glass and plastic to some degree.

3. Most of the surveyed individuals expressed a willingness to participate in a recycling program. Many, however, seem unwilling to travel very far to participate; 42 percent would like more recycling bins to be located inside the cafeteria.

4. Awareness and use of the current campus recycling program are low. Only a little over one-third of the respondents knew of any recycling bin locations on campus, and only one-fifth had actually used them.

5. Respondents considered the locations of the campus bins inconvenient. This perceived inconvenience was given as the principal reason for not participating in the campus recycling program.

RECOMMENDATIONS

Supported by the findings and conclusions of this study, the following recommendations are offered in an effort to improve the operations and success of the West Coast recycling program:

1. Increase on-campus awareness and visibility by designing an eye-catching logo that represents the campus recycling program for use in promotions.

2. Enhance comprehension of recycling procedures by teaching users how to recycle. Use posters to explain the recycling program and to inform users of recycling bin locations. Label each bin clearly as to what materials may be deposited.

3. Add bins in several new locations, particularly more in the food service and vending machine areas.

4. Recruit student leaders to promote participation in the recycling program by giving educational talks to classes and other campus groups, informing them of the importance of recycling.

5. Develop an incentive program for student organizations. Offer incentives for meeting recycling goals as determined by OAS. On-campus groups could compete in recycling drives designed to raise money for the group, the college, or a charity. Money from the proceeds of the recycling program could be used to fund the incentive program.

6

Draws conclusions based on survey findings; summarizes previous discussion

Lists specific actions to help solve report problem; suggests practical ways to implement recommendations

(continued)

The most important parts of a report are its conclusions and recommendations. To make them especially clear, Alan enumerated each conclusion and recommendation. Notice that each recommendation starts with a verb and is stated as a command for emphasis and readability.

Report recommendations are most helpful to readers when they not only make suggestions to solve the original research problem but also describe specific actions to be taken. Notice that this report goes beyond merely listing ideas; instead, it makes practical suggestions for ways to implement the recommendations.

Figure 9.5 ▶ *Continued*

Includes copy of survey questionnaire so that report readers can see actual questions

Explains why survey is necessary, emphasizing "you" view

Provides range of answers that will be easy to tabulate

APPENDIX

WEST COAST COLLEGE RECYCLING PROGRAM SURVEY

West Coast College recently implemented a recycling program on campus. Please take a few minutes to answer the following questions so that we can make this program as convenient and helpful as possible for you to use.

1. Please indicate which items you recycle on a regular basis at home or at work.
   (Check *all* that apply.)
   ☐ Aluminum
   ☐ Glass
   ☐ Paper
   ☐ Plastic

2. Do you live in an area where the city/municipality requires separation of waste?
   ☐ Yes ☐ No

3. How important is it to you to recycle each of the following:

	Extremely Important	Somewhat Important	Somewhat Unimportant	Extremely Unimportant
Aluminum				
Glass				
Paper				
Plastic				

4. How likely would it be for you to go out of your way to put something in a recycling bin?

Very Likely	Somewhat Likely	Somewhat Unlikely	Very Unlikely

5. Which of the following items do you recycle *most* often? (Choose *one* item only.)
   ☐ Aluminum
   ☐ Glass
   ☐ Paper
   ☐ Plastic
   ☐ Other

6. The following are locations of the recycling bins on campus.
   (Check *all* those of which you are aware.)
   ☐ Administration building   ☐ Library
   ☐ Bookstore   ☐ Classrooms
   ☐ Athletic centre   ☐ Student union
   ☐ Computer labs   ☐ Department and administrative offices
   ☐ Cafeteria   ☐ I'm unaware of any of these recycling bins.

7

Alan had space to add the word "Appendix" to the top of the survey questionnaire. If space were not available, he could have typed a separate page with that title on it. If more than one item were included, he would have named them Appendix A, Appendix B, and so on.

Notice that the appendix continues the report's pagination.

Figure 9.5 ▶ *Continued*

7. Which of the following recycling bins have you actually used? (Check *all* that you have used.)

☐ Administration building   ☐ Library
☐ Bookstore   ☐ Classrooms
☐ Athletic centre   ☐ Student union
☐ Computer labs   ☐ Department and administrative offices
☐ Cafeteria   ☐ I've not used any of these recycling bins.

8. If you don't recycle on campus, why don't you participate?
☐ I'm not in the habit of recycling.
☐ I don't know where the bins are.
☐ The bins aren't convenient to me.
☐ Other _____

9. How do you rate the convenience of the bins' locations?
☐ Extremely convenient
☐ Somewhat convenient
☐ Somewhat inconvenient
☐ Extremely inconvenient

10. Which of the following possible recycling bin locations would be most convenient for you to use? (Check *one* only.)
☐ Outside each building
☐ Near the food service facilities
☐ Near the vending machines
☐ Does not matter
☐ Other _____

11. Please indicate:
☐ Student
☐ Faculty
☐ Administrator
☐ Staff

COMMENTS:

Thank you for your responses! Please return the questionnaire in the enclosed, stamped envelope to West Coast College, School of Business, Rm. 321. If you have any questions, please call (555) 450-2391.

8

Anticipates responses but also supplies "Other" category

Uses scale questions to capture degrees of feeling

Requests little demographic data to keep survey short

Offers comment section for explanations and remarks

Concludes with appreciation and instructions

(continued)

Figure 9.5 ▶ *Continued*

WORKS CITED

Cahan, Vicky. "Waste Not, Want Not? Not Necessarily." <u>Business Week</u> 17 July 2006: 116. •—————— Magazine

de Blanc, Susan. "Paper Recycling: How to Make It Effective." <u>The Office</u> Dec. 2005: 32–33.

Foster, David. "Recycling: A Green Idea Turns to Gold." <u>The Los Angeles Times</u> 5 Mar. 2006, Bulldog ed., Metro, <u>CyberTimes</u>. Retrieved 7 Mar. 2006 <http://www.times.com/library/cyberweek/y05dat.html>. •—————— Online Newspaper

Freeman, Monique M. Personal interview. 2 Nov. 2006. •—————— Interview

Holusha, John. "Mixed Benefits from Recycling." <u>The New York Times</u> 26 July 2006: D2. <u>The New York Times Online</u>. Online. Nexis. 26 Oct. 2006. •—————— Online Newspaper

Joldine, Lee. <u>Spirit of the Wolf: The Environment and Canada's Future</u>. Ed. Jo Davis. Waterloo: Turnaround Decade Ecological Communications, 2005. •—————— Book—author with an editor

Landsbury, Steve E. "Who Shall Inherit the Earth?" <u>Slate</u> 1 May 2006. Retrieved 2 May 2006 <http://www.slate.com/Economics/06-05-01/ Economics.asp>. •—————— Online Magazine

"Recycling to the Rescue: As Office Paperwork Grows Recycling Programs Become the Norm." <u>Materials Management and Distribution</u> 39 (Sept. 2005). •—————— Journal—unsigned periodical article

Schneider, Keith. "As Recycling Becomes a Growth Industry, Its Paradoxes Also Multiply." <u>The New York Times</u> 20 Jan. 2006, sec. 4: 6.

Steelman, James W., Shirley Desmond, and LeGrand Johnson. <u>Facing Global Limitations</u>. New York: Rockford Press, 2000. •—————— Book

Steuteville, Robert. "The State of Garbage in America," Part 1. <u>BioCycle</u> Apr. 2006. Retrieved 30 Nov. 2006 <http://www.biocycle/recycle/guid. html>. •—————— Online Magazine

"Tips to Reduce, Reuse, and Recycle." <u>Environmental Recycling Hotline</u>. Retrieved 8 July 2006 <http://www.primenet.com/cgi-bin/erh.p1>. •—————— World Wide Web

Weddle, Bruce, and Edward Klein. "A Strategy to Control the Garbage Glut." <u>EPA Journal</u> 12.2 (2004): 28–34. •—————— Journal

9

On this page Alan lists all the references cited in the text as well as others that he examined during his research. (Some authors list only those works cited in the report.) Alan formats his citations following the MLA referencing style. Notice that all entries are arranged alphabetically. He underlines book and periodical titles, but italics could be used. When referring to online items, he shows the full name of the citation and then identifies the path leading to that reference as well as the date on which he accessed the electronic reference.

Most word processing software today automatically updates the numbering of references within the text and prints a complete list for you.

Alan's report illustrates many of the points discussed in this chapter. Although it's a good example of typical report format and style, it should not be viewed as the only way to present a report. Wide variation exists in reports.

WRITING BUSINESS PLANS

A specific type of formal business report, which also contains elements of a business proposal, is the business plan. Whether you work for a small, medium-sized, or large business, or whether you're an entrepreneur running your own business, a business plan is a document you'll have to write or read at a number of points in your career. According to the federal government's Canada Business Service Centres, a business plan is "a written document that describes the future path of a business. A good business plan explains the business concept, summarizes the objectives of the business, identifies the resources (both in terms of money and people) that will be needed by the business, describes how those resources will be obtained, and tells the reader why the business will succeed."[2] What's not stated in this definition is that before an effective business plan can be written, a lot of business research, like that described earlier in this chapter, has to be done.

Usually, a business plan is written as a means to obtain financing for the company. At the same time, most experts on business plans agree that a well-written business plan does more than just get you an appointment with a bank or with a potential investor. Writing business plans, as the Royal Bank of Canada's website proclaims, gives you "a chronology of events... against which you can compare your actual results."[3] In other words, much like the work plan you write before starting the research for a research report, a business plan lets you tick off the things you've done and understand what you haven't achieved yet.

Numerous books and websites exist that can show you how to write a business plan. The common elements, however, don't change much, notwithstanding the book or site you've chosen to use. Here are the major components of a completed business plan, based on the Canada Business Service Centres model:

- **Executive Summary.** Like the executive summary of a formal research report, this part of a business plan summarizes the important parts of the business plan in less than two pages.
- **Introduction.** In this section, the business plan writer provides an overview of the business, describes the products or services (or both) the company provides, and sets the business in a larger context: who are its competitors, what are the current issues affecting this field of business (e.g., if it's an energy-based business, the current upswing in energy stocks and prices would be important here).
- **Marketing Plan.** All business plans explain the basic elements of the business's marketing plan. For example, what are the 3Ps—product, price, promotion—for this business, and how are this business's products or services distributed to consumers?
- **Staffing.** Like the section of a business proposal that describes who will do what if the proposal is accepted, business plans must similarly describe all employees and managers of the business. What is their background? What is their function in the business?
- **Implementation Plan.** The word "plan" as in "business plan" assumes that this document is a map toward a goal. Sometimes, the goal of a plan is to achieve financing (e.g., a bank loan). At other times, the goal is to motivate employees

after a particularly poor business year. Whatever the reason, this section of a business plan tells readers how and when plan goals will be implemented. In this way, it's similar to a progress report.

- **Financial Statements.** The last and most detailed part of a business plan is the financial statements. Here, the writer must have a basic understanding of accounting principles. As the CBSC site says, the financial statements include "balance sheets, income statements and cash flow statements. A balance sheet compares what your business owns to what it owes. A cash flow statement compares how much money will be coming in to how much you will be spending. An income statement compares your revenues to your expenses to see if you are going to make money."[4]

If as a new business communicator you find yourself having to write or help write or research a business plan, keep in mind that the Government of Canada makes it easy to do this. Through the government-run Canada Business Service Centres, you can access a piece of software called the Interactive Business Planner (IBP). The IBP takes you step-by-step through the business plan writing process. It's a template like the other templates we discussed earlier in the book, such as Microsoft Word's professional memo and letter templates. Of course, with templates, it's tempting to think the software will do your work for you. That's not the case. While the software will prompt you and create the various sections of the plan for you, it won't write the document for you. To view IBP, go to <www.cbsc.org/ibp/login_e.cfm>. Examples of completed business plans (not using IBP) can be found at the Royal Bank of Canada's informative and useful site: <www.rbcroyalbank.com/RBC:RDKoRY71A8YAApsE0NI/sme/bigidea/kamiko.html>.

CONCLUSION

In this chapter you learned the steps in the process of writing a formal research report. The three main steps are analysis, interpretation, and organization. When analyzing data, you are essentially dividing it into parts that will make the explanation of the problem more clear. The next step is to interpret what you've analyzed. This means taking an educated guess and saying what the data mean. After you've been able to say what the data mean, you can make recommendations for how to solve the problem. Analyzed and interpreted data must be organized and formatted in a specific way in a formal report. The main components of a formal report are the executive summary, the introduction, the findings, and the conclusions and recommendations. One typical formal business report is a business plan, which is used to help a business plan its operations or to gain financing. The final three chapters of the book move away from written business communication to a similarly important topic, spoken business communication.

Chapter Review

As a way of studying the material in this chapter, imagine you are at a job interview for your dream entry-level job after college or university. You've prepared answers for all the classic interview questions, but to your surprise, your interviewer also asks a number of questions based on formal report writing. How would you answer the following six questions?

1. In our research department we have a fairly high expectation of analytical skills for our new employees. Can you tell us what you understand to make up the process of analysis?

2. Some clients want not just data collection and analysis, but interpretation too. Explain how you define interpretation, and tell us what you'd do in a situation in which you were asked to interpret data in an area you don't know much about.

3. What types of data tabulation are you comfortable with? Which do you think is most useful for business-related research?

4. In your opinion, what's the main difference between a conclusion and a recommendation? Which is more valuable?

5. In the past some of our clients have complained about where we've placed the conclusion and recommendations in some of our reports. What do you think their complaint might be?

6. We notice that you've had training in report writing. What's on your checklist of the essential items in a formal research-based report?

Problems

1. You are a research associate at a market research firm. Your firm has been successful in being hired by a local college to do a research study on the effectiveness of its website. As you learned when you met with the president and VP of Marketing two weeks ago (as part of your firm's "pitch" team), the college recognizes that today more than ever, a postsecondary institution's website is its most important marketing tool in attracting potential students. The college wants to know two things: how well its website stacks up against two of its main competitors, and how effective its own website is against best practices in the field of web design. Your boss has just informed you that because of your participation in the pitch team, he's assigning you to the three-person team that will complete this job for the college. Remembering what you learned in your business communication course, you recognize that the first step in figuring out a research plan is to analyze the problem. In order to fulfill the college's mandate, what sorts of secondary research should your team do? What sorts of primary research should your team do? Within the research, how will you analyze the problem? How will you measure one college's website against the websites of two other colleges? How will you measure the effectiveness of the college's website compared to best practices in the field? Keep in mind that the budget for this project is very tight, and the time frame extremely narrow—only four weeks. (Use your own college or university and two of its competitors to complete the problems in this chapter.)

2. As part of your primary research, you conducted a focus group of 50 potential college students: a mix of high school students and adult learners. Your focus group was asked seven questions and the following answers were given:

Question 1: What is the most important feature of a useful website?
Answers: Content (9); Design (33); Navigation (3); Other (5) e.g., "Colour"

Question 2: What thing most often "turns you off" a website?
Answers: Poor content (16); Poor design (17); Poor navigation (15); Other (2) e.g., "Too much animation"

Question 3: Spend 15 minutes surfing the websites of Colleges A, B, and C. On a scale from 1 to 5 (1 being excellent and 5 being extremely poor), rate College A's content, design, and ease of navigation.
Answers: Content—1 (18), 2 (22), 3 (10), 4 (0), 5 (0);

Design—1 (39), 2 (7), 3 (4), 4 (0), 5 (0);

Ease of navigation—1 (15), 2 (10), 3 (14), 4 (10), 5 (1)

Question 4: On a scale from 1 to 5 (1 being excellent and 5 being extremely poor), rate College B's content, design, and ease of navigation.
Answers: Content—1 (5), 2 (12), 3 (20), 4 (11), 5 (2);

Design—1 (3), 2 (15), 3 (20), 4 (9), 5 (1);

Ease of navigation—1 (10), 2 (9), 3 (25), 4 (4), 5 (0)

Question 5: On a scale from 1 to 5 (1 being excellent and 5 being extremely poor), rate College C's content, design, and ease of navigation.
Answers: Content—1 (0), 2 (8), 3 (32), 4 (7), 5 (3);

Design—1 (0), 2 (5), 3 (35), 4 (4), 5 (6);

Ease of navigation—1 (0), 2 (8), 3 (11), 4 (21), 5 (10)

Question 6: Overall, which of the three websites most appeals to you?
Answers: A (18); B (24); C (8)

Question 7: If you could offer one piece of advice to the web designer of College C, what would it be?
Answers: Improve content (5); Improve design (32); Improve navigation (10); Other (3) e.g., "Move into the 21st century," "Pick some better colours," "Way too many words to read," etc.

Note: College C is your client.

How might you interpret the above data? You want to give the appearance of being neutral in your interpretation, but at the same time, you want to make your client happy.

3. At this point you've completed both your secondary and your primary research. You've interpreted the data, and would now like to format the findings section of your research report. What would be the most effective way of dividing up this section? What will be your primary and secondary headings? What sorts of graphics or illustrations could you include to illustrate these findings? How will you interweave your secondary research with your primary research in each of the sections? Draft a sample part of your findings section.

4. Considering the analysis and interpretation you've completed in the above problems what can you conclude about your research? When you make your conclusion, will you be completely neutral or will you keep some facts about your client in mind? Also, what kinds of recommendations do you feel confident in making? Based on what you know about the situation, should your conclusion and recommendations be stated directly or indirectly? Should they be stated bluntly or subtly? Why?

5. It's been a month since you submitted your research report to the college discussed in the above problems. Your recommendations were straightforward, as it was clear from the data that the college needed to make some radical improvements to its website if it wanted to stay competitive in the marketplace. One day, you get a phone call from the college's VP of Marketing, Cindy Simon. Cindy thanks you for the report, says it was money well spent,

and asks you for some advice. She wants to know if you know of any web design firms that do "good work" at "affordable rates." You tell her there are a number of firms you can think of, and that you'd be glad to summarize them in an e-mail. After hanging up the phone, a thought comes to you: a friend of yours is a recent graduate of a web design program at MacDonald College, which is located in a small city in your province. He's won all sorts of awards for his design work, and he's struggling with his own new web design business. Wouldn't it be great if you could convince the college to use your friend to redevelop its website? Right away, though, you recognize that you'll have to be ethical in making a recommendation to Cindy. Your friend can't get preferential treatment. He can be one of a small number of firms you recommend without bias. You call your friend and tell him to "put together a business plan quickly, if you haven't already." He says, "What do you mean?", and you reply, "Trust me, I'm trying to land you your first big client." As the web-designer friend, draft a business plan (you can make up the numbers in the financial statements) that can be used as a reference by potential clients.

Grammar/Style Review 9

In this review, you will be practising identifying spelling mistakes. There are at least five mistakes in total, plus two non-spelling mistakes. For a brief explanation of this style problem, please read the explanation on page 330. Besides completing the exercise below, be sure to be on the lookout for spelling mistakes in your own writing.

To: amasucci@optrc.ca

From: bmascoll82@hotmail.com

Date: May 27, 2007

Re: Interview scheduling

Hi Antonella,

Thank u for calling me back last week. I apologize I was not feeling real well, I had food poising. I was wondering when you like to scedule a second interview with Mike. Hopefully if Miek is not to busy we can do it sometime this week. Their's something I'm doing Monday afternoon, but I will be available anytime after Tuesday.

Thank you again,

Bryce

Business Communication Lab 9

Bill Vinauskas and a partner are starting a new market research company. Bill knows there's lots of competition out there, from large well-established firms to smaller niche-based firms. Still, as semi-retired business professionals, with 50 years of experience behind them (and large networks in the pharmaceutical and health industries), Bill and his partner are confident it won't take long for them to establish a solid client base. Bill also understands that today, a key to survival in this competitive industry is to have an impressive website. As part of his business plan, Bill needs to conduct some quick research on the website of his potential competitors. He decides to hire a college student with some business research experience for a two-month co-op position. As the co-op student, do some quick research on three of the market research firms mentioned in Rebecca Harris's article (e.g., Leger, Pollara, Ipsos-Reid) in order to analyze the strengths and weaknesses of these sites. Synthesize your analysis in a one-paragraph conclusion and then make three recommendations about what Bill and his partner should do with their new site. Present your findings to Bill in a two-page memo report.

Spoken Business Communication

CHAPTER 10

Business Presentations and Job Interviews

PowerPoint of no return

BY ANDREW WAHL, *CANADIAN BUSINESS*, NOVEMBER 10, 2003, 131–132

THERE'S A SCOURGE upon the boardrooms and conference centres of the corporate world. It's sucking the life out of meetings, inflicting boredom and confusion on audiences large and small, and leaving wasted productivity in its wake. The sickness is all too well-known: the dreaded PowerPoint presentation.

We've all been there, sitting in some dark, airless space, straining to keep our eyes open during a presentation that drones on and on. A screen glows with a seemingly endless series of slides and charts, bullet points and words streaking and spinning round. But it's all in vain. Befuddled by the barrage of information, you fail to glean anything of use. The presentation ends, the lights come up, and you stumble away in a haze, thirsty for comprehension.

What's gone wrong? Since Microsoft released its first version of PowerPoint 16 years ago, some 400 million copies have been installed around the world, and experts figure the software is employed in—get this—some 30 million presentations each day. It's the second-most-used corporate communication tool after e-mail. People are so accustomed to working with PowerPoint, in fact, that it's no longer just getting the big-screen treatment—they're using it in ways Microsoft developers never intended. For instance, PowerPoint files are increasingly being distributed as self-published reports to colleagues or via the web to the public.

But critics—and there are many—argue that few people use PowerPoint effectively even in speeches, let alone in print form. Perhaps it's easy to take something so ubiquitous in the corporate environment, and

seemingly so simple to learn, for granted. Despite its popularity among speakers, though, audiences often end up giving PowerPoint presentations failing grades.

Everyone has his or her own horror stories. "I've been a recipient of a board paper that was 124 PowerPoint slides long," recalls David Beatty, the head of the Canadian Coalition for Good Governance, who says the presentation was even described as a "core dump" by the presenter himself. "I've been on many boards over many years and, generally, people who use PowerPoint cannot make their point and, in the end, do not look good." Beatty calls PowerPointing "the dark force that frustrates strategic discussion and productive communication between consenting adults." Ouch.

So why are so many PowerPoint presentations a bust, and how can you avoid the pitfalls? Beatty teaches a course in strategy in the executive MBA program at the University of Toronto's Joseph L. Rotman School of Management. His first class is a daylong seminar on effective communication—as he describes it, how to make your case in a clear, memorable and compelling way. His lesson includes PowerPoint, but he asserts its use is never necessary and rarely improves a presentation. "There are very few people who can use the medium to communicate effectively," Beatty says. "Entertainment? Fine. Frustration? Terrific—it's a great tool for frustrating your audience. We would all be better off if PowerPoint was abolished from major corporations."

In fact, some corporations, like 3M, are banning PowerPoint from their offices. But Cliff Atkinson, who runs Los Angeles management consultancy Sociable Media, argues that's throwing the baby out with the bathwater. His take on PowerPoint is that its true value as a visual medium isn't being fully tapped. "We've become such a visual culture, with film and television, people want to communicate visually, and this is the most accessible media-creation tool that's available," Atkinson says. "For better or worse, we've fully adopted this as one of the primary ways of communicating."

Trouble is, most corporate cultures place no emphasis on teaching people how to use PowerPoint effectively, and give little thought to the image it presents. "PowerPoint is a mirror that reflects organizations and individuals," says Atkinson. Often, it's not a pretty sight. Many companies set strict templates to maintain consistency; some insist on putting a prominent corporate logo on every slide. "It's really a negative statement, that it's more important for you to establish your presence than it is to communicate," contends Atkinson. "It's almost to the level of a particular arrogance."

In Atkinson's view, the pre-defined borders and logos of PowerPoint templates are the source of many problems. "It forces communication within that box, and minimizes the amount of real estate I have to creatively express my message," he explains. "It's like giving someone a paint-by-numbers palette, and it completely ignores the fact that people need to know how to communicate visually."

Atkinson advocates training, supported by hiring professional graphics designers to remodel corporate PowerPoint libraries with pre-formatted—but ultimately flexible—layouts, charts and style guides. "There are things an individual can do to presentations, but all those things are constrained by what the culture will allow," he notes. Some companies are catching on. Atkinson cites one corporate client that came to him after its board of directors mandated an audit of PowerPoint policies to improve external and internal communication. It wasn't the marketing department, though, trying to make presentations flashier; instead, it was a strategic plan by investor relations to encourage simple, clear messages.

Maybe Atkinson's theory of PowerPoint's effect on corporate culture is a bit rich for your tastes, or perhaps you aren't in a position to change much at your company. But for the sake of your own reputation, it's worth doing what you can to set your own high presentation standards. "Any tool is dangerous if you don't know how to use it," says Dave Paradi, who is based in Mississauga, Ont. and coaches speakers on how to use technology to communicate more effectively. "What happens to your career if you don't use PowerPoint properly? You could significantly damage it."

Paradi recently ran an informal poll on his website (communicateusingtechnology.com) to find out what annoys people most about bad PowerPoint presentations. Topping the list were complaints about presenters simply reading slides, text that was too small, and poor use of colours. "I had one person write in that they actually scan their Word document in, put those graphics on to PowerPoint slides, and then stand there and read them," says Paradi. "Just brutal."

Of course, at the other end of the spectrum were complaints that presenters liked to use special effects too much. "Most of the training that goes on for PowerPoint is simply how to use every feature," says Paradi. "People know how to click all the buttons; they just don't know what to put on a slide."

For his part, Beatty bans the use of all clip art, colourful backgrounds or any distracting text animation—not to mention sound or video clips. He insists that presenters need to know the basics of making a presentation first. "People don't know how to structure an argument or, to make it even simpler, how to tell a story," he contends. Only once you've grasped that can you learn how to translate it effectively to PowerPoint. "It should be used to give the audience context," says Paradi. "It's basically a map of what you're talking about." Good speakers, he insists, know that successful presentations are built on establishing a positive rapport with their audiences. Stories, for example, work well—whether they're humorous or dramatic—to engage listeners by revealing you are human. But relationships are not built on endless slides of bullet points...

DIAGNOSING THE PROBLEM

As students of business communication, there's a parallel we can draw between the way technology has affected written communication and oral communication. Earlier in this book, we looked at how e-mail has affected business communication. It has caused people to write more than ever, to be stressed out about communicating more than ever, and to be more informal than ever before. Of course, e-mail also has several advantages, such as speed and efficiency, that have changed our workplace for the better. Similarly, oral communication—the way we speak to each other over the phone, in person, in meetings—has changed due to the widespread use of computer presentation technology, notably Microsoft's PowerPoint software.

As Andrew Wahl makes clear, PowerPoint has caused a number of problems in today's workplace. Without listing all the specific problems he sees with the technology, we can conclude that the overall problem he diagnoses is that PowerPoint, though it has become the new norm in how presentations are given in business (and in other fields), does not necessarily (or even mostly) make for better presentations; in fact, it makes for weaker presentations.

If we read the article carefully we see that three different solutions are advocated for how to deal with this crisis in business presentations. The first solution is the most drastic: do away with PowerPoint in your company or organization completely. Next is the idea of training: teach workers and managers who didn't have the benefit of a Business Communication course such as the one you're in how to use PowerPoint effectively. If that doesn't work, Wahl says, hire professional designers to provide employees with well-designed slides so their presentations don't end up frustrating their audiences. What should we make of these solutions?

in-class
activity 10

IMAGINE THAT YOU and your team work for a large company in which weak presentations are the norm. One day, the VP of Human Resources asks you and your teammates to write a short feasibility report on three solutions that have been proposed by the company's board of directors: abolish PowerPoint, train workers in how to use it properly, or "farm out" the work of designing presentations to a design company. Keep in mind your company has 1500 employees in three different Canadian cities and that, on average, 400 presentations per month are given using PowerPoint technology. What will your report say? Report back to the class in 20 minutes.

Now that you've given some thought to the complexity of the issue of contemporary business presentations, it's time to learn about the importance of business presentations and best practices in how they should be given.

THE IMPORTANCE OF ORAL BUSINESS COMMUNICATION SKILLS

Organizations today are increasingly interested in hiring people with good presentation skills. Why? The business world is changing. Technical skills aren't enough to guarantee success. You also need to be able to communicate ideas effectively in presentations to customers, vendors, members of your team, and management. Your presentations will probably be made to inform, influence, or motivate action. And the opportunities to make these presentations are increasing, even for non-management employees.[1] Powerful speaking skills draw attention to you and advance your career. But reading a textbook is not enough to help you develop solid speaking skills. You also need coaching and chances to practise your skills. In this unit you will learn the fundamentals, and in your course you will be able to try out your skills and develop confidence.

Preparing for an Oral Presentation

In preparing for an oral presentation, you may feel a great deal of anxiety. For many people fear of speaking before a group is almost as great as the fear of pain. We get butterflies in our stomachs just thinking about it. When you feel those butterflies, though, speech coach Dianna Booher advises getting them in formation and visualizing the swarm as a powerful push propelling you to a peak performance.[2] For any presentation, you can reduce your fears and lay the foundation for a professional performance by focusing on five areas: preparation, organization, audience rapport, visual aids, and delivery.

Deciding What You Want to Accomplish

The most important part of your preparation is deciding your purpose. Do you want to sell a group insurance policy to a prospective client? Do you want to persuade management to increase the marketing budget? Do you want to inform customer service reps of three important ways to prevent miscommunication? Whether your goal is to persuade or to inform, you must have a clear idea of where you are going. At the end of your presentation, what do you want your listeners to remember or do?

Eric Evans, a loan officer at TD Canada Trust, faced such questions as he planned a talk for a class in small business management. (You can see the outline for his talk in Figure 10.2 on page 268) Eric's former business professor had asked him to return to campus and give the class advice about borrowing money from banks in order to start new businesses. Because Eric knew so much about this topic, he found it difficult to extract a specific purpose statement for his presentation. After much thought he narrowed his purpose to this: "To inform potential entrepreneurs about three important factors that loan officers consider before granting start-up loans to launch small businesses." His entire presentation focused on ensuring that the class members understood and remembered three principal ideas.

Understanding Your Audience

A second key element in preparation is analyzing your audience, anticipating its reactions, and making appropriate adaptations. Understanding four basic audience types helps you decide how to organize your presentation. A friendly audience, for example, will respond to humour and personal experiences. A neutral audience requires an even, controlled delivery style. The talk would probably be filled with facts, statistics, and expert opinions. An uninterested audience that is forced to attend requires a brief presentation. Such an audience might respond best to humour, cartoons, colourful visuals, and startling statistics. A hostile audience demands a calm, controlled delivery style with objective data and expert opinion.

Other elements, such as age, education, experience, and size of audience, will affect your style and message content. Analyze the following questions to help you determine your organizational pattern, delivery style, and supporting material.

- How will this topic appeal to this audience?
- How can I relate this information to their needs?
- How can I earn respect so that they accept my message?
- What would be most effective in making my point? Facts? Statistics? Personal experiences? Expert opinion? Humour? Cartoons? Graphic illustrations? Demonstrations? Case histories? Analogies?
- What measures must I take to ensure that this audience remembers my main points?

ORGANIZING EFFECTIVE PRESENTATIONS

Once you have determined your purpose and analyzed the audience, you're ready to collect information and organize it logically. Good organization and conscious repetition are the two most powerful keys to audience comprehension and retention. In fact, many speech experts recommend the following admittedly repetitious, but effective, plan:

Step 1: Tell them what you're going to say.
Step 2: Say it.
Step 3: Tell them what you've just said.

In other words, repeat your main points in the introduction, body, and conclusion of your presentation. Although it sounds boring, this strategy works surprisingly well. Let's examine how to construct the three parts of an effective presentation.

Capturing Attention in the Introduction

How many times have you heard a speaker begin with, "It's a pleasure to be here." Or "I'm honoured to be asked to speak." Boring openings such as these get speakers off to a dull start. Avoid such banalities by striving to accomplish three goals in the introduction to your presentation:

- Capture listeners' attention and get them involved.
- Identify yourself and establish your credibility.
- Preview your main points.

If you're able to appeal to listeners and involve them in your presentation right from the start, you're more likely to hold their attention until the finish. Consider some of the same techniques that you used to open sales letters: a question, a startling fact, a joke, a story, or a quotation. Some speakers achieve involvement by opening with a question or command that requires audience members to raise their hands or stand up. You'll find additional techniques for gaining and keeping audience attention in Figure 10.1.

To establish your credibility, you need to describe your position, knowledge, or experience—whatever qualifies you to speak. Try also to connect with your audience. Listeners are particularly drawn to speakers who reveal something of themselves and identify with them. A consultant addressing office workers might reminisce about how he started as a temporary worker; a CEO might tell a funny story in which the joke is on herself.

After capturing attention and establishing yourself, you'll want to preview the main points of your topic, perhaps with a visual aid. You may wish to put off actually

Figure 10.1 ▶ Nine Winning Techniques for Gaining and Keeping Audience Attention

Experienced speakers know how to capture the attention of an audience and how to maintain that attention during a presentation. You can give your presentations a boost by trying these nine proven techniques.

- **A promise.** Begin with a promise that keeps the audience expectant. For example, *By the end of this presentation I will have shown you how you can increase your sales by 50 percent!*
- **Drama.** Open by telling an emotionally moving story or by describing a serious problem that involves the audience. Throughout your talk include other dramatic elements, such as a long pause after a key statement. Change your vocal tone or pitch. Professionals use high-intensity emotions such as anger, joy, sadness, and excitement.
- **Eye contact.** As you begin, command attention by surveying the entire audience to take in all listeners. Take two to five seconds to make eye contact with as many people as possible.
- **Movement.** Leave the lectern area whenever possible. Walk around the conference table or between the aisles of your audience. Try to move toward your audience, especially at the beginning and end of your talk.
- **Questions.** Keep listeners active and involved with rhetorical questions. Ask for a show of hands to get each listener thinking. The response will also give you a quick gauge of audience attention.
- **Demonstrations.** Include a member of the audience in a demonstration. For example, *I'm going to show you exactly how to implement our four-step customer courtesy process, but I need a volunteer from the audience to help me.*
- **Samples/gimmicks.** If you're promoting a product, consider using items to toss out to the audience or to award as prizes to volunteer participants. You can also pass around product samples or promotional literature. Be careful, though, to maintain control.
- **Visuals.** Give your audience something to look at besides yourself. Use a variety of visual aids in a single session. Also consider writing the concerns expressed by your audience on a flipchart or on the board as you go along.
- **Self-interest.** Review your entire presentation to ensure that it meets the critical *What's-in-it-for-me* audience test. Remember that people are most interested in things that benefit them.

writing your introduction until after you have organized the rest of the presentation and crystallized your principal ideas.

Take a look at Eric Evans's introduction, shown in Figure 10.2, to see how he integrated all the elements necessary for a good opening.

Organizing the Body

The biggest problem with most oral presentations is a failure to focus on a few principal ideas. Thus, the body of your short presentation (20 or fewer minutes) should include a limited number of main points, say, two to four. Develop each main point with adequate, but not excessive, explanation and details. Too many details can obscure the main message, so keep your presentation simple and logical. Remember, listeners have no pages to leaf back through should they become confused.

Figure 10.2 ▶ Oral Presentation Outline

What Makes a Loan Officer Say "Yes"?

Captures attention ⎯

I. INTRODUCTION

    A. How many of you expect to start your own businesses one day? How many of you have all the cash available to capitalize that business when you start?

    B. Like you, nearly every entrepreneur needs cash to open a business, and I promise you that by the end of this talk you will have inside information on how to make a loan application that will be successful. ⎯ Involves audience

Identifies speaker ⎯

    C. As a loan officer at TD Canada Trust, which specializes in small business loans, I make decisions on requests from entrepreneurs like you applying for start-up money.

       Transition: Your professor invited me here today to tell you how you can improve your chances of getting a loan from us or from any other lender. I have suggestions in three areas: experience, preparation, and projection. ⎯ Previews three main points

II. BODY

Establishes main points ⎯

    A. First, let's consider experience. You must show that you can hit the ground running.

       1. Demonstrate what experience you have in your proposed business.

       2. Include your résumé when you submit your business plan.

       3. If you have little experience, tell us whom you would hire to supply the skills that you lack.

       Transition: In addition to experience, loan officers will want to see that you have researched your venture thoroughly.

    B. My second suggestion, then, involves preparation. Have you done your homework?

       1. Talk to local businesspeople, especially those in related fields.

       2. Conduct traffic counts or other studies to estimate potential sales.

       3. Analyze the strengths and weaknesses of the competition.

       Transition: Now that we've discussed preparation, we're ready for my final suggestion. ⎯ Develops coherence with planned transitions

    C. My last tip is the most important one. It involves making a realistic projection of your potential sales, cash flow, and equity.

       1. Present detailed monthly cash-flow projections for the first year.

       2. Describe "what-if" scenarios indicating both good and bad possibilities.

       3. Indicate that you intend to supply at least 25 percent of the initial capital yourself.

       Transition: The three major points I've just outlined cover critical points in obtaining start-up loans. Let me review them for you.

III. CONCLUSION

Summarizes main points ⎯

    A. Loan officers are most likely to say yes to your loan application if you do three things: (1) prove that you can hit the ground running when your business opens; (2) demonstrate that you've researched your proposed business seriously; and (3) project a realistic picture of your sales, cash flow, and equity.

    B. Experience, preparation, and projection, then, are the three keys to launching your business with the necessary start-up capital so that you can concentrate on where your customers, not your funds, are coming from. ⎯ Provides final focus

When Eric Evans began planning his presentation, he realized immediately that he could talk for hours on his topic. He also knew that listeners are not good at separating major and minor points. Thus, instead of submerging his listeners in a sea of information, he sorted out a few principal ideas. In the mortgage business, loan officers generally ask the following three questions of each applicant for a small business loan: Are you ready to "hit the ground running" in starting your business? Have you done your homework? Have you made realistic projections of potential sales, cash flow, and equity investment? These questions would become his main points, but Eric wanted to streamline them further so that his audience would be sure to remember them. He capsulized the questions in three words: *experience, preparation,* and *projection.* As you can see in Figure 10.2, Eric prepared a sentence outline showing these three main ideas. Each is supported by examples and explanations.

How to organize and sequence main ideas may not be immediately obvious when you begin working on a presentation. In Chapter 9 you studied a number of patterns for organizing formal reports. Those patterns, expanded here, are equally appropriate for oral presentations:

- **Chronology.** Example: A presentation describing the history of a problem, organized from the first sign of trouble to the present.
- **Geography/space.** Example: A presentation about the changing diversity of the workforce, organized by regions in the country (East Coast, West Coast, and so forth).
- **Topic/function/conventional grouping.** Example: A report discussing mishandled airline baggage, organized by names of airlines.
- **Comparison/contrast (pro/con).** Example: A report comparing organic farming methods with those of modern industrial farming.
- **Journalism pattern.** Example: A report describing how identity thieves can ruin your credit rating. Organized by *who, what, when, where, why,* and *how.*
- **Value/size.** Example: A report describing fluctuations in housing costs, organized by prices of homes.
- **Importance.** Example: A report describing five reasons that a company should move its headquarters to a specific city, organized from the most important reason to the least important.
- **Problem/solution.** Example: A company faces a problem such as declining sales. A solution such as reducing the staff is offered.
- **Simple/complex.** Example: A report explaining genetic modification of plants, organized from simple seed production to complex gene introduction.
- **Best case/worst case.** Example: A report analyzing whether two companies should merge, organized by the best-case result (improved market share, profitability, good employee morale) opposed to the worse-case result (devalued stock, lost market share, poor employee morale).

In the presentation shown in Figure 10.2, Eric arranged the main points by importance, placing the most important point last where it had maximum effect. When organizing any presentation, prepare a little more material than you think you will actually need. Savvy speakers always have something useful in reserve (such as an extra handout, transparency, or idea)—just in case they finish early.

Summarizing in the Conclusion

Nervous speakers often rush to wrap up their presentations because they can't wait to flee the stage. But listeners will remember the conclusion more than any part of a speech. That's why you should spend some time to make it most effective. Strive to achieve two goals:

- Summarize the main themes of the presentation.
- Include a statement that allows you to leave the podium gracefully.

Some speakers end limply with comments such as "I guess that's about all I have to say." This leaves bewildered audience members wondering whether they should continue listening. Skilled speakers alert the audience that they are finishing. They use phrases such as "In conclusion," "As I end this presentation," or "It's time for me to stop." Then they proceed immediately to the conclusion. Audiences become justly irritated with a speaker who announces the conclusion but then digresses with one more story or talks on for ten more minutes.

A straightforward summary should review major points and focus on what you want the listeners to do, think, or remember. You might say, "In bringing my presentation to a close, I will restate my major purpose...." Or "In summary, my major purpose has been to ... ; in support of my purpose, I have presented three major points. They are (a) ... , (b) ... , and (c)...." Notice how Eric Evans, in the conclusion shown in Figure 10.2, summarized his three main points and provided a final focus to listeners.

If you are promoting a recommendation, you might end as follows: "In conclusion, I recommend that we retain Matrixx Marketing to conduct a telemarketing campaign beginning September 1 at a cost of X dollars. To complete this recommendation, I suggest that we (a) finance this campaign from our operations budget, (b) develop a persuasive message describing our new product, and (c) name Lisa Beck to oversee the project."

In your conclusion you might want to use an anecdote, an inspiring quotation, or a statement that ties in the attention-capturing opener and offers a new insight. Whatever you choose, be sure to include a closing thought that indicates you are finished. For example, "This concludes my presentation. After investigating many marketing firms, we are convinced that Matrixx is the best for our purposes. Your authorization of my recommendations will mark the beginning of a very successful campaign for our new product. Thank you."

PRESENTATIONS ARE MORE THAN JUST WELL ORGANIZED...

Good speakers are adept at building audience rapport, as Andrew Wahl notes in his *Canadian Business* article above. They form a bond with the audience; they entertain as well as inform. How do they do it? Based on observations of successful and unsuccessful speakers, we learn that the good ones use a number of verbal and nonverbal techniques to connect with the audience. Some of their helpful techniques include providing effective imagery, supplying verbal signposts, and using body language strategically.

Effective Imagery

You'll lose your audience quickly if your talk is filled with abstractions, generalities, and dry facts. To enliven your presentation and enhance comprehension, try using some of these techniques:

- **Analogies.** A comparison of similar traits between dissimilar things can be effective in explaining and drawing connections. For example, "Product development is similar to the process of conceiving, carrying, and delivering a baby." Or "Downsizing and restructuring are similar to an overweight person undergoing a regimen of dieting, habit changing, and exercise."
- **Metaphors.** A comparison between otherwise dissimilar things without using the words *like* or *as* results in a metaphor. For example, "Our competitor's CEO is a snake when it comes to negotiating" or "My desk is a garbage dump."
- **Similes.** A comparison that includes the words *like* or *as* is a simile. For example, "Building a business team is like building a sports team—you want people not only with the right abilities, but also with the willingness to work together." Or "She's as happy as someone who just won the lottery."
- **Personal anecdotes.** Nothing connects you faster or better with your audience than a good personal story. In a talk about e-mail techniques, you could reveal your own blunders that became painful learning experiences. In a talk to potential investors, the founder of a new ethnic magazine might tell a story about growing up without enough positive ethnic role models.

- **Personalized statistics.** Although often misused, statistics stay with people—particularly when they relate directly to the audience. A speaker discussing job searching might say, "Look around the room. Only three out of five graduates will find a job immediately after graduation." If possible, simplify and personalize facts. For example, "The sales of Creemore Springs Brewery totalled 5 million cases last year. That means a full case of Creemore was consumed by every man, woman, and child in the Greater Toronto area."

- **Worst and best-case scenarios.** Hearing the worst that could happen can be effective in driving home a point. For example, "If we do nothing about our computer backup system now, it's just a matter of time before the entire system crashes and we lose all of our customer contact information. Can you imagine starting from scratch in building all of your customer files again? However, if we fix the system now, we can expand our customer files and actually increase sales at the same time."

- **Examples.** If all else fails, remember that an audience likes to hear specifics. If you're giving a presentation on office etiquette, for example, instead of just saying, "Rudeness in the workplace is a growing problem," it's always better to say something like "Rudeness in the workplace is a growing problem. For example, we've heard from some of our clients that our customer service representatives could improve their tone of voice."

Verbal Signposts

Speakers must remember that listeners, unlike readers of a report, cannot control the rate of presentation or flip back through pages to review main points. As a result, listeners get lost easily. Knowledgeable speakers help the audience recognize the organization and main points in an oral message with verbal signposts. They keep listeners on track by including helpful previews, summaries, and transitions, such as these:

- **Previewing.** "The next segment of my talk presents three reasons for...."
  "Let's now consider the causes of...."

- **Switching directions.** "Thus far we've talked solely about ... ; now let's move to...."
  "I've argued that ... and ... , but an alternate view holds that...."

- **Summarizing.** "Let me review with you the major problems I've just discussed...."
  "You see, then, that the most significant factors are...."

You can further improve any oral presentation by including appropriate transitional expressions such as *first, second, next, then, therefore, moreover, on the other hand, on the contrary,* and *in conclusion.* These expressions lend emphasis and tell listeners where you are headed. Notice in Eric Evans's outline, in Figure 10.2, the specific transitional elements are designed to help listeners recognize each new principal point.

Nonverbal Messages

Although what you say is most important, the nonverbal messages you send can also have a potent effect on how well your message is received. How you look, how you move, and how you speak can make or break your presentation. The following suggestions focus on nonverbal tips to ensure that your verbal message is well received.

- **Look terrific.** Like it or not, you will be judged by your appearance. For everything but small in-house presentations, be sure you dress professionally. The rule of thumb is that you should dress at least as well as the best-dressed person in the company.
- **Animate your body.** Be enthusiastic and let your body show it. Emphasize ideas to enhance points about size, number, and direction. Use a variety of gestures, but try not to consciously plan them in advance.
- **Punctuate your words.** You can keep your audience interested by varying your tone, volume, pitch, and pace. Use pauses before and after important points. Allow the audience to take in your ideas.
- **Get out from behind the podium.** Avoid being planted behind the podium. Movement makes you look natural and comfortable. You might pick a few places in the room to walk to. Even if you must stay close to your visual aids, make a point of leaving them occasionally so that the audience can see your whole body.
- **Vary your facial expression.** Begin with a smile, but change your expressions to correspond with the thoughts you are voicing. You can shake your head to show disagreement, roll your eyes to show disdain, look heavenward for guidance, or wrinkle your brow to show concern or dismay. To see how speakers convey meaning without words, mute the sound on your TV and watch the facial expressions of any well-known talk show host.

PLANNING VISUAL AIDS, HANDOUTS, AND POWERPOINT PRESENTATIONS

Before you give a business presentation, consider this wise Chinese proverb: "Tell me, I forget. Show me, I remember. Involve me, I understand." Your goals as a speaker are to make listeners understand, remember, and act on your ideas. To get them interested and involved, include effective visual aids. Some experts say that we acquire 85 percent of all our knowledge visually. Therefore, an oral presentation that incorporates visual aids is far more likely to be understood and retained than one lacking visual enhancement.

Good visual aids have many purposes. They emphasize and clarify main points, thus improving comprehension and retention. They increase audience interest, and they make the presenter appear more professional, better prepared, and more persuasive. Furthermore, research shows that the use of visual aids actually shortens meetings.[3] Visual aids are particularly helpful for inexperienced speakers because the audience concentrates on the aid rather than on the speaker. Good visuals also serve to jog the memory of a speaker, thus improving self-confidence, poise, and delivery.

Types of Visual Aids

Fortunately for today's speakers, many forms of visual media are available to enhance a presentation. Three of the most popular visuals are overhead projectors, handouts, and computer visuals.

Overhead projectors. Student and professional speakers alike rely on the overhead projector and document camera for many reasons. Most meeting areas are equipped with projectors and screens. Moreover, acetate transparencies for the overhead are cheap, easily prepared on a computer or copier, and simple to use.

Similarly, projecting a page from a book or a newspaper article with a document camera is effective. And, because rooms need not be darkened, a speaker using transparencies or a document camera can maintain eye contact with the audience. A word of caution, though: stand to the side of the projector so that you don't obstruct the audience's view.

Handouts. You can enhance and complement your presentations by distributing pictures, outlines, brochures, articles, charts, summaries, or other supplements. Speakers who use computer presentation programs often prepare a set of their slides along with notes to hand out to viewers with mixed results. Often, the audience doesn't pay attention to the speaker but noisily flips through the printed-out pages of the computer presentation. Timing the distribution of any handout, though, is tricky. If given out during a presentation, your handouts tend to distract the audience, causing you to lose control. Thus, it's probably best to discuss most handouts during the presentation but delay distributing them until after you finish.

Computer visuals. With today's excellent software programs—such as PowerPoint, Harvard Graphics Advanced Presentation, Freelance Graphics, and Corel Presentations—you can create dynamic, colourful presentations with your computer. The output from these programs is generally shown on a monitor or a screen. With a little expertise and advanced equipment, you can create a multimedia presentation that includes stereo sound, video clips, and hyperlinks, as described in the following discussion of electronic presentations.

Designing an Impressive Computer Presentation

The content of most presentations today hasn't changed, but the medium certainly has. At meetings and conferences many speakers now use computer programs, such as PowerPoint, to present, defend, and sell their ideas most effectively. PowerPoint is a software program that facilitates design of text and graphics on slides that can be displayed on a laptop computer or projected to a screen. PowerPoint slides can also be sent out as an e-mail attachment, distributed via web download, or printed as a booklet. The latest gadgets even enable you to plan your PowerPoint presentation on a PDA.[4] Many business speakers use PowerPoint because it helps them organize their thoughts, is relatively inexpensive, and produces flashy high-tech visuals. Used skillfully, PowerPoint can make an impressive, professional presentation. Yet PowerPoint has its critics. PowerPoint, say its detractors, like Andrew Wahl in the article that begins this chapter, is turning the nation's businesspeople into a "mindless gaggle of bullet-pointed morons."[5]

The ease with which most of us use PowerPoint has led to a false sense of security. We seem to have forgotten that to be effective, presenters using PowerPoint must first be effective presenters, period. Effective presenters do not overwhelm an audience by assuming it will be happy to read multiple slides with multiple lines or paragraphs of text, nor do they rely so heavily on a screen image that no one is paying attention to or listening to them. In other words, smart business presenters have to keep the attention of their audience by deploying the skills discussed above.

They cannot assume that simply because they have a well-designed PowerPoint presentation, their actual *presentation* will go well. Of course, learning how to use templates, working with colour, building bullet points, and adding multimedia effects are valuable skills, and the rest of this section examines how best to use computer presentation software.

Using Templates to Your Advantage

To begin your training in using a computer presentation program, you'll want to examine its templates. These professionally designed formats combine harmonious colours, borders, and fonts for pleasing visual effects. One of the biggest problems in corporate presentations is inconsistency. Presentations include a hodgepodge collection of informal slides with different fonts and clashing colours. Templates avoid this problem by showing what fonts should be used for different level headings.

Templates also provide guidance in laying out each slide, as shown in Figure 10.3. You can select a layout for a title page, a bulleted list, a bar chart, a double-column list, an organization chart, and so on. To present a unified and distinctive image, some companies develop a customized template with their logo and a predefined colour scheme. As one expert says, "This prevents salespeople from creating horrid colour combinations on their own."[6] But templates are helpful only if you use them when you first begin preparing your presentation. Applying a template when you are nearly finished involves a lot of rekeying and rewriting.

A final piece of advice about presentation templates is that you should resist the temptation toward tackiness. Some novice businesspeople and students assume that because a template with a palm tree and cactus exists, and because they think it looks good, it will look professional. It won't. Remember that visual professionalism means simplicity, not cuteness or busyness.

Working with Colour

You don't need training in colour theory to create presentation images that impress your audience rather than confuse them. You can use the colour schemes from the design templates that come with your presentation program, or you can

Figure 10.3 ▶ Selecting a Slide Layout in Microsoft PowerPoint

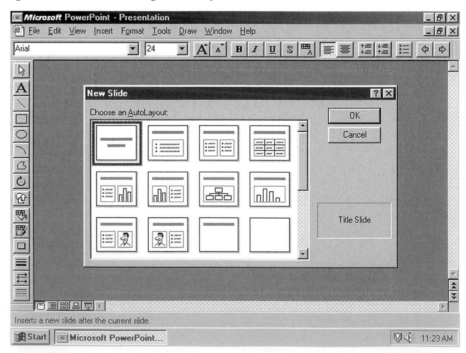

alter them. Generally, it's best to use a colour palette of five or fewer colours for an entire presentation. Use warm colours—reds, oranges, and yellows—to highlight important elements. Use the same colour for like elements. For example, all slide titles should be the same colour. The colour for backgrounds and text depends on where the presentation will be given. Use light text on a dark background for presentations in darkened rooms. Use dark text on a light background for computer presentations in lighted rooms and for projecting transparencies.

When many people are working together to prepare a slide presentation, be sure that they all choose colours that are in PowerPoint's colour scheme menu. When other colours are used, making changes becomes a tedious exercise in individual slide-editing.[7]

Building Bullet Points

When you prepare your slides, translate the major headings in your presentation outline into titles for slides. Then build bullet points using short phrases. In Chapter 4 you learned to improve readability by using graphic highlighting techniques, including bullets, numbers, and headings. In preparing a PowerPoint presentation, you will use those same techniques.

Let's say, for example, that Matt wants to persuade the boss of his small company to install a voice-mail system. His boss is resisting because he says that voice mail will cost too much. Matt wants to emphasize benefits that result in increased productivity. Here is a portion of the text he wrote:

> *Because voice mail allows callers to deliver detailed information to office personnel with just one telephone call, telephone tag can be eliminated. In addition, some research has found that up to 75 percent of all business calls do not reach the desired party. Whatever the actual number, people do tend to make far fewer callbacks when they have a voice mailbox in which their callers can leave messages. Although voice mail can't match the timeliness of a live telephone call, it's the next best thing for getting the word out when time is of the essence. Finally, voice mail frees callers from the prospect of being placed on hold indefinitely when the person they want is temporarily unavailable. Callers can immediately leave a voice message, bypassing the hold interval altogether.*

To convert the preceding text into bullet points, Matt started with a title and then listed the main ideas that related to that title. He made sure all the items were parallel. Matt went through many revisions before creating the following bulleted list. Notice that the heading promotes reader benefits. Notice also that the bullet points are concise. They should be key words or phrases, not complete sentences. This is because the most effective presentations use visuals as signposts along the way. It's up to Matt to speak to each bulleted point, to engage his audience.

> *Voice Mail Can Make Your Calls More Efficient*
> - *Eliminates telephone tag*
> - *Reduces callbacks*
> - *Improves timely communication*
> - *Shortens "hold" times*

One of the best features of electronic presentation programs is the "build" capability. You can focus the viewer's attention on each specific item as you add bullet points line by line. The bulleted items may "fly" in from the left, right, top, or bottom. They can also build or dissolve from the centre. As you add each new bullet point, leave the previous ones on the slide but show them in lightened text.

In building bulleted points or in moving from one slide to the next, you can use slide transition elements, such as "wipe-outs," glitter, ripple, liquid, and vortex effects. But don't overdo it. Experts suggest choosing one transition effect and applying it consistently.[8]

For the most effective presentations, each slide should include no more than seven words in a line. Furthermore, no slide should have more than four lines, plus

Figure 10.4 ▶ Preparing a PowerPoint Presentation

Tips for Preparing and Using Slides

- Keep all visuals simple; spotlight major points only.
- Use the same font size and style for similar headings.
- No more than seven words on a line, and four total lines, plus a title
- Be sure that everyone in the audience can see the slides.
- Show a slide, allow the audience to read it, then paraphrase it. Do NOT read from a slide.
- Rehearse by practising talking to the audience, not to the slides.

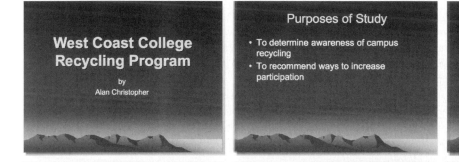

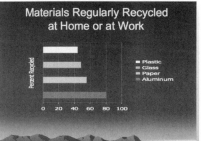

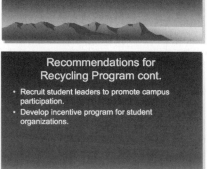

a title. An effective PowerPoint presentation is found in Figure 10.4. Remember that presentation slides summarize; they don't tell the whole story. That's the job of the presenter.

Adding Multimedia and Other Effects

Many presentation programs also provide libraries of multimedia features to enhance your content. These include sound, animation, and video elements. For example, you could use sound effects to "reward" correct answers from your audience. Similarly, video clips—when used judiciously—can add excitement and depth to a presentation. You might use video to capture attention in a stimulating introduction, to show the benefits of a product in use, or to bring the personality of a distant expert or satisfied customer right into the meeting room.

Another way to enliven a presentation is with photographic images, which are now easy to obtain electronically thanks to the prevalence of low-cost scanners and digital cameras. Most programs are also capable of generating hyperlinks ("hot" spots on the screen) that allow you to jump instantly to relevant data or multimedia content.

Producing Speaker's Notes and Handouts

Most computer presentation programs offer a variety of presentation options. In addition to printouts of your slides, you can make speaker's notes, as shown in Figure 10.5. These are wonderful aids for practising your talk; they remind you of the supporting comments for the abbreviated material in your slides. Many programs allow you to print miniature versions of your slides with numerous slides to

Figure 10.5 ▶ Speaker's Notes for a Computer Presentation

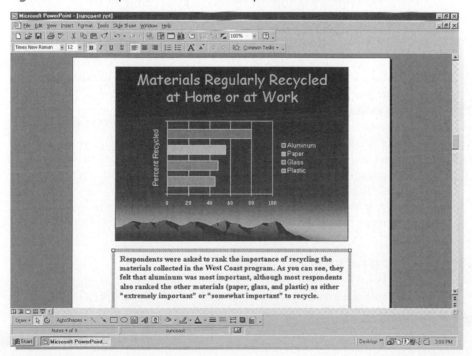

Speaker's notes enable you to print discussion items beneath each slide, thus providing handy review material for practice.

a page, if you wish. These miniatures are handy if you want to preview your talk to a sponsoring organization or if you wish to supply the audience with a summary of your presentation.

Developing Web-Based Presentations and Electronic Handouts

Because of many technological improvements, you can now give a talk without even travelling off-site. In other words, you can put your slides "on the road." Web presentations with slides, narration, and speaker control are emerging as a less costly alternative to videoconferencing, which can be expensive. For example, you could initiate a meeting via a conference call, narrate using a telephone, and have participants see your slides from the browsers on their computers. If you prefer, you could skip the narration and provide a prerecorded presentation.

Web-based presentations have many applications, including providing access to updated training or sales data whenever needed.[9] Larry Magid, computer expert and noted speaker, suggests still another way that speakers can use the Web. He recommends posting your slides on the Web even if you are giving a face-to-face presentation. Attendees appreciate these *electronic handouts* because they don't have to carry them home.[10]

Avoiding Being Upstaged by Your Slides

Although computer presentations are great aids, they cannot replace you. In developing a presentation, don't expect your slides to carry the show. Your goal is to avoid letting PowerPoint "steal your thunder." Here are suggestions for keeping control in your slide presentation:

- Use your slides primarily to summarize important points. For each slide have one or more paragraphs of narration to present to your audience.
- Remember that your responsibility is to *add value* to the information you present. Explain the analyses leading up to the major points and what each point means.
- Look at the audience, not the screen.
- Leave the lights as bright as you can. Make sure the audience can see your face and eyes.
- Darken the screen while you discuss points, tell a story, give an example, or involve the audience.
- Maintain a connection with the audience by using a laser pointer to highlight slide items to discuss.
- Don't rely totally on PowerPoint. Help the audience visualize your points by using other techniques. Drawing a diagram on a whiteboard or flipchart can be more engaging than showing slide after slide of static drawings. Showing real objects is a welcome relief from slides.
- Remember that your slides merely supply a framework for your presentation. Your audience came to see and hear you.[11]

PROFESSIONAL DELIVERY OF PRESENTATIONS

Once you've organized your presentation and prepared visuals, you're ready to practise delivering it. Delivery includes how your voice, eyes, and the rest of your body is used during a presentation. Here are suggestions for selecting a delivery method, along with specific techniques to use before, during, and after your presentation.

Delivery Method

Inexperienced speakers often feel that they must memorize an entire presentation to be effective. Unless you're a professional performer, however, you will sound wooden and unnatural. Moreover, forgetting your place can be embarrassing. Therefore, memorizing an entire oral presentation is not recommended. However, memorizing significant parts—the introduction, the conclusion, and perhaps a meaningful quotation—can be dramatic and impressive.

If memorizing won't work, is reading your presentation the best plan? Definitely not. Reading to an audience is boring and ineffective. Because reading suggests that you don't know your topic well, the audience loses confidence in your expertise. Reading also prevents you from maintaining eye contact. You can't see audience reactions; consequently, you can't benefit from feedback.

Neither the memorizing nor the reading method creates convincing presentations. The best plan, by far, is a "notes" method. Plan your presentation carefully and talk from note cards or an outline containing key sentences and major ideas. By preparing and then practising with your notes, you can talk to your audience in a conversational manner. Your notes should be neither entire paragraphs nor single words. Instead, they should contain a complete sentence or two to introduce each major idea. Below the topic sentence(s), outline subpoints and illustrations. Note cards will keep you on track and prompt your memory, but only if you have rehearsed the presentation thoroughly.

Delivery Techniques

Nearly everyone experiences some degree of stage fright when speaking before a group. "If you hear someone say he or she isn't nervous before a speech, you're talking either to a liar or a very boring speaker," says corporate speech consultant Dianna Booher.[12] In other words, you can capitalize on the adrenaline that is coursing through your body by converting it to excitement and enthusiasm for your performance. But you can't just walk in and "wing it." People who don't prepare suffer the most anxiety and give the worst performances. You can learn to make effective oral presentations by focusing on four areas: preparation, organization, visual aids, and delivery.

Being afraid is quite natural and results from actual physiological changes occurring in your body. Faced with a frightening situation, your body responds with the fight-or-flight response. You can learn to control and reduce stage fright, as well as to incorporate techniques for effective speaking, by using the following strategies and techniques before, during, and after your presentation.

Before Your Presentation

- **Prepare thoroughly.** One of the most effective strategies for reducing stage fright is knowing your subject thoroughly. Research your topic diligently and prepare a careful sentence outline. Those who try to "wing it" usually suffer the worst butterflies—and make the worst presentations.
- **Rehearse repeatedly.** When you rehearse, practise your entire presentation, not just the first half. Place your outline sentences on separate cards. You may also wish to include transitional sentences to help you move to the next topic. Use these cards as you practise, and include your visual aids in your rehearsal. Rehearse alone or before friends and family. Also try rehearsing on audio- or videotape so that you can evaluate your effectiveness.
- **Time yourself.** Most audiences tend to get restless during longer talks. Thus, try to complete your presentation in no more than 20 minutes. Set a timer during your rehearsal to measure your speaking time.

- **Check the room.** If you are using sound equipment or a projector, be certain they are operational. Check electrical outlets and the position of the viewing screen. Ensure that the seating arrangement is appropriate to your needs. If the room has windows, will the sun outside get in the way of your PowerPoint presentation? And what is the set-up for you: is there a table to stand beside or behind? Is there a lectern for you to place your notes on?
- **Greet members of the audience.** Try to make contact with a few members of the audience when you enter the room, while you are waiting to be introduced, or when you walk to the podium. Your body language should convey friendliness, confidence, and enjoyment.
- **Practise stress reduction.** If you feel tension and fear while you are waiting your turn to speak, use stress-reduction techniques, such as deep breathing.

During Your Presentation

- **Begin with a pause.** When you first approach the audience, take a moment to adjust your notes and make yourself comfortable. Establish your control of the situation.
- **Present your first sentence from memory.** By memorizing your opening, you can immediately establish rapport with the audience through eye contact. You'll also sound confident and knowledgeable.
- **Maintain eye contact.** If the size of the audience overwhelms you, pick out two individuals on the right and two on the left. Talk directly to these people.
- **Control your voice and vocabulary.** This means speaking in moderated tones but loudly enough to be heard. Eliminate verbal static, such as *ah, er, you know,* and *um.* Silence is preferable to meaningless fillers when you are thinking of your next idea.
- **Put the brakes on.** Many novice speakers talk too rapidly, displaying their nervousness and making it difficult for audience members to understand their ideas. Slow down and listen to what you are saying.
- **Move naturally.** You can use the lectern to hold your notes so that you are free to move about casually and naturally. Avoid fidgeting with your notes, your clothing, or items in your pockets. Learn to use your body to express a point.
- **Use visual aids effectively.** Discuss and interpret each visual aid for the audience. Move aside as you describe it so that it can be seen fully. Use a pointer if necessary.
- **Avoid digressions.** Stick to your outline and notes. Don't suddenly include clever little anecdotes or digressions that occur to you on the spot. If it's not part of your rehearsed material, leave it out so that you can finish on time. Remember, too, that your audience may not be as enthralled with your topic as you are.
- **Summarize your main points.** Conclude your presentation by reiterating your main points or by emphasizing what you want the audience to think or do. Once you have announced your conclusion, proceed to it directly.

After Your Presentation

- **Distribute handouts.** If you prepared handouts with data the audience will need, pass them out when you finish.
- **Encourage questions.** If the situation permits a question-and-answer period, announce it at the beginning of your presentation. Then, when you finish, ask for questions. Set a time limit for questions and answers.

- **Repeat questions.** Although the speaker may hear the question, audience members often do not. Begin each answer with a repetition of the question. This also gives you thinking time. Then, direct your answer to the entire audience.
- **Reinforce your main points.** You can use your answers to restate your primary ideas ("I'm glad you brought that up because it gives me a chance to elaborate on ..."). In answering questions, avoid becoming defensive or debating the questioner.
- **Keep control.** Don't allow one individual to take over. Keep the entire audience involved.
- **Avoid** *Yes, but* **answers.** The word *but* immediately cancels any preceding message. Try replacing it with *and*. For example, *Yes, X has been tried. And Y works even better because....*
- **End with a summary and appreciation.** To signal the end of the session before you take the last question, say something like "We have time for just one more question." As you answer the last question, try to work it into a summary of your main points. Then, express appreciation to the audience for the opportunity to talk with them.

PRESENTING YOURSELF IN JOB INTERVIEWS

Job interviews, for most of us, are intimidating; no one enjoys being judged and, possibly, rejected. You can overcome your fear of the interview process by thinking about it as a business presentation—one in which you are the expert. After all, who knows more about you and your experience than you?

Trained recruiters generally structure the interview in three separate activities: establishing a cordial relationship, eliciting information about the candidate, and giving information about the job and company. During the interview its participants have opposing goals. The interviewer tries to uncover any negative information that would eliminate a candidate. The candidate, of course, tries to minimize faults and emphasize strengths to avoid being eliminated. You can become a more skillful player in the interview game if you know what to do before, during, and after the interview.

Before the Interview

- **Research the organization.** Never enter an interview cold. Visit the library or use your computer to search for information about the target company or its field, service, or product. Visit the company's website and read everything. Call the company to request annual reports, catalogues, or brochures. Ask about the organization and possibly the interviewer. Learn something about the company's size, number of employees, competitors, reputation, and strengths and weaknesses.
- **Learn about the position.** Obtain as much specific information as possible. What are the functions of an individual in this position? What is the typical salary range? What career paths are generally open to this individual? What did the last person in this position do right or wrong?
- **Plan to sell yourself.** Identify three to five of your major selling points regarding skills, training, personal characteristics, and specialized experience. Memorize them; then in the interview be certain to find a place to insert them.

- **Prepare answers to possible questions.** Imagine the kinds of questions you may be asked and work out sample answers. Although you can't anticipate precise questions, you can expect to be asked about your education, skills, previous experiences, strengths, weaknesses, interest in working for the company, and availability.
- **Prepare success stories.** Rehearse two or three incidents that you can relate about your accomplishments. These may focus on problems you have solved, promotions you have earned, or recognition or praise you have received.
- **Arrive early.** Get to the interview five or ten minutes early. If you are unfamiliar with the area where the interview is to be held, you might visit it before the scheduled day. Locate the building, parking facilities, and office. Time yourself.
- **Dress appropriately.** Heed the advice of one expert: "Dress and groom like the interviewer is likely to dress—but cleaner."[13] Don't overdo perfume, jewellery, or after-shave lotion. Avoid loud colours; strive for a coordinated, natural appearance. Favourite "power" colours for interviews are grey and dark blue. It's not a bad idea to check your appearance in a restroom before entering the office.

During the Interview

- **Establish the relationship.** Shake hands firmly. Don't be afraid to offer your hand first. Address the interviewer formally ("Hello, Mrs. Jones"). Allow the interviewer to put you at ease with small talk (discussed in Chapter 12).
- **Act confident but natural.** Establish and maintain eye contact, but don't get into a staring contest. Sit up straight, facing the interviewer. Don't cross your arms and legs at the same time (review body language cues in Chapter 2). Don't manipulate objects, like a pencil or keys, during the interview. Try to remain natural and at ease.
- **Don't criticize.** Avoid making negative comments about previous employers, instructors, or others. Such criticism may be taken to indicate a negative personality. Employers are not eager to hire complainers. Moreover, such criticism may suggest that you would do the same to this organization.
- **Stay focused on your strengths.** If the interviewer asks a question that does not help you promote your strongest qualifications, answer briefly. Alternatively, try to turn your response into a positive selling point, such as this: "I have not had extensive paid training in that area, but I have completed a 50-hour training program that provided hands-on experience using the latest technology and methods. My recent training taught me to be open to new ideas and showed me how I can continue learning on my own. I was commended for being a quick learner."
- **Find out about the job early.** Because your time will be short, try to learn all you can about the target job early in the interview. Ask about its responsibilities and the kinds of people who have done well in the position before. Inquiring about the company's culture will help you decide if your personality fits with this organization.
- **Prepare for salary questions.** Remember that nearly all salaries are negotiable, depending on your qualifications. Knowing the typical salary range for the target position helps. The recruiter can tell you the salary ranges—but you will have to ask. If you've had little experience, you will probably be offered a salary somewhere between the low point and the midpoint in the range. With

more experience you can negotiate for a higher figure. A word of caution, though. One personnel manager warns that candidates who emphasize money are suspect because they may leave if offered a few thousand dollars more elsewhere.

- **Be ready for inappropriate questions.** If you are asked a question that you think is illegal, politely ask the interviewer how that question is related to this job. Ask the purpose of the question. Perhaps valid reasons exist that are not obvious.
- **Ask your own questions.** Often, the interviewer concludes an interview with "Do you have any questions about the position?" Inquire about career paths, orientation or training for new employees, or the company's promotion policies. Have a list of relevant questions prepared. If the interview has gone well, ask the recruiter about his or her career in the company.
- **Conclude positively.** Summarize your strongest qualifications, show your enthusiasm for obtaining this position, and thank the interviewer for a constructive interview. Be sure you understand the next step in the employment process.

After the Interview

- **Make notes on the interview.** While the events are fresh in your mind, jot down the key points—good and bad.
- **Write a thank-you e-mail.** Immediately send an e-mail thanking the interviewer for a pleasant and enlightening discussion. Be sure to spell her or his name correctly.

CONCLUSION

This chapter presented techniques for giving effective oral presentations. Good presentations begin with analysis of your purpose and your audience. Organizing the content involves preparing an effective introduction, body, and closing. The introduction should capture the listener's attention, identify the speaker, establish credibility, and preview the main points. The body should discuss two to four main points, with appropriate explanations, details, and verbal signposts to guide listeners. The conclusion should review the main points, provide a final focus, and allow the speaker to leave the podium gracefully. You can improve audience rapport by using effective imagery, including examples, analogies, metaphors, similes, personal anecdotes, statistics, and worst/best-case scenarios.

In illustrating a presentation, use simple, text-light, easily understood visual aids to emphasize and clarify main points. If you use PowerPoint, you can enhance the presentation by using templates, layout designs, and bullet points.

In delivering your presentation, outline the main points on note cards and rehearse repeatedly. During the presentation consider beginning with a pause and presenting your first sentence from memory. Make eye contact, control your voice, speak and move naturally, and avoid digressions. After your talk distribute handouts and answer questions. End gracefully and express appreciation.

Business presentation skills are transferable to a common situation: the job interview. Here, your audience is smaller than in a presentation, and it's not necessary to plan an introduction, body, and conclusion, but otherwise, participating in a successful interview is similar to giving an effective business presentation.

:: *Chapter Review*

As a way of studying the material in this chapter, imagine you are at a job interview for your dream entry-level job after college or university. You've prepared answers for all the classic interview questions, but to your surprise, your interviewer also asks a number of questions based on business presentation skills. How would you answer the following six questions?

1. In your role here, you'd be responsible for giving business presentations on a fairly regular basis. Besides the actual content of what you're going to say, what else is important as you prepare for a presentation?
2. One of our top performers always tells new recruits that "giving a presentation's like writing a perfect essay." Do you agree with him and if so, what do you think he means?
3. Lots of college and university grads know how to give presentations because they've been doing so for years at school. Besides organizing the content well, what makes you stand out as a presenter? Why will your audiences remember what you've said?
4. What's your opinion of the various visual aids out there used in presentations? Do you always use the same one, and if so why? If not, why not?
5. We see a lot of PowerPoint presentations around here, and opinion in the office is pretty divided. What's your take on the strengths and weaknesses of the technology and how it's used today?
6. Some people have compared what we do to acting or doing comedy. Do you agree with this way of looking at presentation delivery?

:: *Problems*

1. Using the scenario described in the problems section of Chapter 9, in which you were working on a research report comparing your institution's website to two of its competitors' websites, consider how this report could be turned into an effective and engaging presentation. One day the VP of Marketing, Cindy Simon, calls you and says that even though the board has accepted the recommendations of your report, it doesn't want to commit money to a website overhaul without hearing a presentation based on the report. Specifically, the board has asked for hands-on demonstrations of the three websites to be done so that board members can understand for themselves the findings of the report. After negotiating terms for this extra work with Cindy Simon, you agree to give the presentation in two weeks' time. Knowing what you do about this audience, how will you plan this presentation? How would your plan change if you were told that the board had not accepted the recommendations of your report completely? How would your plan change if you were told that there was resistance on the part of some board members to the idea of spending more money on the website? (Keep in mind Cindy Simon has agreed, in principle, to use your friend the graphic designer from problem 5, Chapter 9, to do the work if the board agrees.)
2. For each of the three scenarios described above (i.e., board wants demonstrations to back up its already-made decision, board wants presentation because report recommendations not completely accepted, and board wants presentation and has active resistance to spending more money on website), draft a presentation outline, following the example of Figure 10.2.
3. For each of the three scenarios described in problem 2, design at least one visual aid that is not a PowerPoint presentation. Will your decision of what

visual aid to use depend on the audience? What will you do if during your presentation one of the board members says, "With all due respect, couldn't all this have been made more clear by doing a PowerPoint presentation?"

4. Design an overall effective 10- to 15-minute PowerPoint presentation to be used in *one* of the three scenarios described in problem 2. Ensure that somewhere in the presentation, one error is made, of the kind described in this chapter (e.g., poor colour combinations, too-busy slides, too much text on slides, reading slides instead of facing audience, etc.). Deliver the presentation to your class, and see whether your audience can pick out the errors you've made. When delivering the presentation, try not to give away when the errors are being made. To do this, you'll have to rehearse at least twice so that the presentation is smooth.

5. Open the business section of today's newspaper and find an article that interests you enough to give a short three-minute presentation. Jot down a rough outline for how the presentation will proceed. Then, without rehearsing the presentation, deliver it to your class. Make sure your presentation is either being videotaped or that you have assigned particular students in the class to be on the lookout for specific mistakes in delivery (e.g., Tim will pay attention to voice, Ralph to body language, Tina to eye contact, etc.). Once you've given the presentation, play back the video and make note of your delivery errors or have the students in charge of critiquing you tell you what they found. With the feedback from the video and/or the students, rehearse the same presentation after class three times, and deliver it again in next week's class. Ask your fellow students to tell you whether they notice improvements.

Grammar/Style Review 10

In this review, you will be practising identifying punctuation mistakes. There are at least five mistakes in total, plus at least one non-punctuation mistake. For a brief explanation of this problem, please read the explanation on page 331. Besides completing the exercise below, be sure to be on the lookout for punctuation mistakes in your own writing.

To: jmoffat@stirplex.ca

From: sgupta@stirplex.ca

Date: January 16, 2007

Re: Brochures are late

Hi June,

I know—you said—the brochures were coming yesterday, but, I haven't recieved them yet, and, time's running out!!!

Although, it might not seem like a high-priority on your list of to do items; please put a rush on this!!!

Thanks!

Sal

:: *Business Communication Lab 10*

Reread the last third of Andrew Wahl's article on PowerPoint, focusing especially on what Dave Paradi, the Mississauga, Ontario-based communications trainer, has to say. Now imagine you have applied for a job, recently advertised by Dave's company. The position is for an assistant corporate trainer. He's just picked up a new client, a large engineering company. One day Dave calls you to offer you an interview. He says that part of the interview will be to give a 10- to 15-minute presentation to a new client on effective business presentations. Using what Dave said to Andrew Wahl in the article above, and what this chapter has taught you about presentations and interviews, script the presentation you will give during your interview next week with Dave Paradi. Be prepared to act your script in front of the class, and include an appropriate PowerPoint presentation to go along with the script.

Business Meetings and Negotiations

Meeting madness
Our workplace is changing and anecdotal evidence suggests we're attending more meetings than a decade ago

BY STEPHANIE WHITTAKER, *MONTREAL GAZETTE*, DECEMBER 10, 2005, B5

THERE WAS A time when Anne-Lisa de Forest was attending as many as four meetings a week at work.

"Each one would last an hour. At the beginning, I used to think that being invited to so many meetings was flattering because it meant people were interested in my opinions," she said. "But I realized that it was too many and that when I was at meetings, I wasn't focusing on my main task, which is to generate revenue."

De Forest is the business development manager at Messaging Architects, a Montreal company that develops email software.

These days, thanks to changes made by her company's CEO, de Forest's presence is required at only one meeting per week.

Do you ever feel as if your workday is a blur of one meeting after another? Worse, do you ever have to set aside important tasks to attend meetings?

While it's difficult to find statistics about the frequency of workplace meetings, anecdotal observations suggest that we attend a lot of them and that they're not all productive.

EffectiveMeetings.com, an online resource centre that teaches people how to have productive meetings, cites studies that say most professionals attend an average of 61.8 meetings per month and that more than 50 per cent of their meeting time is wasted.

Toronto productivity expert Mark Ellwood says anecdotal evidence suggests that people are attending more workplace meetings than they did a decade ago.

There are probably two contributing factors, he said.

"Work is status; leisure is not," Ellwood said. "We define ourselves by our work. There's a great attachment to the busyness of work, to getting a lot of phone calls and emails.

"Have you ever heard anyone boast that he received only two emails today? Likewise, there's a lot of credibility attached to attending a lot of meetings."

Another reason for the frequency of meetings, he said, is the flattening out of workplace hierarchies in the past 15 years.

"We're seeing less hierarchy and more project teams," he said. "Project teams have to meet to collaborate.

"Historically, a farmer or an artisan, for instance, could work alone. But contemporary work is much more collaborative. People need to share information and come together to solve problems. Bosses used to be directive. Now, the team comes together to discuss," he said.

Productivity expert Ann Searles, president of the Canada-Caribbean arm of the Institute for Business Technology, said the U.S. end of her organization surveys its clients on meeting attendance.

"It didn't change that much between 1996 and 2005," she said. "In 1996, people reported spending 5.74 hours a week in meetings. By 2005, they were spending 6.07 hours. It's an increase of 20 minutes.

"But when we asked respondents how much time they spent in ineffective or useless meetings, the number jumped to 2.1 hours in 2004 from 0.7 hours in 2000. So the question is, are people attending more meetings or are they just attending more useless meetings?"

Either way, Searles said, she hears plenty of complaints about meetings and many people grumble that there are simply too many.

Ellwood said it's possible that "people are calling too many meetings. What's more, it's also possible that some meetings are attended by the wrong people," he said.

"You should attend meetings in which you can make a difference," he said.

Searles has noticed that in some workplaces, workers receive invitations for as many as three concurrent meetings.

"Usually, they agree to attend all three because they know that one of them is likely to be moved to a different time slot. But at the last minute, they'll have to insult one of the meeting organizers."

She urges her clients to attend meetings only if they have agendas, since the meetings that lack them tend to be unproductive.

"If you receive an invitation to a meeting, you have to decide 'yes' or 'no,'" she said. "You should put a price on your 'yes' by replying: 'As soon as I see the agenda, I'll know if I should be there.' The rule is: 'No agenda, no attenda.'"

Conference calls, she added, are also meetings and should have agendas.

DIAGNOSING THE PROBLEM

At the beginning of this book we discussed some of the major changes in today's workplace that are affecting the way we communicate. Not surprisingly, two of those changes appear once again, almost at the end of the book. Team-based workplaces and flattened management hierarchies, the two changes discussed earlier in the book, are an important part of what Stephanie Whittaker is saying in her *Gazette* article. Workplaces that operate using team-based models, where decision making is consensual among the team members, instead of imposed by a manager, are by definition workplaces in which lots of meetings take place.

As a student, you're not a stranger to meetings, either. As part of your college or university education, you have probably been assigned group or team work as part of some of your courses. To get this work done, you have to meet outside of class time. Inevitably, these meetings don't always go smoothly. The same thing happens at work.

There are at least three problems hinted at in Whittaker's article. The first is frequency. It seems as though a common complaint of workers in today's knowledge economy is that they simply have too many meetings to attend. Why is this a complaint? Well, if you're attending meetings a significant portion of the time, then when does all of your work get done? Does it get done after hours or in overtime? Or do you compress your work, thereby damaging its quality, in order to get it done in the time you have left?

Another problem Whittaker looks at in this article is what we might label appropriateness. Do all the people invited to meetings these days need to be there? Often, the reason this problem occurs is that the people who called the meeting haven't given enough thought to the type of meeting they want to run: is it an information-sharing meeting or a problem-solving meeting, for instance? If it's the latter, do you need as many people to attend as if you were having an information-sharing meeting?

The last problem Whittaker describes briefly is productivity. Why are so many of the same people who are complaining about the frequency of meetings (too many) also complaining about the "useless" quality of many of these meetings? Once again, the answer must lie in the kind of audience-profiling skills you've been looking at throughout this book. For example, if a Marketing department meeting has been called to look at the reasons a particular product has been losing a lot of market share over the past six months, who should be at the meeting? Does everyone in the Marketing department need to be there, or should only the people working on that particular product attend? Also, what should be on the agenda for the meeting? Should there be a rehashing of the bad publicity that has surrounded the product over the past six months (and which everyone in the department already knows about and is depressed about), or should the meeting be a problem-solving session with strict parameters (What can we do? How much will it cost? When should we start?)?

The article doesn't provide any meaningful solutions, but it does offer one tantalizing hint, in its discussion of Anne-Lisa de Forest's situation. Perhaps you and your teammates can amplify the solution in your next in-class activity...

in-class activity 11

IN THE ARTICLE above, Stephanie Whittaker briefly mentions the fact that Anne-Lisa de Forest's boss, the CEO of Montreal-based Messaging Architects, has made "changes" that have enabled de Forest to attend only one meeting per week. Imagine you are the CEO. Exactly what are the changes you've made? What are the pros and cons that went into your decision-making process? Is Anne-Lisa the only employee affected by this change, or are there others? How did you communicate your decision to enact this change to the rest of the company? Have there been any problems arising from your decision? If yes, what are they? Report back to the class within 20 minutes.

Now that you understand a bit of what goes on in today's workplaces when it comes to business meetings, you're ready to consider best practices in business meetings, as well as the basics of one specific type of meeting, the negotiation.

THE IMPORTANCE OF BUSINESS MEETINGS

As businesses become more team oriented and management becomes more participatory, people are attending more meetings than ever. One survey of managers found that they were devoting as many as two days a week to various gatherings.[1] Yet meetings are almost universally disliked. Typical comments include "We have too many of them," "They don't accomplish anything," and "What a waste of time!" In spite of employee reluctance and despite terrific advances in communication and team technology, face-to-face meetings are not going to disappear. In discussing the future of meetings, Akio Morita, former chairman of Sony Corporation, said that he expects "face-to-face meetings will still be the number one form of communication in the twenty-first century."[2] So get used to them. Meetings are here to stay. Our task, then, as business communicators, is to learn how to make them efficient, satisfying, and productive.

Meetings, by the way, consist of three or more individuals who gather to pool information, solicit feedback, clarify policy, seek consensus, and solve problems.

But meetings have another important purpose for you. They represent opportunities. Because they are a prime tool for developing staff, they are career-critical. According to one Canadian company's website, "It is ... true that careers (rightly or wrongly) have been made or broken through performance at meetings."[3] At meetings judgments are formed and careers are made. Therefore, instead of treating them as thieves of your valuable time, try to see them as golden opportunities to demonstrate your leadership, communication, and problem-solving skills. So that you can make the most of these opportunities, here are techniques for planning and conducting successful meetings.

PLANNING A MEETING

No meeting should be called unless the topic is important, can't wait, and requires an exchange of ideas. If the flow of information is strictly one way and no immediate feedback will result, then don't schedule a meeting. For example, if people are merely being advised or informed, send an e-mail, memo, or letter. Leave a telephone or voice-mail message, but don't call a costly meeting. Remember, the real expense of a meeting is the lost productivity of all the people attending. To decide whether the purpose of the meeting is valid, it's a good idea to consult the key people who will be attending. Ask them what outcomes are desired and how to achieve those goals. This consultation also sets a collaborative tone and encourages full participation.

The number of meeting participants is determined by the purpose of the meeting, as shown in Figure 11.1. If the meeting purpose is motivational, such as an employee awards ceremony for Bombardier, then the number of participants is unlimited. But to make decisions, according to studies at 3-M Corporation, the best number is five or fewer participants.[4] Ideally, those attending should be people who will make the decision and people with information necessary to make the decision. Also attending should be people who will be responsible for implementing the decision and representatives of groups who will benefit from the decision.

At least two days in advance of a meeting, distribute an agenda of topics to be discussed. Also include any reports or materials that participants should read in advance. For continuing groups, you might also include a copy of the minutes of the previous meeting. To keep meetings productive, limit the number of agenda items. Remember, the narrower the focus, the greater the chances for success. A good agenda, as illustrated in Figure 11.2, covers the following information:

- Date and place of meeting
- Start time and end time
- Brief description of each topic, in order of priority, including the names of individuals who are responsible for performing some action

Figure 11.1 ▶ Meeting Purpose and Number of Participants

Purpose	Ideal Size
Intensive problem solving	5 or fewer
Problem identification	10 or fewer
Information reviews and presentations	30 or fewer
Motivational	Unlimited

Figure 11.2 ▶ Typical Meeting Agenda

AGENDA
Adventure Travel Canada
Staff Meeting
September 4, 2007
10 to 11 a.m.
Conference Room

		Person	Proposed Time
I.	Call to order; roll call		
II.	Approval of agenda		
III.	Approval of minutes from previous meeting		
IV.	Committee reports		
	A. Website update	Kevin	5 minutes
	B. Tour packages	Lisa	10 minutes
V.	Old business		
	A. Equipment maintenance	John	5 minutes
	B. Client escrow accounts	Alicia	5 minutes
	C. Internal newsletter	Adrienne	5 minutes
VI.	New business		
	A. New accounts	Sarah	5 minutes
	B. Pricing policy for trips	Marcus	15 minutes
VII.	Announcements		
VIII.	Chair's summary, adjournment		

- Proposed allotment of time for each topic
- Any pre-meeting preparation expected of participants

ATTENDING A MEETING

To avoid wasting time and irritating attendees, always start meetings on time—even if some participants are missing. Waiting for latecomers causes resentment and sets a bad precedent. For the same reasons, don't give a quick recap to anyone who arrives late. At the appointed time, open the meeting with a three- to five-minute introduction that includes the following:

- Goal and length of the meeting
- Background of topics or problems
- Possible solutions and constraints
- Tentative agenda
- Ground rules to be followed

A typical set of ground rules might include arriving on time, communicating openly, being supportive, listening carefully, participating fully, confronting conflict frankly, and following the agenda. More formal groups follow parliamentary procedures based on Robert's Rules. For example, in a meeting run using Robert's Rules, there is a way to stop a person from talking too long. It's called "calling the question," which means ending the current discussion and voting on the previous question (or motion) right away. Before you can call the question, however, you have to be recognized by the chair of the meeting, move the "previous question," have your motion seconded, and receive a two-thirds majority vote in favour of calling the question. Most business meetings do not follow Robert's Rules, except perhaps at the highest levels (board meetings), because of the specialized knowledge required to run a meeting in this way.

In most typical business meetings, after establishing basic ground rules, the leader should ask whether participants agree thus far. Ideally, the next step is to assign one attendee to take minutes and one to act as a recorder. The recorder stands at a flipchart or whiteboard and lists the main ideas being discussed and agreements reached.

After the preliminaries, the leader should say as little as possible. Like a talk show host, an effective leader makes "sure that each panel member gets some air time while no one member steals the show."[5] Remember that the purpose of a meeting is to exchange views, not to hear one person, even the leader, do all the talking. If the group has one member who monopolizes, the leader might say, "Thanks for that perspective, Kurt, but please hold your next point while we hear how Ann would respond to that." This technique also encourages quieter participants to speak up.

To avoid allowing digressions to sidetrack the group, try generating a "parking lot" list. This is a list of important but divergent issues that should be discussed at a later time. Another way to handle digressions is to say, "Folks, we are getting off track here. Forgive me for pressing on, but I need to bring us back to the central issue of...."[6] It's important to adhere to the agenda and the time schedule. Equally important, when the group seems to have reached a consensus, is to summarize the group's position and check to see whether everyone agrees.

Conflict is natural and even desirable in workplaces, but it can cause awkwardness and uneasiness. In meetings, conflict typically develops when people feel unheard or misunderstood. If two people are in conflict, the best approach is to encourage each to make a complete case while group members give their full attention. Let each one question the other. Then the leader should summarize what was said, and the group should offer comments. The group may modify a recommendation or suggest alternatives before reaching consensus on a direction to follow.

When individuals are performing in a dysfunctional role (such as blocking discussion, attacking other speakers, joking excessively, or withdrawing), they should be handled with care and tact. The following specific techniques can help a meeting leader control some group members and draw others out:

- **Lay down the rules in an opening statement.** Give a specific overall summary of topics, time allotment, and expected behaviour. Warn that speakers who digress will be interrupted.
- **Seat potentially dysfunctional members strategically.** Experts suggest seating a difficult group member immediately next to the leader. It's easier to bypass a person in this position. Make sure the person with dysfunctional behaviour is not seated in a power point, such as at the end of table or across from the leader.
- **Avoid direct eye contact.** Direct eye contact is a nonverbal signal that encourages talking. Thus, when asking a question of the group, look only at those whom you wish to answer.
- **Assign dysfunctional members specific tasks.** Ask a potentially disruptive person, for example, to be the group recorder.
- **Ask members to speak in a specific order.** Ordering comments creates an artificial, rigid climate and should be done only when absolutely

necessary. But such a regimen ensures that everyone gets a chance to participate.

- **Interrupt monopolizers.** If a difficult member dominates a discussion, wait for a pause and then break in. Summarize briefly the previous comments or ask someone else for an opinion.
- **Encourage non-talkers.** Give only positive feedback to the comments of reticent members. Ask them direct questions about which you know they have information or opinions.
- **Give praise and encouragement** to those who seem to need it, including the distracters, the blockers, and the withdrawn.[7]

End the meeting at the agreed time or earlier if possible. The leader should summarize what has been decided, who is going to do what, and by what time. It may be necessary to ask people to volunteer to take responsibility for completing action items agreed to in the meeting. No one should leave the meeting without a full understanding of what was accomplished. One effective technique that encourages full participation is "once around the table." Everyone is asked to summarize briefly his or her interpretation of what was decided and what happens next. Of course, this closure technique works best with smaller groups. The leader should conclude by asking the group to set a time for the next meeting. He or she should also assure the group that a report will follow and thank participants for attending.

FOLLOWING UP AFTER A MEETING

According to business meeting expert Frances Micale, "What you do after the meeting is as important as what you do during the meeting."[8] This is because when meetings end with no follow-up, participants in that meeting are left thinking that the work of that meeting (the decisions made, for example) is not as important as it should be. Numerous communication-related tasks, many of them written, are part of proper meeting follow-up.

First of all, if minutes were taken, they should be distributed within a couple of days after the meeting. An example of a formal minutes report is found in Figure 7.8 on page 184. Even if formal minutes were not recorded, a meeting summary or list of actions decided should always be sent to participants. Figure 11.3 shows an informal minutes report, which is the kind you'll see more often in the business world today. Sending a formal minutes report or even an informal summary or list of action decisions is vital to the integrity of the meeting process. If a follow-up message is not sent to participants, they are less likely to see future meetings as worthwhile uses of their time.

But minutes and summaries are not the only communications that are sent after a meeting. For example, if one member of the team volunteers to take a specific job on—for example, doing some research in time for the next meeting—it's your job as the meeting leader to follow up with this person well before the next meeting, both to remind him of the job he volunteered to do and to ask him if he needs help. Another task that might be part of the follow-up portion of a meeting is sending information to people who asked for it. It's not unusual at a meeting for one of the participants to ask for more information on a topic. As the meeting leader, it's your job to find that information and communicate it to the person who asked for it, or else communicate with someone else who has the information and can get it to your team member.

Figure 11.3 ▶   Minutes of Meeting, Informal—Report Format

Grand Beach Homeowners' Association

Board of Directors Meeting
April 12, 2007

MINUTES

Directors Present: J. Weinstein, A. McGraw, J. Carlson, C. Stefanko,
A. Pettus
Directors Absent: B. Hookym

Summary of Topics Discussed

- Report from Architectural Review Committee. Copy attached.
- Landscaping of centre divider on P.T.H. 59. Three options considered: hiring private landscape designer, seeking volunteers from community, assigning association custodian to complete work.
- Collection of outstanding assessments. Discussion of delinquent accounts •⸺ *Summarizes discussion* and possible actions.
- Use of beach club by film companies. Pros: considerable income. Cons: damage to furnishings, loss of facility to homeowners.
- Nomination of directors to replace those with two-year appointments.

Decisions Reached

- Hire private landscaper to renovate and plant centre divider on P.T.H. 59.
- Attach liens to homes of members with delinquent assessments. •⸺ *Capsulizes decisions rather than showing motions and voting*
- Submit to general membership vote the question of renting the beach club to film companies.

Action Items

Item	Responsibility	Due Date
1. Landscaping bid	J. Carlson	May 1
2. Attorney for liens	B. Hookym	April 20 •⸺ *Highlights items for action*
3. Creation of nominating committee	A. Pettus	May 1

Finally, one of the most important aspects of meeting follow-up is evaluation. Because meetings take up valuable work time, it makes sense to evaluate the usefulness of these meetings and make changes as appropriate. Most often, this evaluation is done by the leader internally—what worked today? What didn't? How can I improve the next meeting? Sometimes, an informal evaluation of the meeting can be done after it has ended, using a short e-mail survey, for example. What did the participants in the meeting think of how it was handled? Do they have any suggestions for how to run meetings more effectively? In essence, it is up to the leader to see that what was decided at the meeting is accomplished as well as to ensure that meetings are continually improving so that the situation described in the article at the beginning of this chapter doesn't occur.

NEGOTIATION AS COMMUNICATION

One of the most common situations that occurs in a meeting, or elsewhere in the workplace, is the negotiation. The Harvard Business School, which was one of the first postsecondary institutions to teach negotiation skills to its students, defines negotiation as "the means by which people deal with their differences" and how they "seek mutual agreement through dialogue."[9] The reason we've included negotiation as a business communication strategy in this book is simple: in a negotiation, you use spoken communication skills—dialogue and listening—to achieve important workplace-related goals.

For example, say that the last item on the agenda of your meeting is to choose the next meeting time for the team. It quickly becomes apparent that your preferred choice as meeting facilitator (same early time, same place, one month from today) is not going to work. Two members of the team can't make it that day at that time. Obviously, an experienced business communicator will not say at this point, "Too bad, we're having the meeting on the date and at the time I choose." Instead, she will probably propose to the team that the meeting be switched to the same day a month from now, but later in the day. This could be expressed positively as: "We definitely want the whole team at the meeting, so what about keeping the day but moving the meeting to after lunch?" Three other team members quickly chime in saying that that new time "won't work for them." What should the team leader say now?

This is a classic negotiation situation in which there is a clear difference between people in the room, and a decision has to be made leading to an agreement that satisfies everyone. Other typical business situations in which negotiation occurs are negotiating salary in a successful job interview situation, negotiating price when making major purchases, negotiating a new contract in a unionized workplace, and negotiating how work will be divided up in a workplace team. If you think about it, in each of these situations, the people doing the negotiating have to know what to say to each other, and how to say it, so that a deal, or decision that everyone can live with, is arrived at.

Not surprisingly, numerous words and phrases in our culture have developed to describe the negotiation situation, such as "making a deal, trading, bargaining, dickering, or ... haggling."[10] The variety of these words is more proof that negotiation happens all the time and in many different situations. So what are the right words to use in a negotiation? Is there a specific methodology we can use to make what we say in a negotiation lead to that elusive mutual agreement?

The Importance of Listening

In fact, negotiation experts point out that unlike business presentations, in which what you say is of paramount importance, in a negotiation situation, what you say is important, but so is how you listen. As mentioned in Chapter 2, we tend to forget that listening is as important a communication skill as reading, writing, and speaking. Nowhere is this truer than in a negotiation. As Steven Cohen, author of *Negotiation Skills for Managers*, points out, "While we can certainly influence others by presenting something to which they pay attention, the attention we pay to them helps us make the greater impact on the communication process."[11] What Cohen goes on to argue is that we tend to take our ability to listen to others for granted, when we should instead recognize it as one important way in which we can be persuasive.

One reason listening is persuasive is that it tends to surprise people these days. As Cohen remarks, the omnipresence of communications media in our lives today (e-mails, text messaging, cell phones, PDAs, iPODs, downloadable television, satellite radio, traditional television and radio, etc.) means we tend to think of ourselves as the audience "rather than as a source of interesting or relevant ideas."[12] In this communication-saturated world, it's like a breath of fresh air when someone decides, instead of texting, e-mailing, talking on the phone, or watching something, to listen to us instead.

Another reason true listening is persuasive is that it happens so rarely. Think of the last argument or debate you found yourself in. Were you really listening to what the other person or other side had to say, or were you in fact formulating the perfect come-back in your mind, and waiting for the right moment (often while your opponent is still talking) to say it? What this sort of non-conversation shows is that we couldn't care less about what the other person is saying; rather, we're only interested in what we can say back to him or her.

According to Cohen, the experienced negotiator uses the following active listening skills to be persuasive:

- **Pay attention.** Learning how people you're negotiating with say what they say is vital. If there was a rolling of the eyes when the three team members said that a Friday afternoon "won't work for them," did they really mean "No sane person calls meetings for Friday afternoons"? And if so, maybe one way to get what you want is to get them onside, for instance, by making a joke, as in "What was I thinking? Let's not even go near Friday afternoons!"

- **Ask open-ended questions and listen to the answers.** Instead of assuming you know why someone has said something, ask an open-ended question that will help you find out. For example, to your co-workers' "won't work for us" comment, an open-ended question might be "Why won't it work, Bill?" Depending on what Bill replies, you'll probably be able to tell whether he truly has a conflict or whether he just doesn't like the time you've proposed.

- **Use silence when appropriate.** In a negotiation, there are two kinds of silence. One kind is unfriendly, often called "the silent treatment." This kind of silence should only be used when it's clear that the other side has acted poorly. Your silence will cause your opponents to reconsider what they've just said. There's also a friendly way to use silence. This is the "I need a minute to think about what you've just proposed" kind of silence. This is a more complimentary silence because it says to the person you're negotiating with that you're listening closely and you need some more time to process what he or she has just said. As a result, what you say next will carry more weight.

- **Employ reframing techniques.** One of the most powerful negotiation skills is the ability to take what someone has just said and reframe it for your own purposes. For example, if someone says something you disagree with, you can stop for a moment and then say, "Did I understand correctly that...?" or "Can you explain what you meant when you said...?" Your ability to reframe what people have just said gives you power for two reasons: you've shown you've listened, which looks good on you, and by repeating what to you is a disagreeable idea, you're more prone to make the other side realize that its position is disagreeable. They may then restate what they said in a way you can both agree upon.[13]

NEGOTIATION STRATEGIES

Conflict requiring negotiation is a normal part of every workplace, but it is not always negative. When managed properly, conflict can improve decision making, clarify values, increase group cohesiveness, stimulate creativity, decrease tensions, and reduce dissatisfaction. Unresolved conflict, however, can destroy productivity and seriously reduce morale.

Conflicts usually fall into two categories. Some experts use the terms "distributive" and "integrative" to classify conflicts while others use the terms "interest-based" and "position-based." We can simplify the technical language of negotiation theory into more concrete terms, by saying that all workplace conflicts are either confrontational or cooperative. In a confrontational conflict, the opponents think there is only one way of winning, and that's if they win (e.g., The meeting has to be on Friday afternoon). In a cooperative conflict, the opponents realize that everyone has to win something (e.g., The meeting has to be next week, and it'll be a better meeting if everyone's there, so let's do it on Thursday afternoon instead). A confrontational conflict leads to gains usually only for one side, while cooperative conflicts can enrich all sides.[14]

You will be better prepared to resolve workplace conflict if you know the five most common response patterns as well as an easy-to-follow procedure for dealing with conflict. Imagine a time when you were upset with a workplace colleague, boss, or teammate. How did you respond? Experts who have studied conflict say that most of us deal with it in one of the following predictable patterns:

- **Avoidance/withdrawal.** Instead of trying to resolve the conflict, one person or the other simply withdraws. Avoidance of conflict generally results in a "lose-lose" situation because the problem festers and no attempt is made to understand the issues causing the conflict. On the other hand, avoidance may be the best response when the issue is trivial, when potential losses from an open conflict outweigh potential gains, or when insufficient time is available to work through the issue adequately.
- **Accommodation/smoothing.** When one person gives in quickly, the conflict is smoothed over and surface harmony results. This may be the best method when the issue is minor, when damage to the relationship would harm both parties, and when tempers are too hot for productive discussion.
- **Compromise.** In this pattern both people give up something of lesser importance to gain something more important. Compromise may be the best approach when both parties stand to gain, when a predetermined "ideal" solution is not required, and when time is short.
- **Competition/forcing.** This approach results in a contest in which one person comes out on top, leaving the other with a sense of failure. This method ends the conflict, but it may result in hurt feelings and potential future problems from the loser. This strategy is appropriate when a decision or action must be immediate and when the parties recognize the power relationship between themselves.
- **Collaboration/problem solving.** In this pattern both parties lay their cards on the table and attempt to reach consensus. This approach works when the

involved people have common goals but they disagree over how to reach them. Conflict may arise from misunderstanding or a communication breakdown. Collaboration works best when all parties are trained in problem-solving techniques.[15]

Probably the best pattern for resolving conflicts entails collaboration and problem-solving procedures. But this method requires a certain amount of training. In addition to the communication skills for negotiation described above, experts in the field of negotiation have developed a four-step pattern that you can try the next time you need to resolve a conflict:

1. **Show a concern for the relationship.** By focusing on the problem, not the person, you can build, maintain, and even improve relationships. Show an understanding of the other person's situation and needs. Show an overall willingness to come to an agreement (e.g., "I understand that Friday afternoons don't work for a number of you, so let's try to find another day that works").

2. **Look for common ground.** Identify your interests and help the other side to identify its interests. Learn what you have in common, and look for a solution to which both sides can agree (e.g., "We're all agreed that holding a meeting each week is vital to our work on this project, so what day works next week?").

3. **Invent new problem-solving options.** Spend time identifying the interests of both sides. Then brainstorm to invent new ways to solve the problem. Be open to new options (e.g., "There's six of us and Thursday afternoon works for all of us except Mandy. How about we take detailed minutes at the meeting and one of us volunteers to spend 15 minutes filling Mandy in on what happened?").

4. **Reach an agreement based on what's fair.** Seek to determine a standard of fairness that is acceptable to both sides. Then weigh the possible solutions, and choose the best option[16] (e.g., "Because we have different schedules and projects we're working on, let's commit to rotating our meeting days and times throughout the summer").

CONCLUSION

In this chapter you learned about two types of spoken business communication in which you engage in a dialogue with other communicators. Unlike presentations and job interviews, where dialogue with the audience or the other person in the room is bound by rules (i.e., audiences ask questions in a presentation and you answer them maintaining control of the situation), in a meeting or a negotiation, you are not always as in control as you would like to be.

For this reason, a number of techniques exist, both for meetings and for negotiations, through which you can control the situation. In meetings, preparation is important, tangibly expressed through the sending out of an agenda beforehand. During meetings, your business communication skills turn into facilitation skills as you move the agenda along, dealing with situations such as no one wanting to talk or too much talking going on. After a meeting, the communication doesn't end, but continues with various follow-up mechanisms such as an informal minutes or summary report sent out to participants.

In a negotiation, your spoken business communication skills are especially important because, by definition, negotiations are about attaining mutual agreement where disagreement exists. You learned that one of the most important methods for changing disagreement to agreement is active listening, interspersed with a healthy dose of reframing and questioning. You also learned there are various responses to conflict, including avoidance/withdrawal, accommodation/smoothing, and competition/forcing, but that the most effective way of attaining a negotiated agreement is by using a collaborative problem-solving method in which negotiators look for common ground in their positions, and brainstorm creative ways to deal with the parts of their positions that are not common.

Chapter Review

As a way of studying the material in this chapter, imagine you are at a job interview for your dream entry-level job after college or university. You've prepared answers for all the classic interview questions, but to your surprise, your interviewer also asks a number of questions based on business meeting and negotiation skills. How would you answer the following six questions?

1. Meetings have a bad rap at a lot of companies, but we look at them as an integral part of our day-to-day business. What do you think some of the fringe benefits of meetings might be?
2. If you're successful in this interview your new position will see you in charge of numerous meetings per week. How will you prepare for the meetings?
3. What are some of the tricks you've learned in your experience so far for how to facilitate a successful meeting?
4. Do you think your job as meeting leader ends when the meeting ends? If not, why not?
5. Another aspect of your job here would be negotiations among various departments in the company as well as with third-party organizations outside the company. What are some of the similarities and differences in how you should communicate in a meeting and in a negotiation?
6. What's your personal negotiation style? Demonstrate what you mean by giving us an example of a time you've had to use your style in a real negotiation.

Problems

1. You work in the IT department for a large financial services company, Investica. There are about 20 full-time employees in the department. You've worked at the company for six years now, and nothing seems to change. The VP of Information Technology, your ultimate boss, instituted weekly meetings when he started with the company three years ago. He said the meetings were about "fostering a team spirit" and "making sure everyone is on the same page." At the time, these sounded like worthwhile goals, so you were happy to attend meetings. Over the past couple of years, however, you've become angry about the weekly meetings. Agendas are never sent out. It's just assumed that because the VP wants things to run this way, everyone must make time in their Friday morning schedule to attend a two-hour meeting. More than 50 percent of the time meetings start late and go over time. The VP (who still leads the meetings, even though he has a director and two managers) usually spends at least half of the two-hour time slot talking so that the meeting becomes like a lecture. Some of your colleagues have started to boycott the odd meeting, though you've always been too anxious to do this. You think your absence will be noticed and might be used against you if layoffs occur

(as they did six years ago). You don't understand the purpose of these weekly meetings, though you feel compelled to attend. In this situation, how can improvement occur? Is it your responsibility to do anything about the poor-quality meetings? If so, what should you do and how should you do it?

2. The head-office Marketing department at Investica holds bi-weekly meetings. The VP of Marketing instituted an innovative system two years ago whereby each month a new member of the Marketing department chairs the meeting. The VP's idea was that employees would feel more loyalty to the company if the company demonstrated its trust in its employees by giving them the responsibility of running meetings. The trouble is that instead of creating loyalty, the VP's system has created a high level of competition among employees. For example, employees try to outdo each other with the quality of their PowerPoint presentations. Similarly, some employees have started to invite high-profile friends to attend meetings as guest speakers. In other words, the essence of the meetings (problem-solving and information-sharing sessions for the department) has been lost, and instead the meetings have become presentations by the rotating employee leaders. One day, you attend a meeting at which the marketing plan for a new suite of mutual funds is being discussed. The meeting leader presents a draft of the plan and asks for comments. It's become par for the course in these meetings for people not to say anything when asked to comment. But today, you decide to inject some life into the meeting by making some concrete suggestions. You tell the leader and the others at the meeting that perhaps the draft should be reconsidered so that it's focused more on ... than on.... The leader of the meeting looks at you in an astonished way and says, "Well perhaps you'd like to chair the meeting instead, since you seem to know everything there is to know?" An uncomfortable silence fills the room. You hadn't intended your suggestions as a personal criticism of the leader. You just figured that meetings were about solving problems as a group. Did you do something wrong? And if so, what was it? If you didn't do anything wrong, then why did the leader react the way he or she did? What can be done to improve what goes on in the Marketing department's bi-weekly meetings? Who needs to institute the change?

3. The financial advisers at the Winnipeg Investica office hold a weekly breakfast meeting at which they discuss trends in the market and the industry in general. The meetings are generally information-sharing and team-building exercises, but every once in a while, the managing partner of the office calls a more structured problem-solving meeting. You've just attended one of these more formal problem-solving meetings. The problem in question this week was how to stem the tide of investors who are leaving Investica for the recently launched Westbank.com, an online bank and investment brokerage. The number of clients leaving Investica is so alarming that the CEO of Strategic Alignment participated in the meeting via conference call from Montreal. It quickly becomes apparent that there are two schools of thought in the room. One group of advisers think Investica should fight back against Westbank.com with its own aggressive marketing campaign. The other advisers think the clients who are leaving are expendable and what Investica should do is change its business model to cater only to high-net-worth individuals (investors with over $500 000 invested). The managing partner is participating in the conversation but isn't taking notes, as he usually does. At one point the Montreal CEO says to the managing partner, "I hope you're getting all of this down, Mort." The meeting ends with the CEO taking over from the managing partner by asking the advisers in the room to put together a couple

of teams to investigate the two options for dealing with the loss in clients. Then he says he has to hang up and take another call. The managing partner, Mort, looks perplexed, as do the advisers. They're not in marketing, after all. The meeting breaks up without any decisive division of responsibility. Usually, these meetings are informal and no minutes or recap are sent out afterwards. How should Mort follow up from the meeting? Considering what took place in the meeting, what sort of documents should Mort send out?

4. You are a financial adviser in the Winnipeg office of Investica. You were at the meeting described above, and you were one of the people who argued that the solution to the problem of clients leaving the firm was to invest in more marketing. You find yourself on an informal team putting together a report for the CEO in Montreal. No one on the team has any marketing experience, and neither Mort nor the CEO seemed to think it was important to involve any head office marketing staff from Montreal. Your team meets a few times over lunch to discuss what needs to be done. Everyone on the team agrees that the report to the CEO can only have one clear recommendation. If the solution is marketing, it has to be crystal clear what kind of marketing has to be done. Unfortunately, there's a deep difference of opinion within the group of three charged with writing this report. You feel that traditional marketing avenues like print, radio, and television advertising are the way to go to boost Investica's profile quickly and effectively. Your teammates, both of whom are young and joined the firm in the past two years, think that new media marketing will work more effectively. They reason that because Investica clients are moving to an online firm, it makes more sense to market using the Web. For example, they think Investica banner ads on high-traffic websites are a good way to go. You argue back and forth over a couple of more lunches, and then, in a fit of anger (your teammates are hardly out of school, after all!), you threaten to bypass the teammates, write the report yourself, and take it straight to the CEO. Your teammates are obviously surprised at your ultimatum and, being relatively new employees, are unsure what to do next. How can the principles of effective negotiation help in this situation? Script an exchange between the young teammates and the experienced teammate as they try to negotiate a solution to their disagreement.

5. The Investica advisers who thought the solution to the loss of clients should be to re-invent Investica as a niche firm, focusing on high-net-worth individuals, also have a report to put together for the CEO. This team is bigger than the other team, with six members. Because of the size of the team, no one can agree on a common time to meet to start working on the report. It's now one week after the meeting with the CEO, five days since Mort sent out his follow-up action items, and the team hasn't produced anything concrete. Kim Tymchuk, one of the team members, decides that something's got to be done, otherwise the whole office is going to incur the wrath of the CEO. She decides to draft a bare-bones report that can be sent to her five teammates as a way of sparking a dialogue. In her draft, she calls for Investica to shed its non-high-net-worth clients in a quick two-year period, and aggressively grow its high-net-worth business, moving beyond just Winnipeg to include Saskatchewan and northern Ontario. She e-mails her draft to her teammates under the subject line "Can I get some feedback please?" and waits for the responses to pour in. After two days, not one of her teammates has responded. It's now the day before Mort's deadline to get the two team reports to the CEO in Montreal. Kim gets on the phone and calls each of her teammates. Each of them, once she reaches them, says the same thing: "Sounds kinda risky," "Are

you sure you want to do this?", "I doubt the CEO'll go for it," or "Why didn't we have any input into your draft?" In other words, they're being completely unhelpful to Kim. In no frame of mind to compromise, Kim sends her draft to Mort, and Mort sends it to the CEO. No one bothers to tell Mort or the CEO that the draft was written by one person, not a team. What's wrong with the way this team handled its conflicts? Imagine the CEO tells Mort the report is a "pile of rubbish" and Mort passes this on to Kim. Knowing what you do about predictable responses to conflict, as well as best practices in negotiation, script an imaginary meeting of this team-that-wouldn't-meet and how it deals with the CEO's criticism.

Grammar/Style Review 11

In this review, you will be practising identifying diction mistakes. There are at least five mistakes in total, plus at least one non-diction mistake. For a brief explanation of this problem, please read the explanation on page 332. Besides completing the exercise below, be sure to be on the lookout for diction mistakes in your own writing.

To: smacri@solutionex.ca

From: rwynne@solutionex.ca

Date: November 18, 2007

Re: Sales conference

Sue—

The folks in my department are totally stoked about are upcoming sales conference.

Just wanted to let u know that while we ramp up to the meeting next week, we'll be

operationalizing a number of strategies so that things run more smoothly than last

year. If you want to talk about any of this, just shoot me a message in the next coupla

days.

Best,

Roger

Business Communication Lab 11

Looking in more detail at the various experts quoted by Stephanie Whittaker in her article on meetings, we uncover one of the slightly controversial aspects of journalism, namely bias. Both EffectiveMeetings.com, which Whittaker discusses, and Mark Ellwood, whom she quotes, are not disinterested experts. They are experts with products to sell. In this lab, imagine that you've been asked by your boss to investigate products that might help your company improve the productivity of its meetings, and to recommend a solution. You decide to use <www.effectivemeetings.com> and <www.getmoredone.com> (Mark Ellwood's site) to complete the task. In an e-mail or a memo, evaluate the products offered at these two sites with regard to their usefulness in your company's situation, and recommend one to your boss.

CHAPTER 12

Workplace Conversation, Telephone Etiquette, and Networking Skills

Sorry, wrong number
Some executives will do anything to avoid returning calls

BY MICHAEL STERN, *NATIONAL POST*, MAY 7, 2005, FW9

THE LEGENDARY WASHINGTON correspondent Jack Anderson once revealed his formula for getting people to return his calls. When assistants asked what his call was about, Anderson would say: "Malfeasance."

Few business people today could get away with a ploy like that—although I know a few who are ready to try.

More and more professionals I meet are lamenting how difficult it is to get calls returned today. This doesn't apply only to annoying sales calls. That might be understandable. Ordinary follow-ups on previous business also frequently get this "silent treatment"—even when someone is simply attempting to move forward an agenda that the call recipient had previously identified as urgent. "All I'm trying to do is be proactive on this project. But I'm being ignored and I feel like a bill collector!" says one frustrated marketing consultant.

Entire business relationships are hanging in the ether as people wonder why longstanding colleagues aren't calling them back. So what's the explanation? Overwhelming time demands? Simple rudeness? Poor prioritizing?

We all know that business people are busier than ever, so that's certainly one reason for this outbreak of inertia. But I also see this as a symptom of the overall deterioration of manners in the workplace. Once, it would have been considered plain rude to ignore business peers and colleagues who are calling on legitimate business. Now, in this era of over-communication and spam, many people feel it's perfectly alright to ignore messages and offer no explanation.

Y'know what? It ain't right! Professionals return calls. Colleagues in your business community deserve a hearing and a response.

Leaders treat other people and their messages seriously, and respond as promptly as they can, even if it is only to say that they cannot help some callers with their problem or request. Increasingly, employers judge executives by their "soft skills," and those include empathy, as well as your ability (and willingness) to communicate with all kinds of people.

The epidemic of unreturned calls could reflect another serious business issue. When it comes to moving ahead, particularly on decisions requiring an investment, many companies in today's scattershot economy are stalling as long as they can. Even trusted contacts may be reluctant to call you back just to admit that they can't get any decisions out of their superiors, their colleagues or their board.

Unfortunately, most people who neglect to return calls don't realize the true impact of their inaction. Deciding not to communicate actually communicates a very clear message—whether or not the sender intends it. No matter what excuses you give yourself for not returning calls, people will consider your decision inconsiderate and disrespectful.

Worse still, it's only human nature to view another person's silence in the worst light possible:

"The deal must have fallen through."

"You don't believe in my project."

"You can't get permissions."

"We're not friends anymore."

"You think you're too good for me."

Are these really the messages you've been meaning to send?

The solution is simple: Call back. Or have someone return calls on your behalf. Even letting callers know that nothing has changed is better than leaving them hanging. Plus, since people's expectations today are so low, imagine the impact you can have simply by returning messages promptly and decisively.

If you're still waiting for callbacks yourself, what can you do to increase the odds of getting your calls returned? Be persistent, be professional, be upbeat. When leaving a message, take the pressure off the person who's dodging you. (Saying "this is the fifth message I've left" does nothing to ease the tension.)

Assure contacts that getting back to you will be easy and painless. Show people you value their time. Let them know the best times to call you, so they won't have to play phone tag. And if all you want is a yes, no, or simple explanation, suggest they e-mail you, or leave a message after hours. That assures them you don't want to waste their time making small talk, asking them to explain their decision or begging them to reconsider.

There is no rule of thumb as to how often you should call. But don't give up; some people may think you're not serious if you don't call back at least three or four times.

Communication is the lifeblood of business. Becoming a better communicator is a sure way to build stronger business relationships—and your career.

DIAGNOSING THE PROBLEM

Of all the articles you've read in this book, the one above by Michael Stern is probably the clearest in articulating a business communication-related problem. Simply put, Stern diagnoses an "epidemic of unreturned calls" that is having adverse effects on businesses and business relationships in offices around the country.

Stern's article would make an excellent choice for your instructor to test you on how well you can summarize. This is because the structure of the article is so clear. After announcing the problem—the epidemic of unreturned calls—Stern goes on to list three possible reasons for why businesspeople have seemingly lost their manners when it comes to phone calls. First, he says businesspeople are busier than ever, which explains why they are deciding not to return calls. Second, he argues that businesspeople's manners have deteriorated to the point where they don't recognize the importance of returning calls. Finally, Stern says that something about the business climate today leads people not to want to make commitments too quickly. Hence, they "stall" on phone calls instead of calling back and being honest about their need for more time.

It's important whenever using secondary research material, such as Stern's article, not to accept everything the author says at face value. For example, we may want to evaluate the three reasons he gives for the epidemic of unreturned calls. Starting with his diagnosis of the problem, we might ask, where is Stern's evidence for the "epidemic"? Does he quote anyone in the article to corroborate his thesis? Does he include reputable statistics to corroborate his thesis? If not, why do we find ourselves believing what he has to say anyway? Similarly, what about his reasons for the epidemic? Should we accept as an explanation the idea that businesspeople are busier than ever? If so, does Stern explain what this busyness consists of?

When it comes to a solution for the problem he diagnoses, Stern is again quite clear, perhaps even simplistic. After detailing the possible consequences not calling back can lead to (a sense of being ignored, a damaged business relationship, etc.), he tells his readers that the solution is simply to make it a best practice to call back. Or, if you're in a position to delegate, have someone call back for you. He also offers a secondary solution—to the people waiting for calls to be returned—which is to make it as easy as possible for the person you've called to get back to you. Stern lists a number of strategies for making it easy for someone to call you back.

in-class
activity 12

IN THE ARTICLE above, Michael Stern makes the issue of non-returned phone calls sound cut-and-dried. In other words, he says there's a problem, he lists the reasons for the problem and the consequences of the problem, and then he gives his readers an easy-to-follow solution. Playing the devil's advocate for a while, your team will brainstorm some reasons that Stern's seemingly simple solution is not such an easy solution after all. Once you've done so, write a five-minute comedic skit in which someone tries to return an important phone call but just can't seem to do so. Present the skit to the class within 30 minutes.

Now that you've been exposed to one of the many problems in today's workplace stemming from spoken communication, you're ready to look at a few more. Even though knowing how to write clearly in business situations is an important skill, employers generally rate speaking and listening skills as the most important for their employees. Besides presentations, meetings, and interviews, speaking happens in office conversations, on the phone, and in special networking and small talk situations.

THE IMPORTANCE OF WORKPLACE CONVERSATION

Because technology provides many alternative communication channels, you may think that face-to-face communication is no longer essential or even important in business and professional transactions. You've already learned that e-mail is now the preferred communication channel because it is faster, cheaper, and easier than telephone, mail, or fax. Yet, despite their popularity and acceptance, alternative communication technologies can't replace the richness or effectiveness of face-to-face interpersonal communication.[1] Imagine that you want to tell your boss how you solved a problem. Would you settle for a one-dimensional phone call, a fax, or an e-mail when you could step into her office and explain in person?

Face-to-face conversation has many advantages. It allows you to be persuasive and expressive because you can use your voice and body language to make a point. You are less likely to be misunderstood because you can read feedback and make needed adjustments. As you learned in Chapter 11, in conflict resolution you can reach a solution more efficiently and cooperate to create greater levels of mutual benefit when communicating face to face.[2] Moreover, people want to see each other to satisfy a deep human need for social interaction. For numerous reasons, communicating in person remains the most effective of all communication channels.

A lot of the best practices advice you'll come across in this chapter walks the fine line between business communication and business etiquette. For many people, the word etiquette has taken on negative connotations. It conjures up images of manners, behaving well, being overly formal and careful, and playing by the rules. As the authors of a leading book on business etiquette point out, however, "etiquette is not about rules; etiquette is about building relationships, plain and simple... [it] gives us clues as to how we should act and what we should do in any given situation, so that we can be as successful as possible in our interactions with the people around us."[3]

So as you read this chapter and learn about best practices in interpersonal spoken communication situations, remember that these best practices have been developed not to take away from your individuality or your cultural background, or to impose formality on you when you'd rather be informal. Instead, they are included for the same reason we included a lot of advice on best practices in written business communication: communicators who follow basic common patterns tend to get their point across and persuade others, whereas those who don't have a much harder time doing so. In this chapter you'll explore helpful business and professional interpersonal speaking techniques, starting with viewing your voice as a communication tool.

USEFUL CONVERSATION SKILLS

It's been said that language provides the words, but your voice is the music that makes words meaningful.[4] You may believe that a beautiful or powerful voice is unattainable. After all, this is the voice you were born with, and it can't be changed. Actually, the voice is a flexible instrument. Actors hire coaches to help them eliminate or acquire accents or proper inflection for challenging roles. Celebrities, business executives, and everyday people consult voice and speech therapists to help them shake bad habits or help them speak so that they can be understood and not sound less intelligent than they are. Rather than consult a high-paid specialist, you can pick up useful tips for using your voice most effectively by learning how to control such elements as pronunciation, tone, pitch, volume, rate, and emphasis.

Pronunciation. Pronunciation involves saying words correctly and clearly with the accepted sounds and accented syllables. You'll be at a distinct advantage in your job if, through training and practice, you learn to pronounce words correctly. Some of the most common errors, shown in Figure 12.1, include adding or omitting vowels, omitting consonants, reversing sounds, and slurring sounds. In casual conversation with your friends, correct pronunciation is not a big deal. But on the job you want to sound intelligent, educated, and competent. If you mispronounce words or slur phrases together, you risk being misunderstood as well as giving a poor impression of yourself. How can you improve your pronunciation skills? The best way is to listen carefully to educated people, read aloud from well-written newspapers like *The Globe and Mail* and the *National Post*, look up words in the dictionary, and avoid errors such as those in Figure 12.1.

Tone. The tone of your voice sends a nonverbal message to listeners. It identifies your personality and your mood. Some voices sound enthusiastic and friendly, conveying the impression of an upbeat person who is happy to be with the listener. But voices can also sound controlling, patronizing, slow-witted, angry, or childish. This doesn't mean that the speaker necessarily has that attribute. It may mean that the speaker is merely carrying on a family tradition or pattern learned in childhood. To check your voice tone, record your voice and listen to it critically. Is it projecting a positive quality about you?

Figure 12.1 ▶ Pronunciation Errors to Avoid

Adding vowel sounds	athlete (NOT ath-a-lete) disastrous (NOT disas-ter-ous)
Omitting vowel sounds	federal (NOT fed-ral) ridiculous (NOT ri-dic-lous) generally (NOT gen-rally)
Substituting vowel sounds	get (NOT git) separate (NOT sep-e-rate)
Adding consonant sounds	butter (NOT budder) statistics (NOT sta-stis-tics) especially (NOT ex-specially)
Omitting consonant sounds	library (NOT libery) perhaps (NOT praps)
Confusing or distorting sounds	ask (NOT aks) hundred (NOT hunderd) accessory (NOT assessory)
Slurring sounds	didn't you (NOT dint ya) going to (NOT gonna)

Pitch. Effective speakers use a relaxed, controlled, well-pitched voice to attract listeners to their message. Pitch refers to sound vibration frequency; that is, it indicates the highness or lowness of a sound. In Canada, speakers and listeners prefer a variety of pitch patterns. Voices are most attractive when they rise and fall in conversational tones. Flat, monotone voices are considered boring and ineffectual. In business, communicators strive for a moderately low voice, which is thought to be pleasing and professional.

Volume and rate. Volume indicates the degree of loudness or the intensity of sound. Just as you adjust the volume on your radio or television, you should adjust the volume of your speaking to the occasion and your listeners. When speaking face to face, you generally know whether you are speaking too loudly or softly by looking at your listeners. Are they straining to hear you? To judge what volume to use, listen carefully to the other person's voice. Use it as a guide for adjusting your voice. Rate refers to the pace of your speech. If you speak too slowly, listeners are bored and their attention wanders. If you speak too quickly, listeners can't understand you. Most people normally talk at about 125 words a minute. If you're the kind of speaker who speeds up when talking in front of a group of people, monitor the nonverbal signs of your listeners and adjust your rate as needed.

Emphasis. By emphasizing or stressing certain words, you can change the meaning you are expressing. For example, read these sentences aloud, emphasizing the italicized words:

> *Matt* said the hard drive failed again. (Matt knows what happened.)
> Matt *said* the hard drive failed again. (But he may be wrong.)
> Matt said the hard drive failed *again*? (Did he really say that?)

As you can see, emphasis affects the meaning of the words and the thought expressed. To make your message interesting and natural, use emphasis appropriately.

You can raise your volume to sound authoritative and raise your pitch to sound disbelieving. Lowering your volume and pitch makes you sound professional or reasonable.

Some speakers today are prone to "uptalk." This is a habit of using a rising inflection at the end of a sentence, resulting in a singsong pattern that makes statements sound like questions. Once used exclusively by teenagers, uptalk is increasingly found in the workplace, with negative results. When statements sound like questions, speakers seem weak and tentative. Their messages lack conviction and authority. On the job, managers afflicted by uptalk may have difficulty convincing staff members to follow directions because their voice inflection implies that other valid options are available. If you want to sound confident and competent, avoid uptalk.

In the workplace, conversations may involve giving and taking instructions, providing feedback, exchanging ideas on products and services, participating in performance appraisals, or engaging in small talk about such things as families and sports. Face-to-face conversation helps people work together harmoniously and feel that they are part of the larger organization. There are several guidelines, starting with using correct names and titles, that promote positive workplace conversations.

Use correct names and titles. Although the world seems increasingly informal, it's still wise to use titles and last names when addressing professional adults (*Mrs. Smith, Mr. Rivera*). In some organizations senior staff members will speak to junior employees on a first-name basis, but the reverse may not be encouraged. Probably the safest plan is to ask your superiors how they want to be addressed. Customers and others outside the organization should always be addressed by title and last name.

When you meet strangers, do you have trouble remembering their names? You can improve your memory considerably if you associate the person with an object, place, colour, animal, job, adjective, or some other memory hook. For example, *computer pro Kevin, Miami Kim, silver-haired Mr. Lee, bull-dog Chris, bookkeeper Lynn, traveller Ms. Janis.* The person's name will also be more deeply imbedded in your memory if you use it immediately after being introduced, in subsequent conversation, and when you part.

Choose appropriate topics. In some workplace activities, such as social gatherings or interviews, you will be expected to engage in small talk. Be sure to stay away from controversial topics with someone you don't know very well. Avoid politics, religion, or current event items that can start heated arguments until you know the person better. To initiate appropriate conversations, read newspapers and listen to radio and TV shows discussing current events. Make a mental note of items that you can use in conversation, taking care to remember where you saw or heard the news items so that you can report accurately and authoritatively. Try not to be defensive or annoyed if others present information that upsets you.

Avoid negative remarks. Workplace conversations are not the place to complain about your colleagues, your friends, the organization, or your job. No one enjoys listening to whiners. And your criticism of others may come back to haunt you. A snipe at your boss or a complaint about a fellow worker may reach him or her, sometimes embellished or distorted with meanings you did not intend. Be circumspect in all negative judgments. Remember, some people love to repeat statements that will stir up trouble or set off internal workplace wars. It's best not to give them the ammunition.

Listen to learn. In conversations with colleagues, subordinates, and customers, train yourself to expect to learn something from what you are hearing. Being attentive is not only instructive but also courteous. Beyond displaying good manners, you'll probably find that your conversation partner has information that you don't have. Being receptive and listening with an open mind means not interrupting or prejudging. Let's say you very much want to be able to work at home for part of your workweek. You try to explain your ideas to your boss, but he cuts you off shortly after you start. He says, "It's out of the question; we need you here every day." Suppose instead he says, "I have strong reservations about your telecommuting, but maybe you'll change my mind," and he settles in to listen to your presentation. Even if your boss decides against your request, you will feel that your ideas were heard and respected.

Give sincere and specific praise. A wise person once said, "Man does not live by bread alone. He needs to be buttered up once in a while." Probably nothing promotes positive workplace relationships better than sincere and specific praise. Whether the compliments and appreciation are travelling upward to management, downward to workers, or horizontally to colleagues, everyone responds well to recognition. Organizations run more smoothly and morale is higher when people feel appreciated. In your workplace conversations, look for ways to recognize good work and good people. And try to be specific. Instead of "You did a good job in leading that meeting," try something more specific, such as "Your leadership skills certainly kept that meeting short, focused, and productive."

Respect space and rank. According to Peggy and Peter Post, face-to-face conversations can be positive when space and rank are respected. What these business etiquette experts mean is that in conversations, it's not just what you say and how you say it that counts, it's what your body is doing at the same time. For example, one of the biggest body language mistakes you can make in a conversation is to crowd the person you're talking to. Always keep about half a metre between you and the person you're speaking with. Similarly, don't forget that the person you're speaking with may be your superior. In other words, although the conversation topic may be casual (e.g., you may be talking about a movie you saw last night), this doesn't mean you should make wild hand gestures or rest your foot on a nearby chair. Your body should still say "I respect you as my superior" even though the words coming out of it are on an informal topic.[5]

GIVING AND RECEIVING CONSTRUCTIVE CRITICISM

No one likes to receive criticism, and most of us don't like to give it either. In the workplace, however, cooperative endeavours demand feedback and evaluation. How are we doing on a project? What went well? What failed? How can we improve our efforts? Today's workplace often involves team projects. As a team member, you will be called on to judge the work of others.

In addition to working on teams, you can also expect to become a supervisor or manager one day. As such, you will need to evaluate subordinates. Good employees seek good feedback from their supervisors. They want and need timely, detailed observations about their work to reinforce what they do well and help them overcome weak spots. But making that feedback palatable and constructive is not always easy. Depending on your situation, you may find some or all of the following suggestions helpful when you must deliver constructive criticism:

- **Mentally outline your conversation.** Think carefully about what you want to accomplish and what you will say. Find the right words at the right time and in the right setting.
- **Generally, use face-to-face communication.** Most constructive criticism is better delivered in person rather than in e-mail messages or memos. Personal feedback offers an opportunity for the listener to ask questions and give explanations. Occasionally, however, complex situations may require a different strategy. You might prefer to write out your opinions and deliver them by telephone or in writing. A written document enables you to organize your thoughts, include all the details, and be sure of keeping your cool. Remember, though, that written documents create permanent records—for better or worse.
- **Focus on improvement.** Instead of attacking, use language that offers alternative behaviour. Use phrases such as "Next time, you could...."
- **Offer to help.** Criticism is accepted more readily if you volunteer to help in eliminating or solving the problem.
- **Be specific.** Instead of a vague assertion such as "Your work is often late," be more specific: "The specs on the Riverside job were due Thursday at 5 p.m., and you didn't hand them in until Friday." Explain how the person's performance jeopardized the entire project.
- **Avoid broad generalizations.** Don't use words such as *should, never, always,* and other encompassing expressions as they may cause the listener to shut down and become defensive.
- **Discuss the behaviour, not the person.** Instead of "You seem to think you can come to work any time you want," focus on the behaviour: "Coming to work late means that we have to fill in with someone else until you arrive."
- **Use the word *we* rather than *you*.** "We need to meet project deadlines" is better than saying "You need to meet project deadlines." Emphasize organizational expectations rather than personal ones. Avoid sounding accusatory.
- **Encourage two-way communication.** Even if well planned, criticism is still hard to deliver. It may surprise or hurt the feelings of the employee. Consider ending your message with "It can be hard to hear this type of feedback. If you would like to share your thoughts, I'm listening."
- **Avoid anger, sarcasm, and a raised voice.** Criticism is rarely constructive when tempers flare. Plan in advance what you will say and deliver it in low, controlled, and sincere tones.
- **Keep it private.** Offer praise in public; offer criticism in private. "Setting an example" through public criticism is never a wise management policy.

Responding Professionally to Workplace Criticism

As much as we hate giving criticism, we dislike receiving it even more. Yet, the workplace requires that you not only provide it but also be able to accept it. When being criticized, you probably will feel that you are being attacked. You can't just sit back and relax. Your heart beats faster, your temperature shoots up, your face reddens, and you respond with the classic "fight or flight" syndrome. You feel that you want to instantly retaliate or escape from the attacker. But focusing on your feelings distracts you from hearing the content of what is being said, and it prevents you from responding professionally. Some or all of the following suggestions will guide you in reacting positively to criticism so that you can benefit from it:

- **Listen without interrupting.** Even though you might want to protest, make yourself hear the speaker out.
- **Determine the speaker's intent.** Unskilled communicators may throw "verbal bricks" with unintended negative-sounding expressions. If you think the intent is positive, focus on what is being said rather than reacting to poorly chosen words.
- **Acknowledge what you are hearing.** Respond with a pause, a nod, or a neutral statement such as "I understand you have a concern." This buys you time. Do not disagree, counterattack, or blame, which may escalate the situation and harden the speaker's position.
- **Paraphrase what was said.** In your own words restate objectively what you are hearing; for example, "So what you're saying is ..."
- **Ask for more information if necessary.** Clarify what is being said. Stay focused on the main idea rather than interjecting side issues.
- **Agree—if the comments are accurate.** If an apology is in order, give it. Explain what you plan to do differently. If the criticism is on target, the sooner you agree, the more likely you will engender respect from the other person.
- **Disagree respectfully and constructively—if you feel the comments are unfair.** After hearing the criticism, you might say, "May I tell you my perspective?" Or you could try to solve the problem by saying, "How can we improve this situation in a way you believe we can both accept?" If the other person continues to criticize, say, "I want to find a way to resolve your concern. When do you want to talk about it next?"
- **Look for a middle position.** Search for a middle position or a compromise. Be genial even if you don't like the person or the situation.

PROFESSIONAL TELEPHONE AND VOICE-MAIL SKILLS

The telephone is the most universal—and some would say the most important—piece of equipment in offices today.[6] For many businesspeople, it is a primary contact with the outside world. Some observers predicted that e-mail and faxes would "kill off phone calls."[7] In fact, the amazing expansion of wireless communication has given the telephone a new and vigorous lease on life. Telephones are definitely here to stay. But many of us do not use them efficiently or effectively, as Michael Stern demonstrates in his article at the beginning of this chapter. Besides the important problem Stern discusses (i.e., people who don't return phone calls), this section focuses on other best practices in traditional and cellular telephone use as well as on voice-mail efficiency.

Making Productive Telephone Calls

Before making a telephone call, decide whether the intended call is necessary. Could you find the information yourself? If you wait a while, would the problem resolve itself? Perhaps your message could be delivered more efficiently by some other means. One company found that telephone interruptions consumed about 18 percent of staff members' workdays. Another study found that two-thirds of all calls were less important than the work they interrupted.[8] Alternatives to telephone calls include e-mail, memos, or calls to voice-mail systems. If a telephone call must be made, consider using the following suggestions to make it fully productive.

- **Plan a mini-agenda.** Have you ever been embarrassed when you had to make a second telephone call because you forgot an important item the first time? Before placing a call, jot down notes regarding all the topics you need to discuss. Following an agenda guarantees not only a complete call but also a quick one. You'll be less likely to wander from the business at hand while rummaging through your mind trying to remember everything.

- **Use a three-point introduction.** When placing a call, immediately name the person you are calling, identify yourself and your affiliation, and give a brief explanation of your reason for calling. For example: "Hello. May I speak to Larry Levin? This is Hillary Dahl of Acme Ltd., and I'm looking for information about a software program called Power Presentations." This kind of introduction enables the receiving individual to respond immediately without asking further questions.

- **Be brisk if you are rushed.** For business calls when your time is limited, avoid questions such as "How are you?" Instead, say, "Lisa, I knew you'd be the only one who could answer these two questions for me." Another efficient strategy is to set a "contract" with the caller: "Hi, Lisa, I have only ten minutes, but I really wanted to get back to you."

- **Be cheerful and accurate.** Let your voice show the same kind of animation that you radiate when you greet people in person. In your mind try to envision the individual answering the telephone. A smile can certainly affect the tone of your voice, so smile at that person. Moreover, be accurate about what you say. "Hang on a second; I'll be right back" rarely is true. Better to say, "It may take me two or three minutes to get that information. Would you prefer to hold or have me call you back?"

- **Bring it to a close.** The responsibility for ending a call lies with the caller. This is sometimes difficult to do if the other person rambles on. You may need to use suggestive closing language, such as "I've certainly enjoyed talking with you," "I've learned what I needed to know, and now I can proceed with my work," "Thanks for your help," or "I must go now, but may I call you again in the future if I need ... ?"

- **Avoid telephone tag.** If you call someone who's not in, ask when it would be best for you to call again. State that you will call at a specific time—and do it. If you ask a person to call you, give a time when you can be reached—and then be sure you are in at that time.

- **Leave complete voice-mail messages.** Remember that there's no rush when you leave a voice-mail message. Always enunciate clearly. And be sure to provide a complete message, including your name, telephone number, and the time and date of your call. Explain your purpose so that the receiver can be ready with the required information when returning your call.

Receiving Productive Telephone Calls

With a little forethought you can make your telephone a productive, efficient work tool. Developing good telephone manners also reflects well on you and on your organization.

- **Identify yourself immediately.** In answering your telephone or someone else's, provide your name, title or affiliation, and, possibly, a greeting. For example, "Larry Levin, Proteus Software. How can I help you?" Force yourself to speak clearly and slowly. Remember that the caller may be unfamiliar with what you are saying and fail to recognize slurred syllables.

- **Be responsive, positive, and helpful.** If you are in a support role, be sympathetic to callers' needs. Instead of "I don't know," try "That's a good question; let me investigate." Instead of "We can't do that," try "That's a tough one; let's see what we can do." Avoid "No" at the beginning of a sentence. It sounds especially abrasive and displeasing because it suggests total rejection. As customer service expert Andrew Griffiths notes, "People will always comment on a positive telephone manner, simply because it's so refreshing."[9]

- **Be cautious when answering calls for others.** Be courteous and helpful, but don't give out confidential information. Better to say, "She's away from her desk" or "He's out of the office" than to report a colleague's exact whereabouts.

- **Take messages carefully.** Few things are as frustrating as receiving a potentially important phone message that is illegible. Repeat the spelling of names and verify telephone numbers. Write messages legibly and record their time and date. Promise to give the messages to intended recipients, but don't guarantee return calls.

- **Explain what you're doing when transferring calls.** Give a reason for transferring, and identify the extension to which you are directing the call in case the caller is disconnected.

- **Avoid phone call rudeness.** If you're engaging in any of the following activities, you should seriously reconsider: listening to your messages or calls using a speakerphone in an office with no walls; surfing the net, chewing gum, eating, typing, filing, or doing other loud things while talking on the phone; sending messages directly to voice mail instead of speaking live with someone as a way of avoiding them.[10]

Making the Best Use of Voice Mail

Voice mail links a telephone system to a computer that digitizes and stores incoming messages. Some systems also provide functions such as automated attendant menus, allowing callers to reach any associated extension by pushing specific buttons on a touch-tone telephone. For example, a ski resort in British Columbia uses voice mail to answer routine questions that once were routed through an operator: "Welcome to Panorama. For information on accommodations, press 1; for snow conditions, press 2; for ski equipment rental, press 3," and so forth.

Within some companies, voice mail accounts for 90 percent of all telephone messages.[11] Its popularity results from serving many functions, the most important of which is message storage. Because as many as half of all business calls require no discussion or feedback, the messaging capabilities of voice mail can mean huge savings for businesses. Incoming information is delivered without interrupting potential receivers and without all the niceties that most two-way conversations require.

Stripped of superfluous chitchat, voice-mail messages allow communicators to focus on essentials. Voice mail also eliminates telephone tag, inaccurate message taking, and time-zone barriers. Critics complain, nevertheless, that automated systems seem cold and impersonal and are sometimes confusing and irritating. In any event, here are some ways that you can make voice mail work more effectively for you.

- **Announce your voice mail.** If you rely principally on a voice-mail message system, identify it on your business stationery and cards. Then, when people call, they will be ready to leave a message.
- **Prepare a warm and informative greeting.** Make your mechanical greeting sound warm and inviting, both in tone and content. Identify yourself and your organization so that callers know they have reached the right number. Thank the caller and briefly explain that you are unavailable. Invite the caller to leave a message or, if appropriate, call back. Here's a typical voice-mail greeting: "Hi! This is Larry Levin of Proteus Software, and I appreciate your call. You've reached my voice mailbox because I'm either working with customers or talking on another line at the moment. Please leave your name, number, and reason for calling so that I can be prepared when I return your call." Give callers an idea of when you will be available, such as "I'll be back at 2:30" or "I'll be out of my office until Wednesday, May 20." If you screen your calls as a time-management technique, try this message: "I'm not near my phone right now, but I should be able to return calls after 3:30."
- **Test your message.** Call your number and assess your message. Does it sound inviting? Sincere? Understandable? Are you pleased with your tone? If not, says one consultant, have someone else, perhaps a professional, record a message for you.

CELL PHONE ETIQUETTE

Cell phones enable you to conduct business from virtually anywhere at any time. More than a plaything or a mere convenience, the cell phone has become an essential part of communication in many of today's workplaces. As with many new technologies, a set of rules or protocol on usage is still evolving for cell phones. How are they best used? When is it acceptable to take calls? Where should calls be made? Most of us have experienced thoughtless and rude cell phone behaviour. To avoid offending, smart business communicators practise cell phone etiquette, as outlined in Figure 12.2. In projecting a professional image, they are careful about location, time, and volume in relation to their cell phone calls.

Location. Use good judgment in placing or accepting cell phone calls. Some places are dangerous or inappropriate for cell phone use. Turn off your cell phone when entering a conference room, interview, theatre, place of worship, or any other place where it could be distracting or disruptive to others. Taking a call in a crowded room or bar makes it difficult to hear and reflects poorly on you as a professional. A bad connection also makes a bad impression. Static or dropped signals create frustration and miscommunication. Don't sacrifice professionalism for the sake of a garbled phone call. It's smarter to turn off your phone in an area where the signal is weak and when you are likely to have interference. Use voice mail and return the call when conditions are better.

Time. Often what you are doing is more important than whatever may come over the airwaves to you on your phone. For example, when you are having an important discussion with a business partner, customer, or superior, it is rude to allow yourself to be interrupted by an incoming call. It's also poor manners to practise multitasking while on the phone. What's more, it's dangerous. Although you might be able to read and print out e-mail messages, deal with a customer at the counter, and talk on your cell phone simultaneously, it's impolite and risky. Lack of attention results in errors

Figure 12.2 ▶ Practising Courteous and Responsible Cell Phone Use

Business communicators find cell phones to be enormously convenient and real time-savers. But rude users have generated a backlash against inconsiderate callers. Here are specific suggestions for using cell phones safely and responsibly:

- Be courteous to those around you. Don't force those near you to hear your business. Apologize and make amends gracefully for occasional cell phone blunders.

- Observe wireless-free quiet areas. Don't allow your cell phone to ring in theatres, restaurants, museums, classrooms, important meetings, and similar places. Use the cell phone's silent/vibrating ring option. A majority of travellers prefer that cell phone conversations not be held on most forms of public transportation.

- Speak in low, conversational tones. Microphones on cell phones are quite sensitive, thus making it unnecessary to talk loudly. Avoid "cell yell."

- Take only urgent calls. Make full use of your cell phone's caller ID feature to screen incoming calls. Let voice mail take those calls that are not pressing.

- Drive now, talk later. Pull over if you must make a call. Talking while driving increases the chance of accidents fourfold, about the same as driving while intoxicated.

and a lack of respect. If a phone call is important enough to accept, then it's important enough to stop what you are doing and attend to the conversation.

Volume. Many people raise their voices when using their cell phones. "Cell yell" results, much to the annoyance of anyone nearby. Raising your voice is unnecessary since most phones have excellent microphones that can pick up even a whisper. If the connection is bad, louder volume will not improve the sound quality. As in face-to-face conversations, a low, modulated voice sounds professional and projects the proper image.

NETWORKING AS A COMMUNICATION SKILL

Besides face-to-face conversations and telephone calls, other important venues for spoken business communication are networking and small talk situations. Networking through conversation can occur almost anywhere. For example, you might be riding the bus to work and notice that a friend of yours from college days (whom you haven't seen for five years) is sitting near the back of the bus. Instead of ignoring the friend because you might not know what to say, why not turn this into a networking opportunity? Who knows where your friend works and socializes? Perhaps he works for a company that you could see yourself moving to in a few years. Or perhaps he's a small business owner who might need the product or service you sell in your own job?

Not all jobs are advertised in classified newspaper ads or listed in online job databases. The "hidden" job market, according to some estimates, accounts for as much as two-thirds of all positions available. Companies don't always announce openings publicly because it's time consuming and expensive to interview all the qualified applicants. But the real reason that companies resist announcing jobs is that they dislike hiring "strangers." One recruiter says that when she needs to hire, she first looks around among her friends and acquaintances. If she can't find anyone suitable, she then turns to advertising.[12] It's clear that many employers are more comfortable hiring a person they know.

The key to finding a good job, then, is converting yourself from a "stranger" into a known quantity. One way to become a known quantity is by networking. You can use either traditional or online networking methods to achieve results.

Traditional Networking

The following steps will help you develop a network, whether you're looking for a job at this time or not. The important thing to remember about the steps listed below is that they can be followed smartly or poorly. As Peggy and Peter Post argue, smart networkers make sure they help other people, not just themselves, and that they become friendly with other people before they ask for favours. On the other hand, poor networkers think networking is a one-way street; in other words, they see only what others can do for them.[13] Poor networkers, like friends who are always demanding and never giving, are eventually shut out by their contacts.

Develop a list. Make a list of anyone who would be willing to talk with you about finding a job or creating an opportunity. List your friends, relatives, former employers, former co-workers, classmates from grade school and high school, college or university friends, members of your religious affiliation, people in social and athletic clubs you belong to, present and former teachers, neighbours, and friends of your parents.

Make contacts. Use your excellent telephone skills to call the people on your list, or, what's even better, try to arrange to meet with them in person so you can use your strong conversation skills. To set up a meeting, say something like "Hi, Aunt Martha! I'm looking for a job and I wonder if you could help me out. Could I come over to talk about it?" During your visit be friendly, well organized, polite, and interested in what your contact has to say. Provide a copy of your résumé and try to keep the conversation centred on your job search. Your goal is to get referrals. In pinpointing your request, ask two questions. "Do you know of anyone who might have an opening for a person with my skills?" If not, "Do you know of anyone else who might know of someone who would?"

Follow up on your referrals. Call the people whose names are on your referral list. Say something like "Hello, I'm Carlos Ramos, a friend of Connie Cole. She suggested that I might call and ask for your help. I'm looking for a position as a marketing intern, and she thought you might be willing to see me and give me a few ideas." Don't ask for the job. During your referral interview, ask how the individual got started in his job, what she likes best about the job, and what problems a newcomer must overcome. Most important, ask how a person with your background and skills can get started in the field. Send an informal thank-you e-mail to anyone who helps you in your job search. It's also important to recognize that the follow-up process does not only happen once. You need to stay in regular touch (even if it's only once a year) with your most promising referral contacts. One way to make this easier on yourself is to ask the contact whether it's okay to keep in touch.

Online Networking

As with traditional networking, the goal is to make connections with people who are advanced in their fields. Ask for their advice about finding a job. Most people like talking about themselves, and asking them about their experiences is an excellent way to begin an online correspondence that might lead to a mentoring relationship or a letter of recommendation. Checking out various online forums, discussion groups, or newsgroups where industry professionals can be found is also a great way to keep tabs on the latest business trends and potential job leads.

Web-based discussion groups, forums, and boards. A useful discussion group resource for beginners is Yahoo! Groups <http://groups.yahoo.com>. You can choose from groups ranging from Business/Finance to Science/Technology and everything in between. In any listing you will see sub-listings for more specialized groups. For example, clicking on "Employment and work," you will find career groups including construction, customer service, court reporting, interior design, and so on.

Mailing lists and newsgroups. The most relevant Internet discussions can be found on mailing lists. You can subscribe to an e-mail newsletter or discussion group at Topica <http://www.topica.com>. To post and read newsgroup messages, try the Google website <http://www.google.com> and click "Groups."

BECOMING AN EFFECTIVE SMALL TALKER

Networking does not always happen in the structured step-by-step way suggested above. Sometimes you're not prepared with interview questions and requests. Instead, you may be on an elevator, in a cafeteria, at a cocktail party, at the movies, on public transit, or in a shopping mall, when a networking opportunity comes up. What skills do you need to turn these everyday occurrences into networking opportunities?

The most important skill required is the ability to engage in small talk. Small talk is the conversation we engage in during social occasions with people we may not know very well. Often, because these situations make us nervous, we shut down and don't say anything at all. Instead, we stand by ourselves at the party or walk by, pretending we don't see anyone. The smart networker recognizes this nervousness as a normal reaction and moves past it to take advantage of the various connections there are to be made from the small talk situation.

Networking usually can't happen without some form of small talk. Imagine walking into a room in which the only person you know is the workplace friend who invited you. Other people are sitting on sofas, leaning against tables, drinks in hand, and talking. They notice you as you walk in, but quickly return to their own private conversations. You chat for a few minutes with the host, but you soon sense that she needs to move to the kitchen to prepare some food. You let her go, and now you're left alone, standing in the middle of a room. What should you do?

Common sense dictates that the worst thing to do is to continue standing there and looking like exactly what you are: alone and nervous. Instead, you need to make the move to turn your nervousness into a small talk opportunity. The best way to do this is to move over to a group or pair of people who are chatting and, with a smile on your face, start listening to what they're saying. When the opportunity arises, stick out your hand and introduce yourself: "Hi, I'm Bill, a friend of Jessica's from work." Usually, you'll be met by smiles in return and invited into the conversation. Now the small talk begins. Experts in the area offer the following suggestions for engaging in useful small talk:

- Join the conversation instead of taking it over by asking questions of the person you're small-talking with and demonstrating interest in what he or she has to say (e.g., "Is the restaurant you're talking about in this neighbourhood?").

- Be on the lookout for others wanting to join in your small talk conversation; get them involved even if it means changing subjects (e.g., "Hi there, we were just talking about good places to eat in the east end").
- Talk about topics of general interest instead of overly personal topics; don't make it look as though you only want to talk about work (e.g., "One of the reasons I was comfortable moving here for my job was because there's just so many restaurants, theatres, and clubs. You're never bored!").
- End your small talk conversation by excusing yourself, but only after you've said something like "Well, it was great meeting you"—never leave the conversation after the person you're talking to has said something.
- Know when you've overstayed your welcome, even when strangers have shown they're interested in chatting with you (e.g., "Well, I'm going to see what Jessica's up to in the kitchen. It was good to meet you").
- Sense whether it's appropriate to swap business cards or ask for a contact address or phone number (e.g., "We should definitely keep in touch. Here's my card, send me an e-mail and we'll make plans to have a coffee next week").[14]

CONCLUSION

This chapter covered interpersonal spoken communication skills. The three skills discussed were workplace conversation, telephone skills, and networking skills. Workplace conversation is important because it provides a sense of immediacy and personal contact that is often missing in today's hyper-wired world. Conversation skills you should master include the use of your own voice as a tool, including pronunciation and tone, through to knowing when to offer praise in a conversation. At the same time, workplace conversations sometimes have to do with offering criticism and reacting to that criticism. Understanding best practices in offering and receiving criticism is important, especially knowing how not to take criticism personally.

When it comes to telephone skills, the most important skill you can learn is to treat phone calls as mini-presentations. They should be prepared for, and they should have an introduction, a body with your message, and an ending where you consciously close the conversation. The same goes for voice-mail messages you leave. They shouldn't ramble; rather, they should be well structured and concise. Cell phone etiquette dictates that you take into consideration your location and the volume of your voice before making a call.

Finally, networking and small talk are important spoken interpersonal skills for the effective business communicator. Networking is the process by which you use your acquaintance or friendship with other people to help you (and them) in the world of work. The successful networker methodically lists contacts and gets in touch with them frequently, realizing that networking goes both ways. Contacts cannot just be asked for help and information; they have to be given help and information too. Small talk helps the effective networker by turning sometimes awkward social situations into opportunities to develop contacts.

Chapter Review

As a way of studying the material in this chapter, imagine you are at a job interview for your dream entry-level job after college or university. You've prepared answers for all the classic interview questions, but to your surprise, your interviewer also asks a number of questions based on interpersonal speaking skills. How would you answer the following six questions?

1. Although we give all our employees BlackBerrys and of course everyone has an e-mail account and a telephone extension, we also try to instill the importance of face-to-face communication in our employees. Can you give us an example of a situation in which a face-to-face conversation would be more preferable than a phone call or an e-mail? Why?

2. Recently our company hired a meetings consultant to try to improve our productivity at meetings. The consultant recommended that employees be open to criticism during meetings, in other words, that we treat meetings as times when we can all be honest. The first time we tried this, however, the person leading the meeting was personally insulted by one of his co-workers. What should we be doing differently?

3. About 50 percent of your time in this job will be spent talking on the phone with clients, many of whom are very busy. What tips would you employ to make the best use of your precious telephone time with clients?

4. We participate in about four trade fairs per year, and as a marketing assistant you'll be attending all four. How do you balance your need to stay in touch with the company via cell phone and your need to be available to the people who visit your booth at the trade fair?

5. The real estate business is all about networking. While it's great to sell one high-priced house every few months, it's even better to sell five medium-priced houses during the same time. How will you develop your network as a new agent with our firm?

6. As a marketing assistant working trade fairs regularly and coming into contact with thousands of strangers and potential clients, what interpersonal skill do you think you'll need to differentiate yourself from the other hundred vendors at the same trade fair? How will you use this skill in a trade fair scenario?

Problems

1. You are the manager of the Customer Service division at a large Canadian company's customer service office in Moncton, New Brunswick. Until recently, the company operated without any form of performance review for its employees. One day a directive comes from head office in Montreal informing the Moncton team that a performance review system will have to be implemented in its customer service operations. The system will be made up of bi-annual reviews by managers and peers for each employee. In other words, every two years, each customer service representative at the company will be subject to a performance review conducted both by his or her manager, but also by an unspecified number of his or her peers. When the performance review system is first discussed at a staff meeting, comments from employees are largely positive. They like the fact that good reviews will lead to bonuses, something the company has never offered before. No one seems to be worried about the opposite policy, which is that a series of three poor reviews in a row will be considered grounds for dismissal. Two years later, as the manager, you are conducting between 50 and 75 performance reviews a year—a heavy task. You've noticed recently that during performance reviews you've started to receive "push-back" from many employees. They've said things like "You can't criticize me" or "You don't have any proof of that" or "If

you write that in my review, I'm going to file a harassment complaint with the province," among other comments. You're scratching your head trying to understand how a process that was initially greeted as a positive step is now being viewed with suspicion by employees who are refusing to cooperate in large numbers. How can you solve this problem?

2. The company described in problem 1 has another issue on its hands. The number of complaints that have been lodged against it is growing exponentially. Most of the customer complaints have to do with level of telephone service. For example, a large percentage of customers say that when they call to ask questions about their accounts, they're being rushed through the conversation, and being made to feel as if their questions are not important. Another large percentage of customers say that they're having trouble understanding what the Customer Service agents are saying because of their accents. A final group of customers say that they're having trouble making their way through the maze of automated instructions when all they really want is to talk to a live person. What's the most important problem of the three? Can the solution to the most important problem also be used to solve the other two problems? If not, what else besides the skills learned in this chapter may be necessary to ensure effective telephone service at this company?

3. Bob is a new sales representative with the company described in problems 1 and 2. His job is to travel around his territory and meet with existing clients as well as potential clients, in order to maintain and increase the sales level of the company's product in the territory. Eager to please his boss and ensure his future with the company, Bob recently purchased a cell phone. He's also had his cell phone number listed on his business card (instead of his regular landline). Marge Picton of the MacDonald County School Board, one of Bob's largest existing clients, has been trying to reach Bob for days now. She's called the number on his business card three times, left three messages, but hasn't heard back. She's tried e-mailing Bob twice, and once again, there's been no response. Marge decides to try one more time (an important piece of software isn't working, and it's causing an administrative headache at the school board's headquarters), and finally Bob picks up the phone. It's 5:30 on a Thursday afternoon. Marge can hear a lot of noise and music in the background—loud voices, yelps, laughter. Bob asks Marge to "hold on a minute so I can move to a quieter place" before resuming the call. Marge is disconcerted because she's pretty sure that Bob is in a bar. Bob apologizes for the noise and asks what he can do for Marge. Marge proceeds to tell him about the three unreturned messages. Bob apologizes again and says he's been forgetting to check his cell phone messages. The rest of the phone call goes downhill from there. Bob promises to visit the school board first thing Friday morning, but not before Marge has sent an e-mail to Bob's boss complaining about the sales rep's interpersonal skills. What's gone wrong here and what are the solutions? What's the first piece of advice Bob's boss will give him?

4. Bob the sales rep from problem 3 has been let go from his job, now that the maternity leave he was covering is over. He has six months of experience as a software sales rep under his belt, as well as his business degree from a local college, and some part-time customer service experience from his student years. Because he lives in a rural part of the province, there aren't lots of jobs to be had, and for the first time, he's considering moving over 200 kilometres away to the provincial capital. Most of the jobs he finds advertised online are located there, so the move seems to make sense. However, his grandmother and his father are both in poor health, and as an only child, he feels it's

important at this time to also be living close to them so he can help take care of them. It strikes Bob that what he needs to do is use his contacts to see if there are any local jobs—even if they're outside his area of expertise—for which he can apply. One day in September at the county fair, he sees Marge Picton. She's with a man Bob assumes is Marge's husband. Bob desperately wants to talk to Marge—she might be able to "get him into" the school board, where there are a lot of different job categories. Unfortunately, he remembers that his last exchange with Marge went pretty badly, and he's still embarrassed by his ineptitude. Is the above situation going to cause problems for Bob? If so, why? If not, why not? Ideally, what should Bob do if his first priority is to find a local job?

5. As he approaches Marge Picton on the grounds of the county fair, Bob keeps in mind what his Business Communication professor at MacDonald College kept insisting: it's never too late to network with someone you've come across before. Bob decides that even if Marge stares at him in disgust, he's going to soldier through the awkwardness and turn the opportunity to his advantage. Walking up to Marge, Bob smiles and says, "Hi there, Marge, do you remember me?" Marge turns around, as does the man with her, and to Bob's surprise, she smiles at him. "Hello, Bob, it's been a while. This is my husband, Reg." Bob extends his hand and shakes Reg's hand, saying, "Pleased to meet you, Reg." Marge doesn't allude to Bob's history at the software company, and the three soon find out they have quite a bit in common, including the fact Reg knows Bob's father from their time at the local high school. Soon, Bob is focusing his conversation on Reg, who, besides the connection with Bob's father, turns out to also be the owner of the local Ford car dealership. Marge stands by while the two men talk. Soon, she is visibly shifting her body weight from one foot to another. Then she puts her hand on Reg's left hand. Bob sees these gestures of slight impatience but he continues to ask Reg questions about the car dealership business. Marge eventually interrupts their conversation with another smile, saying, "Reg and I have to be off now Bob, but perhaps you can pay Reg a visit at the dealership if you have any other questions." Knowing what you do about Bob and Marge, what are Bob's chances at succeeding in attaining a position at Reg's car dealership? What could he have done differently in his encounter with Marge and Reg at the county fair to ensure success?

Grammar/Style Review 12

In this review, you will be practising identifying various mistakes discussed throughout this book. There are at least ten mistakes in total, and possibly other errors not explicitly covered. If you can find between eight and ten of the mistakes, consider yourself an effective editor!

To: jchoi@canexhibits.ca

From: kkarim@canexhibits.ca

Date: September 4, 2007

Re: Exibit rules!

Hey Jase,

Did u hear about the new rules on expenses, phone calls, and the protocol at booths.

Turns out that everyone have to get there expenses okayed by Steve before leaving a show and wear a uniform! It doesn't matter if he's an assistant or a director, looks like the company's not trusting no one these days.

Anyways, whatever rules they make get broken anyway, right? :) But what I'm really writeing about is the party on Friday. You still going?

K

⠂⠂ *Business Communication Lab 12*

At a recent monthly staff meeting at your company, the CEO mentions that productivity levels have dipped in recent months and that one reason for the dip is e-mail addiction among employees. In other words, people are spending so much time writing and replying to e-mails that they're not getting as much work done as they should. The CEO says that his solution to the problem will be to take a step back and "re-engage the company in interpersonal communication." As a first step, he says he's struck a team that will produce guidelines on interpersonal communication. The guidelines will be easy to use and written in a checklist and scenario-based manner. You've been asked to join the team, along with a few of your co-workers. Using the skills you've learned about in this chapter, including in Michael Stern's article, design a guideline document that helps employees understand when to engage in conversation and phone calls instead of e-mails, and how to do so effectively.

Grammar, Mechanics, and Style Tutorials and Exercises

TUTORIAL 1: SUBJECT–VERB AGREEMENT

Subjects and verbs must agree to be grammatically correct. This means they match in person (first, second, and third), as well as in number (singular or plural).

a. A singular subject requires a singular verb:

The stock market opens at 10 a.m. (The singular verb *opens* agrees with the singular subject *market*.)

He doesn't (not *don't*) work on Saturday.

b. A plural subject requires a plural verb:

On the packing slip several items seem (not *seems*) to be missing.

c. A verb agrees with its subject regardless of prepositional phrases that may intervene:

This list of management objectives is extensive. (The singular verb *is* agrees with the singular subject *list*.)

Every one of the letters shows (not *show*) proper form.

d. A verb agrees with its subject regardless of intervening phrases introduced by *as well as, in addition to, such as, including, together with,* and similar expressions:

An important memo, together with several letters, was misplaced. (The singular verb *was* agrees with the singular subject *memo*.)

The president as well as several other top-level executives approves of our proposal. (The singular verb *approves* agrees with the subject *president*.)

e. A verb agrees with its subject regardless of the location of the subject:

Here is one of the letters about which you asked. (The verb *is* agrees with its subject *one*, even though it precedes *one*. The adverb *here* cannot function as a subject.)

There are many problems yet to be resolved. (The verb *are* agrees with the subject *problems*. The adverb *there* cannot function as a subject.)

In the next office are several printers. (In this inverted sentence the verb *are* must agree with the subject *printers*.)

f. Subjects joined by *and* require a plural verb:

Analyzing the reader and organizing a strategy are the first steps in letter writing. (The plural verb *are* agrees with the two subjects, *analyzing* and *organizing*.)

The tone and the wording of the letter were persuasive. (The plural verb *were* agrees with the two subjects, *tone* and *wording*.)

g. Subjects joined by *or* or *nor* may require singular or plural verbs. Make the verb agree with the closer subject:

Neither the memos nor the report is ready. (The singular verb *is* agrees with *report*, the closer of the two subjects.)

h. The following indefinite pronouns are singular and require singular verbs: *anyone, anybody, anything, each, either, every, everyone, everybody, everything, many a, neither, nobody, nothing, someone, somebody,* and *something*:

Either of the alternatives that you present is acceptable. (The verb *is* agrees with the singular subject *either*.)

i. Collective nouns may take singular or plural verbs, depending on whether the members of the group are operating as a unit or individually:

Our management team is united in its goal.

The faculty are sharply divided on the tuition issue. (Although acceptable, this sentence sounds better recast: *The faculty members are sharply divided on the tuition issue.*)

j. Organization names and titles of publications, although they may appear to be plural, are singular and require singular verbs:

Deme, Sokolov, and Horne, Inc., has (not *have*) hired a marketing consultant.

Thousands of Investment Tips is (not *are*) again on the best-seller list.

Tutorial 1 Exercises

Edit the following sentences to eliminate subject-verb agreement errors.

1. The keyboard, printer, and monitor costs less than I expected.
2. A description of the property, together with several other legal documents, were submitted by my lawyer.
3. There was only two enclosures and the letter in the envelope.
4. A manager's time and energy has to be focused on important issues.
5. We're not sure whether Mr. Murphy or Ms. Wagner are in charge of the program.

TUTORIAL 2: PRONOUN-ANTECEDENT AGREEMENT

To be grammatically correct, pronouns must agree with the words to which they refer (their antecedents) in gender and in number.

a. Use masculine pronouns to refer to masculine antecedents, feminine pronouns to refer to feminine antecedents, and neutral pronouns to refer to antecedents without gender:

The woman opened her office door. (Feminine gender applies.)

A man sat at his desk. (Masculine gender applies.)

This computer and its programs fit our needs. (Neutral gender applies.)

b. Use singular pronouns to refer to singular antecedents:

Common-gender pronouns (such as *him* or *his*) traditionally have been used when the gender of the antecedent is unknown. Business writers construct sentences to avoid the need for common-gender pronouns. Study these examples for alternatives to the use of common-gender pronouns:

Each student must submit a report on Monday.

All students must submit their reports on Monday.

Each student must submit his or her report on Monday. (This alternative is least acceptable, since it is wordy and calls attention to itself.)

    c. Use singular pronouns to refer to singular indefinite subjects and plural pronouns for plural indefinite subjects. Words such as *anyone, something,* and *anybody* are considered indefinite because they refer to no specific person or object. Some indefinite pronouns are always singular; others are always plural.

Always Singular			**Always Plural**
anybody	everyone	somebody	both
anyone	everything	someone	few
anything	neither		many
each	nobody		several
either	no one		

Somebody in the group of touring women left her (not *their*) purse in the museum. Either of the companies has the right to exercise its (not *their*) option to sell shares.

    d. Use singular pronouns to refer to collective nouns and organization names:

The engineering staff is moving its (not *their*) facilities on Friday. (The singular pronoun *its* agrees with the collective noun *staff* because the members of staff function as a single unit.)

Jones, Cohen, & James, Inc., has (not *have*) cancelled its (not *their*) contract with us. (The singular pronoun *its* agrees with *Jones, Cohen, & James, Inc.*, because the members of the organization are operating as a single unit.)

    e. Use a plural pronoun to refer to two antecedents joined by *and*, whether the antecedents are singular or plural:

Our company president and our vice president will be submitting their expenses shortly.

    f. Ignore intervening phrases—introduced by expressions such as *together with*, *as well as*, and *in addition to*—that separate a pronoun from its antecedent:

One of our managers, along with several salespeople, is planning his retirement. (If you wish to emphasize both subjects equally, join them with *and*: *One of our managers and several salespeople are planning their retirements.*)

    g. When antecedents are joined by *or* or *nor*, make the pronoun agree with the antecedent closest to it.

Neither Jackie nor Kim wanted her (not *their*) desk moved.

Tutorial 2 Exercises

Edit the following sentences to eliminate pronoun-antecedent agreement errors.

1. When you visit Mutual Trust, inquire about their GICs and RRSPs.
2. A manager in our company has responsibilities that they have to take seriously.
3. Everyone on the team is accountable for their section of the report.
4. Every employee is entitled to have their tuition reimbursed.
5. Flexible working hours may mean slower career advancement, but it appeals to me anyway.

TUTORIAL 3: SENTENCE FRAGMENTS AND RUN-ON SENTENCES

A sentence fragment starts with a capital letter and ends with a period but is missing an integral element to make it grammatically correct. On the other hand, a run-on sentence is one in which two independent clauses are improperly joined together.

a. Fragment due to lack of verb

There are numerous causes of workplace stress. For example, rudeness in the workplace. [**Correction:** There are numerous causes of workplace stress, including rudeness in the workplace.]

b. Fragment due to lack of subject

Rudeness in the workplace has been increasing. Which sometimes causes workers to get angry. [**Correction:** Rudeness in the workplace has been increasing, sometimes causing workers to get angry.]

c. Run-on sentence (due to comma splice)

There are numerous causes of workplace stress, for example rudeness in the workplace is an important cause of stress. [Both *There are numerous causes of workplace stress* and *rudeness in the workplace is an important cause* are independent clauses; a comma is not the correct punctuation mark to join them.]

d. Run-on corrected by adding a comma and a coordinating conjunction

There are numerous causes of workplace stress, but rudeness in the workplace is one of the most important.

e. Run-on corrected by adding a semicolon, colon, or dash

There are numerous causes of workplace stress; rudeness in the workplace is one of the most important.

f. Run-on corrected by creating separate sentences

There are numerous causes of workplace stress. Chief among them is rudeness in the workplace.

g. Run-on corrected by re-writing sentences

Rudeness in the workplace is one of the numerous causes of workplace stress.

Tutorial 3 Exercises

Edit the following sentences to eliminate fragment and run-on errors.

1. Although UTS is renowned internationally, our staff consists of only nine people. All of which have different attributes.
2. I have a number of telephone lines. One for business, one for personal calls, one for the fax machine, and one for the Internet.
3. Junk faxes are like a virus that's out of control, the virus is living off my time and fax paper!
4. Quotation marks are important because the reader is assured that the article is accurate and logical because he or she recognizes that the quotation is not the columnist's, but the voice of an expert.
5. Profit derived from Grapealicious bubblegum is 15 percent higher than profit from Breath-X gum, the former is more popular with the teenage demographic, which exercises significant buying power.

TUTORIAL 4: PREPOSITIONS

Prepositions are connecting words that join nouns or pronouns to other words in a sentence. The words *about*, *at*, *from*, *in*, and *to* are examples of prepositions.

a. Include necessary prepositions:

What type of software do you need? (Not *What type software ...*)

I graduated from high school two years ago. (Not *I graduated high school ...*)

b. Omit unnecessary prepositions:

Where is the meeting? (**Not** *Where is the meeting at?*)

Both printers work well. (**Not** *Both of the printers.*)

Where are you going? (**Not** *Where are you going to?*)

c. Avoid the overuse of prepositional phrases:

Weak: We have received your application for credit at our branch in the Halifax area.

Improved: We have received your credit application at our Halifax office.

d. Repeat the preposition before the second of two related elements:

Applicants use the résumé effectively by summarizing their most important experiences and by relating their education to the jobs sought.

e. Include the second preposition when two prepositions modify a single object:

George's appreciation of and aptitude for computers led to a promising career.

Tutorial 4 Exercises

Edit the following sentences to eliminate preposition errors.

1. Mr. Samuels graduated college last June.
2. By putting the wrong address to the address box, e-mail wastes people's time.
3. The trouble with the proposal is in the section about the budget, which is confusing.
4. As much as I would enjoy attending to your seminar, I'm busy that day.
5. I cannot predict at what day I will be available to meet.

TUTORIAL 5: ARTICLES

Articles (*a, an, the*) along with quantifiers (*some, many, a number of*) are used to introduce nouns. In English grammar, articles and quantifiers have to suit (i.e., go together correctly with) the nouns they introduce.

a. Non-specific nouns that can be counted (e.g., student, teacher, car, books, cities) should be introduced with *a* or *an*, depending on whether the noun begins with a consonant or a vowel.

A teacher's job is to help students learn. [**Not** Teacher's job is to help students learn. **Not** An teacher's job is to help students learn.]

b. Non-count nouns name things that cannot be plural (e.g., clothing, furniture), as well as things that cannot be counted, only measured (e.g., courage, bravery). They should not be introduced with *a* or *an*.

She looked nice with a jewellery around her neck. [**Correction:** She looked nice with a jewel around her neck. **Correction:** The piece of jewellery looked nice around her neck.]

    c. Use the article *the* to name specific people, places, or things.

The ingredients of that dish include onions and garlic. [**Not** An ingredient of that dish includes onions and garlic.]

    d. Don't use the article *the* to name proper nouns or generalized statements.

High Park is a large urban park in Toronto. [**Not** The High Park is a large urban park in Toronto.]

People today have a low tolerance for waiting in line. [**Not** The people today have a low tolerance for waiting in line.]

    e. Correct quantifiers must be used to match count or non-count nouns.

Every computer is security-tagged at the college. [**Not** Much computers are security-tagged at the college. **But** Much snow fell overnight.]

Tutorial 5 Exercises

Edit the following sentences to eliminate article errors.

1. These are just a few of many exciting features of the Woodside Condominiums.
2. This new and exciting program is the only one of its kind in Alberta that covers all the three important aspects of financial planning.
3. Allow me to introduce the Macdonald College's Financial Services Post-Diploma program, which boasts numerous direct links with large number of local financial services firms.
4. It is pleasure to work with Chinese Student Association at Macdonald College.
5. We all use the technology to save the time but the technology does not always work well.

TUTORIAL 6: WORDINESS

Wordiness is a style error by which too many words are used to achieve your aim as a writer—the communication of meaning. Always strive to eliminate wordiness in your writing.

    a. Wordiness through redundancy

The colour blue is my boss's most favourite colour. [**Correct:** Blue is my boss's favourite colour.]

    b. Wordiness through repetition

I flipped through the food preparation manual before putting the manual down on the counter. [**Correct:** I flipped through the food preparation manual before putting it down on the counter.]

    c. Wordiness through empty language

We should definitely be on the lookout for cost-cutting opportunities. [**Correct:** We should be on the lookout for cost-cutting opportunities.]

    d. Wordiness through inflated writing

In spite of the fact that attrition is an important factor, it's not our only consideration. [**Correct:** Although attrition is an important factor, it's not our only consideration.]

Tutorial 6 Exercises

Edit the following sentences to eliminate wordiness errors.

1. The reason UTS started operations about six years ago was due to the fact that there was a need for its services.
2. Customers do not like when they have questions and they are not answered right away.
3. A lot of the success of the magazine is credited in part to the fact that the authors are free to express themselves.
4. In summary, I conclude from past experience that mutual cooperation is the most basic requirement of any successful team.
5. For all intents and purposes, the memo is essentially an out-of-date, seldom-used method of business communication.

TUTORIAL 7: IMPRECISION

Imprecision in writing is a style error in which you fail to write what you mean, and instead confuse or irritate the reader. You can achieve precision by making sure what you've written is understandable to a general readership.

    a. Imprecision due to connotation

The whiff of scandal comes after the bank CEO to this day. [**Correct:** The whiff of scandal follows the bank CEO to this day. "Come after" means the same thing as follow, but it also has the connotation of hunting down as in "I'm going to come after you!"]

    b. Imprecision due to misused words

We could of won the competition with a more experienced team. [**Correct:** We could have won the competition with a more experienced team. *"Could of" is an incorrect spoken form of "could have" and should not be used in writing.*]

Tutorial 7 Exercises

Edit the following sentences to eliminate imprecision errors.

1. *Fortune* magazine uses a lot of advertisements.
2. In making the perfect résumé there are a number of factors that come into play.
3. I will suggest him to do the work immediately.
4. Secondly, the columnists of both articles have different points of view about gender.
5. Imageco's fee for developing and facilitating this course comes up to $8000.

TUTORIAL 8: PARALLELISM

Parallelism is a style rule stating that your writing will have more emphasis and impact if you ensure that linked words (in a sentence or in a list) have the same grammatical form.

    a. Parallelism with items in a list or series

Most management theories emphasize being flexible, responsible, plus the ability to cooperate. [The linked adjectives in this sentence—flexible, responsible—are disrupted by "plus the ability to cooperate," which is not an adjective. **Correct:** Most management theories emphasize being flexible, responsible, and cooperative.]

> **b.** Parallelism of items in a bulleted list

Please follow this procedure when writing accident reports:
- Fill out the date, time, and location information at the top of the form
- Describe in 50–100 words what happened, including names of people involved and actions taken
- The form must be signed at the bottom and handed in to your supervisor within two hours of the accident.

Two of the three items in the above list begin with a verb, while the third item begins with an article. **Correct:**

Please follow this procedure when writing accident reports:
- Fill out the date, time, and location information at the top of the form
- Describe in 50–100 words what happened, including names of people involved and actions taken
- Sign the form at the bottom and hand it in to your supervisor within two hours of the accident.

> **c.** Parallelism of paired items

Deciding what needs to be done is easier than to tell people about it. [The paired items in this sentence—"what needs to be done" and "to tell people about it"—should be introduced by parallel grammatical forms. **Correct:** Deciding what needs to be done is easier than telling people about it.]

Tutorial 8 Exercises

Edit the following sentences to eliminate parallelism errors.

1. E-commerce websites should be built with many language options, compatible systems, and be easily connectible to related websites.
2. Executives lead their employees by instilling loyalty and they set a good example.
3. The corporate executive faced his trial confidently, insisting that he was innocent and he rejected any offers of a plea bargain.
4. Some of the major skills are being able to provide value to customers, provide service and performance, provide an attractive site, and providing a sense of community.
5. The following are services that UTS can offer you:
   - Auditing freight bills
   - Checking all shipping and receiving charges for over-charging
   - Our staff will advise you on which trucking companies offer superior service
   - We will file freight claims and fight wrongful claims against you.

TUTORIAL 9: SPELLING

Along with punctuation, spelling is an important mechanical aspect of your writing. The reason spelling (and other mechanics) is important is that when it's done incorrectly, it takes away from your credibility as a writer. In a business situation, your credibility is an intangible though highly important "soft skill" necessary for a successful career.

a. Canadian spelling

The catalog shoot was canceled due to a missing roll of color film. [**Correct:** The catalogue shoot was cancelled due to a missing roll of colour film.]

b. Confusing usage

The medication should not produce any side affects, but if this happens, please call me as soon as possible. [**Correct:** The medication should not produce any side effects, but if this happens, please call me as soon as possible.]

c. Spelling rules

It's almost unbelieveable, but the recievables have increased by 75 percent! [**Correct:** It's almost unbelievable, but the receivables have increased by 75 percent!]

Tutorial 9 Exercises

Edit the following sentences to eliminate spelling errors.

1. Many of our clients have had there products damaged due to poor packaging.
2. It doesn't appear that any one has a viable solution to the problem.
3. While each paper has a special pull out section, the *Post*'s is completely separate while the *Globe*'s is part of the front section.
4. This course investigates the history of labor unions in Canada.
5. "Park your car at the shipping and recieving loading dock," he said.

TUTORIAL 10: PUNCTUATION

Like spelling, when used correctly, punctuation gives you a lot of credibility as a writer. Because there are so many punctuation rules— for periods, commas, semicolons, colons, dashes, hyphens, exclamation marks, question marks, etc.—you're wise to keep your punctuation simple. Use the following common sense rule: if you're not 100 percent sure the punctuation has to be there, then don't use it.

a. Use commas to set off transitions and signal statements.

On the other hand as Smith states clearly "employee morale is part of the bottom line." [**Correct:** On the other hand, as Smith states clearly, "employee morale is part of the bottom line."

b. Avoid comma splices by using semicolons.

Some of my favourite restaurants are in New York, some are in Montreal. [**Correct:** Some of my favourite restaurants are in New York; some are in Montreal.]

c. Only use colons if a period could also work.

Our office has all the up-to-date gadgets such as: laptops, wireless Internet, and flat-screen TVs. [**Correct:** Our office has all the up-to-date gadgets such as laptops, wireless Internet, and flat-screen TVs.]

d. Joint and individual ownership using apostrophes.

Finally, I'd like to acknowledge Tim and Randy's contribution to the project. [Tim and Randy individually own their contributions to the project. **Correct:** Finally, I'd like to acknowledge Tim's and Randy's contributions to the project.]

e. Avoid unnecessary dashes.

The results of the survey indicate that most employers—79 percent—think writing skills are "very important." [**Correct:** The results of the survey indicate that most employers (79 percent) think writing skills are "very important."]

Tutorial 10 Exercises

Edit the following sentences to eliminate punctuation errors.

1. Although, I don't see eye to eye with you, I'm willing to work together to get this project done.
2. After you're finished painting the living room; please work on the dining room.
3. Sue and Mitch's joint mortgage is almost paid off.
4. Sometimes—well almost every day—I feel the urge to take a long—really long—vacation.
5. However some commentators suggest that the country may be moving into a period of inflation.

TUTORIAL 11: DICTION

Diction refers to the language you choose to use when you write and when you speak. In general, business writing and speech should fall somewhere between informal and formal, and they should avoid the following diction errors unless such diction is necessary in the context of the communication.

a. Slangy diction

If you're down with my suggestions, we can move to the next step. [**Correct:** If you agree with my suggestions, we can move to the next step. *"Down with" is slang because it's not a phrase every group in society will understand.*]

b. Jargony diction

Let's operationalize those recommendations! [**Correct:** Let's act on those recommendations! "Operationalize" is an invented verb sometimes used in business writing and speech.]

c. Pretentious diction

The tendentious speech was intended to antagonize the high-powered audience. [**Correct:** The opinionated speech was intended to annoy the high-powered audience.]

d. Discourteous diction

We have a number of girls working for us as administrative assistants. [**Correct:** A number of women work here as administrative assistants.]

Tutorial 11 Exercises

Edit the following sentences to eliminate diction errors.

1. Accountants are not just about calculating taxes and amortization figures.
2. Cryptography also ensures that neither party to the transaction can deny its participation in the exchange of information.
3. My practice focuses on high net-worth individuals; I'm not interested in small-time investors.
4. Fear of being conned out of their money is making consumers hesitant to purchase online.
5. They finalized judging on *Canadian Idol* by prioritizing candidates according to pre-established talent parameters and in due course selected the optimal contestant.

Proofreading Marks

PROOFREADING MARK	DRAFT COPY	FINAL COPY
⸗ Align horizontally	TO: Rick Munoz	TO: Rick Munoz
‖ Align vertically	‖166.32 132.45	166.32 132.45
≢ Capitalize	Coca-cola runs on ms–dos	Coca-Cola runs on MS-DOS
◠ Close up space	meeting at 3 p. m.	meeting at 3 p.m.
⏌ ⊏ Centre	⏌Recommendations⊏	Recommendations
ℛ Delete	in my final judgement	in my judgment
ⱽ Insert apostrophe	our companys product	our company's product
⋏ Insert comma	you will of course	you will, of course,
⋏ Insert semicolon	value therefore, we feel	value; therefore, we feel
⹀ Insert hyphen	tax free income	tax-free income
⊙ Insert period	Ms Holly Hines	Ms. Holly Hines
ⱽ Insert quotation mark	shareholders receive a bonus	shareholders receive a "bonus"
# Insert space	wordprocessing program	word processing program
/ Lowercase (remove capitals)	the Vice-President	the vice-president
⊏ Move to left	HUMAN RESOURCES	Human Resources
⊐ Move to right	⊏I. Labour costs	I. Labour costs
○ Spell out	A. Findings of study⊐ aimed at ②depts	A. Findings of study aimed at two departments
¶ Start new paragraph	¶Keep the screen height at eye level.	Keep the screen height at eye level.
⋯⋯ Stet (don't delete)	officials talked openly	officials talked openly
∽ Transpose	accounts receivable	accounts receivable
〰 Use boldface	Conclusions	**Conclusions**
— Use italics	The Perfect Résumé	*The Perfect Résumé*
⌐ Start new line	Globex, 23 Acorn Lane	Globex 23 Acorn Lane
⊃ Run lines together	Invoice No. 122059	Invoice No. 122059

Document Formats

Business documents carry two kinds of messages. The meaning is conveyed by the words chosen to express the writer's ideas. The level of professionalism is conveyed by the appearance of a document. If you compare an assortment of letters from various organizations, you will notice immediately that some look more attractive and more professional than others. The message of the professional-looking documents suggests that they were sent by people who are careful, informed, intelligent, and successful. Understandably, you're more likely to take seriously documents that use attractive stationery and professional formatting techniques.

Over the years a number of conventions have arisen regarding the appearance and formatting of business documents. To ensure that your documents transmit professionalism from you and your organization, you'll want to give special attention to the appearance and formatting of your letters, envelopes, e-mails, memos, and fax cover sheets.

APPEARANCE

To ensure that a message is read and valued, you need to give it a professional appearance. Important elements in achieving a professional appearance are stationery, spacing after punctuation, and placement of the message on the page.

Stationery. Most organizations use high-quality stationery for business documents. This stationery is printed on paper with good weight and cotton-fibre content. Paper is measured by weight and may range from 9 pounds (thin onionskin paper) to 32 pounds (thick card and cover stock). Most office stationery is in the 16-to-24-pound range. Lighter 16-pound paper is generally sufficient for internal documents. Heavier 20-to-24-pound paper is used for printed letterhead stationery. Paper is also judged by its cotton-fibre content. Cotton fibre makes paper stronger, softer in texture, and less likely to yellow. Good-quality stationery contains 25 percent or more cotton fibre.

Spacing after punctuation. In the past, typists left two spaces after end punctuation (periods, question marks, and so forth). This practice was necessary, it was thought, because typewriters did not have proportional spacing and sentences were easier to read if two spaces separated them. Fortunately, today's word processors make available the same fonts used by professional typesetters. Influenced by the look of typeset publications (e.g., this book), many writers now leave only one space after end punctuation. As a practical matter, however, it is not wrong to use two spaces.

Letter placement. The easiest way to place letters on the page is to use the defaults of your word processing program. The defaults are usually set for side margins of 2.5 cm. Many companies today find these margins acceptable. If you want to adjust your margins to better balance shorter letters, use the following chart:

Words in Body of Letter	Side Margins	Blank Lines After Date
Under 200	*4 to 5 cm*	*4 to 10*
Over 200	*2.5 cm*	*2 to 3*

Experts say that a "ragged right" margin is easier to read than a justified (even) margin. You might want to turn off the justification feature of your word processing program if it automatically justifies the right margin.

LETTER PARTS

Professional-looking business letters are arranged in a conventional sequence with standard parts. Following is a discussion of how to use these letter parts properly. Figure A.1 illustrates the parts in a block-style letter.

Letterhead. Most business organizations use 8½-by-11-inch paper printed with a letterhead displaying their official name, street address, website address, e-mail address, and telephone and fax numbers. The letterhead may also include a logo and an advertising tag-line such as *Ebank: A new way to bank.*

Dateline. On letterhead paper you should place the date two blank lines below the last line of the letterhead or 5 cm from the top edge of the paper (line 13). On plain paper place the date immediately below your return address. Since the date goes on line 13, start the return address an appropriate number of lines above it. The most common dateline format is as follows: *June 9, 2006.* Don't use *th* (or *rd*) when the date is written this way. For European or military correspondence, use the following dateline format: *9 June 2006.* Notice that no commas are used.

Addressee and delivery notations. Delivery notations such as *FAX TRANS-MISSION, FEDERAL EXPRESS, MESSENGER DELIVERY, CONFIDENTIAL,* or *CERTIFIED MAIL* are typed in all capital letters two blank lines above the inside address.

Inside address. Type the inside address—that is, the address of the organization or person receiving the letter—single-spaced, starting at the left margin. The number of lines between the dateline and the inside address depends on the size of the letter body, the type size (point or pitch size), and the length of the typing lines. Generally, two to ten lines are appropriate. Be careful to duplicate the exact wording and spelling of the recipient's name and address on your documents. Usually, you can copy this information from the letterhead of the correspondence you are answering. If, for example, you are responding to Jackson & Perkins Company, don't address your letter to Jackson and Perkins Corp.

Always be sure to include a courtesy title such as *Mr., Ms., Mrs., Dr.,* or *Professor* before a person's name in the inside address—for both the letter and the envelope. Although many women in business today favour *Ms.,* you'll want to use whatever title the addressee prefers.

Remember that the inside address is not included for readers (who already know who and where they are). It's there to help writers accurately file a copy of the message. In general, avoid abbreviations (such as *Ave.* or *Co.*) unless they appear in the printed letterhead of the document being answered.

Attention line. An attention line allows you to send your message officially to an organization but to direct it to a specific individual, officer, or department. However, if you know an individual's complete name, it's always better to use it as the first line of the inside address and avoid an attention line. Here are two common formats for attention lines:

MultiMedia Enterprises
931 Calkins Road
Toronto, ON M3W 1E6

MultiMedia Enterprises
Attention: Marketing Director
931 Calkins Road
Toronto, ON M3W 1E6

ATTENTION MARKETING DIRECTOR

Attention lines may be typed in all caps or with upper- and lowercase letters. The colon following *Attention* is optional. Notice that an attention line may be placed two lines below the address block or printed as the second line of the inside address. You'll want to use the latter format if you're composing on a word processor because the address block may be copied to the envelope and the attention line will not interfere with the last-line placement of the postal code. (Mail can be sorted more easily if the postal code appears in the last line of a typed address.)

Whenever possible, use a person's name as the first line of an address instead of putting that name in an attention line. Some writers use an attention line because they fear that letters addressed to individuals at companies may be considered private. They worry that if the addressee is no longer with the company, the letter may be forwarded or not opened. Actually, unless a letter is marked "Personal" or "Confidential," it will very likely be opened as business mail.

Salutation. Place the letter greeting, or salutation, two lines below the last line of the inside address or the attention line (if used). If the letter is addressed to an individual, use that person's courtesy title and last name (*Dear Mr. Lanham*). Even if you are on a first-name basis (*Dear Leslie*), be sure to add a colon (not a comma or a semicolon) after the salutation, unless you are using open punctuation. Do not use an individual's full name in the salutation (not *Dear Mr. Leslie Lanham*) unless you are unsure of gender (*Dear Leslie Lanham*).

For letters with attention lines or those addressed to organizations, the selection of an appropriate salutation has become more difficult. Formerly, *Gentlemen* was used generically for all organizations. With increasing numbers of women in business management today, however, *Gentlemen* is outdated. Because no universally acceptable salutation has emerged as yet, you'll probably be safest with *Ladies and Gentlemen* or *Gentlemen and Ladies*.

One way to avoid the salutation dilemma is to address a document to a specific person. Another alternative is to use the simplified letter style, which conveniently omits the salutation (and the complimentary close).

Subject and reference lines. Although experts suggest placing the subject line one blank line below the salutation, many businesses actually place it above the salutation. Use whatever style your organization prefers. Reference lines often show policy or file numbers; they generally appear two lines above the salutation.

Body. Most business letters and memorandums are single-spaced, with double line spacing between paragraphs. Very short messages may be double-spaced with indented paragraphs.

Complimentary close. Typed two lines below the last line of the letter, the complimentary close may be formal (*Very truly yours*) or informal (*Sincerely* or *Respectfully*). The simplified letter style omits a complimentary close.

Letterhead ——————————

• *peerless* g r a p h i c s
8 9 3   D i l l i n g h a m   B o u l e v a r d   S t o n y   P l a i n ,   A B
Phone (403) 667-8880   Fax (403) 667-8830   www.peergraph.com

↓ line 13, or 2 blank lines below letterhead

Dateline ——————————
• September 13, 2007

↓ 2 to 10 blank lines

Inside address ——————————
• Mr. T. M. Wilson, President
Visual Concept Enterprises
1256 Lumsden Avenue
Nordegg, AB T0M 3T0

↓ 1 blank line

Salutation ——————————
• Dear Mr. Wilson

↓ 1 blank line

Subject line ——————————
• SUBJECT: BLOCK LETTER STYLE

↓ 1 blank line

This letter illustrates block letter style, about which you asked. All typed lines begin at the left margin. The date is usually placed 5 cm from the top edge of the paper or two lines below the last line of the letterhead, whichever position is lower.

This letter also shows open punctuation. No colon follows the salutation, and no comma follows the complimentary close. Although this punctuation style is efficient, we find that most of our customers prefer to include punctuation after the salutation and the complimentary close.

Body ——————————

If a subject line is included, it appears two lines below the salutation. The word SUBJECT is optional. Most readers will recognize a statement in this position as the subject without an identifying label. The complimentary close appears two lines below the end of the last paragraph.

↓ 1 blank line

• Sincerely

Mark H. Wong   ↓ 3 to 4 blank lines

Complimentary close
and signature block

Modified block style,
mixed punctuation

• Mark H. Wong
Graphics Designer

↓ 1 blank line

MHW:pil

In block-style letters, as shown above, all lines begin at the left margin. In modified block-style letters, as shown at the left, the date is centred or aligned with the complimentary close and signature block, which start at the centre. The date may also be backspaced from the right margin. Paragraphs may be blocked or indented. Mixed punctuation includes a colon after the salutation and a comma after the complimentary close. Open punctuation, shown above, omits the colon following the salutation and omits the comma following the complimentary closing.

Signature block. In most letter styles the writer's typed name and optional identification appear three to four blank lines below the complimentary close. The combination of name, title, and organization information should be arranged to achieve a balanced look. The name and title may appear on the same line or on separate lines, depending on the length of each. Use commas to separate categories within the same line, but not to conclude a line.

Sincerely,   Respectfully,

Jeremy M. Wood, Manager   Casandra Baker-Murillo

Technical Sales and Services   Executive Vice-President

Courtesy titles (*Ms.*, *Mrs.*, or *Miss*) should be used before female names that are not readily distinguishable as male or female. They should also be used before names containing only initials and international names. The title is usually placed in parentheses, but it may appear without them.

Yours truly,   Sincerely,

(Ms.) K. C. Tripton   (Mr.) Leslie Hill

Project Manager   Public Policy Department

Some organizations include their names in the signature block. In such cases the organization name appears in all caps two lines below the complimentary close:

Sincerely,

LITTON COMPUTER SERVICES

Ms. Shelina A. Simpson

Executive Assistant

Reference initials. If used, the initials of the typist and writer are typed two lines below the writer's name and title. Generally, the writer's initials are capitalized and the typist's are lowercased, but this format varies.

Enclosure notation. When an enclosure or attachment accompanies a document, a notation to that effect appears two lines below the reference initials. This notation reminds the typist to insert the enclosure in the envelope, and it reminds the recipient to look for the enclosure or attachment. The notation may be spelled out (*Enclosure, Attachment*), or it may be abbreviated (*Enc., Att.*). It may indicate the number of enclosures or attachments, and it may also identify a specific enclosure (*Enclosure: Form 1099*).

Copy notation. If you make copies of correspondence for other individuals, you may use *cc* to indicate carbon copy, *pc* to indicate photocopy, or merely *c* for any kind of copy. A colon following the initial(s) is optional.

Second-page heading. When a letter extends beyond one page, use plain paper of the same quality and colour as the first page. Identify the second and succeeding pages with a heading consisting of the name of the addressee, the page number, and the date. Use either of the following two formats:

Ms. Rachel Ruiz   2   May 3, 2007

Ms. Rachel Ruiz

Page 2

May 3, 2007

Both headings appear on line 7 followed by two blank lines to separate them from the continuing text. Avoid using a second page if you have only one line or the complimentary close and signature block to fill that page.

Plain-paper return address. If you prepare a personal or business letter on plain paper, place your address immediately above the date. Do not include your name; you will type (and sign) your name at the end of your letter. If your return address contains two lines, begin typing it on line 11 so that the date appears on line 13. Avoid abbreviations except for a two-letter province/territory abbreviation.

580 East Leffels Street
Dartmouth, NS B6R 2F3
December 14, 2007

Ms. Ellen Siemens
Retail Credit Department
Union National Bank
1220 Dunsfield Boulevard
Halifax, NS B4L 2E2

Dear Ms. Siemens:

For letters prepared in the block style, type the return address at the left margin. For modified block-style letters, start the return address at the centre to align with the complimentary close.

Business letters are generally prepared in one of three formats. The most popular is the block style, but the simplified style has much to recommend it.

Block style. In the block style, shown in Figure A.1, all lines begin at the left margin. This style is a favourite because it is easy to format.

Modified block style. The modified block style differs from block style in that the date and closing lines appear in the centre, as shown at the bottom of Figure A.1. The date may be (1) centred, (2) begun at the centre of the page (to align with the closing lines), or (3) backspaced from the right margin. The signature block—including the complimentary close, writer's name and title, or organization identification—begins at the centre. The first line of each paragraph may begin at the left margin or may be indented five or ten spaces. All other lines begin at the left margin.

Simplified style. Introduced by the Administrative Management Society a number of years ago, the simplified letter style, shown in Figure A.2, requires little formatting. Like the block style, all lines begin at the left margin. A subject line appears in all caps two blank lines below the inside address and two blank lines above the first paragraph. The salutation and complimentary close are omitted. The signer's name and identification appear in all caps four blank lines below the last paragraph. This letter style is efficient and avoids the problem of appropriate salutations and courtesy titles.

PUNCTUATION STYLES

Two punctuation styles are commonly used for letters. *Open* punctuation, shown with the block-style letter in Figure A.1, contains no punctuation after the salutation or complimentary close. *Mixed* punctuation, shown with the modified block style letter in Figure A.1, requires a colon after the salutation and a comma after the complimentary close. Many business organizations prefer mixed punctuation, even in a block style letter. If you choose mixed punctuation, be sure to use a colon—not a comma or semicolon—after the salutation. Even when the salutation is a first name, the colon is appropriate.

Figure A.2 ▶ Simplified Letter Style

ABC ★ Automation Business Consultants
2682 Roefield Street
Cactus Lake, SK S0K 4L3   (306) 369-1109

↓ line 13 or 1 blank line below letterhead

July 19, 2007

↓ 2 to 7 blank lines

FAX TRANSMISSION   ↓ 1 blank line   ●——— Identifies method of delivery

Ms. Sara Hendricks, Manager
Western Land and Home Realty
17690 Anscombe Avenue
Porcupine Plain, SK S0E 2H1

↓ 2 blank lines

SUBJECT: SIMPLIFIED LETTER STYLE   ●——— Replaces salutation with subject line

↓ 2 blank lines   ●——— Leaves 2 blank lines above and below subject line

You may be interested to learn, Ms. Hendricks, that some years ago the Administrative Management Society recommended the simplified letter format illustrated here. Notice the following efficient features:

1. All lines begin at the left margin.

2. The salutation and complimentary close are omitted.

3. A subject line in all caps appears 3 lines below the inside address and 3 lines above the first paragraph.

4. The writer's name and identification appear 5 lines (i.e., 4 blank lines) below the last paragraph.

In addition to its efficiency, this letter style is helpful in dealing with the problem of appropriate salutations. Since it has no salutation, your writers need not worry about which to choose. For many reasons we recommend this style to your staff.

Holly Higgins   ↓ 4 blank lines   ●——— Omits complimentary close

HOLLY HIGGINS, MANAGER, OFFICE DIVISION   ●——— Highlights writer's name and identification with all caps

HH:tlb   ↓ 1 blank line
                          ↓ 1 blank line

c John Fox   ●——— Identifies copy

ENVELOPES

An envelope should be of the same quality and colour of stationery as the letter it carries. Because the envelope introduces your message and makes the first impression, you need to be especially careful in addressing it. Moreover, how you fold the letter is important.

Return address. The return address is usually printed in the upper left corner of an envelope, as shown in Figure A.3. In large companies some form of identification (the writer's initials, name, or location) may be typed or handwritten above the company name and return address. This identification helps return the letter to the sender in case of nondelivery.

On an envelope without a printed return address, single-space the return address in the upper left corner. Beginning on line 3 on the fourth space (approximately 12 mm or 1/2 inch) from the left edge, type the writer's name, title, company, and mailing address.

Mailing address. On legal-sized No. 10 envelopes (10.5 cm by 24 cm), begin the address on line 13 about 11.5 cm from the left edge, as shown in Figure A.3. For small envelopes (7.5 cm by 15 cm), begin typing on line 12 about 6.2 cm from the left edge.

Canada Post recommends that addresses be typed in all caps without any punctuation. This Postal Service style, shown in the small envelope in Figure A.3, was originally developed to facilitate scanning by optical character readers. Today's OCRs, however, are so sophisticated that they scan upper- and lowercase letters easily. Many companies today prefer to use the same format for the envelope as for the inside address. If the same format is used, writers can take advantage of word processing programs to "copy" the inside address to the envelope, thus saving keystrokes and reducing errors. Having the same format on both the inside address and the envelope also looks more professional and consistent. For these reasons you may choose to use the familiar upper- and lowercase combination format. But you will want to check with your organization to learn its preference.

Figure A.3 ▶ Envelope Formats

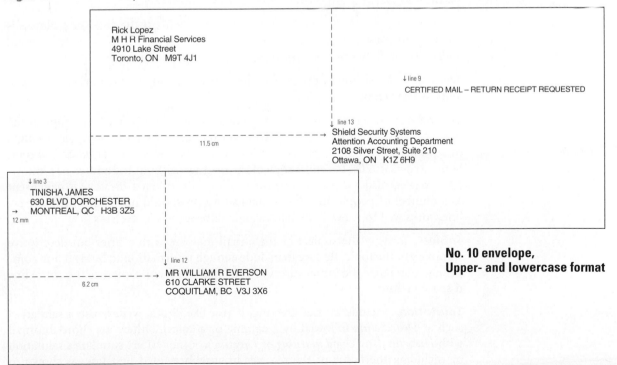

No. 10 envelope,
Upper- and lowercase format

No. 6¾ envelope, uppercase format

In addressing your envelopes for delivery in North America, use the two-letter province, territory, and state abbreviations shown in Figure A.4. Notice that these abbreviations are in capital letters without periods.

Folding. The way a letter is folded and inserted into an envelope sends additional nonverbal messages about a writer's professionalism and carefulness. Most businesspeople follow the procedures shown here, which produce the least number of creases to distract readers.

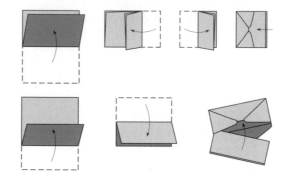

E-MAIL MESSAGES

Because e-mail is an evolving communication medium, formatting and usage are still fluid. The following suggestions, illustrated in Figure A.5, may guide you in setting up the parts of an e-mail message. Always check, however, with your organization so that you can observe its practices.

To line. Include the receiver's e-mail address after *To*. If the receiver's address is recorded in your address book, you just have to click on it. Be sure to enter all addresses carefully since one mistyped letter prevents delivery.

From line. Most e-mail programs automatically include your name and e-mail address after *From*.

Cc and bcc. Insert the e-mail address of anyone who is to receive a copy of the message. *Cc* stands for carbon copy or courtesy copy. Don't be tempted, though, to send needless copies just because it's so easy. *Bcc* stands for *blind carbon copy.* Some writers use *bcc* to send a copy of the message without the addressee's knowledge. Writers also use the *bcc* line for mailing lists. When a message is being sent to a number of people and their e-mail addresses should not be revealed, the *bcc* line works well to conceal the names and addresses of all receivers.

Subject. Identify the subject of the e-mail message with a brief but descriptive summary of the topic. Be sure to include enough information to be clear and compelling. Capitalize the initial letters of principal words, or capitalize the entire line if space permits.

Salutation. Include a brief greeting, if you like. Some writers use a salutation such as *Dear Selina* followed by a comma or a colon. Others are more informal with *Hi, Selina!*, or *Good morning* or *Greetings*. Some writers simulate a salutation by including the name of the receiver in an abbreviated first line, as shown in Figure A.5. Others writers treat an e-mail message like a memo and skip the salutation entirely.

Figure A.4 ▶ Abbreviations of Provinces, Territories, and States

Province or Territory	Two-Letter Abbreviation	Province	Two-Letter Abbreviation
Alberta	AB	Nova Scotia	NS
British Columbia	BC	Nunavut	NU
Manitoba	MB	Ontario	ON
New Brunswick	NB	Prince Edward Island	PE
Newfoundland and Labrador	NL	Quebec	QC
		Saskatchewan	SK
Northwest Territories	NT	Yukon Territory	YT

State or Territory	Two-Letter Abbreviation	State or Territory	Two-Letter Abbreviation
Alabama	AL	Missouri	MO
Alaska	AK	Montana	MT
American Samoa	AS	Nebraska	NE
Arizona	AZ	Nevada	NV
Arkansas	AR	New Hampshire	NH
California	CA	New Jersey	NJ
Colorado	CO	New Mexico	NM
Connecticut	CT	New York	NY
Delaware	DE	North Carolina	NC
District of Columbia	DC	North Dakota	ND
Florida	FL	North Mariana Islands	MP
Georgia	GA	Ohio	OH
Guam	GU	Oklahoma	OK
Hawaii	HI	Oregon	OR
Idaho	ID	Palau	PW
Illinois	IL	Pennsylvania	PA
Indiana	IN	Puerto Rico	PR
Iowa	IA	Rhode Island	RI
Kansas	KS	South Carolina	SC
Kentucky	KY	South Dakota	SD
Louisiana	LA	Tennessee	TN
Maine	ME	Texas	TX
Marshall Islands	MH	Utah	UT
Maryland	MD	Vermont	VT
Massachusetts	MA	Virgin Islands	VI
Michigan	MI	Virginia	VA
Micronesia	FM	Washington	WA
Minnesota	MN	West Virginia	WV
Minor Outlying Islands	UM	Wisconsin	WI
Mississippi	MS	Wyoming	WY

Message. Cover just one topic in your message, and try to keep your total message under one screen in length. Single-space and be sure to use both upper- and lowercase letters. Double-space between paragraphs, and use graphic highlighting (bullets, numbering) whenever you are listing three or more items.

Figure A.5 ▶ E-Mail Message

Annotations on figure:
- Includes descriptive subject line
- Incorporates recipient's name in abbreviated first line
- Uses single spacing within paragraphs and double spacing between
- Closes with name and title to ensure identification

E-mail content shown:

ADDING NEW DEPENDANTS TO YOUR HEALTH COVERAGE

From: Michael E. Wynn <mewynn@mail.onyx.com>   Sent: Nov. 29, 2007
To: <sondra.rios@mail.onyx.com>
Cc:
Subject: ADDING NEW DEPENDANTS TO YOUR HEALTH COVERAGE

Yes, Sondra

You may add new dependants to your health plan coverage. Since you are a regular, active employee, you are eligible to add unmarried dependent children (biological, adopted, step, and foster) under age 19 or under age 26, if they are full-time students. You may also be eligible to enroll your domestic partner or your dependant, as part of a pilot program.

For any new dependant, you must submit a completed Verification of Dependant Eligibility Form. You must also submit a photocopy of a document that verifies their eligibility. An acceptable verification document for a spouse is a photocopy of your marriage certificate. For children, submit a photocopy of a birth certificate, adoption certificate, or guardianship certificate. Please call the Health Insurance Unit at Ext. 2558 for more information or to ask for an application form.

Michael E. Wynn
Health Benefits Coordinator

Closing. Conclude an external message, with *Cheers* or *Best wishes*, followed by your name. If the recipient is unlikely to know you, it's not a bad idea to include your title and organization. Many e-mail users include a signature file with identifying information embellished with keyboard art. Use restraint, however, because signature files take up precious space. Writers of e-mail messages sent within organizations may omit a closing and even skip their names at the ends of messages because receivers recognize them from identification in the opening lines.

Attachment. Use the attachment window or button to select the file name of any file you wish to send with your e-mail message. You can also attach a Web page to your message.

MEMOS

As discussed in Chapter 4, memos deliver messages within organizations. Many offices use computer memo templates imprinted with the organization name and logo and, optionally, the department or division names, as shown in Figure A.6. Although the design and arrangement of memos vary, they usually include the basic elements of *TO, FROM, DATE,* and *SUBJECT.* Large organizations may include other identifying headings, such as *FILE NUMBER, FLOOR, EXTENSION, LOCATION,* and *DISTRIBUTION.*

If no computer template is available, memos may be typed on company letterhead or on plain paper, as shown in Figure A.7. On a full sheet of paper, start

Figure A.6 ▶ Printed Memo Forms

BANK OF MONTREAL
Mortgage Department   BMO ⛰

Interoffice
Memorandum

DATE:

TO:

FROM:

SUBJECT:

PYRAMID INDUSTRIES
Internal Memorandum

TO: DATE:

FROM: FILE:

SUBJECT:

Figure A.7 ▶ Memo on Plain Paper

↓ line 10
MEMO

DATE: February 3, 2007

→
3 cm   TO: Dawn Stewart, Manager
                     Sales and Marketing   *JM*

FROM: Jay Murray, Vice-President
                     Operations

SUBJECT: TELEPHONE SERVICE REQUEST FORMS
                     ↓ 2 blank lines

To speed telephone installation and improve service within the Bremerton facility, we are starting a new application procedure.

Service request forms will be available at various locations within the three buildings. When you require telephone service, obtain a request form at one of the locations that is convenient for you. Fill in the pertinent facts, obtain approval from your division head, and send the form to Brent White. Request forms are available at the following locations:

on line 13; on a half sheet, start on line 7. Double-space and type in all caps the guide words: *TO:, FROM:, DATE:, SUBJECT:*. Align all the fill-in information two spaces after the longest guide word (SUBJECT:). Leave three lines after the last line of the heading and begin typing the body of the memo. Like business letters, memos are single-spaced.

Memos are generally formatted with side margins of 3.5 cm (1 1/4 inches), or they may conform to the printed memo form. For more information about memos, see Chapter 4.

FAXES

Documents transmitted by fax are usually introduced by a cover sheet, such as that shown in Figure A.8. As with memos, the format varies considerably. Important items to include are (1) the name and fax number of the receiver, (2) the name and fax number of the sender, (3) the number of pages being sent, and (4) the name, telephone number, and e-mail address of the person to notify in case of unsatisfactory transmission.

When the document being transmitted requires little explanation, you may prefer to attach an adhesive note (such as a Post-it fax transmittal form) instead of a full cover sheet. These notes carry essentially the same information as shown in our printed fax cover sheet. They are perfectly acceptable in most business organizations and can save considerable paper and transmission costs.

Figure A.8 ▶ Fax Cover Sheet

FAX TRANSMISSION

DATE: _____

TO: _____   FAX
NUMBER: _____
_____
_____

FROM: _____   FAX
NUMBER: _____
_____
_____

NUMBER OF PAGES TRANSMITTED INCLUDING THIS COVER SHEET: _____

MESSAGE:

If any part of this fax transmission is missing or not clearly received, please contact:

NAME: _____
PHONE: _____
E-MAIL: _____

Answers to End-of-Chapter Grammar/Style Reviews

Chapter 1

From: ksmythe@bmo.ca

Sent:

To: mauletti@bmo.ca

Cc:

Subject: Training materials for new hires

Hi Marco,

The new training handbook, along with the brochures and posters, is going to the printer on Friday. What this means is that the copy edit and the proofread are going to be due on the Monday before, which is the 16th. This also means that either you or the members of your team are going to have to put in some extra hours next week. I realize that each of your team members is working at full capacity, so I'd ask you to prioritize your non-handbook tasks. The handbook team is behind you all the way, so just let me know if you need any help over the next week as we work towards this deadline.

Regards,

Kathleen

Chapter 2

File   Edit   View   Insert   Format   Tools   Actions   Help

Reply   Reply to All   Forward

From: gcarere@sobeys.ca   Sent:

To: lzhou@sobeys.ca

Cc:

Subject: Mistakes in last week's flyer

Hi Lucy,

Last week's flyer (Atlantic region) contained so many mistakes that we had to have it reprinted at the last minute. Sobeys stands for quality; its flyers can't be full of mistakes. Unfortunately, each of the pages has its fair share of mistakes. Let me give you some examples:

Page 2: The 12-pack of chicken burgers was listed at $6.98 when it should have been listed at $5.98

Page 4: The juicepacks and cheesesticks were both on sale, but they were on sale for $0.99 cents, not $1.98

Page 5: "Every customer receives $1 off his or her first prescription order" has a spelling mistake (missing t...)

Please ensure that correct proofreading procedure is followed this week.

Best,

George

Chapter 3

From: cbrillstein@harryrosen.ca
To: malamsah@harryrosen.ca
Cc:
Subject: Corporate retreat

Sent:

Hi Mira,

Can we talk about the corporate retreat? We need to discuss the hotel, the accommodations, and also probably the food. Last year's event went really well, so Dave thinks we should use the same place in Niagara-on-the-Lake, as last year. Harry also told me that we should bring in the top-selling employees from all stores this time around. He thinks we could do a small awards ceremony in order to recognize their achievements.

Let me know what you think.

Carl

Chapter 4

From: Susan Schneider
To: All Staff
Cc:
Subject: Christmas Party

Sent:

Hi everyone,

This e-mail is to inform everyone of details of this year's Christmas Party.

At this time of year, the company feels that it's an excellent idea for all employees to get together socially outside of work.

Therefore, I'm happy to announce that this year's Christmas Party will be held on the second Friday of December, the 10th. We have booked the restaurant at the Hotel Eldorado.

Please RSVP to me at the very latest by November 30.

Sincerely,

Susan

Chapter 5

```
File   Edit   View   Insert   Format   Tools   Actions   Help
Reply   Reply to All   Forward
```

From: sli@aventis.ca   Sent:

To: prochefort@aventis.ca

Cc:

Subject: Sales conference in June

Hi Pierre,

A couple of people I know at Biovail and Novopharm have used the Pillar & Post Inn in Niagara-on-the-Lake and they say it's a good hotel. Personally, I think things got out of hand at last year's conference, and anything that will save us money makes sense. If you like, I'd be happy to find out the cost for using the Pillar. I think we want to show the reps a good time but at the same time not go overboard. Let me know.

Best,

Steve

Chapter 6

```
File   Edit   View   Insert   Format   Tools   Actions   Help
Reply   Reply to All   Forward
```

From: tsmith@mesfin.ca   Sent:

To: mmarino@mesfin.ca

Cc:

Subject: Cancelling meeting

Hi Maria,

I'd like to suggest that this week's team meeting be cancelled. Due to a scheduling mix-up and to the fact that I feel we haven't had the necessary time to prepare, I think it would be better if we re-schedule.

I wanted you to know about this early, because you've been preparing a presentation about new CRM software for us. Let's talk in a few days and we can decide when to re-schedule.

Regards,

Ted

Chapter 7

From: m.engle@vmedia.ca Sent:
To: m.muller@vmedia.ca
Cc:
Subject: Potential client?

Hi Mike,

I was reading the Sun yesterday and saw a story on the Whitecaps' plan to build a new soccer stadium downtown. I checked out the Whitecaps' website after reading the article, and found that it could use some work. For example, if you go to the Photo Reel section that has pictures from the stadium press conference, every one of them looks so static! There are no captions and it takes a while to figure out how to navigate the site. I'm not sure what you intend to do about new business, but I would recommend you send them a proposal.

Cheers,

May

Chapter 8

```
From:     mmohammed@rgroup.ca                        Sent:
To:       bflahiff@rgroup.ca
Cc:
Subject:  Problems with our focus group
```

Hi Brenda,

As you know we've been conducting focus groups on nutrition, shopping habits, and fitness of the 18–34 demographic. Our session last night went well, but I wanted to alert you to some potential problems:

- Should we hold another focus group (the responses last night were so-so)?
- Will going this route put us over budget?
- Will choosing not to do another focus group undermine our research?

When you have a minute, can we talk about these potential problems and solutions, and who will communicate with Mike? Thanks a lot.

Best,

Munir

Chapter 9

```
From:     bmascoll82@hotmail.com                     Sent: May 27, 2007
To:       amasucci@optrc.ca
Cc:
Subject:  Interview scheduling
```

Hi Antonella,

Thank you for calling me back last week. I apologize I was not feeling well; I had food poisoning. I was wondering when you would like to schedule a second interview with Mike. Hopefully if Mike is not too busy we can do it sometime this week. There's something I'm doing Monday afternoon, but I will be available any time after Tuesday.

Thank you again,

Bryce

Chapter 10

File	Edit	View	Insert	Format	Tools	Actions	Help

Reply | Reply to All | Forward

From:	sgupta@stirplex.ca	Sent: January 16, 2007
To:	jmoffat@stirplex.ca	
Cc:		
Subject:	Brochures are late	

Hi June,

I know you said the brochures were coming yesterday, but I haven't received them yet, and time's running out!

Although it might not seem like a high priority on your list of to-do items, please put a rush on this.

Thanks!

Sal

Chapter 11

File	Edit	View	Insert	Format	Tools	Actions	Help

Reply | Reply to All | Forward

From:	rwynne@solutionex.ca	Sent: November 18, 2007
To:	smacri@solutionex.ca	
Cc:		
Subject:	Sales conference	

Hi Sue,

The people in my department are excited about our upcoming sales conference. I just wanted to let you know that while we prepare for the meeting next week, we'll be using a number of strategies so that things run more smoothly than last year. If you want to talk about any of this, just send me a message in the next couple of days.

Best,

Roger

Chapter 12

File   Edit   View   Insert   Format   Tools   Actions   Help

Reply | Reply to All | Forward

From: kkarim@canexhibits.ca   September 4, 2007

To: jchoi@canexhibits.ca

Cc:

Subject: Exhibit rules!

Hi Jason,

Did you hear about the new rules on expenses, phone calls, and booth protocol? It turns out that everyone has to get his or her expenses okayed by Steve before leaving a show and wear a uniform. It doesn't matter if he or she is an assistant or a director; it looks like the company isn't trusting anyone these days.

Anyway, whatever rules they make get broken, right? But what I'm really writing about is the party on Friday. Are you still going?

K

Answers to Grammar, Mechanics, and Style Tutorial Exercises

Tutorial 1

1. The keyboard, printer, and monitor cost less than I expected.
2. A description of the property, together with several other legal documents, was submitted by my lawyer.
3. There were only two enclosures and the letter in the envelope.
4. A manager's time and energy have to be focused on important issues.
5. We're not sure whether Mr. Murphy or Ms. Wagner is in charge of the program.

Tutorial 2

1. When you visit Mutual Trust, inquire about its GICs and RRSPs.
2. A manager in our company has responsibilities that he or she has to take seriously.
3. Everyone on the team is accountable for his or her section of the report.
4. Every employee is entitled to have his or her tuition reimbursed.
5. Flexible working hours may mean slower career advancement, but they appeal to me anyway.

Tutorial 3

1. Although UTS is renowned internationally, our staff consists of only nine people, all of whom have different attributes.
2. I have a number of telephone lines: one for business, one for personal calls, one for the fax machine, and one for the Internet.
3. Junk faxes are like a virus that's out of control: the virus is living off my time and fax paper!
4. Quotation marks are important because the reader is assured that the article is accurate and logical. He or she recognizes that the quotation is not the columnist's, but the voice of an expert.
5. Profit derived from Grapealicious bubblegum is 15 percent higher than profit from Breath-X gum. This is partly because the former is more popular with the teenage demographic, which exercises significant buying power.

Tutorial 4

1. Mr. Samuels graduated from college last June.
2. Putting the wrong e-mail address in the address box wastes people's time.
3. The trouble with the proposal is in the budget section, which is confusing.
4. As much as I would enjoy attending your seminar, I'm busy that day.
5. I cannot predict on what day I will be available to meet.

Tutorial 5

1. These are just a few of the many exciting features of Woodside Condominiums.
2. This new and exciting program is the only one of its kind in Alberta that covers all three important aspects of financial planning.
3. Allow me to introduce Macdonald College's Financial Services Post-Diploma program, which boasts numerous direct links with a large number of local financial services firms.
4. It is a pleasure to work with the Chinese Student Association at Macdonald College.
5. We all use technology to save time but the technology does not always work well.

Tutorial 6

1. The reason UTS started operations about six years ago was that there was a need for its services.
2. Customers do not like having questions that are not answered right away.
3. The success of the magazine is due in part to the authors' freedom to express themselves.
4. I conclude from past experience that mutual cooperation is the basic requirement of any successful team.
5. The memo is essentially an out-of-date, seldom-used method of business communication.

Tutorial 7

1. *Fortune* magazine runs a lot of advertisements.
2. In writing the perfect résumé a number of factors come into play.
3. I will ask him to do the work immediately.

4. Secondly, both columnists have different points of view about gender.
5. Imageco's fee for developing and facilitating this course is $8000.

Tutorial 8

1. E-commerce websites should be built with many language options, compatible systems, and easy connectivity to related websites.
2. Executives lead their employees by instilling loyalty and by setting a good example.
3. The corporate executive faced his trial confidently, insisting that he was innocent and rejecting any offers of a plea bargain.
4. Some of the major skills are providing value to customers, service and performance, an attractive site, and a sense of community.
5. The following are services that UTS can offer you:
   • Auditing freight bills
   • Checking all shipping and receiving charges for over-charging
   • Advising you on which trucking companies offer superior service
   • Filing freight claims and fighting wrongful claims against you.

Tutorial 9

1. Many of our clients have had their products damaged due to poor packaging.
2. It doesn't appear that anyone has a viable solution to the problem.

3. While each paper has a special pull-out section, the *Post's* is completely separate while the *Globe's* is part of the front section.
4. This course investigates the history of labour unions in Canada.
5. "Park your car at the shipping and receiving loading dock," he said.

Tutorial 10

1. Although I don't see eye to eye with you, I'm willing to work together to get this project done.
2. After you're finished painting the living room, please work on the dining room.
3. Sue's and Mitch's joint mortgage is almost paid off.
4. Sometimes (well almost everyday) I feel the urge to take a long—really long—vacation.
5. However, some commentators suggest that the country may be moving into a period of inflation.

Tutorial 11

1. Accountants do more than calculating taxes and amortization figures.
2. Cryptography also ensures that neither side can deny its participation in the exchange of information.
3. My practice focuses on high net-worth individuals; I'm not interested in junior investors.
4. Fear of being cheated out of their money is making consumers hesitant to purchase online.
5. The judges on *Canadian Idol* selected the most talented contestants and then chose the best one.

Notes

Preface

1. Peter Schwartz, Stewart Mennin, and Graham Webb, eds., *Problem-Based Learning: Case Studies, Experience and Practice* (London: Kogan Page Limited, 2002), 6.
2. Dave S. Knowlton, "Preparing Students for Educating Living: Virtues of Problem-Based Learning Across the Higher Education Curriculum" in Dave S. Knowlton and David C. Sharp, eds. *Problem-Based Learning in the Information Age* (San Francisco: Josey-Bass, 2003), 6.
3. Charles C. Bonwell and James A. Eison, *Active Learning: Creating Excitement in the Classroom.* ASHE-ERIC Higher Education Report No. 1. Washington, D.C.: The George Washington University, School of Education and Human Development, 1991, 33.
4. Renee E. Weiss, "Designing Problems to Promote Higher-Order Thinking" in Dave S. Knowlton and David C. Sharp, eds. *Problem-Based Learning in the Information Age* (San Francisco: Josey-Bass, 2003), 25.
5. Weiss, 26.
6. Weiss, 27.
7. Bonwell and Eison, 38.

Chapter 1

1. Statistics Canada predicts that by 2017, visible minorities will in fact be the majority of the population in major centres like Toronto, Vancouver, and Montreal. See Statistics Canada, *The Daily*, 22 March 2005, www.statcan.ca/Daily/English/050322/d050322b.htm.
2. Anne Papmehl, "Remote Access," *CMA Management*, 75, no. 3 (May 2001): 11.
3. Desmond Beckstead and Tara Vinodrai, "Dimensions of Occupational Changes in Canada's Knowledge Economy, 1971–1996," The Canadian Economy in Transition Series, Catalogue no. 11-622-MIE—No. 004, Statistics Canada, 2003, www.statcan.ca/cgi-bin/downpub/listpub.cgi?catno=11-622-MIE2003004 (accessed April 26, 2005).
4. Sharon Helldorfer and Michael Daly, "Reengineering Brings Together Units," *Best's Review*, October 1993, 82–85.
5. Marjo Johne, "What Do You Know? The Knowledge Worker and the Knowledge Environment Today Require Synergy and Collaboration More Than Ever Before," *CMA Management*, March 2001, 21–24.
6. Dwight Cunningham, "The Downside of Technology," *Chicago Tribune Internet Edition*, 2 January 2000; "Wire to the Desk," *Fortune*, Summer 1999, 164.
7. Andy Holloway, "Give Like Santa ...," *Canadian Business*, 9 December 2002, 109.

8. Canadian Television Studies *InnoVisions Canada*, available <www.ivc.ca/part12.htm> (accessed 28 May 2003).
9. Kirk Johnson, "Limits on the Work-at-Home Life," *The New York Times*, 17 December 1997, A20.
10. Holloway, "Give Like Santa ..."
11. Rosalind Stefanac, "Brain Drain Is for Real, ITAC's Duncan Argues," *Computing Canada*, 9 July 1999, 29, 33.
12. Hal Lancaster, "Hiring a Full Staff May Be the Next Fad in Management," *The Wall Street Journal*, 4 April 1998, B1.
13. Andrew Denka, "New Office Etiquette Dilemmas," *CPA Journal*, August 1996, 13.

Chapter 2

1. Ray Birdwhistell, *Kinetics and Context* (Philadelphia: University of Pennsylvania Press, 1970).
2. Michael Render, "Better Listening Makes for a Better Marketing Message," *Marketing News*, 11 September 2000, 22–23.
3. Tom W. Harris, "Listen Carefully," *Nation's Business*, June 1989, 78.
4. "Minacs in Profile," Overview, available <www.minacs.com/en/company/about/> (retrieved 2 July 2003).
5. Based on information found at Minacs website, <www.minacs.com> (retrieved 1 July 2003).
6. "Minacs Honored by General Motors as 2002 Supplier of the Year," <www.minacs.com/pdf_uploads/2003/20030414_GM_Award_Rel_Final_Apr14.pdf> (retrieved 2 July 2003).
7. Harvey Robbins and Michael Finley, *Why Teams Don't Work* (Princeton, NJ: Peterson's/Pacesetters Books, 1995), 123.
8. L. E. Penley, E. R. Alexander, I. E. Jerigan, and C. I. Henwood, "Communication Abilities of Managers: The Relationship to Performance," *Journal of Management*, No. 17, 1991, 57–76; R. P. Ramsey and R. S. Sohi, "Listening to Your Customers: The Impact of Perceived Salesperson Listening Behavior on Relationship Outcomes," *Journal of the Academy of Marketing Science*, No. 25 (2) (1997): 127–137; Lynn O. Cooper, "Listening Competency in the Workplace: A Model for Training," *Business Communication Quarterly*, December 1997, 75–84; and Valerie P. Goby and Justice H. Lewis, "The Key Role of Listening in Business: A Study of the Singapore Insurance Industry," *Business Communication Quarterly*, June 2000, 411.
9. Ko DeRutyer and Martin G. M. Wetzels, "The Impact of Perceived Listening Behavior in Voice-to-Voice Service Encounters," *Journal of Service Research*, February 2000, 276–284.
10. L. K. Steil, L. I. Barker, and K. W. Watson, *Effective Listening: Key to Your Success*

(Reading, MA: Addison-Wesley, 1983); and J. A. Harris, "Hear What's Really Being Said," *Management-Auckland*, August 1998, 18.
11. Eric H. Nelson and Jan Gypen, "The Subordinate's Predicament," *Harvard Business Review*, September/October 1979, 133.
12. "Listening Factoids," International Listening Association <http://www.listen.org/pages/factoids.html> (retrieved 7 January 2001).
13. Robert McGarvey, "Now Hear This: Lend Your Employees an Ear—and Boost Productivity," *Entrepreneur*, June 1996, 87.
14. "Good Ideas Go Unheard," *Management Review*, February 1998, 7.
15. Michael Dojc, "Marrying the Media with the Message," *The Toronto Star*, 24 September 2002, E03.
16. Dojc, "Marrying the Media with the Message."
17. Based on Cheryl Hamilton with Cordell Parker, *Communicating for Results*, 6th ed. (Belmont, CA: Wadsworth, 2000), 279; and Robbins and Finley, *Why Teams Don't Work*.
18. Jon R. Katzenbach and Douglas K. Smith, *The Wisdom of Teams* (New York: HarperBusiness and Harvard Business School Press, 1994), 14.
19. Allen C. Amason, Wayne A. Hochwarter, Kenneth R. Thompson, and Allison W. Harrison, "Conflict: An Important Dimension in Successful Management Teams," *Organization Dynamics*, Autumn 1995, 20–35.
20. Kathleen M. Eisenhardt, Jean L. Kahwajy, and L. J. Bourgeios, III, "Conflict and Strategic Choice: How Top Management Teams Disagree," *California Management Review*, Winter, 1997, 42–62.
21. Anthony Wilson-Smith, "A Quiet Passion," *Maclean's*, 1 July 1995, 8–12.
22. Jon P. Alston and Theresa M. Morris, "Comparing Canadian and American Values: New Evidence from National Surveys," *Canadian Review of American Studies*, 26, no. 3 (Autumn 1996): 301–315.
23. Seymour Martin Lipset, *Continental Divide: The Values and Institutions of the United States and Canada* (New York: Routledge, 1991).
24. Norman McGuinness and Nigel Campbell, "Selling Machinery to China: Chinese Perceptions of Strategies and Relationships," *Journal of International Business Studies*, 22, no. 3 (1991): 187.
25. Statistics Canada, CANSIM, Matrices 6367 (estimates), 6900 (projections), www.statcan.ca/English/Pgdb/People/Population/demo23c.htm; and Matrix 3472, available www.statcan.ca/English/Pgdb/People/Labour/labor05.htm (accessed 23 April 2002).
26. Virginia Galt, "Western Union Remakes Canadian Image: Profits from Overseas

Hiring, Staff Diversity," *The Globe and Mail,* 23 November 2004, B1.

27. Lee Gardenswartz and Anita Rowe, "Helping Managers Solve Cultural Conflicts," *Managing Diversity,* August 1996, www.jalmc.org/hlp-mgr.htm (accessed 23 April 2002).

Chapter 3

1. Editorial Staff, "Canadian CEOs Are Big on Communication," *CMA Management,* 74, no. 9 (November 2000): 8.
2. Don Tapscott, "R U N2 It?" *Enroute Magazine,* October 2003, 35–36.
3. Kevin Marron, "Instant Messaging Comes of Age," *The Gobe and Mail,* 1 November 2001, p. B30.
4. Earl N. Harbert, "Knowing Your Audience," in *The Handbook of Executive Communication,* ed. John L. Digaetani (Homewood, IL: Dow Jones/Irwin, 1986), 17.
5. The UVic Writer's Guide, "The First Draft," *UVic English,* http://web.uvic.ca/wguide/Pages/EssayWritingFirstDraft.html (accessed 2 May 2001).
6. Maryann V. Piotrowski, *Effective Business Writing* (New York: Harper Perennial, 1996), 12.

Chapter 4

1. The popularity of e-mail in the workplace is discussed in the Pew Internet & American Life Project's 2002 report entitled *Email at Work.* The report is available at http://www.pewinternet.org/report_display.asp?r=79.
2. The 62 billion figure comes from the popular website Ask.Yahoo.com (http://ask.yahoo.com/20060324.html). The site includes numerous links to private and public research studies on the topic of e-mail usage.
3. Statistics Canada, "Perspectives on Labour and Income," *Working with Computers,* 13, no. 2 (Summer 2001).
4. Sinclair Stewart, "CIBC Turns up Heat as Fight with Genuity Hits Home," *The Globe and Mail,* 17 February 2005, B4.
5. Judith Colbert, Helene Carty, and Paul Beam, "Practice: Assessing Financial Documents for Readability," Task Force on the Future of the Canadian Financial Services Sector, finservtaskforce.fin.gc.ca/research/pdf/RR8_V1b_e.pdf (accessed 29 April 2005).
6. Pamela Gilbert, "Two Words That Can Help a Business Thrive," *The Wall Street Journal,* 30 December 1996, A12.

Chapter 5

1. Editors, Doing Business in Canada website, Section 2.7, www.dbic.com/guide/tm2-7.html (accessed 10 January 2002).
2. Neil Morton, "Some Like It Cold," *Canadian Business,* September 1997, 99.
3. Figure 5.6 is based on a media release on the CTV website dated February 28, 2006,

with the following headline: "Pamela Anderson to Host The 2006 Juno Awards on CTV." <www.ctv.ca/servlet/ArticleNews/show/CTVShows/20060227/ctv_release_20060227_awards/20060228>.
4. Harriett M. Augustin, "The Written Job Search: A Comparison of the Traditional and a Nontraditional Approach," *The Bulletin of the Association for Business Communication,* September 1991, 13.

Chapter 6

1. Elizabeth M. Dorn, "Case Method Instruction in the Business Writing Classroom," *Business Communication Quarterly,* March 1999, 51–52.
2. Based on information found at Hyundai Auto Canada websites, <www.Hyundaicanada.com> and <www.Hyundaiupdate.ca> (retrieved July 2003).
3. Carol David and Margaret Ann Baker, "Rereading Bad News: Compliance-Gaining Features in Management Memos," *The Journal of Business Communications,* 31, no. 4, 268.
4. Robert Mirguet, information security manager, Eastman Kodak Co., Rochester, New York, quoted in *Computerworld,* cited in "Telecommunicating," *Boardroom Reports,* 1 March 1995, 15; Sandy Sampson, "Wild Wild Web: Legal Exposure on the Internet," *Software Magazine,* November 1997, 75–78.
5. Marcia Mascolini, "Another Look at Teaching the External Negative Message," *Bulletin of the Association for Business Communication,* June 1994, 47.
6. Mohan R. Limaye, "Further Conceptualization of Explanations in Negative Messages," *Business Communication Quarterly,* June 1997, 46.
7. This process for handling service-related complaints is described in detail on the Customer Expressions website. Customer Expressions is an Ottawa-based maker of CRM software. <www.customerexpressions.com/CEx/cexweb.nsf/(GetPages)/CAC4DB21930B8EAF852570890045E294>.
8. "Collection Letters," CreditGuru.com, www.creditguru.com/collection.htm (accessed 30 April 2005).
9. Phillip M. Perry, "E-Mail Hell: The Dark Side of the Internet Age," *Folio: The Magazine for Magazine Management,* June 1998, 74–75.
10. Elizabeth A. McCord, "The Business Writer, the Law, and Routine Business Communication: A Legal and Rhetorical Analysis," *Journal of Business and Technical Communication,* April 1991, 183.

Chapter 7

1. The definition of project management comes from the Project Management Institute's website: <www.pmi.org/info/PP_AboutProfessionOverview.asp?nav=0501>.

2. Herman Holtz, *The Consultant's Guide to Proposal Writing* (New York: John Wiley, 1990), 188.

Chapter 8

1. "It Figures: StatsCan's No. 1," *The Financial Post,* 12 November 1994, 16.
2. Melanie Brooks, "The World's Top Number Cruncher: Researchers Last Night Honoured StatsCan Chief Ivan Fellegi for Telling Canada's Story by the Numbers," *The Ottawa Citizen,* 25 October 2002, A2.
3. Haroon Siddiqui, "Ivan Fellegi Has It All Figured Out," *The Toronto Star,* 12 December 2002, A35.
4. Brooks, "The World's Top Number Cruncher."
5. "We Are Statistics Canada," <www.statcan.ca> (accessed 16 June 2003).
6. "What We Do," <www.statcan.ca> (accessed 16 June 2003).
7. "More Than Numbers, Census Tells a Story," *Sudbury Star,* 24 November 2002, A6.
8. "Unlocking History," *The Expositor (Brantford),* 11 February 2003, A10.
9. Kerry Gillespie, "Forget the Sensible Shoes; Librarians Turn a New Leaf," *The Toronto Star,* 14 June 2003, A23.
10. Gillespie, "Forget the Sensible Shoes."
11. Joellen Perry and Janet Tae-Dupree, "Searching the Web Gets Easier with Engines That Try to Read Your Mind," *U.S. News & World Report,* 16 April 2001, 52.

Chapter 9

1. Charlene Marmer Solomon, "Marriott's Family Matters," *Personnel Journal,* October 1991, 40–42; Jennifer Laabs, "They Want More Support—Inside and Outside of Work," *Workforce,* November 1998, 54–56.
2. This definition can be found at <http://www.cbsc.org/ibp/doc/intro_bp.cfm>.
3. The Royal Bank of Canada's business plan information can be found at <www.rbcroyalbank.com/sme/bigidea/>.
4. <http://www.cbsc.org/ibp/doc/intro_bp.cfm>.

Chapter 10

1. Jeff Olson, *The Agile Manager's Guide to Giving Great Presentations* (Bristol, VT: Velocity Printing, 1999), 8.
2. Dianna Booher, *Executive's Portfolio of Model Speeches for All Occasions* (Upper Saddle River, NJ: Prentice Hall, 1991), 260.
3. Wharton Applied Research Center, "A Study of the Effects of the Use of Overhead Transparencies on Business Meetings, Final Report," cited in "Short Snappy Guide to Meaningful Presentations," *Working Woman,* June 1991, 73.
4. "On That Next Business Trip, Leave the Laptop Behind ... And Do It All on Your PDA, New Mobile Software," *Internet Wire,* 18 June 2002. See also "PowerPoint Presentations From Your

Pocket PC," *PC Magazine*, 9 April 2002, p. NA.

5. Tad Simons, "When Was the Last Time PowerPoint Made You Sing?" *Presentations*, July 2001, 6.

6. Jennifer Rotondo, "Customized PowerPoint Templates Make Life Easier," *Presentations*, July 2001, 25–26.

7. Jim Endicott, "It Always Pays to Have a Clean, Professional Package," *Presentations*, June 2002, 26–28.

8. Jim Endicott, "For Better Presentations, Avoid PowerPoint Pitfalls," *Presentations*, June 1998, 36–37.

9. Robert J. Boeri, "Fear of Flying? Or the Main? Try the Web Conferencing Cure," *Emedia Magazine*, March 2002, 49.

10. Victoria Hall Smith, "Gigs by the Gigabyte," *Working Woman*, May 1998, 115.

11. Joan Lloyd, "Engage Your Audience @ Work," *Baltimore Business Journal*, 14 December 2001, 35.

12. Booher, *Executive's Portfolio*, 259.

13. J. Michael Farr, *The Very Quick Job Search* (Indianapolis, IN: JIST Works, 1991), 158.

Chapter 11

1. Hal Lancaster, "Learning Some Ways to Make Meetings Slightly Less Awful," *The Wall Street Journal*, 26 May 1998, B1.

2. Tom McDonald, "Minimizing Meetings," *Successful Meetings*, June 1996, 24.

3. "I've Got to Go to Another ... Meeting," *Interventions: The EFAP Journal of CMR Canada*, November 2000, www.cmrcanada .ca/InterventionsNov2000.html (accessed 25 May 2005).

4. John C. Bruening, "There's Good News About Meetings," *Managing Office Technology*, July 1996, 24–25.

5. Kirsten Schabacker, "A Short, Snappy Guide to Meaningful Meetings," *Working Women*, June 1991, 73.

6. J. Keith Cook, "Try These Eight Guidelines for More Effective Meetings," *Communication Briefings* Bonus Item, April 1995, 8a. See also Morey Stettner, "How to Manage a Corporate Motormouth," *Investor's Business Daily*, 8 October 1998, A1.

7. Cheryl Hamilton with Cordell Parker, *Communication for Success*, 6th ed., (Belmont, CA: Wadsworth, 2001), 100–104.

8. Frances Micale, *Meetings Made Easy* (Madison, WI: Entrepreneur Press, 2004), 16.

9. Herminia Ibarra et al., *Negotiation* (Boston: Harvard Business School Press, 2003), xi.

10. Steven Cohen, *Negotiation Skills for Managers* (Toronto: McGraw-Hill, 2002), 3.

11. Cohen, *Negotiation Skills for Managers*, 85.

12. Cohen, *Negotiation Skills for Managers*, 86.

13. Cohen, *Negotiation Skills for Managers*, 90.

14. Cohen, *Negotiation Skills for Managers*, 5.

15. John R. Katzenbach and Douglas Smith, *The Wisdom of Teams* (New York: HarperBusiness and Harvard Business School Press, 1994), 14.

16. Christine A. Spring, Paul R. Jackson, and Sharon K. Parker, "Production Teamworking: The Importance of Interdependence and Autonomy for Employee Strain and Satisfaction," *Human Relations*, November 2000, 1519.

Chapter 12

1. Shearlean Duke, "E-Mail: Essential in Media Relations, But No Replacement for Face-to-Face Communication," *Public Relations Quarterly* (Winter 2001): 19; Lisa M.

Flaherty, Kevin J. Pearce, and Rebecca B. Rubin, "Internet and Face-to-Face Communication: Not Functional Alternatives," *Communication Quarterly* (Summer 1998): 250.

2. Aimee L. Drolet and Michael W. Morris, "Rapport in Conflict Resolution: Accounting for How Face-to-Face Contact Fosters Mutual Cooperation in Mixed-Motive Conflicts," *Journal of Experimental Social Psychology* (January 2000): 26.

3. Peggy Post and Peter Post, *The Etiquette Advantage in Business* (New York: Harper Resource, 2005), 3.

4. Jean Miculka, *Speaking for Success* (Cincinnati, OH: Southwestern, 1999), 19.

5. Post and Post, *The Etiquette Advantage in Business*, 47.

6. "Fire Up Your Phone Skills," *Successful Meetings*, November 2000, 30.

7. Winston Fletcher, "How to Make Sure It's a Good Call," *Management Today*, February 2000, 34.

8. "Did You Know That ..." *Boardroom Reports*, 15 August 1992.

9. Andrew Griffiths, *101 Ways to Really Satisfy Your Customers* (Crows Nest, N.S.W.: Allen & Unwin, 2002), 93.

10. Post and Post, *The Etiquette Advantage in Business*, 225.

11. Elizabeth Guilday, "Voicemail Like a Pro," *Training & Development*, October 2000, 68.

12. Judith Schroer, "Seek a Job With a Little Help From Your Friends," *USA Today*, 19 November 1990, B1.

13. Post and Post, *The Etiquette Advantage in Business*, 313–314.

14. Post and Post, *The Etiquette Advantage in Business*, 56.

Index

Credits

Unit 1

Chapter 1
Pages 2–3. "Police Exam unsuitable: Race committee members," by Nikhat Ahmed. (*The StarPhoenix*). Page A6. © Copyright November 14, 2005. Material reprinted with the express permission of: Saskatoon Star Phoenix Group Inc, a CanWest Partnership.

Chapter 2
Pages 19–20. Source: "Workers bring culture to their cubicle: As more employees express their ethnicity in their clothing, and more companies recognize their diverse work forces, such dress still raises issues about acceptance in the workplace," by Aparita Bhandari. (*The Globe and Mail*). © Copyright September 28, 2005. Reprinted with permission from *The Globe and Mail.*

Chapter 3
Page 43. Source: "Constipated Mommies and Plush Upholstery," by Richard H. Levey. *Direct.* Reprinted with the permission of Prism Business Media Inc. © Copyright 2005. All rights reserved.

Unit 2

Chapter 4
Pages 74–76. Source: "You've Got Too Much Mail," by Katherine Macklem. © Copyright January 30, 2006. (*Maclean's* magazine). Reprinted with permission of *Maclean's* magazine.

Chapter 5
Pages 108–109. Source: "The Invisible Salesman," by Ian Portsmouth. (*Profit Magazine*). © Copyright Ian Portsmouth, November 2005. Reprinted with permission.

Chapter 6
Pages 135–136. Source: "It became a really hard decision," by Lisa Schmidt. (*Calgary Herald*). © Copyright July 31, 2005. Reprinted with permission of the *Calgary Herald.*

Unit 3

Chapter 7
Page 166. Source: "Whitecaps set sights on 2009 debut for stadium. Best-case scenario detailed for 16,000-seat facility," by Dan Stinston. (*Vancouver Sun*). Page G8. © Copyright February 17, 2006. Reprinted with permission of the *Vancouver Sun.*

Chapter 8
Pages 195–196. Source: "How not to write a research report," by Duncan Stewart. (*National Post*). Page FP9. © Copyright September 1, 2005. Material reprinted with the express permission of: "National Post Company," a CanWest Partnership. Used with permission of the author.

Chapter 9
Pages 222–223. Source: "Go big or stay small," by Rebecca Harris. (*Marketing Magazine,* Rogers Publishing). Pages 19–20. © Copyright September 27, 2004. Used with permission.

Unit 4

Chapter 10
Pages 262–263. Source: "PowerPoint of no return," by Andrew Wahl. (*Canadian Business*). Pages 131–132. © Copyright November 10, 2003. Used with permission.

Chapter 11
Pages 287–288. "Meeting madness: Our Workplace is changing and anecdotal evidence suggests we're attending more meetings than a decade ago," by Stephanie Whittaker. (*The Gazette: Montreal*). Page B5. © Copyright Stephanie Whittaker, December 10, 2005. Reprinted with permission.

Chapter 12.
Pages 303–304. "Sorry, wrong number: Some executives will do anything to avoid returning calls," by Michael Stern. (*National Post*). Page FW9. © Copyright Michael Stern, May 7, 2005. Used with permission.